Philip J. Klass

UFOs
Explained

Random House New York

Library of Congress Cataloging in Publication Data
Klass, Philip J.
    UFOs explained.
    1. Flying saucers.   I. Title.
TL789.K56   1975   001.9'42   74–9054
ISBN 0–394–49215–3

Manufactured in the United States of America

2 3 4 5 6 7 8 9

To my tireless proofreader, publicist and mother, Mrs. Raymond N. Klass

And to Albert Erskine of Random House for his confidence (two books ago) that it made good sense to publish a no-non-sense book on UFOs

Contents

List of Illustrations

UFOs
Explained

Introduction

The persistent mystery of Unidentified Flying Objects (UFOs) is remarkable, if not unique, in the history of modern times. For more than a quarter of a century many thousands of persons in the United States, and around the globe, have reported seeing curious and seemingly unexplainable things in the skies, or coming from the skies. Perhaps you yourself have had such an experience.

Some skeptics dismiss the UFO question without investigation in the belief that reports come only from "kooks." This simply is not so, as numerous UFO cases analyzed in this book will demonstrate. Many come from seemingly honest, intelligent and often well-educated citizens, including scientists, law-enforcement officers and aircraft flight crews. If you are a skeptic, you may be surprised to learn that a number of scientists, some with impressive-sounding credentials, believe that some UFO reports involve extraterrestrial spaceships that are visiting Earth.

If this extraterrestrial hypothesis is correct, the UFO mystery is the most startling and important scientific event of all times. Yet it has been ignored by organized science and by the great majority of scientists. Is it possible that while the scientific community has been building spacecraft to search for primitive life-forms on Mars, and aiming giant radio telescopes at the heavens to search for radio signals from distant civilizations, that the evidence of extraterrestrial intelligent life can be found here on Earth, in abundant quantity?

Those who believe that at least some UFO reports represent extraterrestrial visitations wait impatiently for THE case that will resolve the issue and prove their hopes beyond all doubt. Until this incontrovertible evidence appears, they argue, we must withhold final judgment. This implies that despite more than 10,000 UFO sighting reports in the United States alone, there is little that can be learned from them— *especially those that can, after considerable effort, be explained.* This book will demonstrate that we now have more than enough cases and data to understand and explain the UFO mystery—providing these cases are analyzed objectively and scientifically, and providing the principles derived from such analyses are intelligently applied to similar cases.

This book treats a representative sampling of the more than 10,000 UFO cases on record. To try to report on every one would require an encyclopedia and far more time than a private investigator can ever spend. Nor is it really necessary. Modern public-opinion pollsters have repeatedly demonstrated that a small, representative sample can provide a remarkably accurate profile of the whole. This is the approach that will be used here.

Many of the cases that are included here will be ones that have previously been investigated by experienced UFOlogists, including the very experienced Dr. J. Allen Hynek, Dr. James A. Harder and the late Dr. James E. McDonald, and pronounced by them to be "unexplainable," except in terms of extraterrestrial spaceships or other equally exotic phenomena. Two of the cases were singled out for publication by the American Institute of Aeronautics and Astronautics because they seemed to the AIAA's UFO Subcommittee to defy conventional explanation.

Another case, which reportedly involved a UFO "landing" on a farm outside Delphos, Kansas, was selected as the best of more than a thousand entries in a $50,000 contest staged by the *National Enquirer*. The selection was made by a panel of experienced UFOlogists and investigators, all with Ph.D.'s. The case of the two Pascagoula, Mississippi, shipyard workers who reported that they had been abducted and taken aboard a UFO in October, 1973, will come under critical scrutiny, and the facts may shock you.

In most UFO books the cases selected for inclusion are intended to impress the reader with the seemingly inexplicable nature of UFO reports. In this book the cases have been selected with a different purpose—to help you understand the truly complex nature of the mystery and the many different phenomena involved. In the process of analyzing these representative cases, a number of "UFOlogical Principles" emerge—principles that will enable you to better understand the next UFO report you read or hear about, and why there are periodic rashes of UFO sightings ("flaps").

The famous British mathematician and philosopher Alfred North Whitehead once observed: "The progress of Science consists in observing interconnections and in showing with a patient ingenuity that the events of this ever-shifting world are but examples of a few general relations, called laws. *To see what is general in what is particular, and what is permanent in what is transitory, is the aim of scientific thought.*" (Emphasis added.) The objective of this book is to apply that scientific methodology to the long-standing mystery of Unidentified Flying Objects.

1 · Craft with
Illuminated Windows

It was several hours after midnight on July 24, 1948, when the crew of an Eastern Air Lines DC-3, flying near Montgomery, Alabama, had a terrifying encounter with a giant cigar-shaped Unidentified Flying Object. The incident made headlines around the country; *The Atlanta Constitution*, hardly a sensationalist newspaper, carried a front-page headline that read: "ATLANTA PILOTS REPORT WINGLESS SKY MONSTER."

Only thirteen months earlier, flying saucers had first impacted on the United States public when newspapers carried the report by private flyer Kenneth Arnold that he had seen mysterious disk-shaped objects flying near Mount Rainier in the state of Washington. The following months produced numerous reports from around the country of mysterious flying objects. Barely a year before the Arnold incident, a U.S. Army Air Forces–sponsored study at the RAND Corporation "Think Tank" had concluded that enlarged versions of the V-2 ballistic missiles developed by Germany during World War II could soon make it possible to orbit unmanned spacecraft around the Earth. The next step could be space travel to the moon and planets like Venus and Mars, where scientists as well as science-fiction writers had long speculated there might be intelligent life.

Before the year 1947 was over, the rash of UFO reports had prompted the Army Air Forces (now the U.S. Air Force) to take steps to create a special office to investigate the flying saucer mystery. Then, on January 7, 1948, Captain Thomas Mantell lost his life when his plane crashed while chasing a giant UFO. The July 24 encounter by two experienced airline pilots—Captain Clarence S. Chiles and co-pilot John B. Whitted—added to the growing concern that there were strange craft in our skies whose performance and design were alien to the technology of this Earth.

The twenty-one-passenger airliner was headed east toward Atlanta at the time of the incident, flying at 5,000 feet altitude. The moon was nearly full and visibility was excellent, except for broken clouds at 6,000 feet altitude. Suddenly the crew sighted what appeared to be a giant jet aircraft headed toward them from out of the east. It flashed past the airliner to its right, coming within 700 feet of the DC-3, according to subsequent crew estimates. The UFO's speed was estimated at 500 to 700 mph, and orange-red flame was shooting out from its tail.

Both crew members agreed that the UFO had *two rows of windows* which seemed to be brightly illuminated from inside the object. In subsequent interviews with the press, Captain Chiles was quoted as saying, "You could see right through the windows and out the other side." Whitted, whose co-pilot seat gave him a slightly better view, reported seeing six large square-shaped windows. Both estimated that the UFO was approximately one hundred feet long and perhaps twenty-five to thirty feet in diameter. Sketches of the object drawn by the crew members shortly after the incident were remarkably similar. (See Plates 1a and 1b.) One minor discrepancy was that Chiles' sketch showed cockpit windows in the front, while Whitted observed none. But considering that the whole incident had lasted only ten seconds, this discrepancy was inconsequential.

Because of the early hour, only one of the passengers

aboard the DC-3 had observed the UFO, C. L. McKelvie. He
reported seeing only a sudden streak of light with no physical
shape discernible. Both crew members flatly rejected any
possibility that the UFO might be a meteor, especially since
it seemed to exhibit what would later come to be called
"intelligent control." As Chiles described it, the UFO
"flashed down and we veered to the left and it veered to the
left . . . Then, as if the pilot [of the object] had seen us and
wanted to avoid us, it pulled up with a tremendous burst of
flame out of its rear and zoomed up into the clouds." The
press quoted the crew members as asserting, "It was a
man-made thing, all right."

On the same night, at approximately the same time,
another Eastern Air Lines flight, #573, was en route from
Washington, D.C., to Raleigh-Durham, North Carolina,
when its crew spotted what it later described as "a trail that
appeared to be a jet or rocket trail traveling at a terrific
speed." The object appeared to be moving in a southwesterly
direction, but it was on the distant horizon and did not pose a
possible collision threat. This report appeared to confirm the
other, although it failed to provide any additional details.

The recently formed Air Force UFO investigation office
went into action. Beyond interviewing the airline crew, the
office investigated 225 airline and military flights that had
been aloft that night at approximately the time of the UFO
sighting to determine if one of these aircraft might have been
the UFO. Only one of these, a military C-47, was on a flight
path that could have taken it near the Eastern Air Lines
aircraft, and the military airplane was flying in a northwesterly
direction—opposite to the flight path reported for the UFO.

Six months later, when the Air Force project officer wrote a
final report on the case, his conclusion was that the object
"remains unidentified as to origin, construction and power
source." The report briefly mentioned that an astrophysicist
named Dr. Josef Allen Hynek of Ohio State University, who
had recently been hired as a consultant on UFOs, was
inclined to believe that the object might have been a bright
meteor. Hynek's report, which is part of the official files,
observed: "It will have to be left to the psychologists to tell us

whether the immediate trail of a bright meteor could produce the subjective impression of a ship with lighted windows." But the Air Force project officer rejected this possibility: "It is obvious that this object was not a meteor. There has been no evidence to support any findings of unreliability, nor have there been any major inaccuracies on the part of the witnesses." It would take nearly twenty years to demonstrate that this conclusion was grossly in error.

On March 3, 1968, at approximately 8:45 P.M. Central standard time (CST), the mayor of a large city in Tennessee, another civic official and the latter's wife, had an encounter with a UFO whose description was strikingly similar to the one reported nearly twenty years earlier by the Eastern Air Lines crew. The three adults, all intelligent, well-educated people, were standing outside talking when the woman spotted a distant light in the sky that was moving toward them at high speed. She brought it to the attention of the two men, and the three began to watch the object closely. As the UFO neared, they saw an orange-colored flame thrusting out from behind. Soon the UFO was passing almost directly over them in eerie silence at an altitude they estimated to be only 1,000 feet or less. The UFO seemed to be shaped "like a fat cigar . . . the size of one of our largest airplane fuselages, or larger," the woman later reported in a detailed letter to the U.S. Air Force.

She reported that the giant craft appeared to have at least *ten large square-shaped windows* which were brightly illuminated from inside the object. She observed that "it appeared to me that the fuselage was constructed of many pieces of flat sheets of metal-like material with a 'riveted-together look.'" The woman drew a sketch of the object which bore a remarkable similarity to the sketches drawn two decades earlier by the airline crew. (See Plate 1c.) After the UFO had disappeared to the northeast, the three adults discussed what they had seen and speculated as to what it might be. They agreed, the woman wrote, that the object must have been either a new, top-secret military aircraft or "a craft from outer space."

The same UFO was sighted by a group of six persons, most

of them adults, near Shoals, Indiana, more than two hundred miles north of the Tennessee observation site, at approximately the same time, according to another report submitted to the USAF. The Indiana report described the UFO as being cigar-shaped, with flame emerging from its tail, *and with many brightly illuminated windows.* (See Plate 1d.) The object was estimated to be 150 to 200 feet long, approximately the same size as the object reported by the Tennessee observers. The Indiana report said the object was at treetop level. The person who submitted the report from Indiana added that the morning after the incident "we heard it was supposed to have been a meteor. But the other five observers and myself know the UFO was not a meteor because meteors don't have windows and don't turn corners like IT [*sic*] did. And it didn't make any noise what-so-ever. I believe what we saw was a FLYING SAUCER [*sic*]."

The USAF also received two UFO sighting reports from individuals in Ohio. The sightings also had occurred on March 3, 1968, at approximately the same time as those in Tennessee and Indiana, but the descriptions were different, and for one of the observers, the sighting seemed to produce a strange hypnotic effect. This observer was a mature woman science teacher, with four academic degrees including a Ph.D., who lived near Columbus. She had been out walking her dog when she suddenly spotted a squadron of *three* luminous UFOs flying in formation. The woman was carrying binoculars which she promptly used to get a better look at the mysterious objects. In her very detailed report to the USAF, she said the UFOs were shaped like "inverted saucers," a familiar description in UFO reports. She estimated that the objects were flying very low, at an altitude of 1,500 feet or less.

The woman reported that the presence of the UFOs seemed to have a curious effect on her dog, although the objects emitted no sound audible to her ears. She said that her dog went over and lay down between two trash cans and whimpered "like she was frightened to death." There are many UFO reports which describe such animal reactions. But the UFOs seemed to have an even more curious effect on the woman herself after she had returned to the house. This was an overpowering urge to sleep. The woman reported that this was especially surprising because she had had a full ten hours' sleep the night before and had taken an afternoon nap only a few hours earlier. Because she was expecting a telephone call from a friend and wanted to stay awake, the woman opened the windows wide to admit the cool night air. Despite this, she repeatedly dropped off to sleep until around 11 P.M., when the strange effect disappeared completely.

The sighting by the Columbus teacher was confirmed by an industrial executive from Dayton, who was driving home that night from Cincinnati. The man was a close friend of a top USAF scientist in Dayton, and so he wrote to the USAF official to describe the incident. He observed that the USAF sometimes might have difficulty in determining whether a UFO report came from a crackpot or a credible witness and added: "I shall depend on you as the first witness as to whether I am insane, or highly imaginative, or otherwise unreliable."

The executive described seeing three luminous objects flying in what appeared to be a perfect formation, confirming the report by the Columbus teacher. One object seemed to be in the lead and the others were flying side-by-side to the rear, according to his letter. Then the three objects "executed a distinct curve in their flight path. This was unmistakable; the lead object first entered the curve, swinging out toward the left horizon; then the following two objects together entered the same curving course; then the three of them straightened out again toward the north-northeast." This seemed to indicate that the objects were under "intelligent control," a term that often appears in UFO reports. Because of the speed of the objects, and the absence of noise, it was clear that they could not be military jet aircraft.

The flight path reported for the giant UFO with illuminated windows by observers in Tennessee and Indiana and the approximately coincident time and date of sighting by the two observers in Ohio, raise the possibility if not the likelihood that all of these observers had seen the same thing. If this was true, was there only a single giant UFO, with numerous illuminated windows, or were there really three UFOs flying in a formation? Many UFO investigators automatically conclude that a report from multiple witnesses is more reliable than one from a single witness. If this criterion is used for this case, there are a total of nine observers in Tennessee and Indiana who reported a saucer/cigar-shaped object with illuminated windows and only two in Ohio who reported a squadron of three smaller objects in flight formation, and so one might well decide that there was only one giant UFO with numerous illuminated windows. *But in reality the two lone witnesses in Ohio were far more accurate observers.*

The night before this series of UFO sightings, the Soviet Union had used a giant cluster of rocket boosters to launch the Zond-4 spacecraft into orbit. The following night, March 3, 1968, one of the booster rockets began to lose altitude and finally entered the atmosphere at a speed of roughly 10,000 mph. This caused the booster to break up into pieces which, heated to incandescence, became a series of "man-made meteors." This occurred at approximately 8:45 CST, and the flaming fragments passed on a trajectory that took them over Tennessee in a northeasterly direction until they finally burned up near southern New York State.

This is known with certainty because the North American Air Defense Command (Norad) operates a world-wide network of powerful radars to enable it to keep track of every major object in space. Norad's records show that the reentry of the rocket occurred at the same time as the four UFO sightings, and the trajectory of the debris checks closely not only with these reports but with more than a hundred other observations made by persons on the ground and in aircraft in numerous east-central states. Some of the reports submitted to the USAF referred to the flaming objects as UFOs, while other observers assumed the objects were meteors. When one pilot flying over West Virginia reported the incident to a ground control tower and was asked if the flaming objects could be meteorites, the pilot replied: "It would be the first time I ever saw meteorites flying in formation!"

It is clear that the observers in Tennessee and Indiana were unwitting victims of their imaginations and of information that had been acquired, perhaps unconsciously, by their brains. When the observer sought a logical explanation for the unusual sight, he concluded that what his eyes were really seeing were illuminated windows of a giant craft. Because there was no sound, the craft could not be an ordinary airplane, and so the only other possible explanation was that the object(s) must be a UFO. The brain obligingly supplied the missing details and the observers in Tennessee and Indiana honestly believed that they could see a giant saucer/cigar-shaped craft.

The mature, well-educated science teacher from near Columbus also was a victim of autosuggestion, which fed upon her strong previous interest in UFOs. Her letter disclosed that she had sighted a UFO several years earlier and carried the binoculars on her nightly dog-walks in the hope of seeing another. (She also carried a flashlight and used it to try to communicate with the squadron of UFOs by transmitting Morse-code signals, but without any visible response.) Her sleepiness would seem to have been the result of her exhilaration at having seen three objects which might have been spaceships from another world. But how does this explain the reaction of the dog at the presence of the UFOs? One likely explanation was unwittingly noted in the teacher's report to the USAF. She observed at one point that her dog hated the cold. At another point in her letter she said the night temperature was "clear and cold," and that the temperature was eight degrees below freezing.

Nearly twenty years earlier, Dr. Hynek, the USAF's newly acquired consultant, had suggested that the giant UFO with brightly illuminated windows reported by Chiles and Whitted could have been a bright meteor, and that it might "produce the subjective impression of a ship with lighted windows." So far as is known, the USAF never followed up on his suggestion that psychologists be employed to verify this hypothesis. But the series of UFO sightings that occurred on March 3, 1968, unequivocally demonstrated that Hynek had been correct. The 1968 incident, coupled with the fact that there had been a number of meteor sightings during the week of the Chiles-Whitted encounter as a result of the annual Delta Aquarids meteor shower, clearly enables this case to be removed for all time from the category of "unidentifieds."

The Zond-4 incident and other UFO cases that will be discussed in subsequent chapters demonstrate an important principle that applies to all UFO reports.

> *UFOLOGICAL PRINCIPLE # 1: Basically honest and intelligent persons who are suddenly exposed to a brief, unexpected event, especially one that involves an unfamiliar object, may be grossly inaccurate in trying to describe precisely what they have seen.*

The reason is that what a person *believes* he has seen is very strongly influenced by previously acquired information that has been stored, perhaps unconsciously, in the brain. This UFOlogical Principle #1, in more general terms, has long been recognized by psychologists who have conducted experiments in human perception, and by trial lawyers and criminal investigators experienced in eyewitness testimony. *Its importance in understanding the UFO mystery cannot be overemphasized.*

2 · Mysteriously Behaving UFOs

In late April of 1967, some sharp-eyed residents of Monroe County, Michigan, southwest of Detroit, began to observe an intense white light performing curious maneuvers in the night sky. Several weeks later a second UFO appeared and would seem to cavort with the first. Sometimes the intense white light would mysteriously turn to red, then later back to white. The two UFOs did not appear every night, but one observant woman, Mrs. B., noted that they showed up most frequently on Tuesday nights. They usually arrived around 9 P.M., performed their strange maneuvers until around midnight and then departed. Then, in late July, the UFOs stopped coming to Monroe County.

From newspaper accounts and my own correspondence with some of the observers, there was universal agreement that *the UFOs made absolutely no sound*, except for one night when one observer reported hearing a noise that sounded like a "vacuum-cleaner." This, plus the outlandish capers of one of the UFOs, seemed to rule out any possibility that the UFOs could be airplanes. For example, one of the

UFOs was reported to frequently dive down toward the ground in the vicinity of Milan, Michigan, as if trying to attack something on the surface, and then it would mysteriously disappear, only to reappear some distance away a few minutes later.

One observer reported that on one occasion, one of the UFOs shot straight up into the sky and disappeared. More frequently, Mrs. B. reported, one of the UFOs would "sit in one place for fifteen minutes." She was not only a very observant woman but an adventuresome one as well. One night, on spotting the UFOs, she got into her car and tried to follow one of them, with somewhat frightening consequences. She later reported: "Whoever or whatever flies those things knows you're chasing them, because the object will turn around and follow you." (This apparent reaction of UFOs to human observers on the ground is not uncommon.)

Two other residents of Monroe County had even more unnerving experiences. One woman, who was employed on the night shift in a local hospital, had just parked her car and was walking to the hospital when one of the UFOs flew directly overhead and illuminated her with an intense spotlight, she later reported. A teen-age boy, standing outside his house one night, had a similar experience. Only a few months earlier, *Look* magazine had published a two-part series of articles about Mr. and Mrs. Barney Hill, of Portsmouth, New Hampshire, who said they had been abducted by the crew of a flying saucer and taken aboard the craft. (See Chapter 23.) If their story was true (and *Look* editors implied that they believed the story), then perhaps the UFOs over Monroe County were using spotlights to size up future kidnap victims. One woman later wrote me that the situation had reached the point where she was afraid to venture out alone at night.

On the night of May 12, 1969, two teen-age boys were driving along Illinois Highway #53, near Lake Zurich, when they first spotted a red light that appeared to mark the top of a radio tower. But suddenly there was an intense flash of white light. As the two youths, Greg Lucht and Alan Prouty, drove past a clump of trees toward the lights, they saw what they later described as a saucer-shaped craft which resembled a "World War I English helmet." The object, they said, had a concave indentation in the belly which housed a large white light that flashed on and off repeatedly.

At one point the UFO seemed to nose down, and Lucht later reported that he could clearly make out its oval shape as well as three large headlights in the forward section and numerous small red and white lights around the rim of the saucer-shaped craft which kept blinking on and off. The excited youths drove to Prouty's home and went out on the roof to get a better view of the object. At one point, the youths reported, "we had to lie down on the roof to keep from falling off because it came so close!" Unlike most UFOs, which are reported to be silent, the boys noted an unusual humming noise which seemed to rise and fall in pitch in a regular pattern. They also reported that the UFO's presence seemed to affect a neighbor's dog, which began to bark when the object came near.

This UFO report might be dismissed as a fanciful tale concocted by two youths except that the object was also reported by Morton Konlon, of Lake Zurich, who said he first spotted the curious object around 9 P.M. He said that he and two other men had watched the UFO for almost an hour—which would seem to rule out the possibility that it could be a meteor, or flaming rocket debris. Konlon also reported seeing brilliant flashes of light at intervals of approximately eight seconds which lit up a large area on the ground. This reminded Konlon of a giant camera flash lamp, and he said he "got the impression that it could have been someone taking night photographs from an airplane." But he depreciated this possibility by observing: "I don't know why they would want to photograph this area." Konlon, a private pilot himself, said the UFO made a noise that sounded like a conventional propeller-driven airplane when it was far away, but when the object came closer, the sound mysteriously changed to that of a jet-powered craft. He said he could not make out any shape to the object because of the brilliant flashing light. But it appeared to have two red lights instead of the one red, one green navigation lights of an ordinary airplane.

The case quickly came to the attention of Dr. Hynek, long-time UFO consultant to the USAF, who was now head of the astronomy department at nearby Northwestern University. In the intervening years since Hynek had sought to explain the Chiles-Whitted UFO as a bright meteor, his own views on UFOs had changed radically. Hynek interviewed the two youths and examined a sketch of the UFO which they had drawn showing a saucer-shaped craft with a ring of small lights around its periphery. Hynek then made the following pronouncement, which the *Chicago Tribune* carried in its big feature story on the incident: "The descriptions of the object that flew over Lake Zurich bear striking similarities to other UFOs reported in America and other countries." These similarities, Hynek's statement implied, confirmed the accuracy of the youths' descriptions.

In both the Michigan and Lake Zurich cases, as we shall see, it is possible in retrospect to say with certainty that the reports were submitted by basically honest and intelligent people who were trying their best to describe what they thought they had seen and experienced. And in both instances it would seem logical to rule out the possibility that the UFOs were airplanes. Certainly so for the Monroe County UFOs, which were reported to perform maneuvers that no human pilot seemingly would risk and where the objects made no sound, according to numerous observers.

But in fact the UFOs that attracted so much attention over Monroe County were two fixed-wing aircraft that were being used to test a new experimental military radar that had been developed by the Raytheon Company. The tests were conducted by the University of Michigan's Willow Run Laboratories, just north of Monroe County. They began in late April of 1967, at the time the UFOs first appeared, and the tests ended (temporarily) in late July, the date when the UFOs stopped coming. Both airplanes were outfitted with intense, 20,000-candlepower lights so that the crew of each aircraft could see the other clearly and so that both could be tracked by scientists on the ground.

One of the aircraft, an old World War II piston-engine C-46, functioned as a simulated target while the other, a B-26 of the same vintage which was outfitted with the new Raytheon radar, made simulated air attacks on the C-46. The target aircraft would fly a straight path into Monroe County from the south, and as it came into range, the B-26 would begin a circular-path attack toward the C-46, flying at an altitude of 1,500 feet while the target was several thousand feet higher to provide safe separation. After making the circular-path run against the target, the B-26 would continue to circle around toward the east, away from the target, and would then make a simulated attack against a ground target. This was a special marker located in the field of a farmer outside Milan which had been rented from its owner for the tests.

The B-26 would dive from 1,500 feet to within 500 feet of the ground, at which point the pilot would pull up and return to his original altitude. As the pilot started to pull up, he would turn off the intense white light because that particular test run was concluded. To Mrs. B., who was watching from a distance of some miles, the intense light was the UFO, and this light did indeed disappear shortly after the dive toward the ground near Milan, as she had reported. Meanwhile, the C-46 target aircraft would turn around and fly south to Ohio, to get into position for another mission north into Monroe County. While the B-26 was waiting for the target to return, the pilot would often kill time by flying tight circles near Dundee, Michigan. To Mrs. B., who was viewing this from a distance of five to ten miles, and seeing the aircraft's normal navigation lights, the object seemed to be staying in approximately the same spot. But her particular choice of words suggested that the UFO was literally hovering over one spot.

The intense white light on the C-46 target airplane was installed on its belly, but the light aboard the B-26 was located on the right-hand side of the aircraft. At such times as the B-26 banked sharply for a right-hand turn, the 20,000-candlepower illumination would shine down on the ground.

This explains the two incidents of the woman and teen-age youth who suddenly found themselves caught in the glare of the UFO's spotlight. The B-26 also carried two smaller red lights in its nose, which were visible to ground observers only when the airplane was flying toward them. At any other viewing angle, the red lights would not be visible. This explains why some ground observers reported that the UFO's color would mysteriously change from white to red and then back to white.

Mrs. B. was absolutely correct when she noted that the UFOs seemed to appear most frequently on Tuesday nights. The specific nights on which the tests were conducted depended upon many factors, including the local weather and the operability of the equipment in the B-26. When Raytheon checked its flight-test records, it found that, quite by chance, more flights had indeed been conducted on Tuesday nights than on any other.

On the night that Mrs. B. got into her car and tried to follow one of the UFOs, only to find that it seemed to be turning around to chase after her, the facts were not as they, understandably, appeared to Mrs. B. She was following the B-26, but its pilot was merely following his planned circular flight path. When Mrs. B. started her chase, the B-26 was headed west and northwest toward the target aircraft, and after this part of the run was completed, he simply circled back toward the east, and later south. One Monroe County observer reported that one of the UFOs had flown past her house at treetop level, but the Raytheon pilot assured me that he had never flown below 1,500 feet except for the brief dive to 500 feet outside Milan.

But what explanation is there for the fact that all the observers agreed that the UFOs made no sound (except for the vacuum-cleaner sound one night), when the two aircraft involved are extremely noisy, and the B-26 was flying at only 1,500 feet altitude? One partial explanation may be the distance between the aircraft and the observers. Even when an airplane is moderately close, if the wind is blowing in a direction away from the observer toward the aircraft, little if any sound will be heard. But it also seems likely that the observers were so entranced by the idea that they were privileged to be seeing mysterious spaceships from other worlds that they were oblivious to the aircraft engine sounds.

Shortly after the *Chicago Tribune* carried a big feature story in its May 25, 1969, early editions describing the Lake Zurich UFO sighting, including two sketches of the saucer-shaped object drawn by Alan Prouty, the UFO was very quickly identified by Chicago Aerial Industries of Barrington, Illinois, which produces military photo-reconnaissance equipment. (The company is now Bourns/CAI.) The company reported that the Lake Zurich UFO was a conventional Beech AT-11 twin piston-engine aircraft that was being used to test a new system for illuminating the ground for night photography. The intense flash lamp had been mounted in the belly of the airplane, as the UFO reports stated, and it flashed on and off at five-to-ten-second intervals, as Konlon had accurately noted. Other than this, the airplane carried conventional navigation lights: a red light in one wing tip, a green one in the other and a white light in the tail. Additionally, it carried a conventional rotating red beacon atop the airplane to provide warning against mid-air collisions.

The giant flash lamp required considerable power to operate—more than was available from the aircraft's regular engine-driven generator. So the airplane had been equipped with a small propeller-driven generator suspended from a wing and driven by the windstream. This wind-driven generator emitted a high-pitched sound that would be especially audible when the airplane was near, as Konlon had reported. But contrary to the report by the youths that the UFO had come so low that they had to lie down on the roof, the pilot stated that the aircraft had never flown below an altitude of 1,500 feet except during takeoff and landing. But what of the youths' report that the object had been saucer-shaped? Here again is an example of where the observer's brain supplied details that the eyes did not see, drawing on its store of previously acquired information as to the shape of a UFO, or "flying saucer."

.   .   .

These two cases, as well as the ones discussed in Chapter 1, illustrate another UFOlogical Principle:

> UFOLOGICAL PRINCIPLE #2: *Despite the intrinsic limitations of human perception when exposed to brief, unexpected and unusual events, some details recalled by the observer may be reasonably accurate. The problem facing the UFO investigator is to try to distinguish between those details that are accurate and those that are grossly inaccurate. This may be impossible until the true identity of the UFO can be determined, so that in some cases this poses an insoluble problem.*

For example, Monroe County observers were generally correct about the gross movements, colors and nights of most frequent appearance of the UFOs. But they were grossly in error in their reports about the UFO's sitting in one place, the altitude of the objects, and other details. The Lake Zurich observers were correct in describing the intense flashing light and the sound made by the wind-driven generator, but were seriously in error in describing the object's shape and peripheral lighting.

An interesting postscript to the Monroe County case occurred in November of 1967, when I received a letter from a friend of Mrs. B., who said that she accepted my explanation for the UFO's seen a few months earlier, which I had supplied to original observers who had assisted me in my investigation. But her letter said that UFOs had once again returned to Monroe County and could I explain the new ones. I promptly telephoned a Raytheon public-information official, John Severance, and said, "I'll bet you have recently resumed flight tests of your radar in Michigan." Severance replied, "As a matter of fact, we have, but how did you know?" I replied, "I have a vast network of sources."

We both laughed heartily, because it was through Severance that I had first learned of this case and the identity of the Monroe County UFOs even before I had begun to question the witnesses about their observations. Thus this case had become a valuable controlled experiment in which the observations of multiple witnesses could be checked for accuracy against the known facts. For example, the reported movement of the two UFOs could be compared with the precise flight paths flown by the pilots. When I prepared a report on the case for the witnesses who had cooperated with me, I carefully avoided any ridicule of their inaccuracies and noted that some reported observations were quite accurate. Mrs. B. had accepted the explanation, but she quickly wrote me to describe UFO sightings of previous years during vacation trips and asked if I could explain these. I begged off.

3 · Hand-Made UFOs

During the night of July 7, 1968, thousands of residents of the Seattle area witnessed the strange antics of a squadron of UFOs, and a private pilot approaching the city to land at Boeing Field had a frightening encounter with the objects. The next morning's edition of the *Seattle Post-Intelligencer* carried a banner headline on the front page that read: "UFO MYSTERY HERE," and a two-column subhead that reported: "Eerie Red Lights Chased by Plane." The feature front-page story described how nine ruby-red lights had been seen by thousands of ground observers, including Federal Aviation Administration tower operators, as the UFOs soared back and forth across Puget Sound. Approximately forty minutes after the objects first appeared, they began to mysteriously disappear, one by one, until they were all gone. But despite the many visual sightings, local-area radars failed to detect the objects.

The pilot, Mr. M., had been approaching the city when he suddenly found himself headed directly toward the nine glowing objects, which seemed to be flying in formation, according to his subsequent account. To avoid a mid-air collision, the pilot made a sharp turn to the right, and the nine UFOs simultaneously took evasive action and also made a sharp turn to their right, he reported. The pilot suspected that he had encountered a formation of military aircraft, but when he checked by radio with the local FAA control tower, he was told there were no known military aircraft operating in the area.

It was a clear, moonlit night, and as the pilot watched, he reported that some of the UFOs were *firing rockets* at the ground and that he could even see them impacting near Green Lake. The pilot put his airplane into a 360-degree turn underneath the UFOs, which now seemed to be hovering over West Seattle, so he could get a better look at the objects. Soon, however, the UFOs headed toward the private aircraft, prompting the pilot to turn on his landing lights to warn the UFOs of his presence. At this point the UFOs seemed to react intelligently to his action, and they appeared to halt their head-on approach and back off, the pilot reported. The most mysterious aspect of the whole incident was the apparent effect of the UFOs on two of the cockpit instruments. When the UFOs finally disappeared and the pilot had landed at Boeing Field, he discovered that his gyrocompass was 170 degrees in error—almost completely backward—and the panel clock had stopped at 10:35 P.M. It was as if some mysterious radiation emitted by the UFOs had affected these two instruments. The badly shaken pilot insisted that the UFOs were solid craft: "I wouldn't believe it myself, but I saw it," he added.

Less than four months earlier, on March 25, 1968, a UFO had been sighted near Metuchen, New Jersey, and reported by an impressive collection of twenty-five witnesses that included four policemen and a clergyman. The latter had been the first to see the curious glowing UFO descending, and he had called the police, who dispatched two patrol cars. The clergyman had subsequently described the UFO as resembling a large orange balloon that appeared to have a fire inside. But police officers sharply disagreed with any suggestion that the UFO might have been a balloon because of the seemingly intelligent action the object exhibited. When a squad-car spotlight was pointed toward the UFO, "it began to climb out very fast," one policeman observed. Another officer said: "I thought at first it was the usual plastic-bag gag, but when I turned the lights on it, the orange ball climbed away too fast. It continued to climb until two airplanes converged on it, then it blinked twice and the light went out." Another officer said the UFO appeared to be attached to another, larger object above.

Two years earlier, in late March of 1966, hundreds of citizens of San Gabriel Valley in southern California reported seeing glowing UFOs during several nights. The glowing objects reportedly "zipped along at fantastic speed." Some observers reported that the UFOs made a whistling noise, but others heard no sound at all. The most curious part of the San Gabriel sightings was that some observers reported a *smell of perfume in the air* which seemed to be associated with the presence of the UFOs.

In early April of 1967, glowing UFOs were reported over Boulder, Colorado, by at least six persons. This was shortly after the U.S. Air Force had contracted with the University of Colorado, at Boulder, to conduct a scientific study of unidentified flying objects. It was as if the UFOs were trying to make their presence known to university scientists engaged in the study.

A few months later, in mid-September of 1967, similar glowing UFOs were also spotted in the night skies over Sharon, Pennsylvania. In the large catalog of UFO reports, there are some that tell of electric power system failures that have occurred at the time of UFO sightings, suggesting to some that alien spaceships are bent on sabotage. This speculation seemed to be confirmed by events at Sharon. One evening, shortly after the town had experienced a thirty-minute power outage, a glowing UFO was seen eerily floating over the city just after the lights came back on.

These five cases, that occurred at widely separated locations over a two-year period, are typical of *hundreds* of UFO incidents reported by honest, intelligent persons in which UFOs seemingly caused mysterious effects. In these five cases alone, the effects ranged from throwing airplane instruments out of kilter to creating the odor of perfume and power system failure. In several of these incidents the UFOs seemed to exhibit "intelligent control" or behavior, and possibly even malicious intent.

All five of these cases have one thing in common: the UFOs were hot-air balloons made from large garment plastic bags by practical jokers! Man's first successful flying machine was a fabric balloon whose air was heated by an open flame. All of these UFOs, and hundreds of others, are simply modern implementations of this age-old principle, usually devised by teen-age youths with a scientific bent. We will encounter still more such UFO cases in subsequent chapters.

The day after the *Seattle Post-Intelligencer* carried its front-page story on the UFOs under a banner headline, the newspaper carried the explanation, which *was "buried" on page 12.* Several teen-age boys had admitted that they had launched the plastic balloons, equipped with candles to supply the hot air and ghostly illumination, the night before. The ingenious pranksters had attached to each balloon some railroad flares with long fuses so that the flares would not ignite until some time after launch. When the flares finally ignited and burned free, they fell to earth while still aflame; these were the "rockets" the pilot had reported.

The headline on the story suggested that the newspaper itself was not fully convinced as to this explanation: "BALLOONS . . . OR NOT? UFO VIEWS VARY." The article noted that the prank/balloon explanation had been accepted by the Seattle police, by McCord Air Force Base officials and by the Federal Aviation Administration. But the pilot, Mr. M., disagreed: "Balloons couldn't fly in formation like that, and they certainly couldn't change directions and accelerate so quickly." He also estimated that the objects had been flying faster than 1,000 miles per hour—clearly beyond the capabilities of hot-air balloons.

The newspaper did not attempt to explain how the pilot's gyrocompass might have become so grossly in error. If it had checked with anyone familiar with the relatively inexpensive type of gyro normally used in private aircraft, the explanation could have been found, once it was known that Mr. M. had spent many minutes in flying 360-degree turns to observe the UFOs. Such maneuvers produce gross gyro errors. As for the mysterious stoppage of the cockpit clock, these are a manually wound type. If the pilot forgets to wind his clock, it will stop!

These cases, as well as those discussed in earlier chapters, illustrate two more important UFOlogical Principles:

> UFOLOGICAL PRINCIPLE #3: *If a person observing an unusual or unfamiliar object concludes that it is probably a spaceship from another world, he can readily adduce that the object is reacting to his presence or actions when in reality there is absolutely no cause-effect relationship.**

In the Seattle incident, the pilot concluded that the UFOs reacted first to his own sharp turn and later to his turning on of the landing lights, when in fact the balloons were reacting only to the winds aloft and the vagaries of their own construction. In Metuchen, the same was true of the apparent reaction of the balloon to the squad-car spotlight. In the earlier Monroe County case (Chapter 2), when Mrs. B. was chasing one of the UFOs in her car, and the B-26 aircraft pilot circled around to follow his prescribed flight path, Mrs. B. understandably concluded that the UFO was chasing after her.

The number of UFO reports that have been generated by balloons hoisted by inventive pranksters is unknown, but must surely be in the hundreds. Usually the UFOs are made from plastic garment bags used by dry cleaners. The top of the bag is sealed and the lower opening is held open by wood strips on which candles are mounted. When the candles are

---

* Mark Twain phrased it more colorfully: "You cannot depend on your eyes when your imagination is out of focus."

lighted, the result is a classic hot-air balloon—man's earliest flying machine. But the device is also a potential fire hazard which may be illegal in some communities (and should be outlawed in all). For this reason, those who build and launch this class of UFO are seldom willing to identify themselves.

I had not appreciated the weird, ghostlike appearance of these plastic hot-air balloons until the fall of 1971, when friends in central New York State, Mr. and Mrs. Bruno Spiegler, sent me a newspaper clipping from the *Oneonta Star* with photos of such a device. There had been a rash of UFO sightings which were finally explained when several teen-age boys admitted they had used plastic garment bags as hot-air balloons. One photo (Plate 2b) showed balloon construction while another (Plate 2a) showed one of the balloons in flight at night. The softly illuminated object and its ill-defined shape, silently drifting through the night skies, could readily convince a casual observer that he was seeing a UFO, or an apparition.

Nor does the ingenuity of pranksters stop simply with hot-air balloons of elementary design. On October 6, 1967, hundreds of Los Angeles residents near Griffith Park spotted a weird-looking UFO overhead just at sunset. Traffic along the Golden State Freeway slowed to a near-halt as motorists sought a glimpse of the curious object. Fortunately, a Los Angeles police helicopter was available to investigate and photograph the object. The UFO turned out to be a balloon to which had been attached long sheets of shiny aluminum foil, each piece being about six feet long. These metallic strips, reflecting the rays of the setting sun, created a striking UFO. The prankster, or "artist," who devised and lofted this ingenious UFO has never identified himself, so far as I can determine.

The reaction of the *Seattle Post-Intelligencer* when it found that it had been taken in by a teen-age prank, and the reaction of the *Chicago Tribune* when a prosaic explanation emerged for the Lake Zurich UFO are illuminating. Every reader of the Seattle newspaper on July 8, 1968, knew of the UFO incident because of its front-page, banner-headline treatment. But how many of these readers saw the hot-air balloon explanation the following day when the story was buried on page 12? The *Chicago Tribune* devoted a total of *forty-five column-inches*, including a sketch, to the original Zurich incident. But when the UFO was identified as an ordinary airplane conducting tests, this rated *only two column-inches.*

This points up another UFOlogical Principle which helps to explain why the UFO mystery has persisted for so long:

> *UFOLOGICAL PRINCIPLE #4: News media that give great prominence to a UFO report when it is first received, subsequently devote little if any space or time to reporting a prosaic explanation for the case when all the facts are uncovered.*

As a result, the general public is often left to conclude that there are many unexplainable UFO cases when in reality the news media are usually not interested in devoting space or time to a prosaic explanation—especially if it might prompt readers or viewers to conclude that the media had failed to probe deeply enough before reporting the original incident.

4 · High-Flying UFOs

At 8:52 A.M. on April 30, 1969, the United Press International teletypewriter in our *Aviation Week & Space Technology* magazine Washington offices clattered out an "URGENT" bulletin, datelined Ponce, Puerto Rico:

> THOUSANDS OF PONCENOS ARE HANGING FROM THEIR BALCONIES AND OUT ON THE STREETS STARING AT A STRANGE LIGHT SOUTH OF PONCE. THE ILLUMINATED OBJECT IS SAID TO BE VERY LARGE AND VERY HIGH IN THE SKY. IT WAS REPORTED THAT A PLANE CIRCLED THE OBJECT AND SAID IT WAS ABOUT TEN TIMES LARGER THAN THE PLANE.

At 9:25 A.M., this initial bulletin was followed by another UPI dispatch, this one datelined San Juan:

> HUNDREDS OF PERSONS HERE AND IN THE SOUTH COAST TOWN OF PONCE, INCLUDING AIRLINE PILOTS AND CONTROL TOWER PERSONNEL, ARE MYSTIFIED BY A STRANGE, HIGHLY LUMINOUS UNIDENTIFIED OBJECT APPARENTLY DRIFTING ACROSS THE SKY THIS MORNING.

PETER JACKSON, A CONTROL TOWER OPERATOR AT SAN JUAN INTERNATIONAL AIRPORT, SAID HE SAW THE OBJECT MOVING SLOWLY TOWARD THE SOUTHWEST. "IT WAS COMPLETELY WHITE AND SEEMED TO HAVE A FISHNET TYPE THING HANGING DOWN WITH A WHITE CYLINDRICAL OBJECT INSIDE THE NET. IT WAS DEFINITELY NOT A BALLOON," SAID JACKSON. [Emphasis added.] HE SAID THE OBJECT WAS SPOTTED BY SEVERAL AIRLINE PILOTS. [The earlier report from Ponce was then repeated.] A PUERTO RICO AIR NATIONAL GUARD JET IS BEING SENT TO INVESTIGATE.

JACKSON SAID THE OBJECT APPEARED TO BE OVAL IN SHAPE AND OPEN AT THE TOP. HE SAID IT WAS MOVING VERY SLOWLY BUT HE COULD NOT BE CERTAIN IF IT WAS BEING CARRIED BY THE WIND. . . .

At 11:15 A.M., the UPI provided additional details, datelined San Juan:

"IT'S SOMETHING LIKE I'VE NEVER SEEN BEFORE," SAID PETER JACKSON, CONTROL TOWER MAN AT THE INTERNATIONAL AIRPORT IN RELATION TO AN UNIDENTIFIED FLYING OBJECT SEEN IN SEVERAL PLACES IN PUERTO RICO TODAY. JACKSON DESCRIBED THE UFO AS "BRIGHT WHITE . . . TRANSPARENT AND SOMETHING WAS LAYING BENEATH IT . . . IF IT WAS A BALLOON . . . IT MUST HAVE BEEN FLYING UPSIDE DOWN." JACKSON SAID THAT AN F-104 NATIONAL GUARD JET WAS DISPATCHED TO INVESTIGATE THE OBJECT. HE STATED THAT "EVEN AT 50,000 FEET THE OBJECT WAS STILL FLYING OVER THE JET. IT MUST BE HUGE," SAID THE CONTROL TOWER MAN.

At 11:24 A.M., still another UPI dispatch arrived on the UFO sighting, but this one contained two conflicting reports. Colonel Alberto Nido, of the Air National Guard, was quoted as saying that the UFO had been inspected by two F-104 pilots, who reported that the object was sixty feet long, triangular in shape, apparently made of plastic and was flying at 70,000 feet—far above the ceiling of the F-104s.

But the same UPI report also quoted an Air Force spokesman from Ramey Air Force Base in Puerto Rico, who said: "An Air Force B-52 bomber flew to the object to inspect

it and found it was at 35,000 feet." The object turned out to
be a rubber weather balloon!

At 5:40 P.M., the final UPI dispatch on the incident arrived
on the ticker, datelined Ponce:

> AN UNIDENTIFIED FLYING OBJECT AROUSED CONSIDERABLE
> EXCITEMENT IN PUERTO RICO TODAY BEFORE IT TURNED OUT
> TO BE A COMMON WEATHER BALLOON. THE UFO WAS
> VARIOUSLY DESCRIBED AS BEING ROUND OR TRIANGULAR
> SHAPED . . . RUBBER OR PLASTIC . . . 35,000 FEET HIGH
> OR 70,000 FEET . . . SELF-PROPELLED OR FLOATING IN THE
> WIND. FINALLY, THE NATIONAL GUARD SPOILED THE FUN BY
> ADVISING IT HAD LAUNCHED A WEATHER BALLOON FROM
> SALINAS AND THAT UNDOUBTEDLY WAS WHAT EVERYONE WAS
> LOOKING AT.

This case is only one of many that demonstrate that
balloons do not need to be specially rigged by ingenious
pranksters to induce UFO reports. Usually the balloons are
simply performing routine meteorological functions to aid in
weather forecasting, but occasionally they are performing
more exotic tasks.

Every day the National Oceanic and Atmospheric Administration launches approximately three hundred large, helium-
filled weather balloons. At launch, the balloon measures only
six feet in diameter, but as it rises to less dense air, the size
increases to roughly twenty to twenty-five feet at 100,000 feet
altitude. Approximately half the balloons are launched in the
early morning and the other half in the early evening. Launch
times are 0:00 Greenwich Mean Time (GMT) and 12:00
GMT, which correspond to 7 P.M. and 7 A.M. Eastern
standard time (EST) respectively. The balloons carry a
radiosonde box containing sensors to measure air temperature, pressure and humidity and a radio transmitter to return
this data to the ground. The balloons also carry small lights,
visible for five to ten miles, to alert pilots to their presence.
These same lights, in combination with changing wind
velocity and direction at different altitudes, often generate
UFO reports. The records of the USAF's Project Blue Book
UFO investigative office indicate that approximately 10

percent of all reports received throughout the years can be attributed to balloons.

Still another type of balloon, which was introduced in the United States only three months after the first UFO sighting reported by Kenneth Arnold, has produced a number of UFO reports, including the incident that resulted in the tragic death of Captain Thomas Mantell. These are the giant "Skyhook" balloons, made of partially transparent plastic similar to the material now available to homemakers to keep perishable foods fresh. These giant balloons offered scientists the first opportunity to make measurements at altitudes far above the ceiling of then-existing aircraft, above most of the Earth's obscuring atmosphere.

The first giant Skyhook balloon was launched by the Office of Naval Research on September 25, 1947, from St. Cloud, Minnesota, near the facility of General Mills, Inc., which manufactured it. In the intervening years, much larger Super-Skyhook balloons have been developed and flown both by the Office of Naval Research and the Air Force Cambridge Research Laboratories. One recent design has a volume of 33 million cubic feet, approximately one hundred times that of the first model. It has carried a 3,000-pound payload to an altitude of more than 130,000 feet. In the fall of 1972, the USAF set a new altitude record with a giant-sized 47.8-million-cubic-foot balloon which carried a 250-pound payload to an altitude of 170,000 feet—more than thirty-two miles.

As these giant balloons rise into less dense air, the helium gas fills out the balloon, changing its initial "ice-cream cone" shape to a pear-shaped configuration and finally into a near-circular form. During daylight, the sun's illumination is partially reflected from these giant balloons and partially diffused by the thin plastic, which can produce a rainbow of colors. Under certain illumination conditions, a ground observer may see a "saucer-shaped" patch of sunlight, as indicated by a USAF telephoto picture shown in Plate 3a.

During the past quarter-century the Navy has launched an average of more than one hundred of these giant balloons each year, and in recent years the USAF has lofted a similar number. After launch the balloons are carried by the prevailing winds at the balloon's altitude. At such time as the balloon encounters "jet-stream" winds, which typically move at speeds of 100 to 150 mph, the giant balloon can zip across the sky. But at other times, especially during the warm summer season, there may be strong winds from the east at certain altitudes as well as the traditional westerly wind at different altitudes. Under these conditions the balloon may reverse direction as it changes altitude and can even trace out a roughly circular path, appearing to a ground observer to be hovering in one spot before eventually taking off, possibly at high speed. During the early evening, when the ground observer is in darkness, a balloon cruising above 100,000 feet may still catch the rays of the setting sun and appear as a glowing, multicolored object.

Although the Skyhook balloon had originally been developed as a very high altitude platform for scientific experimentation, it appeared on the scene at a time when relations with the Soviet Union were beginning to deteriorate rapidly and the Cold War was threatening to get hot. Russia's Iron Curtain effectively prevented the West from learning what was taking place in the U.S.S.R. and there was growing concern that preparations for an attack might be under way. If the newly developed Navy Skyhook balloons could lift to very high altitudes scientific payloads which could later be released by radio command to parachute down and be recovered, it seemed logical that the same type of balloon could loft a reconnaissance camera.

During World War II, Japan had devised an ingenious program to retaliate for the 1942 Doolittle bomber raid on Tokyo which would use the prevailing westerly winds to transport balloons carrying explosives and incendiaries to the west coast of the United States. After two years of experimentation, the Japanese began to launch large numbers of these balloons, starting in late 1944, and a significant number reached the United States, some penetrating as far as Michigan, although they did little damage. If Japanese balloons could transit the Pacific ocean with modest-size payloads, then it appeared possible that much larger Skyhook-type balloons, launched from Western Europe, could use the same westerly winds to carry reconnaissance cameras over the Iron Curtain to take photographs of the U.S.S.R. and the Eastern Bloc countries. When such a balloon reached the now-friendly shores of Japan, radio commands could cause the balloon to release the camera and its precious pictures, which would parachute to Earth for recovery. Later, techniques would be developed to enable specially equipped aircraft to locate and recover the camera as it parachuted down—a method subsequently used to recover film capsules from "spy satellites" performing a similar mission.

The program was sponsored by the Central Intelligence Agency and was cloaked in such deep secrecy that only a handful of top military officials were aware of the project— aside from the small number of Navy personnel involved in developing a suitable Skyhook balloon and the USAF scientists at Wright-Patterson Air Force Base who were to develop the required reconnaissance camera and parachute recovery mechanism. Meanwhile, to provide a "cover" for the secret "spy balloons," the Navy would continue to launch Skyhook balloons for scientific purposes. Even today, a quarter-century later, this United States reconnaissance balloon program is still cloaked in secrecy, despite the fact that a number of the vehicles came down in the U.S.S.R., prompting repeated Russian protests at the United Nations. (I first learned of this program while researching my book on spy satellites: *Secret Sentries in Space.*)

In late 1947 a priority effort was under way at Wright-Patterson Air Force Base, near Dayton, Ohio, to develop the recoverable camera payload for the reconnaissance balloons. To test the reconnaissance payload, facilities were established at Wilmington Air Force Base, in Clinton County, Ohio, approximately thirty miles southeast of Dayton, to launch experimental Skyhook balloons. Shortly after noon on January 7, 1948, Kentucky State Police began to receive reports of a high-flying UFO over the central part of the state, which were relayed to the control tower of Godman Air Force Base, near Fort Knox. Soon the tower operators spotted the UFO to the west, moving in a southwesterly direction. Word spread rapidly to bring other observers to the tower, including the base commander. In official reports subsequently prepared by these many observers, the UFO was described in the following way:

- "Object appeared like 'ice-cream cone topped with red'—apparently white with red above."
- "Like tear-drop—round; later, object seemed fluid."
- "Round—at times cone shaped."
- "It was very white and looked like an umbrella."
- "I was unable to tell if it was an object radiating its own light or giving off reflected light [from the sun]. Through binoculars it partially appeared as a parachute does with bright sun shining on top of the silk but there also seemed to be some red light around the lower [part] of it."

All of the observers agreed that the object seemed to be very large, with size estimates ranging up to several hundred feet. As those in the Godman Air Force Base tower watched, a flight of four P-51 fighter planes approached the base. These were Air National Guard aircraft on a ferrying flight from Marietta, Georgia. The tower radioed the flight leader, Captain Thomas Mantell, and asked if the pilots could investigate the mysterious UFO. Mantell and two of the aircraft spotted the UFO and began to climb on a heading of approximately 220 degrees. At approximately 2:45 P.M. (CST), Mantell radioed in to report: "I have an object in sight above and ahead of me and it appears to be moving at about half my speed." When he was asked to describe the object's appearance, Mantell replied: "It appears to be a metallic object or possibly reflection of sun from a metallic object, and it is of tremendous size." A few minutes later, Mantell radioed in: "[object] directly ahead of me and slightly above . . . I am trying to close for a better look." This was the last transmission received from him.

When the three P-51s had climbed to 16,000 feet altitude, Mantell's left wingman, Lieutenant A. W. Clements, had donned his oxygen mask because the P-51s, like other World War II aircraft of that vintage, were not pressurized for operation at high altitudes. But Mantell and his right wingman, Lieutenant B. A. Hammond, carried no oxygen or masks aboard their aircraft because the ferrying flight had been planned to operate at lower altitudes where oxygen would not be required. As the three P-51s neared 20,000 feet, Mantell radioed to his two companions to call their attention to the UFO which was above and ahead, but the transmission was somewhat garbled, his associates would later recall.

As the three aircraft continued to climb, Lieutenant Hammond indicated he was having difficulty because of lack of oxygen and at 22,500 feet, Lieutenant Clements radioed to Mantell that he and Hammond were abandoning the chase to land. *Mantell never acknowledged receiving this message, which is most unusual.* He was last seen continuing to climb toward the UFO. A few minutes later, Mantell's airplane crashed near Franklin, Kentucky, killing the pilot. The cockpit canopy was found in a locked condition, indicating that Mantell had made no attempt to parachute to safety.

Mantell's tragic death and the fact that the accident had occurred while he was chasing a UFO produced sensationalist speculation that his aircraft might have been knocked down by a flying saucer. But the official USAF accident investigation board reached quite a different conclusion. The official report noted that the first symptoms of a lack of oxygen (anoxia) are usually experienced at altitudes above 15,000 feet and that both Lieutenant Hammond and Lieutenant Clements had encountered such effects. (Apparently Clements' oxygen supply was running low.) The official accident report states, "The critical stage is between 20,000 and 25,000 feet at which consciousness can be lost rapidly. . . ." Mantell's last radio transmission at 20,000 feet was somewhat garbled, suggesting that even then he was starting to experience anoxia symptoms without realizing it. Mantell's World War II experience at low altitudes with the Troop Carrier Command did not equip him to know firsthand the dangers of high-altitude operations without oxygen. So he had lost consciousness, his P-51 had slipped into a spiral dive and had crashed.

Beyond the embarrassment over the death of Captain Mantell, those in the then newly created USAF office responsible for investigating UFO reports were unable to offer a plausible explanation for what it was that Mantell had been chasing, because there were few within the USAF who were then privy to the secret reconnaissance balloon project just getting under way. Examination of the Mantell case files, now in the USAF Historical Archives at Maxwell Air Force Base, Alabama, does not reveal when those in the Project Blue Book UFO office, as it was later called, first learned that Navy Skyhook balloons were being launched from Wilmington Air Force Base, approximately 150 miles northeast of where the Mantell UFO chase had occurred. An undated, unsigned summary sheet in the file states: "Found later that 'Skyhook' balloons were launched from Clinton County in Southern Ohio on or about 7 January 1948. These large balloons were unknown, but to very few people [sic] at that time. Wind plots also indicated that the Skyhook would have been brought over or near Godman area."

The fact that the precise date of launch of one of the Skyhook balloons from the southern Ohio site is not known would suggest that the possible relationship of the two incidents was not made known until several years later when the records were no longer available and the memories of those involved in the launch were uncertain. But the descriptions of the UFO as reported by numerous observers at the Godman tower, and those radioed back by Mantell, so closely match the known appearance of Skyhook balloons as to leave no doubt that the UFO the unlucky pilot was chasing was similar to those that would soon be taking pictures behind the Iron Curtain.

Since 1961 this strategic reconnaissance mission has been performed by satellites in one-hundred-mile-high orbit, operated both by the United States and the U.S.S.R. Although satellites have also taken on some of the scientific missions previously performed by Skyhook balloons, there remain a number of experiments which can best, or most economically, be performed by high-altitude balloons. In recent years the French have become extremely active in developing and using balloons for scientific experiments. In a typical year they launch more than one hundred large scientific balloons,

most of them from a site in southern France near the Spanish
border called Aire-sur-l'Adour.

On September 5, 1968, during the early evening hours a
strange-looking UFO was sighted by thousands of citizens of
Madrid. It was still visible at 7:30 P.M., some time after sunset,
moving in a southwesterly direction. Observers said the UFO
was "pyramid-shaped," and a newspaper photo of it taken
with a telephoto lens bears out that description. The Spanish
Air Force dispatched F-104 jet fighters to inspect it, according
to newspaper accounts, but they could not reach the UFO,
which was estimated to be above 50,000 feet altitude. The
fact that the object was moving slowly in a southwesterly
direction and that Madrid is southwest of the French balloon
launch site, in combination with the appearance of the UFO,
strongly suggests that it was a large scientific balloon
launched from Aire-sur-l'Adour. I have twice written to
France's Centre National d'Etudes Spatiales (CNES), which
operates the facility, asking them to check their records to see
if a balloon had been launched on or just before September 5,
but have never received a reply.

The much more commonplace weather balloons are most
likely to be reported as UFOs during a "UFO flap," when the
subject has been given considerable publicity. This prompts
large segments of the public to scan the skies in the hope that
they too may chance to see a UFO. During the nationwide
UFO flap in the fall of 1973 (Chapter 26), Mr. and Mrs.
James Thulke of Chicago were returning home from an auto
trip to the East. They had stopped near Jackson, Michigan,
for food, and when they emerged from the restaurant, they
noticed several groups of people staring at something in the
sky to the north. The sun was just setting, Thulke told me,
but the sky was still light. Looking to the north, Thulke said,
he and his wife saw a curious object which was "too brilliant
and large to be a star." It seemed to be stationary, about 50
degrees above the horizon, and it was glowing too brightly for
him to determine the object's shape with the naked eye.

Fortunately, Thulke had very powerful binoculars in his
car, with a zoom-type lens that could provide variable
magnification, from 7 to 14 power. Viewing the object with

the binoculars set at minimum magnification (7 power), he said the UFO seemed to be tear-drop shaped and *internally illuminated*. But when he shifted to 14 power, he quickly identified the UFO as a weather balloon whose bright illumination came from the setting rays of the sun. When Thulke informed the other puzzled UFO watchers that it was only a weather balloon, some accepted his word and departed. But others wanted to see for themselves, and Thulke obliged. Still some lingered on, not wanting to believe the UFO was only a weather balloon. When the Thulkes departed and headed west, he told me, they saw cars, campers and trucks stopped along the expressway for many miles, with their passengers gazing at the mysterious UFO in the sky. For these people, that weather balloon will always be an Unidentified Flying Object.

5 · UFOs in Flight Formation

Late in the afternoon of June 5, 1969, American Airlines flight #112 was approaching St. Louis, en route to Washington, D.C. The jetliner had departed San Diego several hours earlier, had made an intermediate stop at Phoenix, and now was cruising at 39,000 feet to its destination. The weather was perfectly clear and more than two hours of daylight remained. The airliner's captain had gone back to the passenger cabin, and his seat was temporarily occupied by a senior air traffic controller from the Federal Aviation Administration. The controller had boarded in San Diego and was flying as an observer in the cockpit, a not unusual situation which enables FAA controllers to better understand flight-crew problems.

The traffic controller had turned around to the rear of the cockpit to talk with the flight engineer when, as he later recounted the incident, the co-pilot suddenly hollered: "Damn, look at this." The controller swung around and, in his own words, "there it was—a flight of four—whatever they were—flying in a square formation." There was one large UFO in the lead, followed by three smaller objects. The

UFOs, coming from the east, seemed to be on a near-collision course toward the jetliner, according to the controller.

Each of the UFOs seemed to be shaped like a hydroplane, with the largest appearing to be about eighteen to twenty feet long and about seven to eight feet thick. They were the color of "burnished aluminum," the controller later recalled, and seemed to be propelled by some sort of rocket engines that emitted a long tail of blue-green flame. Fortunately, only moments before it seemed that the UFOs might collide with the jetliner, they appeared to take evasive action. Even so, the UFOs appeared to have come *within three hundred feet of the airliner* as they zoomed past, the controller said. The co-pilot called the nearby St. Louis airport tower on the radio to report the incident, and he asked if the tower had any unidentified targets on the radarscope. Soon a controller in the St. Louis tower radioed back to report that there were unidentified targets on the radar. But the radar showed only two unidentified targets, not the four reported by the American Airlines crew.

An eastbound United Air Lines jetliner was cruising at 37,000 feet approximately eight miles behind the American jetliner, and its crew had monitored the radio report to the St. Louis tower. Suddenly, one of the United crew members radioed down: "We see it too," according to the subsequent report by the traffic controller aboard the American flight. Behind the United flight was an Air National Guard jet fighter, cruising at 41,000 feet, also eastbound. He too had monitored the radio reports of the UFOs, and a few moments later he reported: "Damn, they almost got me." He went on to explain that the squadron of UFOs seemed to be headed directly for his aircraft until, at the last moment, the strange objects abruptly changed course and climbed out of his path. This would seem to indicate that the UFOs were under "intelligent control."

UFO reports that come from experienced airline and military pilots are usually given much greater credence than those that come from laymen, because it is presumed that experienced flight crews are much more accurate observers of any object that moves through the air. If this hypothesis is true, then this UFO case should be a classic, for there were three experienced flight crews, it was a daylight sighting and there was perfect visibility.

I first learned of this case in late March, 1972, when I received a telephone call from Stuart Nixon, then director of the National Investigations Committee on Aerial Phenomena (NICAP), the nation's largest private organization dedicated to UFOs, whose headquarters is located near Washington, D.C. The bulk of NICAP's several thousand members believe, or are inclined to believe, that there are extraterrestrial spaceships visiting Earth which are responsible for at least some UFO reports. Under Nixon's direction, NICAP has become more responsible and scientific in its investigations of UFO reports, and also more willing to expose hoaxes.

Nixon was calling me because of the locale of the St. Louis UFO incident. He knew that a major aircraft company, McDonnell Douglas, was located near the St. Louis airport, and he wondered if perhaps the UFOs were some new experimental rocket-propelled aircraft built there. Because of my position as a senior editor with *Aviation Week & Space Technology* magazine, Nixon assumed I would know if such aircraft had been developed by McDonnell Douglas and were under flight test there. I assured him that, to my knowledge, the company had not developed any such new aircraft. And if the company had, the novel vehicles would almost certainly be tested at remotely situated Air Force/Navy facilities and not in the vicinity of a populated area such as St. Louis.

My curiosity having been aroused, I asked for more details of the incident. These suggested to me, I told Nixon, that the squadron of UFOs might have been a giant meteor and that I would check into that possibility and advise him of my findings. I promptly telephoned the Smithsonian Institution in Cambridge, Massachusetts, a principal center for astrophysics and astronomy which also operates what is called a Center for Short-Lived Phenomena. The latter serves as a collection-distribution center for reports on transient phenomena, such as meteors, earthquakes and unusual wildlife migrations. When such an event occurs, a participating scientist close to the scene transmits the information to the Smithsonian Center for Short-Lived Phenomena, which in turn alerts other scientists interested in that category of events so they can promptly investigate, if they wish, or add to their data on the subject. I was aware of this function because for several years I had been on the center's mailing list to receive reports on meteor sightings, knowing that some of them might help explain some UFO reports.

The Smithsonian Center's public affairs officer, James Cornell, said he would check the records to see if there had been any reports of a meteor in the vicinity of St. Louis in the late afternoon of June 5, 1969. He soon called back to report that there had indeed been a giant meteor, or "fireball," that had been seen by numerous observers on the ground, ranging from Peoria, Illinois, to Glenwood in western Iowa. He added that the fireball had even been photographed by an alert newspaper photographer, named Alan Harkrader, Jr., in Peoria. This served to jog my memory and I recalled that nearly two years earlier I had received a number of post-card reports from the center on the "Iowa Fireball," as it was called, and had written off to Harkrader to obtain a copy of his photos—all of which were sitting at home in my files.

However, there were two seemingly significant discrepancies between the Iowa Fireball and the St. Louis UFO report. According to the traffic controller aboard the American jetliner, the incident had occurred a few minutes before 4 P.M., whereas the numerous observers of the Iowa Fireball agreed that the meteor had flashed by, breaking up into flaming fragments which fell behind the meteor, just before 6 P.M. Central daylight time (CDT). Another seeming discrepancy was that while the traffic controller estimated that the squadron of UFOs had passed within three hundred feet of his aircraft, then flying near St. Louis, a careful analysis by the Smithsonian Institution based on many ground observer reports, indicated that the Iowa Fireball's flight path was *at least 125 miles north of St. Louis*. Could experienced flight crews, in broad daylight, make so gross an error in estimating distance?

My first step was to try to resolve the two-hour discrepancy. The traffic controller had boarded American Airlines flight #112 in San Diego. If he had not yet set his watch ahead to the Central time zone, in which the aircraft was flying at the time, then the correct local time would have been a few minutes before 6 P.M., precisely the time of the Iowa Fireball. I called American Airlines headquarters in New York City and asked them to dig back into their records to provide me with the scheduled time of departure of flight #112 on June 5, 1969, and its scheduled arrival time in Washington, D.C.

American Airlines soon called back to say that flight #112 had been scheduled to depart San Diego at 12:15 P.M. Pacific daylight time (PDT), to land at Phoenix and then depart there at 1:40 P.M. Mountain daylight time (MDT). If the aircraft had been approximately on schedule on June 5, it should have been nearing St. Louis a few minutes before 6 P.M. CDT, not 4 P.M. as the controller had reported. The only possible way that the flight could have been nearing St. Louis at 4 P.M. is if it had departed both San Diego and Phoenix *two hours ahead of schedule*—which is illegal and unprofitable, since there would be no passengers on board. Clearly the traffic controller had simply forgotten to set his watch ahead.

When I queried the headquarters of the Federal Aviation Administration to learn if any other UFO reports had been generated by the Iowa Fireball, their files produced evidence that even in broad daylight, an experienced pilot on the ground can misjudge the distance of an unfamiliar, fleeting object by more than one hundred miles. For example, a private pilot and his friend were standing outside the municipal airport near Cedar Rapids, Iowa, on June 5, 1969, just before 6 P.M., when they spotted the UFOs coming out of the east on a westerly course. After the objects had passed, the two men promptly reported the incident to the FAA office at the airport.

The pilot said the UFOs were circular-shaped and "iridescent" in color. He estimated their altitude to be only 1,000 feet above the ground, based on the altitude of a light plane preparing to land at the airport at the time. And the two men reported that the UFOs had flown *directly over the east-west runway of the Cedar Rapids airport,* approximately 225 miles north of St. Louis! Yet numerous reports from ground observers in Illinois and Iowa, plus Harkrader's photo, indicate that the fireball trajectory was roughly one hundred miles south of Cedar Rapids and 125 miles north of St. Louis! Some of the ground observers, like the two men in Cedar Rapids, estimated the objects to be at an altitude of only 1,000 to 1,500 feet. Yet the three flight crews near St. Louis, all cruising at altitudes above 35,000 feet, reported the UFOs were at or above their own altitude. (Probably the meteor was tens of thousands of feet higher.)

But what of the two unidentified objects that had been spotted on the radarscope in the St. Louis tower following the American Airlines crew report of the visual sighting? Although meteors and their ionized trails can be detected on radar, the Iowa Fireball was beyond the range of the St. Louis radar. At the time of this incident, the type of radar display installed at St. Louis was not equipped to show the altitude or individual identity of each target automatically, a provision that has since been added. In good weather, such as that existing at the time of this incident, it was not necessary for overflying aircraft to identify themselves to the St. Louis tower unless they planned to land there, which none of the three aircraft involved in this incident expected to do. Thus, the two "unidentified targets" reported in the vicinity of the American Airlines flight may well have been the United Air Lines flight and the Air National Guard aircraft, or possibly other overflying airplanes in the vicinity.

Within several days after NICAP's Nixon had first called, I telephoned back to provide the full explanation of the incident and also mailed him a four-page report I had prepared with full documentation. The report included the Harkrader photo, showing a long, luminous tear-drop-shaped UFO, followed by a smaller flaming object of similar shape. (See Plate 3b.) The report included a map showing the estimated trajectory of the fireball and the location of numerous ground observers whose sightings had been used to estimate the trajectory. (See Plate 4.) Although the Harkrader photo showed only the meteor and one object in trail, he reported seeing additional flaming fragments break off and go into trail behind the fireball.

Nixon told me that NICAP had already gone to press on the next issue of its monthly publication, UFO Investigator, which would carry a big feature article on the St. Louis UFO case. (The next issue was dated February, 1972, but was not mailed out until early April.) The case was given feature treatment with a headline that read: "FAA Controller Recounts '69 Sighting." The article concluded by saying: "NICAP intends to investigate this case further." When the March issue arrived, I looked for at least a brief note informing NICAP members that the St. Louis UFO case had been explained, but there was none. Nor was there any mention in the April issue, or May, June, July or August. Finally, in the September, 1972, issue, NICAP found space for a small article informing its members that the St. Louis UFOs had been "tentatively identified as a meteor." The article quoted extensively from my report, but without any indication that NICAP itself had not dug up the new facts.

It is not really surprising that NICAP and similar UFO groups much prefer to devote space to reporting new UFO sightings rather than to informing their members that a previous case has now been explained in terrestrial terms. These organizations depend on dues and contributions from members, most of whom believe or want to believe in extraterrestrial visitors. But the net result is to leave members with the impression that there are many unexplained UFO cases when in fact the explanations simply have never been published.

On April 1, 1972, I also sent a copy of my St. Louis UFO analysis-report, along with other supporting data, to the senior FAA traffic controller who had reported the incident to NICAP. (I had tried to telephone him, but he had an unlisted number.) Neither the report nor my letter attempted to ridicule him for the incident, so I assumed he would be interested in obtaining the explanation. More than two years have elapsed since I wrote the controller, and he has never responded.

The extremely gross errors made by all of the pilots in this incident in estimating the distance to the "UFOs," as well as serious errors made in estimating the altitude of the objects by the Cedar Rapids pilot and some other ground observers, illustrate another important UFOlogical Principle:

> UFOLOGICAL PRINCIPLE #5: No human observer, including experienced flight crews, can accurately estimate either the distance/altitude or the size of an unfamiliar object in the sky, unless it is in very close proximity to a familiar object whose size or altitude is known.

The human brain can make only a rough estimate of the angle subtended by an object, and this is a function of *both* its size and its distance. That is, a given angle can be subtended by a small object at close range or a large object at a considerable distance. This basic principle has long been known to those working in optics and physics. The importance of this principle in dealing with UFO reports is also illustrated by the series of sightings reported in Chapter 1 that occurred on March 3, 1968, as a result of the reentry of Russian rocket debris. The observers in Tennessee estimated the giant UFO was flying at an altitude of only 1,000 feet, and those in Indiana said the cigar-shaped UFO was flying at "treetop level." Yet a pilot flying over Kentucky at an altitude of 10,000 feet estimated that the flaming objects were at an altitude of 18,000 to 20,000 feet. And an airline pilot cruising at 33,000 feet altitude estimated the height of the objects at 60,000 feet.

The way in which the June 5, 1969, fireball incident was treated by different newspapers in the Midwest is interesting, if not revealing. *The Peoria Journal Star*, which ran Harkrader's photo, headlined its story: "Meteorite, Maybe Satellite Streaks Across Illinois Sky." The *Des Moines Register* headlined its brief story: "Seek Meteor Seen Over C.R." (i.e., Cedar Rapids). But *The Cedar Rapids Gazette*'s article bore the headline: "Three Persons Report Seeing UFO at Airport," and the *Omaha World-Herald* headlined its story: "UFOs Seen In 3 States."

.   .   .

During the early evening of June 17, 1968, approximately fifty persons living in the southeast section of Scottsdale, Arizona, reported seeing what appeared to be a small aircraft that suddenly exploded in mid-air. Many of the persons reported seeing "large objects," apparently pieces of the airplane, fall from the ball of fire, as well as what appeared to be two parachutes descending from the object. A number of the witnesses jumped into their cars and searched the area where the object appeared to have exploded, but they found nothing in the darkness. The Scottsdale police and rural fire department were notified and searched the area without finding anything. Authorities at nearby Williams Air Force Base and Luke Air Force Base were contacted, but they reported none of their aircraft were missing.

The *Scottsdale Daily Progress* quoted one woman, who had been sitting with some neighbors, as saying that they had noticed "a plane flying without lights. Two white lights suddenly went on when the plane passed over us. A few seconds later two blinker lights came on. A short time later we saw the ball of fire. The parachutes were easily discernible and were large and grayish in color. The objects that fell from the flames appeared to be about five feet long," she said. The newspaper said that a spokesman at Williams Air Force Base had theorized that the object might have been a meteor, but it added, "Those who saw the explosion ask how the parachutes and the large objects that fell can be explained."

On June 25 the newspaper carried a follow-up story which began: "No one has been able to find traces of a mysterious flying object that reportedly disintegrated in mid-air above southeast Scottsdale last Monday night. Residents in the area . . . have spent hours during the past week searching the desert for what they say was a small aircraft that disintegrated in a large mass of flames. Neither residents of the area nor appropriate agencies have been able to find anything. . . ."

The mysterious object sighted that night over Scottsdale was not reported as a UFO in the usual sense. But it deserves mention here because it seems likely that the object was a meteor. The large objects seen to break off could have been fragments like those that were observed (in broad daylight) to fragment from the Iowa Fireball. If this hypothesis is correct, the two "parachutes" reported by some observers were details unwittingly supplied by their brains, seeking to explain the unfamiliar sight in the belief that a small aircraft was exploding. The Scottsdale incident is still another illustration of UFOlogical Principle #1 at work.

6 · An "Extraterrestrial" UFO

On the night of February 10, 1951, a Navy R5D four-engine transport was flying over the North Atlantic en route from Iceland to Newfoundland. The weather was clear except for a few nearly transparent clouds several thousand feet below the aircraft, which was cruising at 10,000 feet altitude. It had been a routine flight, and the airplane commander was relaxing in the passenger cabin, with a relief pilot at the controls. At 00:55 GMT this pilot, Lieutenant G. E. B., observed what he later described as "a glow of light *below the horizon*" (emphasis added) at an angle that he estimated to be approximately 60 degrees to the right of the airplane's flight path. The pilot called the yellow glow to the attention of the co-pilot, Lieutenant F. W. K., and asked him what he thought it might be. The co-pilot suggested the yellow glow might be coming from a large ship, or possibly the airplane was off-course and the light might be coming from a village on land. But a check with the airplane's navigator, Lieutenant N. J. P. K., ruled out these possibilities. The pilot, co-pilot and navigator watched the yellow glow for several minutes, and it continued to maintain its position of approximately 60 degrees bearing to the right.

Then, according to an account of the incident published in NICAP's *UFO Investigator* in the September and October, 1970, issues, *based on the pilot's recollection more than a decade after the experience:* "Suddenly, the lights went out. There appeared a yellow halo on the water. It turned to an orange, to a fiery red, and then started movement toward us at a fantastic speed, turning to a bluish-red around the perimeter." The pilot said he disengaged the autopilot and prepared to take evasive maneuvers to avoid a mid-air collision. Then, curiously, "it stopped its movement toward us and began moving along with us about 45 degrees off the bow to the right, about 100 feet or so below us and about 200 to 300 feet in front of us. It was not in a level position; it *was tilted about 25 degrees.*" (Emphasis added.) According to the pilot's decade-later recollection: "It stayed in this position [near the Navy airplane] for a minute or two. It appeared to be from 200 to 300 feet in diameter, translucent or metallic, shaped like a saucer, a purple-red fiery ring around the perimeter and a frosted white glow around the entire object."

Then, according to the pilot, the UFO "moved away from us; it made no turns, as though it was backing up . . . [in] the direction that it had approached us and [it] was still tilted." Within a few seconds, the UFO had disappeared over the horizon, traveling at a speed that the pilot estimated to be 1,500 miles per hour. The aircraft radioed to Argentia (Newfoundland) Naval Air Station to report the incident, and when the airplane landed at the field a short time later, crew members were interrogated by intelligence officers to obtain their observations while still fresh. NICAP quoted the pilot as saying: "It was obvious that there had been many sightings in the same area . . ." And he added: "I found out a few months later that the Gander [Newfoundland] radar did track the object in excess of 1,800 mph."

My own attention was first drawn to this case in the late spring of 1972 during correspondence with a writer in the Boston area who had been studying UFOs. He said this case was one of the most convincing he had encountered and he challenged me to explain it. Long experience in investigating older UFO cases has taught me to be wary of depending on details contained in published accounts, especially where witnesses are recalling details of an incident that occurred some years earlier. Because the pilot said that the crew members had been interrogated shortly after the incident at Argentia, I hoped that these original crew reports might be available in the official Air Force Project Blue Book files, now in the archives at the Air University, Maxwell Air Force Base, Alabama. A letter to the Air University's historical research division, plus the payment of a modest fee to cover cost of service and reproduction, quickly produced a copy of the complete file on this case, including the all-important statements made by seven crew members of the R5D within several hours of the unusual incident.

In general terms, the original crew reports corroborated many of the details that had been recalled by the pilot for NICAP nearly two decades after the event. But the pilot's recent recollection contained a number of details *not* found in his or other original crew reports—*and all of these new details added to the impression that the Navy Aircraft had had an encounter with an alien spaceship!* For example, whereas the pilot's recent recollection was that the UFO had flown alongside the Navy aircraft "for a minute or two," the pilot's original report, confirmed by other crew reports, indicated that the UFO had appeared to zoom toward the airplane and then suddenly seemed to reverse its course and head back over the horizon, where it disappeared.

Airplane commander Lieutenant A. L. J., in his original report, said: "I called Gander Tower on VHF [radio] and asked them if Gander A.T.C. [Air Traffic Control] had any information of an aircraft at that position and time. They had no such information and notified the military of our sighting." This is confirmed by a letter dated February 10, 1951, from the North East Air Command, Pepperrell AF Base, Newfoundland, to the Air Force Chief of Staff, which states: "Gander Air Traffic Control reports Navy #6501 only acft [aircraft] in area." This would deny the hearsay report by the pilot, as quoted by NICAP: "I found out a few months later that Gander radar did track the object in excess of 1,800 mph."

Despite these discrepancies between the original reports and the pilot's recent recollections, there was no immediately obvious explanation for the sighting. Nor was I inclined to accept the tentative Project Blue Book explanation that I found in the USAF case files: "Believed to be Aurora [Northern Lights] display by consulting astronomer." (Project Blue Book's consulting astronomer was Dr. Hynek, whose efforts as a UFO investigator will be covered in a number of subsequent case analyses.)

My first step in investigating this case was to try to piece together a chronological sequence of events, using the original crew reports. In this process, two curious things attracted my attention. The first was that the UFO *appeared to maintain the same bearing of approximately 60 degrees to the right of the airplane's flight path for the full duration of the incident*—which appears to have lasted for five to six minutes. Even when the UFO seemed to be heading directly for the Navy aircraft, and when it seemed to head back and disappear over the horizon, *it had maintained this same relative bearing.*

There were two possible explanations for this constant bearing: (1) if there was indeed a craft involved, it always managed to maintain precisely the correct speed so as to hold the constant bearing, or (2) the UFO might be an object at very great distance, in which case the motion of the Navy airplane would result in no perceptible change in bearing.

The second curious feature of the case was the description of the UFO as reported shortly after the incident by the seven crew members and passengers who observed it. These included:

- ". . . huge fiery orange disk on its edge." (Lieutenant A. L. J.)

- ". . . definitely circular and reddish-orange on its perimeter." (Lieutenant G. E. B.)

.   .   .

- ". . . circular, bright orange-red disk . . ." (Lieutenant N. J. P. K.)

- ". . . round object . . . with color of fire." (Chief Aviation Radioman Q. R. S.)

- "It looked very much like an eclipse of the sun, which was about three-fourths of total eclipse, in size, shape and color . . ." (Aviation Electronics Technician Third Class G. R. D.)

- ". . . my first impression was the celestial setting of the moon and the fact that stratus [cloud] layers were present to cause the bright-red glow and the halo effect that was apparent." (Lieutenant J. M. M.)

Was it possible that Lieutenant J. M. M.'s impression was correct and that the giant UFO that seemed to come zooming at the Navy aircraft and then suddenly zoomed back and disappeared over the horizon was only the moon, and that the illusion of movement was produced by some interactive optical effect from the thin cloud layer below the aircraft? Surely an experienced military flight crew could not be so easily misled. Yet if the UFO were the moon, this could explain why it maintained constant bearing throughout the incident.

From earlier work in UFO investigations, I was aware of a curious but readily explainable phenomenon known as a "Sub-Sun." It is occasionally seen by air crews when they are flying over stratus cloud layers consisting of millions of tiny ice crystals, which act as a mirrorlike reflecting surface for the sun. Under such conditions, the airplane crew will see a diffused glowing object—actually a reflection of the sun—ahead or off to the side of the aircraft that appears to be following the airplane. When the airplane reaches a point where the thin layer of ice crystals no longer exists, the glowing "object" suddenly disappears.

This prompted me to wonder whether the UFO that had been reported by the Navy crew might be a "Sub-Moon," i.e., a similar type of reflection of the moon from the stratus clouds known to be below the R5D's flight altitude. If this were the explanation, the bearing of the moon at the time would necessarily have had to be approximately 60 degrees to the right of the airplane's flight path and it would also have had to be moderately high in the sky. To determine whether this was indeed the case, I would need to know the airplane's approximate position, its heading and the time of the incident. Fortunately, all of this information was available because the airplane carried a full-time navigator, who reported the data to investigators at Argentia when the aircraft landed. The incident occurred at approximately 00:55 GMT when the airplane was at 49° 50' north latitude and 50° 03' west longitude. The airplane was on a true heading of 230 degrees with a ground speed of 118 knots. The crew had estimated that the UFO was approximately 60 degrees to the right of the airplane's flight path, which would correspond to a *true azimuth of approximately 290 degrees* (230 + 60).

Armed with this information, I called the U.S. Naval Observatory in Washington and asked them to check back in the almanac records for February 10, 1951, to tell me the azimuth bearing of the moon at 00:55 GMT for an observer located at 49° 50' north latitude and 50° 03' west longitude. I also asked for the elevation angle of the moon at that time and date. Dr. Kenneth Seidelmann of the Nautical Almanac Office called back shortly to inform me that the moon would have been at an azimuth of approximately *280 degrees*. This was a difference of only 10 degrees from the approximate bearing reported for the UFO—an insignificant difference in view of the rough-estimate nature of the crew reports.

But the moon was *not moderately high in the sky* at the time, as would be required for a "Sub-Moon" explanation. Rather, Seidelmann told me, the moon was actually 1.35 degrees *below the horizon* at 00:55 GMT. And it was approximately six-sevenths dark; that is, only a thin "banana-shaped" sliver of the moon was illuminated. If the moon was 1.35 degrees below the horizon, this at first seemed to eliminate it as a possible explanation for the UFO. But then I realized that this figure was based on the horizon for an observer on the *surface* of the ocean, and that the crew in the Navy aircraft at 10,000 feet would have had a higher vantage point. Calculation showed that from 10,000 feet altitude, the crew would have been able to see approximately 0.9 degrees below the horizon of a surface observer. But this still would not be sufficient to see the upper tip of the illuminated sliver of the moon. Then I recalled that the earth's atmosphere has a refraction effect at low grazing angles which makes it possible, even from the surface, to see *below* the physical horizon. A check with two astronomers confirmed this and provided a conservative figure of 0.5 degrees of below-the-horizon coverage due to refraction. This meant that the crew of the Navy airplane should have been able to see at least 1.4 degrees (0.9 + 0.5) *below* the physical horizon of a surface observer, and the upper limb (edge) of the illuminated sliver of the moon was only 1.35 degrees below the physical horizon. (See Plate 5.)

So the crew should have been able to see this tip of the moon at 00:55 GMT at approximately the same bearing at which they thought they saw the UFO. By shortly after 01:00 GMT, when the UFO suddenly seemed to zoom over the horizon and disappear, the moon would have dropped sufficiently below the horizon so that it would no longer be visible to the crew. Thus the disappearance of the UFO corresponded closely to the time of "disappearance" of the moon. If the UFO and the upper limb of the moon were not one and the same, it seems strange that not a single crew member, in the original reports, mentioned seeing the moon, or said that the UFO was observed to be close to the moon. Recall also that one of the pilots had originally observed: ". . . my first impression was the celestial setting of the moon and the fact that stratus [cloud] layers were present to cause the bright-red glow and the halo effect that was apparent." Also, the first report described the UFO as "a glow of light *below* the horizon." (Emphasis added.)

In my numerous years as a UFO investigator I have encountered many cases that proved to be misidentifications of unfamiliar objects, and occasionally of familiar objects seen under unusual conditions. But until my analysis of the Gander case, I would have had difficulty believing that so many experienced pilots and others in a flight crew could mistake the moon for a giant UFO that seemed to be zooming toward them on a collision course. One contributing factor in the Gander case may have been the fact that there had been a considerable number of UFO reports in the press during the several months preceding this incident, and in 1951 the possibility of alien spaceships was still a conceivable hypothesis. There is other evidence to show that even experienced pilots are quite human and therefore subject to the psychological influence of what they read and hear.

In the late 1950s, with the advent of the Space Age, the North American Air Defense Command (Norad) set up an extensive network of radars to enable it to detect and maintain a catalog of all objects in orbit around the Earth. To keep this catalog up to date, it was desirable to be able to predict when satellites had lost sufficient altitude to reenter the atmosphere and burn up. But because of uncertainties in data on the density of the atmosphere at very high altitude, it was difficult to accurately predict the demise of satellites. In 1962, Herbert Roth, employed by the United Air Lines Flight Training Center at Denver, Colorado, not far from Norad Headquarters at Colorado Springs, conceived the idea of making use of the hundreds of airline crews around the globe to assist Norad by reporting any flaming satellite debris spotted in flight.

This resulted in the formation in late 1962 of the Volunteer Flight Officer Network (VFON), operated under Roth's direction. When Norad's computers indicate that a satellite is expected to reenter the atmosphere, the predicted time and location is supplied to Roth. He in turn checks the schedules of the more than one hundred different airlines around the world who participate in VFON to determine which flights will be in the predicted region of reentry at the projected time. Then Roth dispatches telegraphic messages to the operations offices of the airlines involved which in turn are given to the flight crews to alert them to the expected event. Any flight crew member in the VFON participating airlines who sees the spectacular sight of a reentering satellite then reports the incident, the time and location to Roth, who in turn supplies the data to Norad.

VFON flight crews also report back to Roth on any unscheduled sightings they make, some of which may be satellites that have reentered slightly ahead or behind Norad's predictions. Other sightings may prove to be meteors, based on the flight crew's descriptions and subsequent Norad radar tracking data which shows that no satellite reentered at that time and place. And in a few instances, VFON reports have been classified as "unidentified objects" because they do not match any known satellite reentries and the *flight crew's description of the object seems* to rule out the possibility of a meteor or high-flying balloon. At the time that VFON was organized, Roth was also head of the Denver chapter of NICAP and was quite interested in UFOs. Perhaps it was his interest in UFOs that prompted Roth to assure all flight crews participating in VFON that none of their reports would be made public without their written permission.

There are those who claim that airline pilots often see UFOs but are afraid to report them for fear of ridicule or disciplinary action by airline management. If this was true at one time, the claim is no longer valid since the formation of VFON because Roth rigorously adheres to his no-publicity policy. Because all of the major airlines around the world are members of VFON, and their pilots feel free to report everything they see, it is useful to examine the number of "unidentifieds" that Roth has received. During the first three years of VFON's existence (1963–1965), a total of 173 flight crew sighting reports were submitted of which *only one* could not be identified as a satellite, meteor or balloon. This corresponded to only 0.5 percent of the total. During these same three years, public interest in UFOs was fairly low, with the USAF receiving an average of forty UFO reports per month from the general public.

Then, in early 1966, UFO reports from University of Michigan students achieved national fame and prompted a brief Congressional inquiry. *Look* magazine carried its sensational two-part series on the Barney and Betty Hill account of being abducted by the crew of a flying saucer. In the fall of 1966 the USAF announced that it had selected the University of Colorado to conduct an independent scientific study of the UFO issue. In that year the number of UFO reports submitted to the USAF jumped to an average of ninety-three per month, more than double the average of the three previous years. By a curious coincidence, there was also a dramatic increase in the number of VFON reports where crew description left no choice but to classify them as "unidentified." VFON crews submitted thirteen such "unidentifieds," corresponding to 3.3 percent of all crew reports in 1966, compared to only one "unidentified" during the previous three years of VFON's operation.

In 1967, public interest was still running high and the USAF received an average of almost eighty UFO reports per month. The same situation prevailed at VFON, where flight crews submitted fourteen sightings that could not be explained as satellites, meteors or balloons. This represented 2.7 percent of the total VFON reports for 1967. By 1968, public excitement over UFOs had begun to drop, and the number of reports submitted to the USAF dropped sharply to an average of thirty-three per month. VFON experienced a similar drop. Out of a total of nearly four hundred VFON reports, only seven, or 1.8 percent, were classified as "unidentifieds." By 1969, the University of Colorado report had been submitted to the USAF, and its conclusion that there was no evidence of extraterrestrial spaceships had received the endorsement of the respected National Academy of Sciences. In 1969 the number of UFO reports submitted to the USAF experienced another sharp drop, to an average of less than fifteen per month. The same sharp drop occurred in VFON reports, where there was *only one* "unidentified" out of 550 reports, corresponding to only 0.2 percent of the total.

Admittedly one can draw either of two possible conclusions from this very close correlation between UFO interest by the general public and mass-media coverage and the number of "unidentified" reports submitted by VFON flight crews. One could conclude that UFOs were coming in far larger numbers in the mid-1960s and that this explains the larger number of reports both from the general public and from flight crews. And that in the late 1960s, UFOs came in fewer numbers—hence there were fewer reports from the public and from flight crews. The alternative explanation is that flight crews, despite their specialized training, are subject to the same mass-media influences as the general public, and that both are equally vulnerable to UFOlogical Principle #1. Thus at times of strong public interest in UFOs and speculation that they might be spaceships from other worlds, a pilot viewing a meteor or high-altitude scientific balloon is more inclined to endow the object with unusual qualities that leave it "unidentified."

7 · The Brown Mountain UFOs

"COME SEE THE FLYING SAUCERS" was the headline for the story in *Argosy* magazine's December, 1968, issue that began: "Did you know that there is a place right here in this country where anyone can see UFOs on almost any clear night? Their behavior pattern varies from sudden, instantaneous flight, faster than the human eye can follow, to slowly ascending, wandering flights. What they are, no one knows, but they are there and can be seen. . . . Not one investigator has developed a workable hypothesis on these UFOs which cannot be torn completely apart by trained observers in other scientific disciplines," the article by Herbert Bailey stated.

Bailey described his own first encounter with the Brown Mountain Lights, as they are better known, during a visit to the western part of North Carolina. Brown Mountain is part of the lower extremity of the Blue Ridge mountain chain. When Bailey and a friend arrived in the vicinity of Brown Mountain, with its flat top that is at approximately 2,600 feet altitude, he reported seeing two hundred to three hundred lights lined up along the top. Suddenly, as the two men watched, the lights began to blink off, only to reappear a few moments later at a higher altitude, according to the author's account. The lights were a variety of colors that covered much of the spectrum.

"After a minute or two of watching the incredible speed and sudden stops of the lights," Bailey wrote, "I realized there could be nothing less than intelligent direction." He asked his associate to get a camera from the car, adding: "These things, whatever they are, are obviously controlled. We may never get any closer than they want us to be." He added that "this proved to be true, not only on [this] occasion . . . , but on later trips. Each time I went, I never failed to see the lights, but at what obviously seemed to *them* to be the proper distance."

One curious aspect of the Brown Mountain Lights mystery is that they had been observed there for more than fifty years—long before flying saucers had burst upon public awareness in 1947. The mysterious lights had been investigated in 1913 by D. B. Sterrett of the U.S. Geological Survey, who had concluded that they were simply distant locomotive headlights distorted by refractory atmospheric effects. When the Brown Mountain Lights grew in numbers and frequency, the Geological Survey had in 1922 sent another scientist, George R. Mansfield, to conduct an even more extensive investigation.

The detailed report subsequently issued by Mansfield and the Geological Survey, according to author Bailey, "reads like most scientific reports, full of jargon. . . . His conclusions were that the lights were caused by auto headlights (47%); locomotive headlights (33%); stationary lights (towns and houses, 10%); brush fires (10%)." Bailey challenged Mansfield's findings, charging, *"He neglected to mention that there was a great flood throughout that region in 1916 which wiped out all bridges, roads and electricity, making it impossible for trains and autos to run for a week or more. Yet the lights were seen quite regularly during this period."* (Emphasis added.)

Bailey dismissed other attempts to explain the Brown Mountain Lights as a freak natural phenomenon. "There have been various attempts to explain the lights as being caused by temperature inversions, mirages, and swamp gas. Yet how could mirage lights appear night after night long before there were autos, locomotives or electricity? In addition, the lights shine with an inner glow, and the ones I have seen are approximately six feet in diameter, and have not the slightest relationship to the beam of a locomotive or a Model T Ford. That rules out the temperature inversion (which is similar to mirage in that a reflection of *existing* light as well as images would be involved) and mirage hypotheses."

The *Argosy* article naturally sparked my curiosity, and a few months later I obtained a copy of the original Mansfield/Geological Survey report through the kindness of Carsten M. Haaland, a physicist at the Oak Ridge National Laboratory. Haaland, who lives not too far from the Brown Mountain region, had earlier obtained a copy of the original report from the files of the U.S. Forest Service office in Asheville, North Carolina. The seventeen-page report reveals that Mansfield spent a full two weeks in the area and that his investigation was both thorough and scientific. For example, there were some reports indicating that the Brown Mountain Lights had been reported back in the mid 1880s, so Mansfield attempted to determine when they were first observed and reported. The first published account he could find was one dated September 23, 1913, in the *Charlotte Daily Observer*. It credited the "discovery" of the lights to members of the Morganton Fishing Club who reportedly had first seen the lights more than two years earlier, or around 1910 to 1911. This observation described a *single* light which was said to resemble a "toy fire balloon," and which seemed to rise in the far distance *from beyond* Brown Mountain. After rising a short distance, the light would flicker and go out.

Two persons who had spent much time in the vicinity of Brown Mountain during the early 1900s, for business or pleasure, gave positive assurance that they had never seen or heard about the mysterious lights until around 1910. By a curious coincidence, it was just at this time that railroad locomotives began to be equipped with powerful electric headlights, Mansfield found. Also, at about this time the first automobiles began to appear on the roads of this region. Electric lights for street and house illumination had been in use in the region starting back at the turn of the century, Mansfield found. The growing numbers of automobiles, with electric headlights, locomotives and house-city lighting at a time when the Brown Mountain Lights were becoming more numerous and frequent suggested a possible cause-and-effect relationship to Mansfield.

The scientist came well equipped for the investigation. His principal tools were an alidade—a telescope with crosshairs and a ruler attached—and a topographic map of the area, plus a plotting table. The map was attached to the top of the table and was oriented by using the telescope to sight on known landmarks. When a Brown Mountain Light was sighted, the alidade would be trained on it and the precise bearing to the light could then be transferred to the topographic map. Additionally, Mansfield carried two magnetic compasses, binoculars, a barometer for measuring the height of the observation point, and a camera.

Three different observation points, from which the Brown Mountain Lights often were seen, were selected. One of these at Blowing Rock was approximately 1,100 feet higher than Brown Mountain and north of it. The other two sites were both west of Brown Mountain. One, near Loven's Hotel, was approximately 1,000 feet higher than the flat-topped Brown Mountain, while the other, on the east slope of Gingercake Mountain, was about 1,400 feet higher than Brown Mountain. Mansfield arranged with a number of local residents, who had often seen the Brown Mountain Lights, to accompany him during his night observations to assure that the lights he was seeing and measuring were the same as those traditionally reported. He also obtained timetables for the local railroads showing the scheduled times of arrival and departure from towns in the region. The topographic map showed both the location of railroad track and highways for automobiles.

On the evening of March 29, 1922, Mansfield was accompanied by three of the area residents. At approximately 8:40 P.M., lights suddenly appeared over Brown Mountain and a sighting was taken on them. When this was transferred to the map, it intersected a curve in the track of the Southern Railway, about one and one-half miles northwest of Conover, North Carolina. Checking the train schedules, Mansfield wrote, "it was determined that a westbound freight train passed this curve at the time noted." Bearings taken to other lights that appeared later that evening intersected highways, suggesting that the source was an automobile. One of Mansfield's companions that night, Robert Loven, said that the lights observed that night were not as bright as the traditional Brown Mountain Lights, but Joseph Loven disagreed and said that sometimes the lights were brighter and sometimes dimmer than those observed on March 29. According to Mansfield's report, Joseph Loven "was satisfied that the lights observed were a fair average exhibition of the Brown Mountain Light."

On April 2, Mansfield set up his observation station on nearby Gingercake Mountain. At 7:35 P.M., he reported, a light appeared over Brown Mountain and its bearing was taken with the telescope. When drawn on the map, the bearing "coincides practically with the track of the Southern Railway about half a mile west of Catawba station. The station agent reports that on April 2, a westbound train left Catawba at 7:32 P.M. It is therefore clear that the source of this light was a locomotive headlight." Subsequent lights that appeared were traced to westbound freight trains leaving Drexel, or were attributed to automobiles because the bearing lines intersected highways.

On this particular evening, Mansfield decided to remain until after midnight because he was curious to learn whether the headlight from a train at Connally Springs, more than twenty-five miles distant, would appear as a Brown Mountain Light. The train was due to arrive at 12:25 A.M., and ten minutes before its scheduled arrival the telescope was aimed in the direction of Connally Springs. But when the appointed time arrived, no light appeared. Then at 12:33 A.M. a light suddenly flared over Brown Mountain. The next day, Mansfield checked the train register at Connally Springs and found that the train had arrived in town at 12:35 A.M., *ten minutes late.* Allowing two minutes for travel from the curve on the track where the telescope was aimed, this indicated that the Brown Mountain Light had been caused by Train No. 35.

On April 3, Mansfield and his associates set up at Blowing Rock to the north of Brown Mountain. A steady group of lights were dimly visible, he reported. They were reddish in color and were accompanied by what appeared to be smoke. Their bearing located them along a ridge north of Mulberry Creek, and the smoky appearance suggested the source was brush fires. A reddish light that suddenly appeared at 8:35 P.M., which flared twice and then went out, was on a bearing that intersected a curve in the track of the Carolina, Clinchfield & Ohio Railroad, Mansfield reported. The curve was near Sprucepine, but there was no agent on duty at night to confirm the time of the train's arrival. At 9:05 P.M. another light flared. Its bearing suggested that the source was in the streets of the town of Lenoir, probably an auto headlight, Mansfield reported.

On April 5, Mansfield and several others climbed Brown Mountain to see if the lights could be observed from there, but rain and fog hindered observation. Another attempt was made on April 6, again hampered by fog, but from below the summit the party could not see any lights over Brown Mountain itself.

Mansfield's report concludes that he is "confident that the lights he saw were actually a fair average display of the so-called Brown Mountain Light," based on the comments of local residents who accompanied him and earlier published reports of the phenomenon. His hypothesis to explain the unusual illusion notes that the region is a "basinlike area—an area nearly surrounded by mountains." He theorized that "after sunset, cool air begins to creep down the tributary valleys into the basin, but the air currents come from different sources and are of different temperature and density. The atmospheric conditions in the basin are, therefore, very unstable, especially in the earlier part of the evening, before any well-defined circulatory system becomes established. At any given place in the basin the air varies in density during the evening and hence in [its] refractiveness. The denser the air, the more it refracts light or bends waves of light emanating from any source. The humidity of the air affects its density and hence its refractive power. Mist, dust, and other fine particles tend to obscure and scatter the light refracted and to impart to it the reddish or yellowish tints so frequently observed. Thus it is that the [Brown Mountain] light is most active in a clearing spell after a rain, as noted by many observers."

The Mansfield report continues: "Lights that arise from any source in the basin are viewed at low angles. Even those observed from altitudes of 3,700 or 4,000 feet, the heights of the stations on Gingercake or on Blowing Rock Mountain, had vertical angles of less than 3°. Thus the refractive effect of the atmosphere through which the light waves must travel is at a maximum." The seemingly mysterious appearance and disappearance of lights is explainable because the train and auto headlights that produce them are visible only when the vehicle is headed toward the observer; when the track or highway direction shifts, the light suddenly disappears. But other lights from distant houses or streetlamps remain more permanently until atmospheric conditions change. "The valley is fairly well settled, has a network of roads, three railroads, and several large towns, so that the possible sources of light are very numerous," Mansfield noted.

But what of the charge by Bailey in *Argosy* that Mansfield "neglected to mention that there was a great flood through that region in 1916 . . ."? The first paragraph on page 15 of the Mansfield report says: "During the flood of 1916, when train service was temporarily discontinued, the basin east of Marion, where the atmospheric conditions are disturbed, was still the scene of the intermittent flare of favorably situated lights. Automobiles were then in use in the larger towns and on some of the intervening roads, and their headlights were doubtless visible from Loven's [Hotel] over Brown Mountain. One need only remember the network of roads in the valley region . . . to realize the almost infinite number of possibilities for automobile headlights to be pointed toward Brown Mountain and stations of observations beyond."

And what of Bailey's statement that the Brown Mountain

Lights do not resemble "the beam of a locomotive or a Model T Ford"? The fact that many of the lights sighted by Mansfield and experienced local residents were definitely traced to locomotive headlights in terms of location and time flatly contradicts Bailey's implication. Mansfield himself addressed this question in broader terms by telling of his own experience in viewing a lighthouse near Boston from twenty-five miles away. Because the lighthouse had a unique coded flashing sequence (one flash, then four flashes, then three flashes), Mansfield could readily identify the source. During clear weather, he reported, the light can be seen and "there is no beam and there are no rays . . . it has much the same appearance as the Brown Mountain light."

Mansfield's investigation pointed up a principle of broader importance that has application to a number of other UFO sightings to be discussed in Chapter 9. This is the *apparent* motion of an object, or light, which in reality is fixed. During the evening of March 29, two of Mansfield's companions reported that they saw the light move. But when it was viewed through the telescope and its crosshairs, there was no movement. *"The eye is easily deceived at night as to the stability or motion of an object,"* Mansfield wrote. *"And an observer's impressions are to a considerable extent affected by his mental and physical condition at the time of the observation.* It is not surprising that under the circumstances, different eyewitnesses give quite different accounts of the light, especially as the light may appear suddenly against a dark background with nothing near by that can be used as a scale to determine its size or its possible motion." (Emphasis added.) Although Mansfield's caveat was written a quarter-century before UFOs burst on the scene, it is as valid today as it was in 1922.

Mansfield· also considered the question of whether a locomotive headlight could be seen from distances of up to forty-five miles, as indicated by his explanation for the Brown Mountain Lights. The lighthouse near Boston, which he had personally been able to see from a distance of twenty-five miles under favorable conditions, was equipped with a 75,000-candlepower lamp. A check with the engineering

department of the Southern Railway showed that the locomotive headlights then in use, in combination with their
silvered parabolic reflectors, "yield about 600,000 candle-
power. There is therefore no reason to doubt that the
headlights would be visible at a distance of 45 miles."

Mansfield's report contains a subtle hint which may explain
why some of the residents of the area were reluctant to accept
a prosaic explanation for the curious lights. One of the better
spots for viewing the Brown Mountain Lights is near Loven's
Hotel, and as Mansfield observed: "The lights furnish one of
the many attractions afforded by this remarkably well situated and delightful little town." As we will see in subsequent
chapters, towns that are anxious to attract tourists or that
cater to tourists as a key to economic survival are sometimes
"blessed" with a UFO sighting, or, better still, a "UFO
landing."

8 · The Maynard Experiment

On the morning of April 14, 1971, in Maynard, Iowa, West Central high school student Michael Potratz approached a fellow student, Russell Bartz, to inquire if he too had seen a low-flying UFO the previous night that seemed to be heading for a landing near the farm of Mrs. James Bantz on the outskirts of town. Bartz had not, but he suggested they promptly go to the scene to look for evidence that the UFO might have landed. The youths, joined by a third student, headed out for the reported site of the landing. Soon after arrival they spotted a scorched circular area, measuring ten feet in diameter, plus four smaller burned circles which had obviously been made by the "landing pads" of the UFO. The youths went over to ask Mrs. Bantz if she had seen or heard anything unusual the night before. Mrs. Bantz recalled that for a brief interval the whole sky seemed to be brightly illuminated.

Clearly an event of major importance had occurred on the outskirts of Maynard the night before, and so the youths called the local radio station, KOEL. The station, under-

standably, was extremely interested and interviewed young
Potratz for details. Soon the news of the exciting event was
being broadcast by KOEL. Within an hour, Leroy Latham, a
local "UFO expert," arrived at the school to interview the
youths. After visiting the landing site, Latham reported that
he had smelled burned sulfur. Within twenty-four hours news
of the UFO landing had been carried by radio stations in
Chicago and Minneapolis and by a number of Iowa newspapers, and NICAP Headquarters in Washington had called to
investigate.

One newspaper account stated that "The boys have
pictures to prove some sort of 'unidentified flying object'
really did touch down in Fayette County Tuesday evening."
The pictures showed only a burned spot. Additional substantiation came from a number of persons in eastern Iowa.
Persons in Cedar Rapids and Lisbon reported that they too
had seen an object in the sky between 10 P.M. and 11 P.M. the
previous night. A woman in Oelwein said she had seen the
same UFO the preceding night. *And a man in Tripoli
reported that he had seen the UFO for some two weeks and
could tell from its actions "that it was going to land."* Still
another person observed: "We saw marks like these by
Elkader last year. I wonder how they'll explain this. They
won't be able to say it was marsh gas like they have before."

In reality, the Maynard UFO was a hoax perpetrated by
several students in the sociology class of John Forkenbrock. It
had been staged at the suggestion of the teacher as a practical
experiment in mass psychology and to demonstrate the
impact of the news media. On the night of April 13, young
Potratz and several other students, after making arrangements with the farmer who owned the pasture, had poured
gasoline and set it afire to form the ten-foot-diameter circle
and the four smaller "landing pad" circles. Mrs. Bantz had
been informed of the experiment and had agreed to cooperate. When local UFO expert Latham had arrived the next
morning to investigate, he too had been let in on the
experiment and agreed to cooperate. But Russell Bartz, the
student approached by Potratz on the morning of April 14,
had not been aware of the experiment.

Bartz subsequently described his reactions when the youths first spotted the burned circular areas: "I was really stunned for a moment just thinking what it might be. Right away I had to know if anyone else besides us three knew it. Mrs. Bantz [whose house was barely one hundred yards away] could be the only possible one that could have seen this up close, and I had to talk to her. She confirmed that she had seen it and that the whole church was lit up by this thing. I just couldn't believe that something like this could happen to us. On the way back to school, after [we] had called KOEL and told them the whole story, all I could think about was telling more kids about it . . . Later on I told everybody I could see." Several hours later, Bartz was let in on the truth but was asked to cooperate in the experiment, which he did.

Within twenty-four hours the hoax was getting out of hand, and so the teacher informed the press and local radio station that it had all been part of a controlled experiment. Now the students in Forkenbrock's class set about interviewing their classmates and some of the local citizens to determine their initial reactions to the UFO report. These, as detailed in a report subsequently published by the students, were especially revealing. When the UFO incident was first reported, a variety of possible explanations occurred to members of the community. Some accepted the report at face value and concluded that an extraterrestrial spaceship had indeed landed outside the town. Others said they suspected that a secret experimental military vehicle might have been involved, or that the burned circles might have been caused by a meteor or a Russian satellite. Still others suspected a student hoax.

One student remarked: "I didn't believe it at first, but I came to school and heard my friends talking and I began to believe it." Another said: "I believed it and was even fooled into going over and seeing it [burned spots]. The main reason it was so convincing was hearing it on the radio and seeing it on television." Among some, the incident provoked fear. One woman reported: "My husband came home from work and loaded his gun and put it on the shelf, so I knew he was scared . . . I was scared too." Another resident observed: "I hadn't locked the door for twenty-five years; but when I heard that, I ran to my door, locked it, and ran underneath the bed and stayed there until I heard it was a hoax."

One student in Forkenbrock's sociology class, Holly Seegers, who was absent from class the day that the UFO experiment was planned, later summed up her own reactions to the report in these words: "Wednesday, April 14, began as another uneventful school day. . . . After a few minutes, Lona Hennager came down from the library and asked me if I had heard about the UFO. I said 'no' and she proceeded to tell me about the 'thing' Don Ede and Mike Potratz had seen the night before. She also said they went back out to the site and had seen burnt spots in the pasture. My reaction was one of disbelief at first. So the morning went on and I heard firsthand reports and that the news media had been notified, I believed everything with great conviction. I mean, why shouldn't there be people from another planet? Why should we be the only inhabited world in the universe? People are always seeing flying saucers. Why not around here, too? I couldn't see why this story couldn't be true. The stories didn't conflict as I heard them. I thought this was the most exciting thing to ever hit this area. . . ."

The final report written by the students in Forkenbrock's class contained some very sage observations about mass psychology and its implications for the UFO question:

- People caught up in the group reaction with respect to the UFO were found to act on suggestions that they might otherwise reject. Letting their emotions cloud their reasoning resulted in the temporary suspension of the ability to think critically.

- Approximately 500 [people] went to the site of the UFO. This statistic alone shows how excited the people were at a new experience that relieved some of the boredom in the daily routine of life.

- The [news] media give reality to unreality. Without the use of the mass media in our class study, fewer people would have believed in the UFO. The mass media supposedly give the truth; that's why so many people believed that the UFO was real. Even though such adjectives as the word "alleged" may be used in the reporting of news, many people have the tendency to ignore such words, further stretching unreality toward reality.

The media are not always reliable and can be used. The media were responsible for exaggerating the UFO incident before all the facts had been taken into consideration. The media can be misled and can mislead.

What was the reaction of the news media to the experiment after the hoax was revealed? *The Cedar Rapids Gazette,* which reported the initial "UFO landing" and later the story exposing the hoax, carried an editorial which was critical of Forkenbrock's experiment. But radio station WCCO in Minneapolis, which also had been taken in by the experiment, took a different attitude: "A good educational experiment . . . this represents real student involvement in learning."

The ability of the news media to generate, albeit unwittingly, a rash of UFO reports in a localized area—which UFOlogists call a "flap"—was effectively demonstrated by the Maynard experiment. Several typical UFO flaps, set in motion by widespread media coverage, will be analyzed in the next chapter and in chapters 25 and 26.

9 · More "Extraterrestrial" UFOs

No single object has been misinterpreted as a "flying saucer" more often than the planet Venus. The study of these mistakes proves quite instructive, for it shows beyond all possible dispute the limitations of sensory perception and the weakness of the accounts relating shapes and motions of point sources or objects with small apparent diameters.

This sage admonition sounds as if it might have come from Dr. Donald H. Menzel, astronomer and former director of the Harvard Observatory. Menzel was one of the early debunkers of UFOs as extraterrestrial visitors. But in fact the above warning comes from French-born mathematician Dr. Jacques Vallee, who himself leans strongly toward the extraterrestrial view on UFOs, judging from his two books on the subject.* Vallee voiced this note of caution on page 110

* Vallee presently is director of the Parapsychology Research Group of Palo Alto, California. In a recent article, Vallee suggests that UFOs might not be extraterrestrial spaceships but may involve "interpenetrating universes."

of the book he coauthored with his wife Janine: *Challenge to Science: The UFO Enigma* (Chicago, Regnery, 1966). Vallee, who obtained his Ph.D. at Northwestern University, was a close friend of Dr. Hynek while he was there. Vallee followed his admonition with the explanation that UFO reports induced by Venus and other bright celestial bodies can usually be identified by an experienced investigator with some background in astronomy. But he neglected to add that by the time such identification usually occurs, the news media have already given widespread publicity to the initial sightings. This publicity encourages the pranksters to make and release their plastic hot-air balloons, which are not so easily identified, and the hoaxers to concoct their tall tales.

You may find it difficult, perhaps at first impossible, to believe that intelligent people and no-nonsense observers such as police officers can honestly think that they were chased by a UFO which really is Venus or Mars. Once the observer decides that Venus *is a UFO*, he will find that no matter how far or fast he drives, when he looks back the UFO seems just as close and just as bright. The logical conclusion is that the UFO must be following him. I once found this hard to believe. Today I know it can be true. For example, in the fall of 1967 a rash of UFO reports of this type achieved national publicity because many of them came from police officers in more than ten communities in central Georgia.

The first report came from a police lieutenant in Milledgeville, with eleven years of service, who told of spotting a UFO at 4:36 A.M. Eastern daylight time (EDT) on October 20 while on patrol duty. Initially, he said, the object seemed to be only a new streetlight, low on the horizon, but then it appeared to move away. As it did so, the UFO took on the appearance of a "bright-red, football-shaped light." The officer took off in pursuit and followed the UFO, he later reported, for about eight miles into the country until he and his associate lost sight of the object and turned around to head back to town. As they neared Milledgeville, the other officer said he looked back and was shocked to discover that the UFO had reappeared and had "caught up with us." It was so close, he said, that it illuminated the inside of the patrol car brightly enough so that the officers could read the hands on their watches! The officers radioed in that they were being followed by a UFO. Soon the two policemen decided to stop the car and get out for a better view, but when they did, the object seemed to "veer away and disappear behind the trees," the lieutenant reported.

The two policemen returned to headquarters and picked up a third officer. By this time, they noted, the UFO "had started climbing and had gotten about twice the height of the tree line." The three men watched for nearly half an hour as the UFO changed color from bright red to orange and then back to white, while it climbed higher in the sky until it resembled "a star." When the lieutenant finished work at 7 A.M., he reported the UFO was still "hanging" there high in the sky. Earlier, the local radio dispatcher had called the police in a nearby town to report the UFO, and soon they called back to say they could see it also.

The next night, the UFO was not sighted from Milledgeville.* But the following night, shortly after midnight, the police received a call from the outskirts of town from a man who, having read of the earlier UFO sighting, reported that a UFO had followed him down the highway. The lieutenant, now the local UFO expert, was dispatched to the scene, and when he arrived, he reported seeing *two* UFOs, one of which he said appeared to be several thousand feet above the other. The two UFOs remained high in the sky and "were still hanging" there, the officer later reported, when he finished duty the next morning. Both objects, he said, seemed to drift together across the sky with the passage of time, and the lower object resembled a piece of floating tin foil.

During the early morning hours of the fourth day of the local flap, Milledgeville police began to receive reports that the UFO had returned, and so the lieutenant and a companion were dispatched to the scene. Sure enough, they quickly spotted the UFO, which they described as "bright, starlike." Soon a second, similar UFO began to rise above the horizon.

---

* Possibly because of an overcast sky. I have not made an attempt to dig out the weather records for that date.

Earlier, arrangements had been made with a local pilot, who agreed that if the UFO returned he would take off and try to get a closer look at it. So, shortly after 5 A.M., the pilot and a companion were airborne on their UFO search. The pilot maintained radio contact with the police officers so they could direct him to the UFO, but initially he had trouble spotting it because, as he later explained, there were hundreds of lights in the sky. Finally, to guide the pilot, the officers pointed the patrol car spotlight toward the UFO, and the pilot took off in pursuit. Later, the lieutenant said the pilot had erred because he "flew under it [the UFO]."

The pilot later reported that the UFO that he was chasing seemed to "back off" and kept "moving higher and away from us" as the aircraft headed east. At one point, the pilot called the control tower at Robbins Air Force Base, near Macon, to see if the UFO was showing up on the airport surveillance radar. The controller looked and said he had a target, which he believed to be the aircraft chasing the UFO, and that for about one minute he had an unidentified target, which then disappeared. Finally, at about 6 A.M., the pilot gave up the chase and landed. He reported that the brilliant white object he had been chasing was still visible in the sky.

Although the Milledgeville police and the pilot were never able to get a close look at the UFO, a thirteen-year-old local youth claimed to have been much more successful, and he had two Polaroid photos to support his contention. The photos, taken in broad daylight, showed an object that resembled a Mexican sombrero. The boy said he had simply hiked into the woods in search of the UFO, found it and photographed it. It was as simple as that!

The numerous Georgia sightings came during a government-sponsored UFO study at the University of Colorado which had been funded in response to criticism that the USAF had failed to do a competent job of investigating UFO reports, or that it was withholding information from the public. The university dispatched a team of two scientists to Georgia for an on-the-spot investigation, and they arrived while the sightings were still in progress. When the police lieutenant pointed to the UFO he had chased and which had chased his patrol car, University of Colorado scientists quickly identified it as Venus, which was especially bright at that time because of its proximity to the Earth. Venus would start to rise above the eastern horizon at approximately 3:50 A.M., local time, or approximately an hour before it had been spotted on the first night by the policemen. (At the time, Venus was so bright that it had produced numerous other, if less widely publicized, UFO reports across the nation for several weeks.) The second UFO that had been spotted on the third night was the planet Jupiter, which was not quite as bright as Venus.

But what explanation is there for the unidentified target that had appeared briefly on the scope of the radar at Robbins Air Force Base? It could have been an overflying airplane, a swarm of birds, insects or freak atmospheric conditions which can produce radar echoes, as will be discussed in Chapter 18. Although Dr. Hynek is an outspoken critic of most of the conclusions of the University of Colorado UFO study report, he has fully endorsed the findings on the Georgia UFO of 1967, which he said "was most definitely Venus!" Hynek said the "case should be read by all UFO investigators. It is a fantastic example of how persuasive the planet Venus can be as a non-screened UFO. Police officers in 11 counties were 'taken in' by this planet." *

A similar UFO flap developed in central Kansas during the late summer of 1972. A United Press International article, published on August 17, quoted the director of the International UFO Bureau, a small UFO group with headquarters in Oklahoma City, Oklahoma, as theorizing that the sightings involved "scouts from a 'mother ship.' " The article recounted numerous reports from Hays and other Kansas towns. One Hays policeman described the UFO as a "red blinking thing" that periodically turned white and sometimes had a greenish tint. This UFO had been spotted first around 10 P.M., and reports continued to come in until around 4:35 A.M., just as dawn was breaking. Police in another town,

* From Hynek's book, *The UFO Experience* (Chicago, Reguery, 1972).

twenty-five miles away, had also sighted the UFO and reported that it hovered in one spot, giving off white flashes that resembled a camera flash lamp. There were numerous other reports from the area during the predawn hours.

On August 18, local newspapers carried an Associated Press dispatch telling of mysterious lights that had been reported by observers near Lyons. One came from a truckdriver who said a light had moved alongside his vehicle for three miles at approximately 4:45 A.M. *The Kansas City Star*, in its August 19 edition, carried an article, datelined Hays, quoting Ellis County sheriff Clarence Werth as saying that the mysterious UFOs being reported in the area *were nothing more than stars*. The sheriff explained that the flashes and apparent movement were simply illusions caused by the high moisture content of the air. But this explanation apparently failed to impress *The Kansas City Star*, because on August 20 the newspaper carried a feature story on its *front page* under the headline: "Ranks of U.F.O. Believers Grow." This story, and a follow-up article that appeared two days later, described how the police at Colby had been alerted at 2:07 A.M. by a telephone call from John Calkins, who lived in a mobile home some eight miles outside of town. The man told of a giant UFO that appeared to be landing nearby.

This report was relayed to a patrol car, manned by a twenty-two-year-old officer named Paul Carter. Carter quickly spotted a UFO, and as he later described it, the object was coming out of the northeast. The UFO was "very bright, changing from red and green-blinking colors to white." It was "so bright you couldn't look at it. It lit up the pasture," the officer said. He called for assistance and soon was joined by another twenty-two-year-old officer, Dennis Brown. As he arrived, Brown later reported, the entire area was illuminated "like daytime." When he got out of his own car to climb into the patrol car, Brown said, "I saw a shot of light go straight up into the air and then veer or level off to travel in a southeasterly direction." Carter said the UFO was oval-shaped, resembling "a cereal bowl turned upside down." It seemed, he said, to be about thirty to thirty-five feet wide and twenty to twenty-five feet high, and appeared to be hovering only ten to fifteen feet above the horizon.

As the two officers drove out toward the Calkins residence, they said they observed a "very bright, colored object in the sky" in the vicinity of the Calkins mobile home. This UFO appeared as a bright, white light when it was moving rapidly, but when the UFO stopped, the officers later reported, there were red and green lights. As the officers drove along and scanned the skies, they noticed numerous other smaller UFOs, higher in the sky, that appeared as fast-moving lights which streaked across the sky in only a few seconds. It is not surprising that when the two young policemen arrived, they were "as white as sheets," according to Calkins. "I never seen [sic] police officers as scared as that in my life," the newspaper quoted him as saying.

As Calkins described his own experience, he said he had been awakened at approximately 2 A.M. by barking dogs. When he looked outside, he said, he saw a giant saucer-shaped object, blazing with light, that seemed to be descending on a Quonset building barely 150 feet away. This had prompted his call to the police. But according to the Kansas City newspaper story of August 22, on the morning following the incident, when Calkins had searched for any signs that a UFO had landed nearby, he found nothing. The two young policemen had attempted to photograph the UFO(s) using both an Eastman Instamatic and a Polaroid camera. The pictures from the former failed to show any image while the Polaroid print had an unclear image that one of the officers conceded "could be anything."

The August 20 article in *The Kansas City Star* told of numerous other UFO reports from central Kansas. For instance, the police radio dispatcher at Hays had logged a telephone call received at 10:03 P.M. in the following words: "Unknown female advised there was an unknown object over northeast part of Hays with a big red light." A few minutes later, the log showed, another woman had called to say that a UFO had illuminated her whole house, and this was followed by a similar report from a local man. All of the reports indicated that the UFO was either a large red light or a bright white light. In most reports, the UFO was said to have hovered in one spot in the sky, moved upward slowly and finally disappeared.

The same article disclosed that the UFO flap had begun to envelop Kansas City itself. A UFO reportedly seen over the city at approximately 8 P.M. the previous night was described by some as being wedge-shaped, while others said it resembled a sausage. Some reports said the UFO was white, others that it was orange. The article concluded by quoting unidentified officials as suggesting that the object might have been a weather balloon or a vapor trail from a high-flying jet aircraft.

The August 23 edition of the same newspaper carried a brief article, datelined Wichita, under a headline that read: "Saucer Sightings Linked With Helium Balloon Sales." It disclosed that a military surplus store in Wichita had been experiencing booming sales of surplus Army weather balloons for several weeks! Mrs. Harold Friedman, who operated the store with her husband, said she hadn't noticed at first how fast the surplus weather balloons were selling "until we ran out of them and we kept getting calls for more." The balloons, made of translucent plastic, inflate to a diameter of about six feet when filled with helium. At a price of only $3.98 they were selling like hotcakes. When Mrs. Friedman read about the mysterious lights being reported in central Kansas skies, she became suspicious. So when two teen-age boys came in to buy balloons, she asked what they would be used for, and the boys replied: "Don't you know, we fill them with helium and attach batteries and flashlight bulbs and make flying saucers." The boys explained that the effect could be made even more mysterious by using colored lights and adding a mechanism which would cause the balloon-borne lights to flash off and on.

The following day, *The Kansas City Star* carried still another major feature on the current UFO flap in Kansas, under the headline: "Strange Lights in Kansas Skies." It was not until a reader got down to the ninth paragraph in the article that there was a brief mention of the possibility that some of the UFO reports might be the result of surplus weather balloons launched by ingenious teen-agers. The article did, however, give a little more prominence to another possible explanation for some UFO reports. This came from a meteorologist at Colby who suggested that temperature inversions might be producing extreme refraction, so that lights from distant autos and towns far beyond the local horizon could be visible. (This is the same sort of phenomenon that causes the Brown Mountain Lights, discussed in Chapter 7.)

On August 25 the Associated Press reported UFO sightings from still another Kansas town, Arkansas City. The sighting by three police officers had occurred during the early morning hours, and the officers had called a local newspaper reporter, Ms. Beth Lilley. When she joined the three policemen on a small hill at 4:20 A.M., the UFO was still clearly visible in the form of a large, bright light that appeared to be round with beams of light extending outward from the edges. A few moments later, Ms. Lilley later reported, the UFO was suddenly surrounded by a glowing circle, and red twinkling lights appeared in front of it. Then after a few minutes the bright glow seemed to be absorbed into the UFO, and it appeared to change to a triangular shape. When Ms. Lilley finally returned home at 5:20 A.M., near dawn, the UFO was still visible, and she decided to get her camera and photograph it. By 6:40 A.M., the UFO had climbed much higher in the sky and now was no larger than a star. By 7:05 P.M., in full daylight, the UFO was still there, but only barely visible.

Following the news that UFOs were now to be seen over Arkansas City, many hopeful observers turned out the following night, and despite partly cloudy conditions the UFO was again sighted by such prominent persons as the city manager and a city commissioner. According to one observer who watched the UFO for thirty minutes, the object seemed to be surrounded by a red ring. Another published report, from an unidentified man, said that shortly after he had sighted the UFO over his house, the entire structure began to shake. But when he went outside to take a closer look, he reported that the UFO had disappeared completely.

An important break in the UFO mystery was reported in

the August 27 edition of *The Kansas City Star,* but *not* on the front page, where UFO articles had previously been featured. *This was only a brief news item, buried on page 4.* It reported that the UFO pictures that had been made by Ms. Lilley in Arkansas City had been analyzed by Joseph Olivarez, director of the Hutchinson planetarium and an astronomy teacher at Hutchinson Junior College. The photos showed enough stars in the background so that Olivarez could precisely determine the direction in which the camera had been aimed, and thus the position of the UFO. From this, plus the known time at which the photo had been taken, Olivarez could positively identify the mysterious UFO. *It was the planet Venus.* He added that when Venus is viewed through thin cloud layers or haze, it often seems to be surrounded by a halo and to emit radiant beams of light.

It was about this time that the national press services and *The Kansas City Star* began to lose interest in UFOs, and that the 1972 Kansas flap began to run out of steam. The newspaper's September 4 edition did, however, carry an interesting photo which shed additional light on the mystery. The picture showed the sheriff of Sedgwick County (in which Wichita is located) holding a large inflated weather balloon that had come down intact and had been recovered. *The balloon had been outfitted with a battery-powered light plus a mechanism to cause it to flash on and off.* To make the balloon's appearance even more mysterious, metallic reflectors had been taped to the sides of the balloon. These would magnify the apparent size of the flashing light and also make the balloon more readily visible during daylight. How many such balloons were launched by Wichita teen-agers, how far they traveled and how many UFO reports they generated will never be known. Because winds aloft can change direction with altitude, these "UFOs" could readily exhibit mysterious behavior that would seem inexplicable to unsuspecting observers on the ground.

During the Kansas UFO flap, Lawrence R. Brandt, an assistant professor at the University of Wisconsin at Stevens Point, was returning from a vacation trip out west with his son. In a subsequent letter to me, he described how, during the drive east through Kansas, he and his son had seen a very bright celestial body—he wasn't sure of its identity—which "was fantastic in brightness, alternating red and green flashes and practically dancing" in the sky. Brandt wrote me that when he first pointed the object out to his son, "I told him that the newspapers would be full of UFOs on the [Kansas] plains that night. They were! The next evening's newspaper was full of [accounts of] low-flying, hovering UFOs all over the region," Brandt wrote.

But what is the explanation for the tiny UFOs which the two Colby policemen reported seeing zipping across the sky? Only a few days earlier, the Smithsonian Astrophysical Observatory had issued a press release announcing that observers were being treated to a "spectacular display . . . as the Earth passes through a meteor shower this month." During the Perseids meteor shower, which occurs every August, an observer can expect to see numerous "shooting stars." Undoubtedly these were the tiny UFOs that the two Colby officers reported.

So there were at least three different types of visual stimuli involved in the 1972 flap in Kansas: Venus, hoax balloons and meteors. Perhaps there were others. For example, there are a number of Strategic Air Command bomber bases in Kansas, and their aircraft occasionally conduct night training exercises, including mid-air refueling missions. Still other UFO reports may have been generated by ordinary civil aircraft, which not only carry red, green and white navigation lights, but also rotating red-neon anticollision beacons. Some of the newer airliners also carry very bright white xenon anticollision lights which flash periodically and resemble a camera flash lamp.

In the spring of 1973, the town of Piedmont, in southeast Missouri, experienced an extended local UFO flap which made headlines around the country, and may have helped to spark the major nationwide flap in the fall of that year. The continuing UFO sighting reports sparked the curiosity of Dr. John H. Mullen, a scientist in the McDonnell Douglas Corporation's research laboratories in St. Louis. When the Piedmont radio station reported that a UFO had actually landed just outside of town, leaving behind incontrovertible evidence of its visit, Mullen decided he might go down to conduct his first UFO investigation. But before doing so, he called the manager of the Piedmont radio station to be sure the story was as reported. When the account was confirmed, Mullen, his wife and a friend drove to Piedmont.

When Mullen arrived at the Piedmont radio station so he could be taken to the site of the UFO landing, he was met not only by the station manager but also by the president of the Clearwater Lake Association, which promotes tourism in the area. The latter informed Mullen that *tourists were Piedmont's principal source of income.* (Clearly the UFO report had brought in at least three—Mullen, his wife and friend.) The group proceeded to the reported UFO landing site, where, as Mullen later wrote me, they found "the remnant of a large bonfire, made of wood chips." The radio station manager apologized to Mullen for bringing him on a wild-goose chase and admitted that he had not previously visited the site. But the station manager urged Mullen to visit Mrs. J., *an instructor in photography* at the local high school, who had allegedly taken numerous pictures of the UFOs.

Later, when Mullen visited Mrs. J., he was not impressed by any of her UFO pictures, most of which seemed to him to be simply time exposures of stars or meteors. Mrs. J. was undaunted and suggested that the Mullen party return that night to see the UFOs for themselves. Because Mullen is an amateur astronomer, he had come well equipped to see UFOs, or celestial bodies. He had brought along a four-and-one-quarter-inch Questar telescope and a four-and-one-quarter-inch Kutter Schifspiegler astronomical telescope with a large equatorial mount. The Mullen party returned at 10 P.M. and Mrs. J., waiting with several neighbors, told Mullen that he was in luck because the principal UFO, which she called "Grandpa," was directly overhead and that many of its small UFOs also were visible.

As Mullen was setting up his two telescopes, he observed that the objects did indeed seem to change color, from white to red to blue, and that they seemed to be scintillating like spinning tops. But for the next two hours, he wrote me, whenever he focused his telescopes on one of Mrs. J.'s UFOs, it turned out to move at precisely the rate at which the earth turns. This, plus the fact that the object was in focus when the telescope was set at infinity, indicated that the UFOs were simply celestial bodies. When Mullen finally explained to Mrs. J. that her UFOs were simply stars and planets, she seemed neither surprised nor disappointed. Instead, she thanked him and invited the group to come in for coffee and cookies.

The next morning, when Mullen returned to the radio station to report his findings to the manager, he had another surprise. Before Mullen could speak, the station manager said, "Don't tell me. I know. They are stars." The manager explained that two physics students from Washington University in St. Louis had come down to Piedmont *the previous week* and had informed Mrs. J. of the true identity of her UFOs!

The three cases discussed in this chapter, and others that will follow, demonstrate another important UFOlogical Principle:

> UFOLOGICAL PRINCIPLE #6: *Once news media coverage leads the public to believe that UFOs may be in the vicinity, there are numerous natural and man-made objects which, especially when seen at night, can take on unusual characteristics in the minds of hopeful viewers. Their UFO reports in turn add to the mass excitement which encourages still more observers to watch for UFOs. This situation feeds upon itself until such time as the news media lose interest in the subject, and then the "flap" quickly runs out of steam.*

Even before the "discovery" of UFOs in 1947, the brilliant planet Venus had been seducing terrestrial observers into thinking it was something other than a celestial body. During World War II, United States newspapers agreed to not publish anything on the Japanese balloons, loaded with explosives and firebombs, which were reaching this country—to prevent Japan from appraising the success of this novel weapon. Despite this voluntary censorship, the existence of the Japanese balloons became known, at least in some circles. During the summer of 1945, a group of nuclear scientists based at the then secret Los Alamos laboratory in New Mexico observed an extremely bright object in the sky, prompting suspicion that it might be one of the Japanese balloons. The scientists got binoculars to better observe the object, and some thought they could see a basket suspended from the object, indicating it was a balloon. A nearby air base was alerted, and it dispatched two aircraft, which reported that they could not intercept the object because it was at such high altitude.

As the excited group of scientists watched the object, the famous nuclear physicist Dr. Enrico Fermi returned to his office, pulled out an almanac and did a few calculations. He returned to report that the mysterious object was—Venus! One of the scientists involved, George L. Weil, who described the incident in a letter published in the November 8, 1973, edition of *The Washington Post*, explained that in the clear mountain air of New Mexico, Venus was readily visible even during bright sunlight conditions.

It was at about the same time that B-29 crews making night bombing raids on Japan began to report they were being "followed" by a "ball of fire." One of the earliest recorded incidents occurred on April 3, 1945, during a night raid over Kawasaki, according to a former B-29 officer, Richard M. Keenan. A few days later, another crew reported a similar observation, and now the reports began to come in thick and fast. Intelligence officers tried to figure out what the new secret weapon might be and speculated that the Japanese might have outfitted an aircraft with a powerful searchlight to illuminate the B-29s for attack by fighter planes. Gunners aboard the B-29 were alerted to watch for the "searchlight airplanes." Some reported that their bomber had been followed by the bright light for hundreds of miles, despite evasive maneuvers taken by the B-29 pilots to try to shake the mysterious object, Keenan told me. Some of the B-29 gunners reported that they had opened fire on the object, but none ever claimed to have hit it.

The most curious aspect of the mysterious ball of fire,

intelligence officers began to note, was that it always appeared off the right wing—to the east—when the B-29s were flying north toward Japan. And it was always off the left wing—also to the east—when they returned to their bases on the Mariana Islands. Then, in mid-July, according to Keenan, all B-29 crews were briefed as follows: "Fire all you want. You're not going to shoot this one down. That 'ball of fire' out there is the planet Venus, which is now extremely brilliant."

10 · UFOs and Ghosts

"Flying Saucer Over Freeport Reported" was the headline for the story that appeared in the March 25, 1966, edition of *The Houston Post*. The article described an incident that had occurred shortly after midnight on March 20 and involved members of the crew of the U.S. Coast Guard Cutter *Legare* which had been anchored off Freeport, Texas. The article noted that the sightings near Freeport had occurred on the same night as a rash of UFO sightings in Michigan, which seemingly added credibility to the Freeport sightings.

The newspaper had been informed of the incident by the National Investigations Committee for Aerial Phenomena (NICAP), which had learned of the sightings from one of its members who was on the crew of the *Legare*. Rather than quote the newspaper account here, I will use a firsthand source—the official reports filed by the principals involved, which were sent to the USAF's Project Blue Book office. Radioman Third Class John R. Weitlich, who was first to see the UFO, described the incident as follows: "While standing on the bridge on Quartermaster Watch at 01:25 on the

morning of 3/20/66, I had been staring unthinkingly out
through the portholes when I noticed that the lights in two
houses about 100 yards apart from each other and approx.
one mile direct from our ship, blinked on and off very rapidly
and at an intensity extremely brighter than normal, as if these
two houses in particular were completely flooded from within
by fluorescent lights.

"Immediately following this, all power was cut in the area,
which I noticed after a tremendous blue flash of light had
occurred approx. center of these two houses. To get a clearer
look at the situation, I then went out to the port side wing of
the bridge and noticed a distinct whitish glow about 45 deg.
to the right of where I had noticed the blue flash. This object
appeared to be about from 300 to 500 feet above the ground,
and emitted an 'eerie' glow of white light that appeared to
pulsate in its intensity. I must say now I tried to kid myself
into believing this was an object of some earthly form but
ruled this out and informed my supervisor who was sitting in
the radio shack at this time, that I saw a U.F.O. and I then
pointed it out to him. I was ordered to immediately get a
camera but upon my return the U.F.O. had disappeared, thus
my story ends here."

His supervisor was Radioman First Class Glenn A. Mushett, whose official account reads as follows: "I was in the radio
shack working when the Quartermaster of the Watch reported seeing a blue flash in the sky. This was about 1:35 A.M.
local time. A few seconds later the ship and entire area had a
power failure [i.e., the ship had been connected to land power
at the time]. The Quartermaster went out on the bridge, and
as he walked out he reported seeing a UFO in the sky. He
hollered for someone else so I went out.

"As soon as I walked out I saw a very large object in the
sky. It was oval in shape. It was giving off an orange glow and
around the object itself it was giving off a blue light, shortly
after seeing it the blue stopped. I told the Quartermaster to
get some binoculars, and then to go below and get a camera.
As I observed the UFO through binoculars, I could see it had
ports or windows. These windows were open. As I could see
coming from inside the UFO, it was giving off a dark orange

glow. I must have observed it for about a minute or longer. Then it started to move up from about 500 feet to about a thousand feet very slowly. As it reached somewhere around a thousand feet the orange glow it was giving off got larger, then there was another blue flash; the orange glow subsided and the UFO moved away at a high rate of speed, and was out of sight in several seconds. The Quartermaster and another member of the crew and myself was [sic] watching the area, two objects shot up from the ground at a high rate of speed. The objects gave off a white glow, but they gave no trail or stream as they moved up. Also in several seconds they were out of sight."

The third observer who witnessed only the last two objects was Fireman Apprentice Keith Van Orden. His account is very brief: "At 01:35, two objects very bright shot up into the sky and disappeared quickly at about one and one-half miles from our ship, 350 deg. magnetic [bearing]." In reporting the incident, the Houston newspaper noted that UFOs are sometimes reported during times of electrical power failure. It did *not*, however, go on to explain that some UFOlogists believe that the power outages are caused by alien spaceships bent on sabotage.

In my first book, *UFOs—Identified* (New York, Random House, 1968), I proposed that some of the most perplexing and seemingly inexplicable UFO reports might involve a family of freak atmospheric electrical phenomena related to "ball lightning," which is occasionally seen during stormy weather conditions and more rarely during fair weather. Ball lightning is a phenomenon known as a "plasma"—a collection of highly electrified air which glows intensely in a spectrum of colors that include white, blue, orange and red. Ball lightning has been reported to penetrate a window and enter a house without breaking the glass and to behave in mysterious ways. Science is not able to explain how ball lightning forms or sustains itself for periods of up to several minutes, but it is accepted as an atmospheric electrical freak which one day, perhaps in another decade, will be explainable as a result of growing knowledge in the complex field of plasma physics.

My training as an electrical engineer, and knowledge of similar plasmas that can form on or near high-tension power lines during a system malfunction, prompted me to believe that the glowing UFOs that were sometimes reported near power lines during an outage were plasmas produced by the malfunction itself—not alien spaceships that were maliciously sabotaging our power systems. I referred to this phenomenon as a "plasma-UFO." At the time my first book was written, I was not aware of the *Legare* sightings near Freeport, which provide further support for my hypothesis.

Investigation of the Freeport incident, supplemented by my own correspondence with J. M. McReynolds, vice-president for engineering at the Houston Lighting & Power Company, revealed the following: At approximately 11:15 P.M. on the night of March 19, the company received a report that there had been a power outage in the Surfside area, not far from where the *Legare* was anchored. A repair crew was dispatched, and they found that a primary conductor on the 7,200-volt line had broken and short-circuited, and this had blown a line fuse which had interrupted service to the area, including the Coast Guard Station. Repairs were made and service was restored at approximately 1:00 A.M. on March 20. The repair crew thought it had solved the problem, but a detailed inspection was difficult because of the *heavy fog present*, McReynolds wrote.

At approximately 1:30 A.M., the power company received another call reporting trouble. (This was approximately the time that Radioman Weitlich had observed flickering lights in the two houses, followed by what appeared to be intense illumination.) The repair crew was dispatched to the area, and this time they found a faulty transformer, *which was situated directly in front of the two houses cited by Weitlich.* The transformer malfunction had resulted from a short circuit on the primary bushing which created such intense flame and pressure that the transformer cover was blown off, according to the company official. These are precisely the sort of conditions that could, in my opinion, have produced a ball-lightning-type glowing plasma that would be blown out of the transformer case when its cover was expelled. The rising ball of fire, seen through the fog and from a distance, was most likely the UFO reported by Weitlich and Mushett.

But what of the other two objects that were observed by Mushett and Van Orden some distance from where the first UFO was observed? The Houston power company official told me that the repair crew, during its second visit, found that the transformer malfunction had also blown a line-fuse approximately one-half mile from the transformer. The fuse was housed in a cylindrical container, open at both ends, so that hot gases and metal fuse fragments generated during a short-circuit could rapidly escape. When the fuse "blew," the gases and fragments would have been extremely hot, making them luminous, which explains the two small UFOs briefly spotted. There were no more faults in the Surfside area power system that night. Nor were there any more UFO observations by the *Legare* crew members.

It was a cool, misty night in October in the small town of Aguilar, located in southeastern Colorado. It was past midnight and the main street was all but deserted when suddenly a woman's scream rang out. Men in a local saloon rushed outside and found a woman near hysteria. She said she had seen a white shining "thing" moving along the electric power lines. If this incident had occurred after June 25, 1947, when UFOs were first "discovered," the object reported by the woman would have been a "UFO." But this was October, 1946, and so the shimmering object moving along the power line could only be a "ghost."

Aguilar had been founded by the Spanish, and in Spanish-American folklore there is a legend of La Llorona—the spirit of a woman who drowned her own children and was therefore doomed to wander forever. (These and other details of the incident were reported in a feature article by Olga Curtis that appeared in the October 20, 1968, edition of *The Denver Post*.) The hysterical woman said that the shimmering white thing she had seen moving along the power lines resembled a

woman in a flowing gown—the Lady in White of the La
Llorona legend!

There were many skeptics when the incident was first
reported in 1946, but not for long. The ghost was associated
with a sound like a crying baby, and one night a man
allegedly went into the fields to investigate such a noise.
Hours later the man was found, reportedly in a state of shock
with a broken leg and no recollection of how he had been
hurt. On another night, a youth reportedly went into a
woodshed and failed to return. When his family went to
investigate, they reportedly found him huddled in a corner,
babbling about a bony thing that had tried to drag him away.
One woman, who had been a girl of sixteen in Augilar at the
time, recalled the incident twenty-two years later. She said
that she too had seen a "shimmering white thing, hanging
above the ground . . . *it was shapeless, yet it looked like a
woman.*" (Emphasis added.) Another woman said her son
had seen the ghost "plain as day—a white thing swirling up
high . . . and we heard that crying baby." The swirling white
thing had been seen *near a power line.*

Anthony Tessari, who had been the marshal in Aguilar at
the time, later recalled: "I had one man I trusted completely,
a reliable witness, swear to me that he had actually seen the
ghost lady." Small wonder that before the month was over,
the main streets of Aguilar were being patrolled by armed
guards and at least a few citizens preferred to stay inside after
dark. There were a few casualties—stray *white* dogs. Tessari's
own view is that "it was just a story that snowballed . . . It
got so people were seeing ghosts everywhere, every night, for
more than a month." Then, after a nervous month, Aguilar's
ghost scare died out—not unlike a typical "UFO flap." The
initial report of a shining white thing moving along the power
lines strongly suggests a plasma, or "corona" as it is usually
called by power company engineers.

It never occurred to the citizens of Aguilar that the
mysterious white object reportedly seen near the electric
power lines might be a spaceship from another world, because
UFOs had not yet been discovered. ("Invented" might be a
more precise term.) The only choice available in 1946 was a

"ghost," and specifically the "Lady in White" of the local legend. A few years later, in a different locale, it never occurred to members of the crew of the USCG *Legare* that they had seen a ghost. What they saw was clearly a UFO, complete with portholes.

In the 1890s the United States experienced what today would be called a UFO flap through the Midwest and Pacific coast. But the UFOs reported in the 1890s were said to resemble gas-filled fabric airships and to carry ordinary humans in gondolas, rather than being metallic and saucer-shaped. In other words, the UFOs of the 1890s were described in terms of the advanced technology of that era that was familiar to the public. The story of these "mysterious airships," and their relationship to the modern UFOs, will be discussed in Chapter 24.

11 · A Close Encounter

The telephone rang just as I was leaving my apartment during the early evening hours of August 3, 1972, on my way to attend an important technical meeting. My first impulse was not to answer because I was already late for the conference, but curiosity overwhelmed judgment and I answered. The male voice on the other end said, "Mr. Klass, my name is Leonard D——, and I think I saw one of your plasma-UFOs last night." My first reaction was to skip the technical meeting, but it was a business assignment for *Aviation Week & Space Technology* magazine, so even plasma-UFOs would have to wait. I explained the situation to my caller, assured him of my keen interest, and asked that he write me the details of the incident. He agreed to do so.

Several days later Leonard's letter arrived. I learned he was fifteen years old, in the eleventh grade and lived in a large mid-Atlantic city. His hobby, he explained, was radio astronomy, an extremely ambitious (and expensive) one for a young man his age. (Radio astronomy employs a sensitive radio receiver and antenna to receive a noiselike signal radiated by the sun and other stars.) Leonard's letter explained that on August 2 he had heard a report on the radio that a solar storm (sunspots) had been detected, and this would provide a strong signal for his radio telescope. He said that he had telephoned the National Bureau of Standards Solar Forecasts division at Boulder, Colorado, for more details and prepared to monitor the solar storm. But first, he said, he decided to check the antenna on the roof of his house to be sure it was in readiness and well-supported, because of an approaching thunderstorm. So he opened a second-story window, which faced south-southwest, and then, he said, he thought to look at his watch to see how much time remained before the predicted time of the solar storm. The time, he wrote, was 4:43 P.M. EST. "I'll never forget that because of what was going to happen in the next few seconds was like nothing that ever happened before, at least to me."

Out of the corner of his eye, he spotted "something luminous and glowing." He turned and "then I just stopped cold and stared at it for a few seconds. . . . It was a ball you could see into, although not reflecting, it was glowing . . . red around the outside, shifting to red-orange and getting brighter near the center. It was 3 feet in diameter and 15 feet above my head. It drifted downward slowly, as if blown by the wind toward our lightning rod. It began to fade slowly in brightness, not color, shrinking in size and collapsing toward an imaginary center." By 4:47 P.M., he wrote, after four minutes of observation, the glowing object had disappeared. According to his letter, he had not wasted those four minutes simply watching. He said he had checked the radio receiver and found a buzzing type of static. When he tuned the dial, he found the static over a wide frequency band, from 7 megacycles to 245 megacycles. He added that the buzzing static did not seem to decrease in intensity as the glowing object lost brightness, but the noise did disappear completely when the object disappeared. He also reported making an observation of the object through a prism.

At first reading, it was an exciting report. The object, as described, exhibited many of the characteristics of a plasma-UFO, or ball lightning. And so far as I knew, there had never before been an incident near a radio telescope, albeit a modest amateur's rig, to permit measurement of the spectrum of radio noise emitted by the plasma. Only at the end of the letter did I encounter an unsettling comment. Leonard had written: "Too bad my mother was at the store and not home to witness all this. You'll just have to take my word for it." Why, I wondered, should he think that I might not believe him? I was not always so suspicious—but numerous years of investigating UFO reports and many encounters with hoaxers have left me sadder and cautious, if not suspicious.

As I mulled over his comment, another disturbing question came to mind. The incident reportedly had occurred in the late afternoon of August 2, and the youth had telephoned me barely twenty-four hours later. How had he so quickly learned of my interest and background in such phenomena—unless he had earlier read *UFOs—Identified*? And if he had read my book, his description was sufficiently close to others in the book that the whole incident could be only a flight of youthful fancy, with a few new details added to distinguish his report from others. Yet he had gone to the expense of calling me long distance and had not attempted to obtain publicity in the local news media. This tended to ease my suspicions.

In my letter of reply to Leonard, I asked for some additional details and complimented him on his good scientific instincts in thinking to make the radio receiver measurements. Then I asked how he had learned of my background in such phenomena so quickly and inquired if he had read my first book. I added that if he had not seen my book, I would send him an autographed copy so he could read of other reports similar to his own.

Leonard replied on August 16, and his letter responded to all of my questions except the one asking how he had learned of me and whether he had read the book. His failure to respond to an offer of a free autographed copy seemed a strange oversight. On August 21 I decided to telephone the youth. (His letter provided two telephone numbers—one for his mother and one for him—suggesting that he came from a family of means.) I asked Leonard if he planned to study science in college and was surprised to hear him say that he could not afford to go to college. I offered to try to get him a job as a technician at Westinghouse, through several officials who are acquaintances, telling him that I thought the company provided scholarships to promising youths on their payroll, but this evoked scant interest as far as I could tell. Then we went over the reports he had sent me. Finally, I asked to speak with his mother.

When his mother came on the line, I explained that I was very impressed with her son's scientific aptitude and that I had no reason to question the truthfulness of his report. But I added that my experience with reports from teen-age boys required that I probe thoroughly. I asked her to recount what had happened when she returned from the store on the evening of August 2—had Leonard rushed up to tell her of the curious incident? She replied, "Yes, sort of, he did. But you see I always tell him, 'I'm not interested. I don't want to hear. I'm tired . . .'" and she proceeded into a lengthy discussion of her poor health.

A few moments later, I tried a more direct approach and asked if she had any doubt that Leonard's story was true or whether it could be a product of his imagination. She replied, "Oh, I don't know. I believe him." Then she went on to say that a few years earlier she herself had been quite interested in UFOs and had read some books on the subject but had since lost interest. She gave only a brief and somewhat qualified endorsement of Leonard's story. When Leonard and I resumed our discussion, he volunteered that he had "once seen your book, *UFOs—Identified*, in the school library. I just glanced at the pictures about corona and power lines. Then, after this [August 2 incident] happened, I took out the book the very next day and glanced at some of the stories that were similar to mine." (He added that he had also read another UFO book.) It was clear then that Leonard had at least skimmed my book prior to the date of the alleged incident, so his description could have come either from firsthand observation or from my book.

Seeking other means to try to check Leonard's account, I asked if he had reported the incident to any of his friends or

neighbors at the time, to see if they might have seen the
glowing object. Leonard replied that he had checked with a
next-door neighbor, a woman, shortly after the incident. He
said he had "tried to make sure not to hint as to what it might
be and just see if they noticed anything." When he said the
neighbor said she had not seen anything unusual, I asked if
Leonard had then described the incident to her? "Yes, I
started to, and then she got kind of fussy about something
else." I told Leonard that I would like to call his neighbor
and asked for her name and address. He was a bit reluctant
but did provide them. Then, as if to prepare me, he
volunteered, "We haven't been around here too long, so I
don't know if she is going to be too friendly."

As soon as I finished talking with Leonard, I called the
neighbor, Mrs. Chester P., explained the reason for my call
and asked if the young man had come over to report his
sighting to her on the late afternoon of Wednesday, August
2. Without hesitation she replied, "No, he didn't." When I
asked, "Are you sure of that?" she replied, "As sure as God is
in heaven." Knowing that the incident, if it had occurred, had
happened nearly three weeks before, I told her that I would
terminate this call and give her a few minutes to recollect her
thoughts and to check with her husband, then I would call
back.

When I called back, Mr. P. answered, and he confirmed his
wife's earlier statement that Leonard had not come over to
make any such report. He explained that he and his wife both
work in their furniture store until 5 P.M. and return home
together, so he would have been present had such a visit by
Leonard occurred. Then he added, "That boy, he reads a lot
of books, and, ah, he is very bright in electronics—but I think
he's kinda nutty." Mr. P. went on to explain that during an
Apollo lunar landing mission, Leonard was not content to
receive progress reports from radio and television stations; he
had personally called NASA's Manned Space Center in
Houston "to see how the astronauts were doing," and he also
called NASA headquarters in Washington "to ask some
questions," Mr. P. said, running up a big telephone bill that
added to his mother's financial problems. Mr. P. explained

that he was familiar with the situation because he owned the house in which Leonard and his mother lived.

After two lengthy discussions with Mr. and Mrs. P., I could only conclude that this scientifically talented, if somewhat erratic, young man had concocted his story after having read about plasma-UFOs and ball lightning in my book. I asked the neighbors not to ridicule Leonard, and expressed the hope that they would not discuss the matter with him or with other neighbors. Whether they respected my request I do not know, for I never wrote or called Leonard to tell him the result of my check with his neighbors. He never called or wrote to inquire.

It was not my first encounter with a UFO hoax, and it would not be my last, as we shall discuss in subsequent chapters. Invariably the perpetrator of the hoax is a nice, gentle, seemingly forthright individual and never an "obvious" hoaxer. People who are basically dishonest, I have found, normally do *not* engage in staging UFO hoaxes. They prefer to devote their skills and efforts to more financially rewarding ventures.

12 · The "Landing" at Socorro

The small town of Socorro in central New Mexico achieved international fame almost overnight as a result of a widely publicized report that an egg-shaped UFO had landed on the outskirts of town, leaving behind evidence on the ground that seemingly confirmed the story.* The incident reportedly occurred on April 24, 1964, at 5:45 P.M., in broad daylight, as young police officer Lonnie Zamora was chasing a speeding motorist heading south on the outskirts of town. Suddenly, over the sound of his own racing car, Zamora said he heard a loud "roar." Looking for the source, he said he spotted a "flame in the sky" which seemed to be coming from a flat-top hill (mesa) approximately three-quarters of a mile southwest of his position.

Zamora said he recalled that there was a small shack on the

* This case is discussed in more detail in my previous book *UFOs—Identified* but will be highlighted here to provide a benchmark for the similar "landing" case discussed in the following chapter, and for the benefit of readers who are unfamiliar with the Socorro case.

mesa near where the flame appeared which was used to store dynamite, so he assumed the dynamite had exploded. He said he abandoned the chase after the speeding motorist and headed up the steep, rough road to the top of the mesa. Reaching the mesa top, he drove southwest, seeing nothing at first except the undulating topography, partially covered by mesquite bushes. Then, he said, he spotted a "shiny-type object" in the distance and alongside the object what appeared to be "two people in white coveralls." Zamora said the object appeared to be "a car turned upside down." As he drove toward it, Zamora said, he called in by radio to headquarters to say that he was proceeding to investigate what appeared to be an auto accident.

By the time Zamora finished his radio call, he said, he had reached a clearing that was only one hundred feet from the object, which was sitting in an arroyo—a small gully which gradually sloped away from the road. Zamora said he did not try to get a good look at the object from the car because he planned to get out and walk over for a closer observation. But as he got out of the car, Zamora said, he heard "a very loud roar," and a giant blast of flame shot out from the underside of the object as it began to slowly rise straight up.

Zamora said the roar and flame made him fear an explosion and prompted him to run back toward the car in such haste that he bumped into the car, knocking off his prescription glasses, which he did not stop to recover. He said the roar soon subsided and was replaced by a "sharp-tone whine" which lasted only briefly. Then, he reported, the UFO flew off silently in a southwesterly direction, barely clearing the nearby dynamite shack, sailed over Highway #60 to the west and disappeared over the nearby mountains.

Then, Zamora said, he ran back to his car and called in to headquarters to report the incident and to ask for assistance. Curiously, Zamora specifically asked that Sergeant Sam Chavez of the New Mexico State Police be sent out, rather than a local police officer or someone from the sheriff's office. Zamora said that while he waited for Chavez to arrive, he went into the gully to investigate, and then he drew several sketches of the UFO. These showed an egg-shaped object with two legs protruding and on the side of the object an insignia containing an arrow. The sketches showed no other details and resembled drawings made by a young child. Earlier, when Zamora had called in to report the incident and was asked to describe the object, he had said that it "looks like a balloon."

When Chavez arrived approximately ten minutes later, the two men explored the arroyo and reported finding four indentations in the soft sand as well as some slight evidence of burning on a mesquite bush and a clump of grass. Soon they were joined by Socorro Deputy Sheriff James Luckie, who had overheard Zamora's radio message and had decided to investigate. Another visitor who drove to the site was Federal Bureau of Investigation Agent J. Arthur Byrnes, Jr., who had been in Chavez' office at the time of Zamora's request for assistance. Out of curiosity, Byrnes had decided to drive out—in an unofficial capacity, he later emphasized to me.

The four indentations, or "pad-prints" as they were soon referred to in subsequent reports on the case, plus the slight evidence of burning on a mesquite bush and a clump of grass, ruled out any possibility that Zamora's UFO might really have been only Venus, a weather balloon or a meteor. Either a craft of extraordinary design had landed briefly on the outskirts of Socorro, or the case was a hoax. (During my subsequent investigation of the case, I briefly entertained the possibility that a plasma-UFO might be involved, but soon found a much more plausible explanation.)

Dr. J. Allen Hynek, the USAF's UFO consultant, was quickly requested to visit Socorro, and he arrived four days after the reported incident. Hynek was deeply impressed by the case, and this is evident in his official report to the USAF. He said the Socorro case was "one of the major UFO sightings in the history of the Air Force's consideration of this subject." And he warned that NICAP and other UFO groups "would consider this the best authenticated landing sighting on record," and would use it as leverage to try to obtain a long-sought Congressional investigation of the whole UFO question. Hynek's report said that Zamora was "basically sincere, honest and reliable. He would not be capable of contriving a complex hoax. . . ." Hynek apparently failed to consider the possibility that *a hoax might have been contrived by others* and that Zamora might only have been an "accomplice."

Hynek's report indicates that in the spring of 1964 he did not even consider the possibility that the case might involve an extraterrestrial spaceship. Instead, he concluded that the object that Zamora had reported must have been a supersecret new military craft. Hynek therefore urged the USAF to locate the unusual egg-shaped craft and bring it back to Socorro so "movies [can] be taken of it departing in the manner described by Zamora. . . . This could then be played at any future [Congressional] hearings on flying saucers." The USAF followed Hynek's advice and even canvassed all of the nation's aerospace companies to see if any of them had secretly developed such a strange craft on their own, without telling the Defense Department. But no such craft was found, nor has one turned up since that time to match Zamora's account.

In recent years, since the USAF terminated its contract with Hynek to serve as a UFO consultant, he has repeatedly criticized the Air Force for its failure to conduct a thorough investigation of important cases. Yet despite Hynek's own recognition of the critical import of the Socorro case, he spent less than one day on the scene during his first visit. And it was not until nearly four months later that Hynek found time to return to Socorro for an equally brief visit.

During Hynek's second visit, he talked with one local resident who suggested that the case might be a hoax. The man was Mr. Felix Phillips, whose house is located only one thousand feet south of the spot where the UFO allegedly landed. Phillips said that he and his wife had been home at the time of the reported incident, and that several windows and doors had been open—yet neither of them had heard the loud roar that Zamora reported during UFO landing and later during takeoff. This was especially curious because Zamora's speeding car was four thousand feet away from the site and *the Phillips home was only one-quarter this distance.*

Hynek briefly mentioned the man's suspicions in his second trip report to the USAF, but he strongly rejected all possibility of a hoax.

Immediately following Hynek's first visit to Socorro, he was interviewed by the Associated Press to obtain his appraisal. Hynek was quoted as saying that the Socorro case was "one of the soundest, best substantiated reports as far as it goes. Usually one finds many contradictions or omissions in these reports. But Mr. Zamora's story is simply told, certainly without any intent to perpetuate a hoax." In the early 1960s, Hynek had the reputation of being a "debunker" of most UFO reports, so his acceptance of Zamora's account as being literally true and the inability of the USAF to locate a supersecret craft that matched Zamora's account quickly elevated the Socorra case to the status of a "classic." For UFO "believers," it seemed to be *the* long-awaited case that would prove beyond all doubt the existence of extraterrestrial spaceships. When UFOlogist Jacques Vallee surveyed numerous UFO groups and asked them to list the most impressive UFO case on record, their overwhelming first choice was Socorro.

At the time the Socorro incident had occurred, I had not been active in the field of UFOlogy, but soon after I entered it in mid-1966, it became apparent that I ought to visit Socorro for a firsthand investigation. This I did on December 16, 1966, spending two full days there interviewing all of the principals plus a number of other Socorro residents. My investigation led me to disagree sharply with Hynek's statement that the Socorro case was "one of the soundest, best substantiated reports." Contrary to Hynek's observation, I found "many contradictions or omissions."

For example, Zamora had reported seeing intense flame when he first heard the roar from atop the mesa, and again he reported a blast of intense flame when the UFO took off. *Yet there was no evidence of intense or widespread heat, or blast effects*, at the "landing site." Pictures taken by Sergeant Chavez on the following morning show only traces of burning on a mesquite bush and a clump of grass, while other bushes and grass at the site show absolutely no sign of intense heat!

The Chavez pictures also show small twigs that should have been burned to a crisp or blown away by the intense blast of flame reported by Zamora, still lying in the middle of the site unscathed. Both Byrnes and Phillips, who had also visited the site shortly after the incident, emphasized this discrepancy in our discussions. (See Plates 6a, 6b.)

Another curious discrepancy was that the "pad-print" indentations were significantly different from one another. The northeast indentation was shallow and irregular in shape and could be duplicated simply by removing one of the large rocks that abound in the sandy arroyo. The southwest indentation, however, was a moderately deep V-shaped trench that looked as if it had been formed using a small shovel. (At the time of my visit, I had not yet obtained copies of the original Chavez photos. When I asked Chavez to describe the appearance of the indentations, he went to his car and took out a small shovel and used it to make a V-shaped indentation which, I later found, closely matched the appearance of the southwest indentation and the more shallow northwest indentation.) The southeast indentation was a broader, irregular-shaped trench. If the indentations had been made by the landing pads of a craft, it was a curiously unsymmetrical set of landing gear because of the widely different distances between adjacent pairs of indentations. These range from 115.5 inches to 177.5 inches, based on measurements made shortly after the incident.

Another curious thing was that from the clearing where Zamora said he viewed the object, and from the position of the indentations, if they had been made by landing pads, Zamora would have been able to see at least three if not four legs. Yet his sketches showed only two legs. If a large egg-shaped craft had departed the arroyo shortly before 6 P.M., in broad daylight, and flown over Highway #60 to the west as Zamora reported, it seemed curious that it had not been seen by any motorists on that major highway.

There was a secondhand report of an unnamed motorist who had allegedly seen the UFO approaching from the east *before* it landed atop the mesa, which Hynek learned of during his first visit. The report came from the operator of a filling station on the northern outskirts of the town, who said a motorist had stopped shortly before 6 P.M. and had commented about the strange craft that had flown low over Highway #85 as he drove north. The filling station operator told Hynek that the motorist said the UFO was headed west *toward* the mesa and that the motorist also reported seeing a police car driving up the mesa. Presumably this was Zamora's. In his recent book, Hynek sharply criticized the USAF for its failure to launch an all-out search to find this "missing witness."

In reality, the alleged report by this "missing witness" must be false because the sequence of events really contradicts rather than supports Zamora's account. (The reader is referred to Plate 7, which shows a map of Socorro.) Recall that while Zamora said he was still chasing the speeding motorist, he reported seeing flame which indicated that the UFO was then in the process of landing atop the mesa— some two thousand feet west of Highway #85. Not until some time later—I would estimate nearly a minute, from having personally retraced Zamora's path—could the police car have been seen driving up the mesa. So the "missing witness" could not possibly have seen a UFO fly over the highway and at the same time have seen Zamora driving up the mesa. Zamora could not have started up the mesa until some time later when he reportedly saw evidence of the "landing" far to the west. It therefore seems lucky that the USAF decided to ignore Hynek's suggestion that it launch an all-out search for the "missing witness," because it would have had no more success than it had in following Hynek's advice to search for a secret United States craft shaped like an egg.

During my two days in Socorro, I talked with many residents in addition to Zamora and Chavez, including several scientist-professors at the New Mexico Institute of Mining and Technology, the town's principal "industry." I was amazed to find that with one exception, these scientists exhibited no interest in the Socorro UFO case, despite the fact that it had achieved international fame and had brought thousands of curious tourists to the town. If the story was true, the most exciting scientific event of all time—a visit

from an extraterrestrial spaceship—had occurred almost
within sight of the institute. How could these scientists be so
uninterested?

When I pressed one man for an explanation, he urged me
to "nose around a bit." When I sought clarification, he
pointed out that except for the Institute of Mining and
Technology, Socorro had no industry, and some citizens
feared that the town was "going to seed." He noted that
Socorro had a colorful history, having been one of the first
Spanish settlements in what is now New Mexico. Although
many tourists passed through town on the two highways (#60
and #85), few bothered to stop unless they needed gas or
food. That night I came across a brief but interesting item in
the Socorro newspaper, *El Defensor Chieftain*, the sort of
item that is timeless and runs repeatedly. It read:

> One of the best ways a community can boost its
> economy is to attract new industry. *Today, the fastest,
> most effective way to attract new industry is by first
> attracting tourists.* The reason is that industrialists, in
> selecting plant locations, are seeking for their employees
> the same kind of "community atmosphere" that appeals
> to tourists. (Emphasis added.)

An article that appeared in the *El Paso Times* on April 24,
1965, on the first anniversary of the Socorro UFO report,
revealed that officials of the town were quick to recognize the
tourist potential of the UFO incident. The article, by Jake
Booher, Jr., who had visited Socorro prior to writing the story,
was headlined: "Socorro To Use Flying Object As Tourist
Catch." Booher wrote that Zamora said he prefers to forget
the whole incident, "but regardless of how much Zamora says
he wants to forget, many of Socorro's 7,000 residents have
other ideas." The article quoted City Clerk Ray Senn as
saying, "We frankly intend to use it as a tourist attraction."
The article noted that "the road to the site, almost impassa-
ble last year, has been graded. Posters are being planned by
the Chamber of Commerce for placement within Socorro's
businesses to alert tourists to the town's claim to fame."

The article reported that "a portion of a movie on UFOs was filmed earlier this year at Socorro. Much of the town's hope for additional tourist dollars is based on this film, which Empire Films Studio of Hollywood had planned to premier at Socorro soon. Mayor Holm Bursum, Jr., said he had to go to Zamora and persuade him to re-enact the experience for Empire's cameras. . . . Senn said he had spent $200 out of his own pocket in assisting the film crews."

If a spaceship from distant worlds just happened to land outside a town that was sorely in need of a tourist attraction to stop passing motorists, the officials of that town should not be blamed for promptly acting to exploit their good fortune. But my own investigation turned up several other curious "fortuitous" coincidences. The place where the UFO reportedly landed was especially convenient—almost midway between the two highways that bring tourists through Socorro— so it was relatively easy and inexpensive for city officials to provide an improved road that connected the site to the two highways. If the UFO had chanced to land only a few miles to the east or west, behind nearby mountain ranges, the site would have been all but inaccessible to tourists passing through Socorro.

The property where the UFO reportedly landed had, prior to the incident, been next to worthless "scrub land." But now, if the site became a long-lived tourist attraction, there could be need for refreshment stands, perhaps even a motel for those who might like to spend the night near the spot where an extraterrestrial spaceship had seemingly landed. By a curious coincidence, the property where the UFO reportedly landed was owned by Mayor Bursum, officer Zamora's boss! The mayor's principal business? He is the town banker and as such would not be unhappy to see an influx of tourist dollars.

On March 16, 1972, *The New York Times* reported that the United States government had decided to build the world's largest scientific instrument, a mammoth radio telescope, in the vicinity of Socorro. The reporter who wrote the article had talked with Mayor Bursum to get his reaction to the remarkable scientific facility to be constructed near

Socorro. Bursum's comment: "[It] will definitely help our economy and give the area some publicity." In view of Socorro's economically depressed condition, one cannot blame its mayor for seeking publicity for his community.

13 • Another "Landing" at South Hill

On April 21, 1967, the small town of South Hill in southern Virginia, like Socorro nearly three years earlier, achieved instant fame when one of its respected residents reported that a UFO had landed on the outskirts of town, then taken off, leaving behind physical evidence of its visit. The following account of the incident was first carried by the *Richmond News Leader* and subsequently distributed by the Associated Press, appearing in numerous newspapers throughout the United States.

SOUTH HILL (AP)—A blackened circle of road tar remained as mute testimony Saturday to a report by a South Hill warehouse manager of an unidentified flying object that shot straight up with "a tremendous burst of white-looking fire." C. N. Crowder, manager of the Mobil Chemical Co. warehouse in this Mecklenburg County community, said he encountered the strange-looking object as he was driving home from the warehouse Friday about 9 P.M.

"You can imagine how it felt to see a big thing like that sitting in the road in front of you, and all of a sudden a ball of fire flies out and it disappears," Crowder exclaimed. He said it looked like an aluminum-colored storage tank about 12 feet in diameter sitting on legs three to three and a half feet high.

When he switched on his lights to high beam, Crowder said, "a tremendous burst of white-looking fire came from the bottom of the object and it went right straight up in the air like a bullet. I got a perfect look at it," he said. A section of the road where the object had been sitting caught fire, Crowder said, and he waited until the blaze died down before going to the police station to report the incident. When police returned with Crowder to the scene, they found a burned spot in the black macadam several feet in diameter.

Crowder said he was puzzled by what he saw but assumed it "may be some object the government is experimenting with and that the general public knows nothing about."

Within twenty-four hours of the reported incident, three investigators from NICAP's Washington Headquarters, including Assistant Director Gordon Lore, had driven to South Hill. There they learned that additional evidence had been found the morning after the incident—four tiny holes, each approximately one-half inch in diameter, surrounding the burned area on the road. These, obviously, were "pad-prints" made by the legs of the giant tank-shaped UFO that Crowder had reported.

Following the widespread publicity given to the Crowder incident, NICAP investigators learned of additional reported UFO sighting from local residents, some of which turned out to have been flares fired from a nearby Army base, Fort Pickett. More impressive was a report from Norman Martin, a farmer who lived near the road where Crowder had reported seeing the UFO. Martin said he and Mrs. Martin had just returned from visiting his ailing mother in the local hospital, and while standing outside his house in the dark, he saw a large tree briefly illuminated near the UFO burned spot.

1a

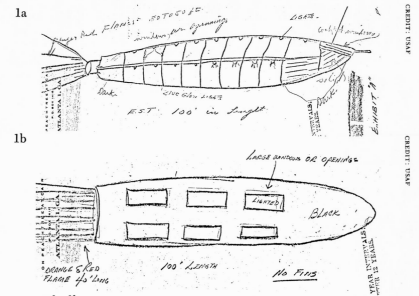

1b

PLATES 1a, 1b:
Sketches by airline pilot C. S. Chiles and co-pilot John B. Whitted, made shortly after their encounter with a giant UFO on the night of July 24, 1948, show object with many illuminated windows and an orange-red jetlike exhaust. The two experienced flight officers estimated object was 100 feet long. USAF classified the case as "Unidentified."

1c

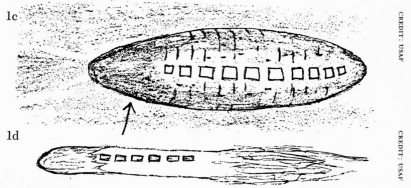

1d

PLATES 1c, 1d:
Sketches submitted nearly twenty years later by observers in Tennessee (Plate 1c) and Indiana (Plate 1d) of UFO sighted on March 3, 1968, are remarkably similar to the Chiles-Whitted UFO sketches. Note especially the numerous illuminated windows. The 1968 UFO incident resulted from flaming pieces of debris from a Russian rocket that reentered the atmosphere, becoming in effect a "man-made meteor." The Chiles-Whitted UFO incident occurred during the annual Aquarids meteor shower and without doubt involved a giant meteor (fireball). The nonexistent fuselage details in both cases were unwittingly supplied by the observers' brains. (See Chapter 1.)

2a

2b

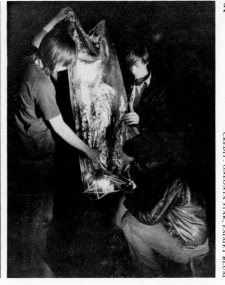

PLATES 2a, 2b:

Hundreds of reports of glowing, multicolored UFOs that perform mysterious maneuvers are the result of hot-air balloons fabricated from plastic garment bags, usually built by ingenious teen-agers. Plate 2a shows the ghostlike appearance of this type of UFO which mystified residents near Oneonta, New York, until several teen-age boys admitted the prank and demonstrated the construction technique for an Oneonta *Star* newspaper photographer. More often, the pranksters do not own up to their handiwork —because such balloons are an illegal fire-hazard—leaving the UFO sighting unexplained. (See Chapter 3.)

PLATE 3a:

Giant scientific balloons, made from thin plastic material, are another source of many UFO reports. The balloons can rise to altitudes of more than thirty miles, making them visible for great distances, especially shortly after sunset when they catch and reflect the rays of the departing sun. The USAF and Navy normally launch a total of nearly two hundred of these giant balloons each year, some with a volume of more than 45 million cubic feet. Depending on winds at very high altitude, the balloons can hover, move in circles, then suddenly depart at very high speed. Note two "saucer-shaped" reflections from this USAF balloon. (See Chapter 4.)

PLATE 3b:

Large, bright meteors such as this one—and a flaming fragment following behind—often generate UFO reports, especially when the fireball is on a near-horizontal trajectory. This "Iowa Fireball" was photographed by Alan Harkrader on June 5, 1969, near Peoria shortly before 6 P.M. on a clear day. Fireballs often seem much lower and closer than they really are because observers have no means of estimating their size, or distance, and this can lead to very gross errors, as shown in Plate 4.

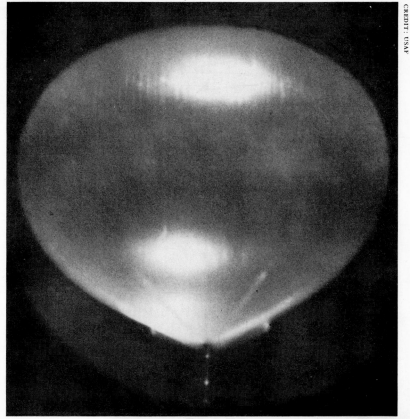

3a

3b

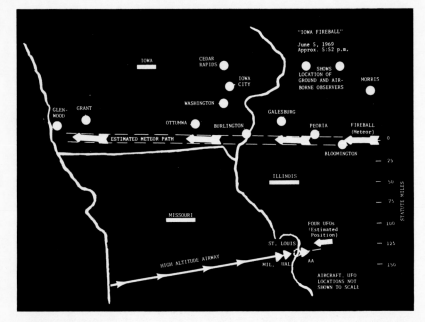

PLATE 4:

The Iowa Fireball of June 5, 1969, and its fragments were sighted by three experienced airplane crews flying near St. Louis. At least one crew, aboard an airliner, concluded the objects were a squadron of UFOs that was about to collide with their airliner. A private pilot at the Cedar Rapids, Iowa, airport saw the flaming objects and he reported that the objects passed directly over the local airport runway. The St. Louis flight crews erred by *125 miles* in estimating the distance to the fireball, while the pilot in Cedar Rapids made nearly as great an error. A reasonably accurate estimate of the fireball trajectory was determined from numerous reports by ground observers in Illinois and Iowa, shown by white dots, plus the Harkrader photo. (See Chapter 5.)

7

PLATE 5:

Even the Moon, when viewed at night through clouds, can play tricks on the imaginations of an experienced flight crew. A Navy crew, approaching Gander after a long night flight, thought they saw a glowing UFO on the ocean surface that was pacing them. Later the UFO, seemingly tipped on its edge, appeared to come zooming toward the Navy airplane, then to back away and disappear over the horizon. From airplane's known position, the time, and the reported bearing angle to the UFO, it can be identified as the upper tip of the partially illuminated Moon, which was visible just below the horizon. The zooming effect may have been caused by ice crystals in the clouds. (See Chapter 6.) This case was classified by USAF as "Unidentified" prior to the author's investigation.

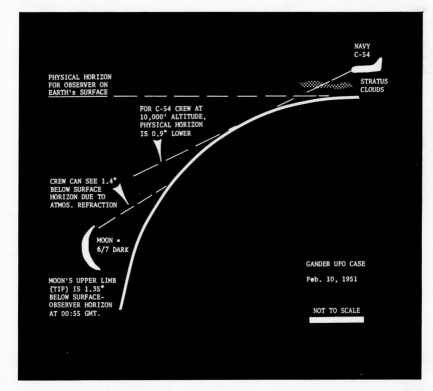

PHYSICAL HORIZON
FOR OBSERVER ON
EARTH's SURFACE

FOR C-54 CREW AT
10,000' ALTITUDE,
PHYSICAL HORIZON
IS 0.9° LOWER

CREW CAN SEE 1.4°
BELOW SURFACE
HORIZON DUE TO
ATMOS. REFRACTION

MOON =
6/7 DARK

MOON'S UPPER LIMB
(TIP) IS 1.35°
BELOW SURFACE-
OBSERVER HORIZON
AT 00:55 GMT.

NAVY
C-54

STRATUS
CLOUDS

GANDER UFO CASE

Feb. 10, 1951

NOT TO SCALE

6

8a

BURNED
SPOT

ROAD TO
VACANT
FARM

8b

PLATE 8a:

The UFO "landing" that allegedly occurred on the outskirts of South Hill, Virginia, on April 21, 1967, like the Socorro incident just three years earlier, left behind evidence which seemed to some investigators to substantiate the report. The irregularly shaped burned spot on the macadam road (arrow) was presumed to have been made by a giant UFO that reportedly landed and took off from the road. Several months after the incident achieved national fame, some unknown local resident painted his own appraisal of the case near the burned spot—"HOAX." The "PV '67" refers to Park View High School, where the daughter of C. N. Crowder, who reported the incident, was then a student. Earlier, Dr. J. Allen Hynek was quoted as saying: "[I] can't think of it being a hoax." Car shown is parked near where Crowder said he stopped his auto.

PLATE 8b:

One of many curious aspects of the South Hill case was Crowder's description of the UFO's appearance. Rather than being the traditional saucer shape, the UFO, Crowder said, was a large cylindrical tank-shaped object which looked very much like this storage tank that stands just outside the warehouse that Crowder operates.

9

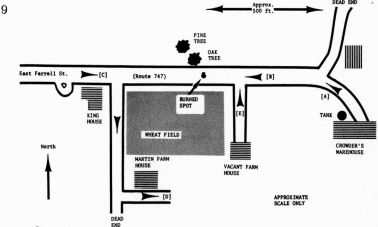

PLATE 9:

According to Crowder's account of the UFO incident, he had left his warehouse a few minutes before 9 P.M. to drive home. As he turned west on East Farrell Street (A), he said, his headlights illuminated a giant tank-shaped object in the middle of the road, several hundred feet ahead. As he neared the object, he said, it took off with a blast of flame that left the macadam road aflame, and he stopped his car (B) until the fire burned out before driving into South Hill to report the incident to the police. While Crowder waited for the fire to go out, with his car headlights on high beam, he said, he saw another car driving east on the same road (C). The car turned south on the road leading to the house of Norman Martin (D). The author's investigation showed that this car was driven by Norman Martin, who, with his wife, was returning from a visit to the local hospital.

Although Crowder reported seeing lights from the Martins' car on the dark, little-traveled road, neither Martin nor his wife saw the lights fom Crowder's car, nor the flames on the macadam road, even though they would have been only several hundred feet away. These and other curious anomalies become explainable if Crowder had actually parked his car on the road leading to a then-unoccupied farm house (E), and had turned off the car lights so he could pour gasoline (or other flammable liquid) on the road and light it to produce the burned spot. With his car parked off the main road, Crowder could avoid being seen and the risk of his car being struck by another motorist. (See Chapter 13.)

10a

PLATE 10a:

Hundreds of UFO photos of this type have been published through the years and seem to show a craftlike object either hovering or flying through the sky. This one, taken by three brothers ranging in age from ten to twelve, consists of a small model, carved out of Styrofoam, which was then suspended from a very thin wire from one of the tree branches and photographed. The boys did not try to pass the photo off as authentic but simply wanted to show how easy it is to produce UFO pictures.

10b

PLATE 10b:

Robert Sheaffer, an experienced camera buff and UFO skeptic, has produced many hoax photos using a variety of techniques to demonstrate how easy it is to make impressive-looking UFO photos. This example shows what seems to be two glowing saucer-shaped UFOs flying over suburban houses at night. It is simply a triple exposure in which the glowing UFOs were produced by shining a light through the center hole of a 45 rpm phonograph record which was tilted to make the illumination passing through elliptical in shape.

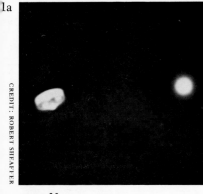

CREDIT: ROBERT SHEAFFER

CREDIT: ROBERT SHEAFFER

PLATE 11a:
This glowing UFO, with three landing pads visible, was fabricated from two aluminum plates by Sheaffer so it could be sailed through the air and then photographed, alongside the Moon, using a strobe-type flash lamp to illuminate the UFO-model.

PLATE 11b:
This UFO, whose upper compartment provides portholes so its crew can look out, was made from an aluminum pie-tin to which Sheaffer attached an empty cottage-cheese container. Black circles were added to create the porthole effect.

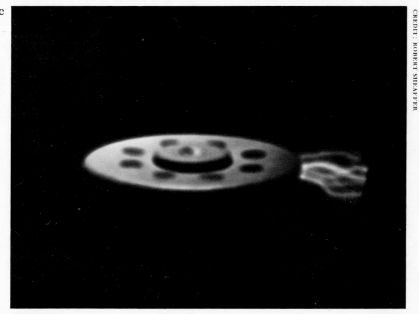

CREDIT: ROBERT SHEAFFER

PLATE 11c:
This UFO seemingly employs some sort of electrical propulsion system, judging from the electrical sparks shooting out the aft end. Sheaffer fabricated it from miscellaneous parts and rigged up a high-voltage transformer to generate the electrical sparks. The model is suspended by a thin thread not visible in the dark background.

PLATES 12a, 12b:
These two UFO photos, made near McMinnville, Oregon, have been widely acclaimed as being authentic and were endorsed by the University of Colorado's photo analyst. The pictures were allegedly taken during the evening of May 11, 1950, shortly *after sunset*. But there are strong shadows on the east wall of the garage (arrows) which prove the picture must have been taken in the early morning, not after sunset as claimed. Furthermore, the pictures show a hazy sky, and official Weather Bureau records for May 11, 1950, show that the sky near McMinnville was clear during the evening hours but was smoky during the early morning. These and other inconsistencies in the account given by Mr. and Mrs. Paul Trent, who took the photos, indicate the pictures are a hoax. (See Chapter 15.)

NICAP investigators concluded that Martin had seen the illumination produced when the UFO had taken off.

Dr. J. Allen Hynek was asked by the USAF to visit South Hill to investigate the case, but he had other commitments. Instead, Hynek sent a trusted associate from Northwestern University, William T. Powers, who is also an experienced UFOlogist. The official report that Powers later sent to the USAF said he was met on his arrival at South Hill by Sergeant S. H. Raines, head of the Virginia State Police office there, who provided "valuable assistance and advice during the entire investigation." When Powers was interviewed by *The South Hill Enterprise*, the town's weekly newspaper, he said that Sergeant Raines had "speeded up the investigation tremendously." Raines told Powers that he had known Crowder for seven years and had a high opinion of him. (Later I would learn that Raines and Crowder were good friends and members of the same church.)

In his report Powers said that during his investigation "many people, including all the police, indicated that Crowder has excellent standing in the community, is a responsible citizen, and would by no means be involved in a hoax or a falsehood." Powers said that a typical comment was, "If anyone but C. N. Crowder had made the report, I wouldn't have believed him, but if C. N. Crowder says it happened, it happened." When I visited South Hill in mid-December of 1967, I heard the same favorable comments on Crowder—almost verbatim. Crowder, then a man in his mid-fifties, has a slightly rural Lincolnesque quality. He is the sort of man who could walk up to you on the street as a complete stranger, and if he asked to borrow twenty dollars, you would not hesitate to give it to him. And I am certain he would promptly repay the loan. Without doubt, he is basically an honest man.

During his visit Powers learned of *some curious artifacts that had been found in the middle of the irregularly shaped burned area on the road but which had not been reported in the original newspaper story.* Police and deputy sheriffs whom Crowder brought back to the site, and a state trooper from Raines' office who joined them, had found *four completely charred paper matches in the burned area. All*

*the matches were completely burned from one end to the
other, and three of them were sitting side by side,* so close
together that "they could have been covered with a half
dollar," according to officer B. O. Murphy, who discovered
them. These three charred matches were sitting approximately six inches inside the northeast edge of the burned
area, and the fourth match was near the center.

In his report to the USAF, Powers wrote: "At this writing,
in the absence of any additional clues or the results of
chemical analysis, the only conclusion that can be drawn is
that the witness probably did see something out of the
ordinary, but that we cannot rule out the possibility that a
hoax was perpetrated by some person or persons *other than
the principal witness.*" (Emphasis added.) Based on the
Powers investigation and report, the USAF officially classified
the South Hill case as "Unidentified" a few weeks later.

The April 27 edition of *The South Hill Enterprise,* the first
published following the incident, quoted Powers as saying
that he could not rule out the possibility of a hoax by some
other party. But he added that "Crowder is telling exactly
what he saw and there is no reason to disbelieve him. . . ." *
This suggests that Powers was convinced that a giant, metallic
tank-shaped object, approximately twelve feet in diameter
and sixteen to eighteen feet tall, sitting on four large legs, had
indeed landed and taken off from the macadam road. If such
an object had been built, and launched, by pranksters, this
was itself a feat of remarkable proportions.

When I studied the Powers report before my own visit to
South Hill, and pondered the implications of the charred
matches, I reached a very different conclusion. It seemed to
me that no giant object, either terrestrial or extraterrestrial,
could have taken off with a blast of fire so intense as to set fire
to the road, without having blasted the matches far away.
Anyone who has been waiting at an airport to board an

* Later, after Powers had returned to Northwestern and reported on his
investigation of the South Hill case to Dr. Hynek, the latter was interviewed
by the *Richmond Times-Dispatch.* The May 10, 1967, edition of the
newspaper quoted Hynek as saying he "can't think of it being a hoax."

airplane when a nearby jet aircraft has turned to taxi away knows that the blast forces from even idling jet engines are sufficient to blow off a person's hat from a distance of several hundred feet. If the three paper matches had just happened to be sitting side by side on the road at the spot where a giant craft decided to land, they would probably have been blown away during the landing process, or certainly by the blast of flame during takeoff.

But I decided to conduct a simple test-demonstration on a deserted macadam road near Washington. I ignited three paper matches, held them as long as I could without burning my fingers so they were three-quarters burned, and then I placed them side by side on the road several hundred feet ahead of my waiting car. After taking a photo of the matches, I got into my car and drove "over" them so the wheels of the car did not touch the matches and they were exposed only to the forces of car-induced wind. I could not hope to duplicate the bulletlike takeoff speeds that Crowder had reported and limited myself to a velocity of twelve to eighteen miles per hour in the several trial runs. In each instance, when I stopped the car and returned to photograph and examine the matches, I found they had been dispersed over a very wide area, and the previously side-by-side matches were separated by many inches.

If the incident was a hoax, Crowder might have been the victim of pranksters who could have used a large weather balloon with something resembling "legs" attached that could have been released as his car approached. Then the pranksters could have set fire to a pool of flammable liquid previously poured on the road. I knew that observers of sudden, unexpected events could be grossly in error in trying to reconstruct what they have seen. (UFOlogical Principle #1.) The only alternative to this hypothesis was that the hoax had been perpetrated by Crowder himself.

Before visiting South Hill, I had written to Crowder and he agreed to meet with me. A friend and I drove down on December 16, 1967, arriving shortly after noon. We called Crowder, he drove to meet us and we then followed his car to the site on Route 747, locally known as East Farrell Street, which runs east from U.S. Highway #1. Approximately three-quarters of a mile east of Highway #1, Crowder stopped at the burned area, which was still visible eight months after the incident. We stopped to briefly inspect the irregular egg-shaped darkened area, which measured approximately thirty-nine inches by twenty-six inches. It was immediately obvious that something new had been added, although Crowder did not mention it nor did I at the time. Adjacent to the burned area, painted in giant bold white letters, was the cryptic message: "PV '67 HOAX?" Later I learned that "PV" referred to Park View High School, where Crowder's teen-age daughter was a student. (See Plate 8a.) It was clear that someone else shared my suspicions of a hoax; later I would learn of others among the South Hill residents.

The "pad-print" holes were no longer there. NICAP investigators had obtained approval to dig them out of the macadam for chemical analysis. After a brief discussion, we proceeded to follow Crowder to his warehouse. Route 747 continues east for approximately several hundred feet before it jogs northeast and soon dead-ends. At the jog in 747, Crowder turned right (south) onto a dirt road, and in a few seconds we were at the warehouse. My attention was instantly attracted to a large metal storage tank standing alongside the warehouse, because it so closely resembled Crowder's original description of the UFO. (When I first read of the South Hill case, I was curious about the unusual tank-shaped configuration because most UFOs are said to be saucer- or cigar-shaped. But this discrepancy had not seemed to bother NICAP or Powers.)

Crowder recounted the original incident as we sat in his warehouse office. He said he had been working late on his financial books, and around 8 P.M. he had decided to drive into town to get a soft drink, stopping to buy it *at a gas station*. Then, he said, he returned to the warehouse and continued working until a few minutes before 9 P.M., when he decided to call it a night. As he drove out of the dirt road from the warehouse and turned onto Route 747, his auto headlights, aimed west, showed some object sitting in the middle of the road—approximately five hundred feet away.

He said he continued along the road, and when he had approached to within approximately 250 feet, he switched his headlights to high beam. For about five seconds Crowder had a good view of the object, he said, until suddenly it emitted the brilliant ball of fire from its underside and took off like a bullet, disappearing in the night. (Refer to the map, Plate 9.)

There was a curious change in Crowder's description of the object since he had first reported it to the police and drawn a sketch on an official USAF report form. Instead of the original metallic, cylindrical tank-shaped object with four legs approximately six inches in diameter, he now said the object was more like a bag or a balloon. After the UFO took off, Crowder said, he stopped near a dirt access road to an unoccupied farm house to let the high flames die down and because he said he feared the blast might have left a gaping hole in the road. *As he waited, Crowder said, he saw the lights of another car coming toward him.* But the other car then turned south onto a dirt access road approximately six hundred feet west of the burning area. This road led to the farm of Norman Martin.

When the flames had finally died down, Crowder said he drove into South Hill to report the incident to the local police, who in turn alerted the county sheriff's office and the local office of the Virginia State Police. Within a few minutes, Crowder and five law enforcement officers were at the site, where the burned area was still warm to the touch. Soon they were joined by Harry Nanny, publisher of the local newspaper, and by Robert Harris, a part-time reporter-photographer for *The Richmond News Leader*. Both had been alerted by the police. Harris took several photographs of Crowder examining the burned spot on the road, after which Crowder decided to go home to tell his wife and daughter of the exciting event. It was while Crowder was absent that the four charred matches were found by police officer B. O. Murphy. They were discovered as the officers painstakingly searched the area with powerful flashlights, looking for clues to the mysterious UFO. When Crowder returned to the site with his wife and daughter, he learned of the newly discovered artifacts.

Early the next morning, Crowder drove to the farm of Norman Martin, onto whose access road Crowder had reported seeing a car turn as he waited for the flaming spot on the road to die out. Crowder learned that Martin and his wife had indeed returned to their farm shortly before 9 P.M., after having visited Martin's mother in the local hospital. Then Crowder asked whether Martin and his wife had noticed anything unusual at the time, but neither recalled anything of note. When Crowder proceeded to describe the UFO incident of the previous night, Martin then said he recalled that he had lingered outside on arriving home, and while looking north toward Route 747 (approximately six hundred feet away), he had seen a large tree near the road become brightly illuminated for a brief time. But it had not been sufficiently unusual to prompt him to go and investigate, and he had soon retired to the house. Some investigators quickly concluded that this reported observation by Martin confirmed Crowder's account and that the illumination of the tree must have been caused by the UFO during takeoff.

But in fact, by the time the Martin car had turned onto the access road, the UFO had already departed, according to Crowder's account, and it would not be until several minutes later that Martin saw the large tree being briefly illuminated. From where Martin was standing, he could not see the road itself because of the intervening field of growing wheat and the topography, I learned when I interviewed the Martins. *But the curious thing is why neither Mr. Martin nor his wife reported seeing the burning spot on Route 747, or the high-beam headlights of Crowder's car, which should have been directed toward them. If Crowder readily saw the lights of the Martin car, it is curious that neither Mr. nor Mrs. Martin recalled seeing the lights of Crowder's car.*

During my first interview with Crowder, he told me that after his short discussion with Martin on the morning following the incident, he then drove to his warehouse. *In doing so, Crowder drove directly past the burned spot on the road where the exciting event of the previous night had reportedly occurred. One might have expected Crowder to be curious and anxious to examine the scene for the first time in daylight. Yet, strangely, Crowder said he did not bother to stop, even for a moment.* Instead, he proceeded directly to the warehouse.

Local radio station WJWS first heard of the exciting UFO report before it had gone off the air at 1 A.M. the preceding night, but it had withheld any announcement pending confirmation. But on the first newscast the following day, at 6 A.M., the station carried the details of the UFO incident. Stories of UFO sightings were not unusual for the station because it broadcast daily a syndicated (taped) radio program by veteran UFOlogist Frank Edwards which was devoted in part to strange UFO tales.

Sergeant Raines of the Virginia State Police did not learn of the UFO incident until Saturday morning, when he stopped for gas and heard the news from the attendant, the officer told me during our subsequent interview. Raines had more than a professional interest because of his friendship with Crowder. (Both are also active in the South Hills Methodist Church.) So Raines drove to the site of the burned area for a brief inspection and then proceeded on to the warehouse to discuss the incident with Crowder. It was while Raines and Crowder were discussing the incident that Raines received word that important new evidence had been found at the site—the four tiny holes punched in the macadam. (The holes formed the corners of an irregular rectangle with the distance between adjacent holes varying from 137 inches to 145 inches.) Raines quickly decided to drive back to the site, only a few hundred yards away, and invited Crowder to join him. But, curiously, as Crowder explained to me, he decided instead to stay on the job. It would not be until several hours later when Crowder returned home for lunch that he would stop to briefly inspect the new finding. (Shortly after lunch, Crowder left town to visit his sister in Lynchburg, Virginia.)

While Crowder showed scant interest in inspecting the original burned area or the new "pad-prints," hundreds of local residents who had learned of the incident from the local radio newscasts showed a great deal more curiosity and flocked to the site. (During subsequent weeks thousands of visitors would come to the site on the usually deserted road, forcing the police to direct the heavy traffic.) *But on the morning of April 22, barely twelve hours after the exciting incident, Crowder was not sufficiently interested to take off ten minutes and drive a few hundred yards to the site.*

If the discovery of the four tiny holes seemed to some to confirm Crowder's story, it raised further doubts in other quarters. For example, State Trooper James A. Crawford, one of the officers who had searched the area the previous night, *could not believe that the holes had been there the night before.* Crawford told me that he and officer Murphy had searched the whole area, side by side, bending over close to the road and using powerful flashlights. They had, as a result, discovered the small charred paper matches against the black burned spot on the dark macadam road. And if they had discovered even one of the four holes the previous night, they undoubtedly would have found all of them. Crawford was so skeptical that he told me he had returned to the site the following night to see if he could spot the holes during darkness. He added, "I could see them without being shown where they were." Sergeant Raines, Crawford's superior, told me, "Crawford will argue for half a day with you that they [the holes] weren't there, and he is a right thorough fellow, and ordinarily I'd say when he said they weren't there, they weren't there . . . But I won't buy anyone going back there afterwards. Well, maybe they did, but I just don't believe it."

But Crawford's suspicions are supported by physical evidence, or, to be more precise, the lack of certain physical evidence. During my first interview with Crowder, he chanced to mention that "it poured down rain that night, after this happened . . . it came a good hard rain." When I later dug out the official records of the Weather Bureau for April 21–22, I found that there had indeed been a moderate rainfall during the predawn hours of April 22. All of the "pad-print" holes were so shallow that none penetrated the macadam to the ground below. *Thus, if the four holes had been at the site prior to midnight, there should have been rain water at the bottom of the holes. Yet no liquid of any kind had been found in any of the holes, so far as I could learn.*

It is easy to understand why a hoaxer would be tempted to return and create "pad-print" holes in the predawn hours, because when the charred matches were found, *they immediately suggested a hoax to many of those present at the site.* What was Crawford's reaction when the matches were discovered? "I wasn't interested any more," he told me. I asked whether anyone else had become suspicious of a hoax, and Crawford replied, "I think everyone was." He added, "If something had taken off, it would have blown everything out [including] the matches." Crawford's suspicions explain why he did not bother to officially notify his superior, Sergeant Raines, of the incident either that night or early the next morning.

During my interview with Harris, who had already taken photos of Crowder near the burned spot when the matches were found, I asked him for his reactions to the discovery of the curious artifacts. Harris replied, "I said, 'I've wasted my film' . . . I just went and put my camera away." Then Harris discussed his suspicions with Harry Nanny, publisher of the local newspaper. "Between the two of us," Harris later told me, "we decided that, ah, Crowder had seen us take these pictures and expects to see something in the paper, you know, . . . and so we decided to go ahead. So, at 2 A.M., I sent these films in by bus to *The Richmond News Leader.*" *But the story, as published and later distributed by the Associated Press, made no mention of the charred matches, or of the resulting suspicions of a hoax!*

Harris explained to me that the Crowders are a prominent family clan in South Hill. Clifton Crowder's brother was then a member of the County Board of Supervisors and running for reelection. Another brother was in the Virginia State Highway Department. Still another member of the clan had a large insurance agency, which advertised in the South Hill newspaper, and a more distant member was a doctor. Personal considerations may have been another factor in Harris's decision to file his story despite misgivings of a hoax.

As he explained to me, shortly after he was married, Harris
and his wife had rented an apartment in Clifton Crowder's
house, and the two had become good friends. Harris explained to me that after his talk with Nanny, "we knew that
he [Crowder] had seen something; we didn't know what it
was." When I asked Harris if he thought Crowder was the
victim of a hoax, he replied, "Oh, I'm sure he didn't do it.
Whatever has been done, he didn't do it. He is a victim of
circumstances."

During my interview with Nanny, he indicated that when
the charred matches were found "everybody [at the site] sort
of thought it was a hoax or something. But Mr. Crowder is a
very reliable man, a respected man in the community, which
substantiated the story quite a bit." When Crowder returned
to the site with his wife and daughter, he was informed of the
discovery of the charred matches. It is not certain whether
any of those at the site privately or publicly told him of their
suspicions of a hoax, but Crowder must certainly have sensed
the changed atmosphere on his return.

During my numerous interviews with those involved in the
South Hill case, I discovered *only one person who did not
consider the charred matches significant. That person was
Clifton Crowder himself.* When he casually mentioned the
matches during our first interview, Crowder said, "To me that
didn't mean a thing on God's earth, you know, so far as
somebody starting a fire was concerned. As many people as
were around there smoking cigarettes and dropping matches,
don't you see." Then he switched to another subject. Was it
possible that the charred matches had simply been dropped
by persons who had rushed to the site, and three of them just
chanced to fall side by side? I posed this question to officer
Murphy, who had found the matches. He responded, "No,
no, no. They had to have been there. It would have been
impossible for someone to have lit a cigarette and the
matches to have burned like that. It couldn't have been
possible." Murphy explained to me that the matches were so
completely burned that they crumbled when he picked them
up. Thus, if they had been used to light a cigarette and had
then been dropped, they would have crumbled upon impact

with the road—*yet they were intact when found.* But later in our discussion, in what was intended as an expression of support for Crowder's word, Murphy volunteered, "I don't doubt that Mr. Crowder didn't see something."

These widespread suspicions among the handful of persons present at the site shortly after the incident explain why a hoaxer would recognize the need to create additional evidence during the few remaining hours of darkness to try to confirm that a giant craft with four legs had indeed landed on the road. *This would indicate that the perpetrator of the hoax either was among the persons present at the site that night, or else had been promptly informed of what had happened by someone who had been there.*

During my interview with Crowder at his warehouse, I had asked him to decipher the meaning of the "PV '67 HOAX?" that had been painted near the burned spot, and he had said he assumed it had been done by students from Park View High School. This prompted me to ask whether he thought that the whole incident might have been a prank by the students. He rejected this possibility, explaining that "it was too complicated for some high school kids to have built some balloon—that's what I always thought it was—it appeared to be the size of the upper half of that nitrogen tank [outside his warehouse] and it had those legs." (See Plate 8b.) (Crowder's own original sketches had shown a cylindrical tank-shaped object, not a balloon or bag-shaped object.)

Later, Crowder willingly agreed to let me test his visual acuity using the special slides I had brought. I had made these 35 mm color slides at night using two floodlights to simulate the illumination from the headlights of Crowder's car. The object selected for each slide was one with which Crowder was unlikely to be familiar—for example, one was an ancient Persian military helmet. I also included several slides of unusual technical devices from my existing files. My plan called for giving Crowder approximately five seconds to view each slide—the time he said he had to view the UFO at close quarters. Then I would turn off the slide and ask him to *describe* what he had seen—its shape and color—but *not* to try to identify what the object was. This would help

determine whether Crowder's visual acuity had begun to
deteriorate as the result of age. Within several minutes the
test was over, and Crowder had passed with flying colors. He
had described with remarkable accuracy the object on each
slide—including an unusual type of laser operating inside a
laboratory, a device which I'm sure he had never seen before.
I could only conclude that Crowder's visual acuity was much
too good for him to mistake a small weather balloon and a
prankster lighting a pool of flammable liquid for a giant
tank-shaped object with four legs standing in the road and
later emitting an intense blast of flame.

At the end of our second day in South Hill, we departed
for Washington. During the several-hour drive my friend and
I discussed every possible hypothesis we could conceive that
might explain this curious case. *But there was only one* that
could stand up and that enabled every mysterious piece of
the puzzle to fall neatly into place. We both wished we could
find another hypothesis, because in the few hours we had
spent with Crowder we had both become very fond of him,
and we could understand why he was so well-liked by the
citizens of his community. If Clifton Crowder were the
perpetrator of the hoax, it would have been very easy to
produce the original evidence—the burned spot. When
Crowder drove into town and stopped at a gas station around
8 P.M. to buy a soft drink, he could also have filled a container
with gasoline, or purchased a large can of lighter fluid. *The
book of paper matches was something that Crowder normally carried with him to light his cigarettes, as I frequently
observed during our two interviews.*

When he drove from his warehouse to the site to produce
the burned spot, there would be a minor problem—where to
park his car. If he left the car parked on Route 747 with its
headlights on, they would illuminate him as he went about
his work, and if another driver should come down the road
toward him—as did indeed occur with the Martin car—the
other motorist might see what was under way. But if Crowder
turned off his car lights completely, and if another car came
down the road from the east, it might collide from the rear
with Crowder's unilluminated car. There was a handy solu-

tion to this problem because there was a dirt access road running south to a farm house that was not occupied at the time. (This access road ran parallel to the one to Martin's farm, as shown in Plate 9.)

So Crowder could back his car onto this dirt access road and shut off all the lights without risk of being hit by another car, since no one would be driving out from the deserted farm house. Being concerned lest he be seen pouring the flammable liquid on the macadam road, Crowder would keep alert to any other car coming down Route 747. And so he would be sure to notice the Martin car coming toward him—possibly even moving off the road to avoid being seen. *If Crowder's car was in fact parked on the access road to the deserted farm with its lights off, this would explain why he had seen the Martin car but neither Mr. Martin nor his wife had seen the headlights of Crowder's car, or the fire on the road which he said was burning with high flames at the time.*

From the road, Crowder would have been able to see the Martins drive into their yard and shut off the car lights, and he would assume that they had retired to their house—not knowing that Mr. Martin was lingering in his backyard. At that point, Crowder would feel it was safe to return to his task. After the fire had been ignited, and had burned out, Crowder would return to his car on the access road, turn on its headlights, and drive out—turning left onto Route 747 toward South Hill. *As he turned onto Route 747, the headlights of his car would briefly illuminate the large tree that Martin would subsequently report had been lit up for a few moments.* As Martin told me during our interview, when the nearby farm house was occupied, "many times I've seen them [previous residents] come out, and the car would shine on the trees there." But since Martin knew the adjacent farm was now vacant and there should not be any resident driving out of the access road, he was naturally puzzled when the large tree was briefly illuminated.

Why did it require four matches to ignite the pool of flammable liquid? During Powers' visit to South Hill, he had poured a quart of gasoline onto the macadam and tried to set fire to it using a single match, which he dropped into the center of the pool of liquid. To his surprise, the match went out instantly—quenched by the flammable liquid for lack of oxygen. In his next attempt, which was successful, Powers placed the burning match near the edge of the pool of gasoline where the fluid was not so deep. If Crowder had made the same mistake, this would explain the single charred match found near the center of the burned area. Then, to be sure of achieving ignition, he might logically use three lighted matches to produce a bigger, stronger flame and would gently place the matches near the edge of the pool of liquid—corresponding to the location in which the three charred matches were found. Without previous experience in such matters, one might well expect that an intense fire of this sort would completely destroy the matches. If Crowder normally carried a cigarette lighter and had used it, there would have been no curious artifacts found, but he uses paper matches to light his cigarettes, as noted earlier.

If Crowder was the perpetrator of the hoax, perhaps he was motivated by the desire to obtain some publicity for the Crowder name which might help reelect his brother to the Board of Supervisors in the soon-to-be-held elections. But once the charred matches were discovered, and prompted suspicions of a hoax, it was clear that the incident could hurt his brother's political future as well as the family's good name. During the hours following the incident, this would have been a disturbing prospect and he would have sought means to substantiate the original story.

Crowder was the only person of the many I interviewed who knew that it had rained during the predawn hours. It had not been a sufficient downpour or thunderstorm to awaken others and make them aware of the rain. This suggests that Crowder was up in the predawn hours and that it was at that time that the four tiny holes were created—perhaps by hammering a railroad spike into the macadam. The new evidence would need to be created hurriedly, to avoid all risk of discovery, and this could explain why the distances between adjacent holes varied by several inches. This hypothesis would also explain why Crowder was sufficiently interested in the incident to take time to visit the Martins, to find out if the car he saw had been theirs and if they had seen "anything unusual," and why Crowder showed so little interest a few moments later that he did not bother to stop for a daylight inspection of the site as he drove to his warehouse. For if Crowder had stopped and inspected the site, he would have been the first to discover the four tiny holes, and this might have raised suspicions that he himself had created them. And it would also explain why Crowder showed so little interest in the holes when they were later discovered and reported to Sergeant Raines as the two men talked about the UFO incident.

At the time of the South Hill incident, the Socorro case was still widely accepted at face value, and a number of UFOlogists saw a remarkable parallel between the two. For example, when investigator Powers was interviewed by the local South Hill newspaper, he said that Crowder's UFO bore many similarities to the one reported by Zamora, and that both had left behind "pad-prints" and evidence of burning. There seem to me to be similarities beyond those Powers cited. The May 3, 1967, edition of *The Richmond News Leader*, in one of many follow-up stories on the South Hill incident, reported that barely two weeks after the incident had made headlines around the country, the site had been visited by persons from as far away as California and France! (Crowder later told me he had gotten telephone calls from as far away as Australia.) The story concluded: "Members of the South Hill Development Commission, long eager to increase tourist trade, never imagined that South Hill would one day 'make world news.'"

The pastor of Crowder's own church referred to the UFO incident in his weekly column in the April 27, 1967, edition of the South Hill newspaper in the following way: "The important thing is that one [UFO] made the scene at South Hill and South Hill is now really on the map." The column concluded with a joke about nuclear scientists who had decided to get away from their work and relax at Las Vegas. During the holiday, one of the nuclear scientists said to an associate: " 'What's gotten into Harry? Have you noticed the

way he's been living it up . . . as if there would be no
tomorrow?' " To this his companion replied: " 'Maybe Harry
knows something *we don't know.*' " (Italics in original.) This
prompted me to wonder if the pastor knew something that
some local residents had only begun to suspect.

The Socorro and South Hill cases, and numerous others,
illustrate another important UFOlogical Principle:

> UFOLOGICAL PRINCIPLE #7: *In attempting to determine
> whether a UFO report is a hoax, an investigator should
> rely on physical evidence, or the lack of it where
> evidence should exist, and should not depend on charac-
> ter endorsements of the principals involved.*

People who are basically honest and law-abiding can
become involved in a UFO hoax. At the time it may seem
like only an innocent prank which they fully intend to
promptly expose as such—only to find themselves trapped by
events into keeping up the pretense. Banks employ only
people who look honest and come well-recommended. Yet
every year there are numerous instances of embezzlement by
just such seemingly honest employees. As I write this, the
Senate Watergate hearings are in progress. A few months ago,
all of the principals in the hearings would have been able to
get character testimonials from many prominent people. Yet
today some of them admit to perjury and obstruction of
justice.

A final footnote to this case at South Hill was the reaction
of *The Richmond News Leader*, which had widely publicized
the incident. Before tackling the case, I had written to the
newspaper to obtain the name of their man in South Hill who
had first investigated the case (Robert Harris), and to obtain
any additional information they had acquired on the case
since the original articles. In reply, State Editor John A.
Gunn told me they had published all the facts they had
obtained. He added, "And if we'd had more, we would have
used them, too." Clearly *The Richmond News Leader* was
extremely interested in the South Hill case.

My report on the case, prepared early in 1968, was sent to the USAF Project Blue Book office and to the University of Colorado UFO study group, headed by Dr. Condon. In the summer of 1971, while straightening up my UFO files, I came across my correspondence with State Editor Gunn and decided he might be interested in my analysis of the South Hill case. So, on July 24, I sent him a copy of the report with the idea that the newspaper might be interested in explaining the case to its readers. When I failed to hear from Gunn by early September, I wrote to ask for his reactions to my report. He replied promptly to say that my report had somehow gone astray and he had never received it. On September 19, I mailed him another copy of the report, and in my covering letter I explained that all quotations in the report were based on tape-recorded interviews and could therefore be validated. I assured him that he was free to show the report to both Harris and Crowder for their comments.

In the summer of 1972, some nine months later, having failed to hear further from Gunn, I wrote to ask what had happened. The reply, from David L. Burton, state editor, explained that Gunn had left the newspaper the previous November. Burton said he had searched Gunn's files but could not find my report or my letters. I replied on July 30, 1972, providing Burton with the full background of the matter. I did not send the report, explaining that I had already gone to the expense of duplicating and mailing two copies earlier—both of which had "disappeared"—but I would be happy to send a third copy if the newspaper was interested in learning the explanation for the UFO case that had occupied its attention several years earlier. I never received a reply.

14 · UFOs As Brutal Killers

Some UFO cases require much less investigatory effort to explain than did Socorro and South Hill. Some require only a few inquiries by telephone and/or letter. For example, in the fall of 1967, a man in New Jersey challenged me to explain a bizarre case that had been reported in the book *Flying Saucers Are Hostile* by Brad Steiger and Joan Writenour. Steiger is the pseudonym of Eugene Olson, a former English teacher at Luther College in Decorah, Iowa.

According to Steiger and Writenour, three men were mysteriously cremated at precisely the same time on the same day under unexplainable circumstances at three widely separated geographic locations. According to the authors, it was April 7, 1938, at 1:14 P.M. in the time zone west of Ireland where the tramp steamer the S.S. *Ulrich* was sailing, when the second mate, F. E. Phillips, noted the ship was wandering off course. He went to the wheelhouse to investigate, and to his horror he discovered that the helmsman, John Greeley, "had been transformed into a human cinder." But, curiously, there was absolutely no other sign of fire in the wheelhouse. Even the man's shoes were reported to be unmarked by flame. According to the two authors, medical examiners later reported that the poor helmsman had been "fried from inside out."

Several hundred miles east of the S.S. *Ulrich*, in the adjacent time zone, the police went to investigate a crash of a runaway truck near the village of Upton-by-Chester. Inside the truck cab they found the incinerated body of the driver, George Turner. The clock on the dashboard had stopped at 2:14 P.M.—the same time as the death of the helmsman in the S.S. *Ulrich*, one time zone west. There was absolutely no sign of any fire inside the truck—except for poor George Turner's charred body, the authors emphasized.

In the next time zone to the east, in Nijmegen, Netherlands, the authors reported that a young man eventually identified as William Ten Bruik was found in his Volkswagen burned beyond recognition but with absolutely no other sign of fire in the car—the upholstery was not even smudged, the authors noted. The Nijmegen incident had occurred, they reported, at 3:14 P.M., exactly the same moment as the two mysterious deaths in Upton-by-Chester and aboard the S.S. *Ulrich*.

The authors did not attempt to show a direct relationship between the three reported tragedies and UFOs, since it would not be until 1947 that UFOs were officially discovered. But the authors implied that so bizarre a tragedy, in which three men were cremated without any evidence of fire around them, must necessarily involve the black magic of extraterrestrial visitors.

The first step in my investigation of this case was to telephone the public information office at the U.S. Maritime Administration headquarters in Washington. I asked Harry Hamann of that office if he had access to records that would show the country of registry of a ship named the S.S. *Ulrich*. I told him that I was not absolutely positive that there was such a ship, but if it existed, it had been afloat in April of 1938. Hamann assured me that he could get me an answer quickly. But it was several hours before he called back. He explained that he had first checked with the Lloyds of

London register of shipping for the year 1938. When he failed to find any S.S. *Ulrich,* he checked for 1939, then for 1940. Then he began going in the opposite direction, back to 1928—without finding any S.S. *Ulrich.* Undaunted, Hamann turned to an American counterpart of the Lloyds register called the American Shipping Register, which he had searched from 1940 back to 1928, also without success. Finally, he had checked the Merchant Marine list prepared by the U.S. Customs Department, with similar results.

He ended by saying that if a ship named the S.S. *Ulrich* had existed, it somehow escaped being listed by three different organizations that pride themselves on a complete listing of every ship afloat. I could only conclude that there was no ship named the S.S. *Ulrich* and that at least this part of the Steiger-Writenour story was pure fiction. I wrote to the man in New Jersey to report the initial findings and suggested he confront Steiger for the author's reactions. This he did and Steiger replied by suggesting that I might not be telling the truth or that it was all part of a "CIA cover-up." Why the CIA would be interested was not made clear by Steiger, nor how that agency could manage to replace all existing volumes of ship listings with counterfeits in which the name of the S.S. *Ulrich* was missing.

Meanwhile, I had written letters to the police departments at Nijmegen and Upton-by-Chester asking each to check its records to confirm or deny the part of the story that had allegedly happened in their respective cities. Shortly, I received a reply from Mr. F. Perrick of the Nijmegen police department. He reported that it was not possible to check records dating back to 1938 because these had been destroyed during the subsequent war. But Perrick did point out that *no Volkswagens had appeared on the highways of Netherlands until 1947—approximately nine years after the incident had allegedly occurred in such a car!* Later I learned that the first Volkswagen factory had not even been constructed by April, 1938; Adolph Hitler personally laid the cornerstone for the first factory in May of 1938!

Soon I also had a reply from the superintendent of the Cheshire constabulary, who had turned to the local newspaper—*The Cheshire Observer*—for assistance in responding to my request. The newspaper had found that a truck driver had indeed been burned to death in April, 1938, and it had supplied a photostatic copy of the original news account, which in turn was forwarded to me. This revealed that Steiger and Writenour had made a few errors in their account of the incident. For example, the driver's name was not George Turner, but Edgar Beattie. The incident had happened not at 2:14 P.M., but around 5 P.M. And it had not occurred on April 7, but on April 4. But the most significant discrepancy was that the whole truck had been consumed by flame when it crashed against a small bridge. The newspaper article quoted an eyewitness, named Norman Cheers, who had rushed to the scene to try to rescue the driver, but found the raging fire had made the door handle red-hot, frustrating any attempt to save the driver.

These findings I also forwarded to the man in New Jersey, and he in turn passed them along to Steiger for comment. In Steiger's reply, he suggested that instead of the S.S. *Ulrich* having been involved in the first incident, it might really have been the S.S. *Turtledove.* As for the reply from Nijmegen, Steiger said there was nothing to have prevented someone in Germany from having driven a Volkswagen across the border in April, 1938—nothing except that the factory that would later manufacture the car had not yet been constructed! Steiger did not try to suggest that the Nijmegen police were participating in a "CIA cover-up."

Someday, when I have nothing better to do, I might call the Maritime Administration and ask them to check on the S.S. *Turtledove,* and also on the S.S. *Nonsense.*

15 · UFO Photographs

In the more than twenty-five years since unidentified flying objects burst upon the public, many hundreds of pictures that purport to show a UFO have been published, often in respected national news media, including even *The New York Times*. In the early years, typical photos often showed an elliptical or pentagonal-shaped blob of light which resulted from internal reflection of sunlight in the lens system, known to professionals as a "lens-flare." Others, taken at night, showed a blob of light that might be anything from a streetlamp to a time exposure of the Moon or a bright star.

Then, in the early 1950s, a more interesting type of UFO photo began to appear that showed a craftlike object, sometimes called a "structured object," that typically was circular. Thousands of UFO photos have been submitted to NICAP during the first sixteen years of its existence. But in a remarkably candid admission, NICAP director Stuart Nixon wrote in the November, 1972, issue of the organization's monthly publication: *"NICAP has never analyzed a structured object picture that is fully consistent with the claim*

[*that*] *an extraordinary flying device was photographed.*"
(Emphasis added.)

The NICAP publication explained: "In every case, there has been some small detail, or group of details, that raised the *suspicion of a hoax* or a mistake." (Emphasis added.) Most of the photos submitted to NICAP came from males, often from a teen-ager. Photos of a craftlike UFO are usually taken in broad daylight, often near a populated area. If the craftlike UFO is really a giant vehicle, and not a small model, it might be expected that there would be other sighting reports from independent witnesses in the area, yet there never are. This, understandably, raises suspicions of a hoax at NICAP.

If giant saucer-shaped craft with exotic flight characteristics have been operating in our skies for more than twenty-five years, it is surprising that there is not a single authentic photo of such an object. In the United States alone, there are approximately 80 million cameras (not counting movie cameras), and Americans currently shoot approximately 5 *billion* still photos every year. Since the discovery of UFOs in 1947, Americans have taken approximately 50 *billion* pictures and have managed to photograph such brief, unexpected events as meteors, tornadoes and aircraft accidents. Yet there is not a single photo showing a craftlike UFO which can withstand close analysis. This explains the remarkably candid admission in the Nixon/NICAP article: "Statistically speaking, an unimpeachable photograph must sooner or later appear if UFOs are a physical reality. *Every year that passes without such a photograph being produced is evidence against the position that unknown objects are operating in the Earth's atmosphere.*" * (Emphasis added.)

The reason there are so many hoax UFO pictures is that they are so easy to make. Plate 10a shows a typical UFO

---

* Stuart Nixon's candor aroused the ire of Donald Keyhoe, one of NICAP's founders and a member of its Board of Governors. When Nixon was interviewed on station KFI in Los Angeles, and was asked if NICAP had proof of extraterrestrial visitors, he replied, "NICAP doesn't have actual proof. As a matter of fact, we don't really feel we've ever come up with solid proof that something extraordinary occurred." A few months later, on December 31, 1973, Nixon and NICAP parted company.

picture that was produced by three brothers: Gary, Kenneth and Brad Baum, ages ten, eleven and twelve, at the time. The boys, who happen to be my cousins, simply carved a saucer-shaped object from a block of styrofoam, suspended it from a tree limb with a thin wire, and then photographed the model, without any prompting from me. Their UFO picture is as good as most I have seen. Fortunately, they did not attempt to pass off the picture as authentic, as many teen-agers do—not realizing the forces they will set in motion.

I believe that many who make UFO hoax photos, using models, a hub cap or other handy object, do not originally intend to try to pass the pictures off as authentic. Rather, like my young cousins, they have seen published UFO photos which they recognize as hoaxes, and they believe they can do as well or better. When the pictures turn out well, the photographer—perhaps encouraged by friends—decides to see if he can fool the news media. If the pictures are subsequently published, because the local newspaper fails to investigate the case thoroughly or the editor welcomes the opportunity to enliven the front page, the photographer quickly becomes a national UFO celebrity and then finds it awkward to confess the picture is a hoax.

There are so many possible ways to produce hoax UFO photos that it is not always possible for even an experienced investigator to explain, or duplicate exactly, every picture—even when he is certain that a hoax is involved. One of the more ingenious producers of hoax UFO photos is Robert Sheaffer, a UFO skeptic, camera buff and, at the time he first sent me samples of his handiwork, a Northwestern University student. He never tried to pass the photos off as authentic. If he had, and had concocted a well-devised story to accompany some of his better UFO photos, I have no doubt that he could have become famous overnight.

One of Sheaffer's pictures (Plate 10b) shows two glowing saucer-shaped UFOs in formation flight at night over suburban houses. This picture is a triple exposure in which the two UFOs were created by shining a light through the center hole of a 45 rpm phonograph record that had been tilted so its circular hole would appear saucer-shaped. After superimposing the first UFO on the original scene, Sheaffer shifted the position of the camera slightly and repeated the process. Another of his hoax photos shows a glowing craftlike object, with three landing pads, in flight at night near the Moon. This UFO was fabricated from two aluminum plates which enabled it to be sailed through the air like a Frisbee. He had then photographed it in flight, using a strobe-type flash lamp, while taking a time exposure of the Moon (Plate 11a).

Still another Sheaffer picture (Plate 11b), taken in daylight, shows a saucer-shaped craft complete with an upper compartment that contains circular portholes—obviously to allow the crew to look out. He had fashioned this UFO from an old aluminum pie-tin to which he had attached an empty cottage-cheese container. Black circles were added to create the illusion of portholes. Still another Sheaffer photo (Plate 11c) surely qualifies as one of the most exotic UFO photos ever taken. It shows a circular, metallic craftlike object flying through the night sky, with portholes visible on the upper surface and electrical sparks shooting out from the rear— seemingly the UFO used an electrical propulsion system. Sheaffer explained that he had fabricated this UFO from scrap-metal parts, suspended the model in a dark room with only the model illuminated. Then he had rigged up a high-voltage transformer to produce the electrical sparks from the rear.

Because it is so easy to produce hoax UFO photos, serious investigators always try to obtain the original negative or the original print, in the case of a Polaroid photo which has no negative. Using the original negative or print, and with the aid of an instrument called a "densitometer," it is *sometimes* possible to detect the presence of a thread or wire used to support a model. But if the model is sufficiently aerodynamic, it can be sailed through the air. Still, whenever the person who took the UFO photo refuses to submit the original negative or print for analysis, NICAP is suspicious and I fully share their suspicions. In the final analysis, *the integrity of any UFO photo is no better than the truthfulness of the photographer when he describes the incident that led to the photo.* If an investigator catches him in one or more overt falsehoods, as distinguished from a momentary lapse of memory, then invariably the picture turns out to be a hoax, as numerous cases have demonstrated.

For example, early in January, 1967, two teen-age brothers living in Macomb County, Michigan, reported that a flying saucer had been spotted near their home and that they had taken four photos of the object with a Polaroid camera. The boys said the UFO had moved rapidly but noiselessly, and had remained in view for approximately ten minutes. They also reported that approximately five minutes *after* the UFO had departed, a military helicopter from a nearby Air Force base had flown over, and they had decided to photograph it also. When the incident was publicized, the USAF helicopter pilot said he had not seen the UFO—but if the boys' account was correct, the UFO had departed five minutes earlier.

The sighting was reported by the Associated Press in a dispatch dated January 10, 1967, and the story and photo(s) appeared in many newspapers around the country, including *The New York Times*, which seldom carries UFO reports. None of the newspapers that carried the AP dispatch seemed to attach much importance to a curious inconsistency in the boys' story which was contained far down in the account. The reporter who first investigated the case had asked to examine the backing sheet on which Polaroid prints are developed and processed, which contains a faint image of the print itself. When the backing sheet was examined, the reporter discovered that the picture of the USAF helicopter was not sequenced *after* the four UFO photos, but was sandwiched in between them. That is, the backing sheet showed the boys had taken two pictures of the UFO, then the photo of the USAF helicopter, then two more pictures of the UFO. Clearly the boys had not told the truth when they said the UFO had departed five minutes before the helicopter arrived!

The Detroit News, seeking the opinion of an experienced UFOlogist, interviewed Dr. J. Allen Hynek. An article based on the Hynek interview, published in the newspaper on January 16, was headlined, "Expert Sees 'No Hoax' in Boys' UFO Photos." The long feature story, extended for more than fifty column-inches, including a second headline: "Expert Sees 'No Hoax' in St. Clair UFO Photos." The article began: "One of the nation's leading unidentified flying objects (UFO) experts believes the 'flying saucer' photographs taken last week by two Macomb County brothers are 'strikingly similar' to other UFO reports he has investigated." The article said that Hynek had examined negatives made from the original Polaroid prints and had observed that "analysis so far does not show any indication of an obvious hoax." The credibility of the photos, according to Hynek, was enhanced because the boys had taken four pictures instead of only one.

"The striking thing to me," Hynek was quoted as saying, "is the similarity these pictures have to other photos I have seen, and also to verbal descriptions I've taken from ostensibly reliable people." The UFO in the Michigan photos did bear a striking similarity to the object that had been photographed nearly a decade earlier by Z. T. Fogl, a radio officer on the S.S. *Ramsey*. For many years, Fogl's UFO pictures had been widely accepted as being among the few truly authentic photos of a UFO. What Hynek perhaps did not know was that only a few months before the Michigan UFO pictures were taken, Fogl had admitted in England that his UFO pictures were a hoax, taken of a small model he had built himself and suspended from a thin thread!

The same article in *The Detroit News* which carried Hynek's strong endorsement of the authenticity of the Michigan pictures also contained a brief report of interest. *The mother of the two teen-agers who had taken the pictures was still flatly refusing to allow anyone, including the USAF, to borrow the original Polaroid prints for careful analysis.* Did the mother know something that Hynek did not? Some months later, when Hynek spoke on UFOs in Washington, I learned from him that the two boys had finally agreed to take a "lie-detector" (polygraph) test. He said they had "flunked."

When there is significant inconsistency in the photographer's reported behavior, this is usually an indication of a hoax. The behavior need not be logical by the investigator's standards, but it must be *self-consistent*. For example, if a person reports that he became so absorbed in watching a UFO that he forgot to go get his camera and photograph it, this is *not* necessarily cause for suspicion. However, if the person says that upon sighting the UFO he ran to his house or car to get a camera to photograph the object, this action clearly indicates that he recognized the rare nature of the event and the considerable value of obtaining a photo.

If, after photographing the UFO, the person later says he let the valuable pictures sit in his camera for many days or weeks because he didn't want to waste a few cents' worth of unexposed film to obtain the valuable photos of the UFO and to examine them for details he might earlier have missed, this is "inconsistent" behavior and cause for grave suspicion of a hoax. When a photographer is lucky enough to capture pictures of a rare event, such as a meteor or airplane accident, these pictures are invariably developed promptly and made public, if only for their monetary value. It should be clear to every person intelligent enough to operate a camera that an authentic picture of a spaceship from other worlds would be vastly more important, and more valuable, than a picture of an airplane crash or a meteor. Otherwise, why exert so much effort to get the camera and photograph the object?

Dr. William K. Hartmann, who served as the principal photo analyst for the University of Colorado UFO study, generally did an excellent job. He explained a number of UFO photos, many of them hoaxes. But there was a pair of UFO pictures showing an object resembling an inverted pie pan, that had been taken by Mr. and Mrs. Paul Trent on May 11, 1950, near McMinnville, Oregon, which Hartmann found extremely impressive. This is evidenced by Hartmann's conclusion in his analysis of the McMinnville photos that appeared in the final University of Colorado UFO report. Hartmann wrote: "This is one of the few UFO reports in which all factors investigated, geometric, psychological and physical, appear to be consistent with the assertion that an extraordinary flying object, silvery, metallic, disk-shaped, tens of meters in diameter, and evidently artificial [i.e., manufactured], flew within sight of two witnesses. *It cannot be said that the evidence positively rules out a fabrication [hoax], although there are some physical factors such as the accuracy of certain photometric measures of the original negatives which argue against fabrication."* (Emphasis added.)

Hartmann explained that the shadowed bottom of the object, visible in one of the photos, "has a particularly pale look, suggestive of [atmospheric] scattering between the observer [camera] and object. . . ." He noted that the apparent brightness ("luminance") of an object increases with its distance and that "if an object is sufficiently far away, its brightness equals the sky brightness." Hartmann used a densitometer to measure the luminance, relative to that of the sky, of objects on the ground, such as a distant barn whose range was known. On this basis, Hartmann found that the technique appeared to be accurate for the Trent photos within an error of no more than 4 to 1. This would be accurate enough to determine if the UFO was only a few dozen yards away from the camera, and hence a small object, or many hundreds of feet away, in which case it must have been a giant craft. It was the latter conclusion that emerged from his photometric analysis.

When I learned in the summer of 1969 that the Trent photos were the only ones showing a structured-type object that Hartmann had endorsed as authentic, I was prompted to launch my own investigation. I contacted Hartmann to obtain good prints of the Trent photos, and he referred me to United Press International's Compix department. He told me he had earlier tracked down the original negatives and found that Compix had them in its files. He had borrowed them to make prints for use in his analysis.

The Trent photo prints that I obtained from Compix (Plates 12a, 12b) were forwarded to Bob Sheaffer for his expert analysis while I proceeded to probe for possible "soft spots" in the Trents' story of events that had led to the UFO photos—using references that Hartmann had cited in his Colorado UFO report. From McMinnville, I obtained a copy of the June 8, 1950, edition of *The Telephone Register*, where the Trent photos and story had first been published— on the front page—under a banner headline that read: "At Long Last—Authentic Photographs of Flying Saucer [?]" It quoted Mrs. Trent as saying: "*It was getting along toward evening*—about a quarter to eight. We'd been out in the back yard. *Both of us saw the object at the same time.* The camera! Paul thought it was in the car but I was sure it was in the house. I was right—and the Kodak was loaded with film. Paul took the first picture. The object was coming in toward us and seemed to be tipped up a bit. It was very bright—almost silvery—and there was no noise or smoke." (Emphasis added.) Mr. Trent, she said, wound the film to the next frame and took a second picture before the UFO zoomed away toward the northwest.

Although the Trents were not sophisticated big-city folks, it is clear that they had read enough about UFOs to recognize the importance of what—allegedly—they were watching, as evidenced by their dash to find the camera. But having photographed this remarkable flying craft, did they promptly process the film and turn it over to the local newspaper or to the USAF? Hardly. The pictures remained in the camera for some time, to avoid wasting three unused frames of film. Even after the roll was developed, the Trents did nothing with the photos except show them to friends, including local bankers Ralph and Frank Wortman. It was the latter who finally persuaded Trent to offer the photos to the local newspaper, which published them nearly a month after they had been taken. The local newspaper explained the reason for the delay as follows: "Trent was reluctant to allow the use of the pictures." It quoted him as saying, "I'm afraid I'll get into trouble with the government." If Trent really feared that he had photographed some top-secret United States craft, he could get into as much trouble by releasing the picture in June as he would have a month earlier.

Another curious detail emerged two days later when the incident was reported by *The Oregonian*, the Portland newspaper. When McMinnville newspaper reporter William Powell first visited the Trents to obtain the UFO negatives, he said they were found "on the floor under a davenport where the Trent children had been playing with them," according to the Portland newspaper account. This was a curious way to treat the first authentic pictures of an extraterrestrial spaceship, if the Trents' story was true. It was much more understandable if the pictures were a hoax and the Trents knew they could readily be duplicated. The Portland newspaper story also revealed some significant discrepancies in the Trents' account of the incident, based on a tape-recorded interview with them on station KMCM, compared to their original version given to the McMinnville newspaper. Where originally Mrs. Trent had said that both she and her husband had been outside and had spotted the UFO at the same time, now Mrs. Trent said that she had been outside *alone* when the object was first seen. She said she hollered for her husband, who was inside the house, and when he failed to reply, she had run inside to get him and the camera.

Experienced UFO investigators, even those who believe in extraterrestrial spaceships, are very suspicious of reports that come from "repeaters"—a term applied to persons who claim to see UFOs frequently. NICAP itself, in the previously cited article, warned that one criterion for rejection should be "pictures taken by individuals with a history of UFO sightings." The Portland newspaper article revealed that the Trents were "repeaters" and quoted Mrs. Trent as saying that "she had seen similar objects on the coast three different times, *'but no one would believe me.'*" (Emphasis added.) Now, thanks to the photos, skeptical friends would be convinced. Nearly two decades later, in the summer of 1967, after Hartmann had visited the Trents for his investigation, *The Oregonian* carried a follow-up story in its August 3 edition which quoted Mrs. Trent as saying: "We've seen quite a few [UFOs] since then [1950] but we didn't get any pictures, they disappeared too fast." (Later, when I wrote Hartmann to ask if he had been aware that the Trents were "repeaters," he replied that he had known this and that during his visit he had discovered that the whole area was a veritable "hotbed" of UFO sighting reports.)

Meanwhile, Sheaffer's analysis of the Trent photos had turned up other significant discrepancies. From Hartmann's visit to the Trent farm, it had been established that the camera had been pointed in a northerly direction when the photos were taken. Sheaffer's keen eye noted that there were distinct shadows on the *east* wall of the Trent garage, caused by the overhanging eaves of the roof. This indicated that the pictures had been taken *in the morning*, and not shortly after sunset as the Trents had claimed. Sheaffer used his training in astronomy and mathematics to calculate the time of day when the photos were made, based on the position of the shadows. He concluded that the pictures had been taken at approximately 7:30 A.M., not at 7:45 P.M. Furthermore, his analysis indicated that the photo which the Trents claimed had been taken first had really been shot *several minutes after the other picture, and not a few seconds earlier as the Trents said.**

Hartmann had observed the same shadows on the east wall of the Trent garage during his own analysis, as well as other shadows faintly visible on the south wall of a white farm house in the distance. But he had been so impressed with the seeming integrity of the Trents that he was inclined to accept their story as factual. So he had sought another possible explanation for the shadows on the east and south walls of the buildings. Both Trent photos show what appears to be an overcast or hazy sky, and so Hartmann assumed that the light from the setting sun somehow was being reflected off the overcast sky so as to provide illumination from the east. Hartmann had never tried to check this hypothesis by taking photos under similar conditions. If he had, Sheaffer emphasized to me, he could not have succeeded in obtaining such distinct shadows as appeared on the garage wall. Such strong shadows could be produced only by a bright "point source"— the sun—and not by sunlight being diffused and reflected from an overcast sky.

Hartmann's hypothesis became completely untenable when I obtained a copy of the weather records for McMinnville for May 11, 1950, from the National Weather Records Center in Asheville, North Carolina. These records showed

---

* If the object had been in the vicinity for at least several minutes, the Trents would have had plenty of time to take additional photos since there were three more unused frames then on the roll of film.

that there had *not* been a high-overcast sky during the evening of May 11. *Instead the sky had been perfectly clear.* Beyond all doubt, the Trents' story that the pictures had been taken in the early evening of May 11, 1950, *could not possibly be true.* The same records disclosed that during the early morning of May 11, however, the air around McMinnville had been "smoky"—which is what the Trent photos show. (Perhaps these smoky conditions played a role in the erroneous conclusions that Hartmann reached via his photometric analysis.)

Hartmann's original analysis had mentioned the shadows and the fact that they suggested that the photos might have been taken in the morning, but he questioned why the Trents would falsify the time even if a hoax were involved. It seems to me that there is a plausible reason. Most farmers are out working in the fields around 7:30 A.M., when the photos were actually taken, and Trent's neighbors would think it odd that they too had not seen the giant UFO that the Trents claimed to have seen and photographed. But to claim that the pictures were taken at 7:45 P.M., when most farmers have retired to their houses for dinner, would eliminate most potential witnesses who might dispute the story and photos.

Sheaffer hit upon another possible explanation for the photometric anomalies that could have thrown off Hartmann's appraisal, and he decided to test the idea with an experiment. Sheaffer speculated that if the lens of the Trent camera had not been perfectly clean, light scattering could occur that might produce effects like those that Hartmann had observed. The camera used by the Trents was an Eastman folding type which sometimes needed a hard push to get it folded. The lens offered a handy point against which to push, and it might thus have accumulated a thin film of body oil on the lens surface. For Sheaffer's experiments, he used an ordinary streetlamp, suspended from a pole, to simulate a small model UFO at close range. He first photographed it against a bright sky using a clean lens. Then he smeared a thin layer of petroleum jelly on the lens and repeated the shot. This was followed by another, thicker layer of jelly, and still another photo. When he developed the negatives and examined them with a densitometer, the results confirmed his hypothesis. Light from the bright sky surrounding the simulated UFO had been diffused by the oily film on the lens, and this had increased the luminance of the "UFO." Using the same technique that Hartmann had employed on the Trent photos, Sheaffer could "prove" that the top of the streetlamp pole was at a much greater distance from the camera than the bottom of the same pole, even though both were actually at the same distance.

Everitt Merritt, a professional photometric analyst employed by Raytheon's Autometrics division in the Washington, D.C., area, had been employed by Hartmann and the University of Colorado to analyze two UFO pictures taken by a barber in Zanesville, Ohio, which seemed to show a giant UFO hovering near his house. Merritt, using the techniques of his trade, soon proved that the photos were a hoax. Merritt told me that he had been asked by Hartmann to make a similar photometric analysis of the Trent photos. But he said this proved impossible because Hartmann had failed to obtain sufficiently precise measurements when he visited the Trent farm. However, Merritt had examined the Trent photos casually, and he told me that he "radically disagreed" with Hartmann's views on their authenticity.

It is a tribute to Hartmann that when Sheaffer and I presented him with the results of our investigation, he promptly revised his earlier views on the Trent pictures. Hartmann seemed especially impressed with Sheaffer's efforts in demonstrating that the pictures had been taken around 7:30 A.M. "I think Sheaffer's work removes the McMinnville case from consideration as evidence for the existence of disklike artificial aircraft," Hartmann said, using his favorite euphemism for extraterrestrial spacecraft. He added that the McMinnville case "proves once again how difficult it is for any one investigator . . . to solve all the cases. Perhaps no one has the experience for that, because there are too many phenomena and methods for hoaxing."

Hartmann's observation served to remind me that I too may have been the victim of a photo fabrication, early in my career in UFOlogy, which he had quickly spotted as a hoax.

The case involved two pictures taken at night by two teen-age boys in Beaver, Pennsylvania, that seemed to show a glowing, plasmalike UFO. After spending two full days in Beaver investigating the case and later trying to re-create the photos, without success, I had concluded that the pictures were probably authentic. Hartmann, however, had been suspicious of the photos from the start. Although he had never visited Beaver or inspected the original negatives, he became convinced that the photos were a hoax when he himself was moderately successful in duplicating them using a white plate. Later, when I met Sheaffer, I learned that he too was suspicious of the photos. Subsequently, when Sheaffer produced a much more convincing replica of the pictures, it caused me to have serious doubts about my original appraisal. Undoubtedly, it was this early experience, plus my subsequent encounters with so many other hoaxes, that has made me an ever-suspicious UFO investigator. It had also made me especially appreciative of having the assistance of someone with Sheaffer's expertise in UFO photo cases.*

* Sheaffer studied astronomy under Dr. Hynek at Northwestern, and they often discussed UFOs, with Sheaffer in the role of the skeptic. Sheaffer gave copies of his hoax UFO photos to Hynek, to demonstrate how easily they can be made, and he volunteered to assist Hynek in UFO investigations. It seems a pity that Hynek all but ignored Sheaffer's offer, for it could have saved him the embarrassment of publicly endorsing the authenticity of UFO photos, like the ones taken in Michigan, that later turn out to be hoaxes.

16 · The Great Falls
UFO Movies

In contrast with the many hundreds of still photos that purport to show UFOs, there are only a handful of amateur ("home") movies that make the same claim. This might at first seem strange, since there are more than 8 million home-movie cameras in the United States. The explanation is that it is extremely difficult for an amateur to make a convincing hoax UFO movie without a well-equipped special-effects department that is available only to commercial motion-picture producers. This intrinsic constraint on making hoax UFO movies does, however, focus attention on the tiny handful that do exist. Aside from several which were obviously made by hanging a small model by a thin thread from the end of a fishpole, the only seemingly authentic amateur movies simply show one or more "blobs of light"—not structured or craftlike objects, even in those taken in broad daylight.

The most impressive and famous UFO movie (excluding those made in commercial studios) is a 16 mm color film of approximately sixteen seconds' duration that was shot near

Great Falls, Montana, on August 15, 1950, at approximately 11:25 A.M. Mountain standard time (MST). Taken on a clear, sunny day, the film shows two nearly circular, gleaming white bloblike images that seem to be flying in close formation and in nearly horizontal flight. As the brief film proceeds, the images become fainter against the deep-blue sky until finally they are no longer visible. (See Plate 14a.) The film was taken by Nicholas Mariana, then aged thirty-eight and the general manager of the Great Falls baseball team. Mariana was also a radio sportscaster and produced a weekly syndicated program that was purchased by a number of stations in the area. He had graduated in journalism from the University of Montana and had served for two years during World War II in the Army Air Corps.

In the spring of 1968 I first learned of a rigorous scientific analysis of the Mariana/Great Falls film through a paper written by Dr. Robert M. L. Baker, Jr., published in the January–February, 1968, issue of *The Journal of the Astronautical Sciences.* The analysis had been conducted at Douglas Aircraft Company in 1955–1956, with Baker as the principal investigator. In 1968, when Baker wrote the paper, he was a senior scientist with System Sciences Corporation (whose name subsequently was changed to Computer Sciences Corporation). Following an exchange of correspondence with Baker in early 1968, we met on July 29 of that year when he came to Washington to testify before a "Symposium on Unidentified Flying Objects," sponsored by the House Science and Astronautics Committee, to be discussed in Chapter 30. His journal paper on the Great Falls film was included in the published transcript of the Congressional UFO symposium.

Baker's views in 1968 on the Great Falls film were summarized in the abstract to his paper, entitled "Observational Evidence of Anomalistic Phenomena." He wrote: "It is concluded that, *on the basis of the photographic evidence, the images cannot be explained by any presently known natural phenomena.*" (Emphasis added.) Coming from a man with Baker's credentials, this was an impressive endorsement. At the time Baker had conducted the analysis in 1955–1956, at the age of twenty-four, he had recently graduated with highest honors in physics and mathematics from the University of California at Los Angeles. In 1956, Baker had received his master's degree and in 1958 his Ph.D. in engineering with a specialty in astronautics.

Baker's published paper revealed that he had quickly ruled out any possibility that the two UFO images on the film could have resulted from balloons or other wind-borne objects. The reason was that the UFOs appeared to be moving in a southerly direction, opposite to the direction of winds reported for Great Falls on August 15, 1950. He had also ruled out the possibility that the UFOs could be meteor fragments because of the appearance of the images and their reported long-duration visibility. And so Baker's investigation focused on the question of whether the two white blobs could possibly have been the result of sunlight reflecting off two F-94 aircraft which had reportedly been in the vicinity of Great Falls at the time.

Baker wrote: "This explanation seemed attractive since *it was rumored (although not verified)* that two jet airplanes (F-94s) were landing at Malstrom [*sic*] Air Force Base at the approximate time of the sighting." (Emphasis added.) In a footnote, Baker added that in late 1955, some five years after the incident, he had made inquiry to the commanding officer of the Great Falls Air Force Base, later renamed Malmstrom Air Force Base. Baker had been informed that there were no F-94s stationed at the base in 1950 and "if any were in the air, they would have been transients." Baker also quoted from a book written by the late Edward J. Ruppelt, a former USAF officer who had been named to head Project Blue Book a few months after the Great Falls incident. Ruppelt had written: "The intelligence officer at Great Falls had dug through huge stacks of files and found that only two airplanes, two F-94s, were near the city during the sighting and that they had landed about two minutes afterwards. . . . We knew the landing pattern that was being used on the day of the sighting and . . . the two jets just weren't anywhere close to where the two UFOs had been."

Despite Baker's apparent doubts over whether there had

indeed been two F-94s in the area at the time of the filming, the possibility that the UFO images might have been caused by sunlight reflections from the aircraft was the only hypothesis that was amenable to investigation. So Baker painstakingly analyzed the Mariana film, frame by frame, using a *copy* of a *copy* obtained from a Hollywood producer who was then making a commercial movie on UFOs. For convenience, Baker assumed that the two objects had maintained a constant separation between them for the duration of the sixteen-second film and that the objects were flying essentially a straight path. Based on these assumptions, Baker's analysis showed that the UFOs appeared to be flying on a heading of 171 degrees—*slightly east* of south. Malmstrom Air Force Base was approximately three miles due *east* of where the film was taken.

The presence of a water tower and other buildings in the foreground of some of the film frames enabled Baker to determine the elevation angle of the UFOs and their approximate angular velocity. From this data it was possible to calculate the altitude and speed of the UFOs for each of several different possible distances of the objects from the camera. (No determination of even approximate distance was possible from the film.) If, for example, the UFOs had been two miles from the camera, their altitude would have been approximately 2,730 feet (above local terrain) and their velocity would have been 177 mph (on a 171-degree heading), according to Baker's paper. If the objects were six and one-half miles away, their altitude would have been 8,860 feet and their ground speed would have been nearly 600 mph, close to the top speed of the F-94. Thus, if the UFO images were sunlight reflections from two F-94s, the aircraft could not have been more than six and one-half miles away. (Baker's published figures are used here even though my calculations indicate a small arithmetic error.)

One crucial question for the F-94 hypothesis was this: if the two airplanes had been within six and one-half miles of the camera, would portions of the aircraft fuselage still have been visible on the film to identify the source? If so, this would seem to rule out the F-94 explanation, for no craftlike structure was visible around the gleaming white blobs on the Mariana film. To check this point, the investigators obtained a Revere 16 mm movie camera with a three-inch telephoto lens of the same type used by Mariana. They measured its resolving power and other optical characteristics. In one key experiment, the camera was used to photograph four jet fighters, comparable in size to an F-94, that were flying in close formation at a distance estimated to be approximately two and one-half miles. These movies showed a strong sunlight reflection off the aircraft fuselages which was similar to but somewhat more elongated than the near-circular Mariana images. But more important, Baker reported, was the fact that the aircraft structures were clearly discernible at *two and one-half miles,* leaving no doubt as to the source of the reflection.

Assuming that the optical quality of Mariana's camera lens was comparable to that used in the experiments, the data obtained prompted Baker to write *in his 1968 paper:* "Thus, theoretically, and as borne out by the author's experiments, *the F-94s would have been identifiable even at 6-1/2 miles."* (Emphasis added.)

It was in the summer of 1973 that I had my first opportunity to examine the Project Blue Book file on the Great Falls case, now stored in the USAF Historic Research Center archives at Maxwell Air Force Base, Alabama. My attention was drawn first to the original report, written by Baker on March 24, 1956, which Douglas Aircraft had submitted without charge to the Project Blue Book office. To my surprise, I discovered that Baker had succeeded in producing a Mariana-type UFO blob of light by photograph-ing a one-hundred-foot-long airliner at a distance of approxi-mately twelve miles using the Revere camera and three-inch telephoto lens. This would be the approximate equivalent of photographing a forty-foot-long F-94 from a distance of approximately five miles—well within the six-and-one-half-mile "speed limit" cited earlier.* *The airliner showed up*

---

* The one-hundred-foot airliner at a distance of twelve miles would not be exactly equivalent to a forty-foot F-94 at a distance of five miles because of

simply as an intense blob of light, with no structural details visible to identify it as an airplane! (This photo is shown in Plate 13b.) The picture of the airliner appeared directly above a similar-size enlargement of one frame from the Mariana movies. The similarity between the two was so pronounced that someone in the Project Blue Book Office had been prompted to draw in a sweeping arrow pointing to both photos, with the notation "Compare!"

The Great Falls case file contained convincing evidence that there had indeed been two F-94s in the vicinity at the time of filming which were preparing to land at the nearby air base. There was a letter, dated October 6, 1950, from the 15th District Office of Special Investigations at the Great Falls Air Force Base that reported the result of examination of records at Base Operations, which logs all incoming and departing aircraft. These records showed that one F-94 had landed at 11:30 A.M. and the other at 11:33 A.M., several minutes after the time Mariana shot his movies. The two jet interceptors were assigned to the 449th Fighter Squadron at Ladd Air Force Base in Alaska. The log even showed their individual registration numbers: 2502 and 2503.

The surprising thing to me was the striking contrast between the conclusions Baker had drawn in 1956 in his original Douglas report and those in his 1968 paper, *both based on exactly the same evidence.* In 1968, Baker had written: ". . . on the basis of the photographic evidence, the images *cannot be explained* by any presently known natural phenomena." Twelve years earlier Baker's report had stated: "The photographs shown in Appendix II *do seem to indicate that airplane reflections might possibly look like the images shown on the film."* * (Emphasis added.)

---

atmospheric scattering effects which are roughly proportional to the square (second power) of distance. This would serve to make the fuselage of the airliner less discernible as well as reducing the intensity of the spot of reflected sunlight.

* Baker later explained to me that this wording in the original report was a compromise used to placate his boss, Dr. W. B. Klemperer, who disagreed with Baker on the key issue of whether the images could have been caused by reflections off the two F-94 aircraft.

In fairness to Baker, another factor must be considered. Granted that sunlight reflecting off an airplane could produce the white-blob-type image on the Mariana film, this would occur only when the airplane was in a favorable position relative to the sun and the ground observer or camera. If an airplane were flying a curved (parabolic) path, as would be the case if the objects were F-94s circling in the customary counterclockwise direction to land on the southwest runway (into the direction of the prevailing wind on that day), then a sunlight reflection could conceivably persist for an extended time. But if the objects were flying a straight path, as Baker's calculations suggested, they could reflect sunlight to Mariana's camera for only approximately twenty seconds. The film that Baker analyzed was approximately sixteen seconds long—well within the twenty-second "limit." But there is some uncertainty over the total duration of the incident—from initial sighting to UFO disappearance.

The October 6, 1950, report prepared by intelligence officer Captain John P. Brynildsen, based on a lengthy interview with Mariana, gave the following account: "Mr. Mariana made these pictures on 15 August 1950 between the hours of 11:25 and 11:30 A.M., at Great Falls, Montana . . . *he stated that he first sighted the objects while standing in the grandstand of the ball park* . . . and that he saw two bright disc shaped objects proceeding in a southerly direction at an altitude of approximately ten thousand feet and at a distance of about three-quarters of a mile in a westerly direction, from the observer's viewpoint. Mr. Mariana then stated that he ran downstairs and outside to his car from which he obtained his camera and made the pictures shown in the film. *From the time of first sighting to the completion of taking of the pictures, Mr. Mariana estimated consumed approximately twenty seconds.*" (Emphasis added.)

This is not consistent with Mariana's statement that he had to run down to his car to get his camera—which subsequent tests indicated might have consumed up to thirty seconds. Perhaps Brynildsen misunderstood and the twenty-second figure is the total time that Mariana said he personally had the two objects in view, which included several seconds in the stands before he decided to run for his camera plus the sixteen seconds during the filming. Allowing thirty seconds for Mariana to recover his camera would mean that the two UFOs had been present for a total of fifty seconds. *If they had maintained their mysterious bloblike appearance for this full fifty seconds,* this would justify Baker's doubts that the images could be sunlight reflections from F-94s.

Thus the accuracy of Mariana's story *in all details* seems crucial in trying to assess whether two jet aircraft could have produced the bloblike images. Brynildsen's report states: "He enjoys an excellent reputation in the local community and is regarded as a reliable, trustworthy and honest individual." Brynildsen also noted that Mariana told him "he had read numerous newspaper articles on the subject of flying discs and flying saucers and had not attached very much significance to them. However, Mr. Mariana almost invariably carries a camera in order that he may make 'opportunity pictures' and had previously thought that if he could see such unconventional aircraft in flight, he would take motion pictures of them."

Mariana told Brynildsen that his nineteen-year-old secretary, Miss Virginia Raunig, had been present during the filming, but according to the officer's report the UFOs were observed by her for *only about seven seconds.* This seemed to indicate that she had not been with Mariana at the time he reported being in the grandstand and had only spotted the objects while Mariana was taking his movies. After interviewing the secretary, Brynildsen appraised her as being a "fairly reliable individual." One possible explanation for this qualified endorsement was volunteered by Mariana during our telephone conversation in mid-1973. He explained that "she was one of those kind of people who would just go into a tizzy when she was questioned about it . . ."

It seems certain that the Mariana UFO movies are not a staged hoax, aside from the great difficulty of staging them. One typical characteristic of hoax UFO photos is that the incident is almost never reported until the pictures have been developed to see how well they turned out. In Mariana's case, he promptly reported the incident to the local newspaper immediately afterward and at least two weeks before the films were processed. Mariana called his friend Raymond Fenton, sports editor for the *Great Falls Leader,* and the following story appeared in that evening's edition on the front page under the headline "Mariana Reports Flying Discs."

> Could it be that even baseballs now come home to roost?
>
> Nick Mariana, general manager of the Selectrics [baseball team] was asking himself that question this morning. Two objects—for all the world like the "long gone" ball slugged out of the Twin Falls ball park last night by Lou Briganti and Joe Nally—sailed across the sky at Legion park this morning.
>
> At least so the troubled Brewers' general manager reported today—even while admitting he could have been seeing things. Only he hopes to have photographic proof for skeptics.
>
> It all happened at 11:30 A.M. while Mariana was out taking a look around the reserved seat section at Legion park—and there sailing smoothly above the smelter stack at the ACM plant were two spherical silvery objects at a height he estimated at 5,000 feet. After a quick double-take and a minute lost while he brushed the cobwebs from his eyes, he called his secretary as a witness.
>
> Very opportunely he remembered his movie camera and shot the movies he hopes will verify what he hopes isn't failing eyesight.
>
> No report is available on possible weather balloons floating in the atmosphere today—but it is feared that the high-flying baseball version may be more acceptable to Great Falls residents than "flying saucers."

The article has a tongue-in-cheek tone, but this could simply have been the result of its having been written by the sports editor. Perhaps sports editor Fenton was slightly suspicious at the time that the story was an attempt to get a little publicity for the local ball club and its manager. In a telephone conversation with Fenton in the summer of 1973, he recalled that Mariana was "very public-relations conscious . . . that's the way Nick is . . ."

Since the two objects in Mariana's film had flown over the edge of Great Falls shortly before noon in perfectly clear weather, and the city then had a population of nearly 40,000, it would be logical to expect that at least a few other observers might have seen the objects. Yet even after the front-page prominence given to the Mariana sighting in the August 15 edition of the *Great Falls Leader,* there were no other confirming reports submitted to the newspaper, so far as its subsequent editions disclose. If the two objects were jet interceptors, *they would be clearly identifiable as aircraft to other ground observers in Great Falls,* unless the observers chanced to have the same viewing angle as Mariana. This could explain the lack of other confirming sightings. It was not until two weeks later, on August 30, that the Great Falls newspapers carried another UFO report. This one came from two local men who reported that while in the vicinity of Geyser, Montana, they had sighted something with "a long tail, flying at high altitude," that had streaked across the sky and then disappeared. Their description strongly suggests that the object was a meteor.

Mariana promptly finished the roll of film and sent it off to be processed. He does not recall exactly when the film was returned, but processing in those days usually required seven to ten days, he told me. So it was late August or early September when he first viewed his film. He recalled his reactions for me: "I was just stunned." At the time that Mariana received his film, there was some concern in high government circles that UFOs might be spaceships from other worlds, whose intent was unknown, or more possibly some secret type of Russian vehicle that was being used for covert reconnaissance of United States military bases. The United States had already started to employ high-altitude balloons to try to take photos behind the Iron Curtain, and perhaps the Russians were doing the same. Two and a half years later, the Central Intelligence Agency would secretly sponsor a panel of specialists to examine UFO reports because of these potential national security implications.

Some of these national security implications would not have been known to Mariana. But he was well aware of "flying saucers" from articles he had read on the subject, as he later acknowledged to Captain Brynildsen. And it was general knowledge that the USAF had created a special office to receive and investigate UFO reports at Wright-Patterson Air Force Base in Dayton, Ohio. If the source of the images on the film was truly unknown to Mariana, one might have expected him to have promptly visited the nearby USAF base to show the UFO movies to the base commander and to offer them for detailed analysis. But as Mariana recalled for me in mid-1973, "it just never occurred to me."

Instead, he arranged to show the UFO movies at local club meetings. For example, the September 12 edition of the *Great Falls Leader* reported, in a brief item that appeared in the sports section, that Mariana had showed the film the previous night to the Central Roundtable. At approximately the same time he was invited by the publisher of the *Great Falls Tribune*, the morning newspaper, to show the film to members of the staff of that newspaper and of the associated *Great Falls Leader*, which he did. If Mariana failed to recognize the potential national security import of the films, the city editor of the *Leader*, C. T. Sullivan, was more alert. On September 13, Sullivan wrote a letter to the commanding general at Wright-Patterson Air Force Base in Dayton, bringing the incident to his attention. Sullivan wrote that Mariana was willing to "give the films to any government agency which may be interested."

It strikes me as odd that it was Sullivan who wrote the letter. Surely he would not have written and stated that Mariana was willing to lend the films unless he had first discussed the matter with Mariana and obtained his permission. Assuming that Mariana had earlier simply overlooked potential USAF interest in his films in the initial excitement, once Sullivan had pointed out the possible national security implications of the movies, it seems strange that Mariana himself would not have written the letter. As a graduate in journalism, he should not have been fazed by the task of writing a letter, nor was he known as a shy, retiring person.

One *possible* explanation is that Mariana really knew, or suspected, that the two UFO images on his film were only sunlight reflections off two jet aircraft. If so, he would, understandably, be reluctant to personally try to pass them off to high USAF officials as "authentic UFOs." If this hypothesis is correct, perhaps Mariana had originally intended to use the incident and film only as a means of getting a little local publicity for himself and the ball team. If so, things were about to get out of hand, for it would have been embarrassing to admit to Sullivan that the images were only sunlight reflections off two aircraft, yet equally awkward to try to stop Sullivan from writing to the USAF.

In response to Sullivan's letter, the USAF had dispatched Brynildsen from the local air base to interview Mariana and to borrow the film. Brynildsen's report of October 6, along with the film, was sent to Dayton on that date. Based on this evidence of official USAF interest, the local newspapers filed a story on the Associated Press wire on October 6. Now Mariana and his UFO films were world-famous. In the AP story, Mariana seemed to have tried to play down any possible relationship between the two UFO images and the two F-94s. He was quoted as saying: "Two jets that flew over in another direction about the same time seemed to be going much faster [than the two UFOs]." Within several days, Mariana was approached by representatives from *Life* and *True* magazines and from Movietone News, to obtain copies of his film when it was returned by the USAF.

On October 10, in response to press inquiries, USAF officials in Dayton announced that the "film is too dark to distinguish any recognizable objects," and added that the film was being returned to Mariana. This suggests that the USAF had decided that the two UFO images were simply sunlight reflections off the two F-94s, but found it awkward to publicly state that a reputable citizen had mistaken two jet interceptors for UFOs, or was attempting to mislead the USAF.

Mariana later charged that the USAF had not returned all of his original film and that the "missing" portion offered the best view of the UFOs, including frames that indicated that the UFOs had hovered briefly. The USAF flatly denied the charge. Two years later, in preparation for the CIA-sponsored Robertson Panel, which would evaluate key UFO cases, the

USAF asked Mariana if it could again borrow his film, and he agreed. The original film, now somewhat the worse for wear, was then duplicated by the USAF and returned to Mariana without further incident. The Robertson Panel agreed with the earlier appraisal that the UFO images probably were sunlight reflections off the two F-94s. This would indicate that the USAF did not have in its possession any "missing frames" which showed the UFOs hovering, for they would have ruled out the F-94 explanation.

It is conceivable that someone in the Project Blue Book office originally might have snipped out the early frames as a private venture. But this would have had to be done before anyone else in the office viewed the film, which seems unlikely. The alleged "missing frames" have never come to light, despite a $50,000 prize later offered by the *National Enquirer* for outstanding UFO evidence. (Chapter 28).

The Sullivan letter of September 13 served to set in motion still other events that would commit Mariana to defend the white-blob images as "authentic UFOs." For example, columnist Bob Considine, during a radio program, reportedly ridiculed persons who claimed to have seen UFOs and he mentioned Mariana and his film. According to the official USAF case files, this resulted in Mariana losing some subscribers to his syndicated radio sportcasts. Mariana filed suit against Considine and his sponsors, but the legal action was later dropped. Eventually, Mariana moved to Portland, Oregon, where he is presently engaged in selling automobiles.

Some months after I first began investigating the Great Falls case, while glancing through the January, 1969, issue of *Air Progress* magazine, my attention was drawn to a photo showing an F-4K jet fighter making a low-altitude pass during the British Farnborough Air Show. The jet fighter was enveloped in a glowing, white circular "blob," perhaps forty feet in diameter, which instantly reminded me of Mariana's UFO images. The brief caption for the photo, and an adjoining one showing a similar effect on another aircraft, explained that this was an unusual shock-wave pattern that resulted from high humidity of the air and sunlight reflecting off this shock wave. The effect was so unusual that the magazine had devoted a full page to the two pictures of commonplace aircraft in otherwise routine flight.

This prompted me to wonder if this, or some other unusual atmospheric effect, could have produced a similar visual phenomenon at Great Falls—a phenomenon that would be unfamiliar to Mariana and could have obscured the identity of the two F-94s. The official Weather Bureau records for Great Falls for August 15 showed that at 11:27 A.M. the surface temperature was 77° F. and the dew-point temperature was 45° F. (Dew-point temperature is the temperature at which the air would have 100 percent humidity.) Thus, August 15 was not an especially humid day in Great Falls. More recently, a similar "localized fog" effect was observed to form around the fuselage of a USAF B-52 during Boeing flight tests and was photographed by the crew of a nearby "chase-plane." (See Plate 14b.) The B-52 had been flying at 21,000 feet altitude at around 600 mph. Boeing scientists, after investigating the effect, concluded that the temperature of the air was lowered by flowing over the wings, which thereby increased its relative humidity. Under the prevailing atmospheric conditions, this caused water droplets to form in the wake of the airplane, creating a localized fog which reflected the rays of the sun. Just such a condition could explain the Great Falls "white blobs" and why they remained visible for a time considerably longer than the allowable twenty seconds calculated by Baker for simple reflections off the F-94 fuselages.

So we are left with two possible explanations for the two UFO images on the Mariana film:

(1) That they resulted from sunlight reflecting off the fuselages or off freak shock/moisture patterns produced by the two F-94s that are known to have been in the vicinity at the time the film was shot. Mariana was quoted by Captain Brynildsen as saying that the UFOs made a "swooshing sound." This is the sound produced by jet aircraft.

(2) That the images are of two extraterrestrial spaceships that just happened to visit Great Falls on the very same day and at the very same time as the two F-94s. This is conceivable, but certainly would be a very remarkable coincidence.

If the images were produced by the two F-94s, as I believe, the secondary question of whether Mariana really knew what produced the UFO blobs on his film may never be resolved. It is not always possible to fully resolve every question, every ambiguity in every UFO case, as the Great Falls film and the curious case to be described in the next chapter demonstrate.

17 · A Curious UFO

In early August of 1968, the Air Force received the following letter, addressed to the USAF Chief of Staff in Washington. The letter was written by William C. Rogers, a diesel-locomotive specialist and test engineer with the Union Pacific Railroad who then lived in Cheyenne, Wyoming.

Dear Sir:

This is to report an Unidentified Flying Object as follows: At about 2 P.M. July 28, on the Ada Crouter farm in Cuming County, Nebr. [approximately 70 miles northwest of Omaha], I became aware of a tear-drop shaped object in the sky, more or less 100 feet from me in an Easterly direction and at about the height of the electric power lines which cross the farm.

The object could have been 6–12 feet in length, but it was not an object—it was a phenomenon of light or electricity. The heavy end of the tear-drop was toward the earth and the tapered end was up. The color was shining-blue. As I watched, it burst open with blinding light and then disintegrated into fragments of light.

There was no noise. Nothing came down to earth. No one saw this but me and I have told no one except Mrs. Crouter.

At the time I was on the shore of a small lake on her farm doing some brush clearing work for her. Temperature was approximately 88° F. Sky was cloudless. Sun was very hot. The incident occupied a small but indeterminate number of seconds. There was no noise. This was not a man-made object nor was any human associated with it.

If you wish to question me, I am available.

Very sincerely,
William C. Rogers

The USAF sent Rogers one of its official UFO report forms, which he promptly filled out and returned in early August. In this detailed questionnaire, Rogers described the UFO's appearance as follows: "Incandescent—ultraviolet. Self-luminous. Edges sharp. The phenomenon hung in the sky, slightly higher than the high-tension electric lines, but beyond them and in no way connected with them." In response to one question that asks that the UFO's appearance be described in terms of a commonplace object, if possible, Rogers said it resembled "a blown-glass Christmas tree ornament, ultraviolet colored and tear-drop or pear shaped. But the object I saw was incandescent light, [like] the arc from electric welding—the object glowed steadily with exceptional brightness. It did not flicker. *It did not move.*" (Emphasis added.)

Rogers estimated that the UFO remained in view for approximately thirty seconds before it "burst open revealing gold colors. Almost simultaneously it disintegrated into many fragments, each disappearing in a separate flash. Complete silence throughout." The only change from the original letter was that Rogers now estimated the distance to the UFO at two hundred yards, rather than one hundred feet. (Later he measured the distance to be 750 feet.) Rogers said he was sixty-one years old and noted that he had served as a colonel during World War II in the Army Transportation Corps.

The USAF's Project Blue Book office sent me copies of

Rogers' original letter and his official report a few weeks later because the UFO seemed to have many of the characteristics of a plasma and had been reported to be in the vicinity of a high-tension power line. Some UFO investigators, such as Dr. Hynek, are inclined to place little credence in a UFO report when there is only a single "witness" and to automatically give the account a high credibility rating if there are multiple witnesses. Such simple criteria may be convenient, but my own experience indicates that a UFO investigator should at least attempt to probe each case carefully, regardless of the number of "witnesses," to establish its credibility. This I attempted to do when I first wrote to Rogers to seek more details and during our subsequent correspondence. Neither in Rogers' original letter nor in his official report had he used the term "plasma" to describe what he had seen, as had young Leonard (Chapter 11) in his first telephone call. This suggested that Rogers had not read about plasma-UFOs in my book or elsewhere. The fact that Rogers replied promptly to my first letter of inquiry was also reassuring, for UFO hoaxers usually do not welcome the efforts of experienced investigators to probe their account and often do not reply to repeated letters, although this by itself is not necessarily proof of a hoax.

In my first letter I casually asked Rogers if he had ever before seen a UFO, or a phenomenon similar to that in the reported July 28 incident. He replied by describing an incident that had occurred about three years earlier during a train run through the Black Hills of South Dakota. There had been an intense thunderstorm with extensive lightning, and he said he had seen small tear-drop-shaped "droplets of lightning" in the dark sky that had appeared briefly. But he recognized that these were some unusual form of lightning and *he had not submitted a report of a UFO sighting.* He also recalled that roughly twenty years before, while driving along a highway with friends, he had briefly observed a ball of fire rolling along a high-tension line on a clear afternoon. In a few moments the ball had disintegrated and disappeared. He had never bothered to report the incident, recognizing that it was probably some freak electrical phenomenon related to the power lines. The July 28 incident was the first that he had characterized as a UFO and had bothered to report.

In Rogers' first letter to me, he volunteered, "If you would like to question me the next time I am in New York, let me know and I will be glad to answer any questions whatsoever." Rogers seemed a credible, intelligent individual, and the case itself seemed to provide one more report to confirm the existence of plasma-UFOs.

Then, in early October, I received a large envelope from Project Blue Book containing new data which provided a different perspective on this case. The new data consisted of numerous reports of a giant meteor (fireball) that had passed over central Nebraska, heading east, on July 28, 1968, at approximately the time that Rogers had reported seeing the UFO. The time of the Omaha Fireball, as it was officially called, was precisely known from a report that had been filed by a United Air Lines jetliner crew that had been cruising at 31,000 feet, headed west toward Omaha. The time the crew spotted the fiery-red meteor was 1:45 P.M., while the aircraft was over Iowa City, Iowa. Subsequent investigation by the Smithsonian Institution's Center for Short-Lived Phenomena and the Smithsonian's Meteorite Recovery Project indicated that the meteor had come to a fiery end in the vicinity of Atlantic, Iowa, *approximately 110 miles southeast* of where Rogers had been standing when he first spotted the UFO, at "approximately 2 P.M."

Knowing that railroad men pride themselves on the accuracy of their watches, I promptly wrote to Rogers to ask if he had looked at his watch immediately after the UFO sighting to fix the time, or if he had later tried to estimate the time to arrive at the 2 P.M. figure. I did not explain the reason for my question or mention the fireball incident. Rogers replied that his 2 P.M. figure was only an estimate, made some time after the incident, based on the fact that he had gone in for lunch shortly before noon and had taken a leisurely lunch-period before returning to his brush-clearing task. The UFO incident had occurred shortly afterward. This raised the possibility that the pear-shaped UFO that Rogers had reported seeing and which seemed to be only a couple

hundred yards away might really have been the Omaha
Fireball disintegrating near Atlantic, Iowa, approximately *110
miles away.* At the time it was difficult for me to imagine that
a mature adult could make so gross an error during broad
daylight in estimating distance. It was not until a year later
that the St. Louis UFO sighting (Chapter 5) would conclusively show that even experienced flight crews could make
such gross misestimates of distance.

But there were several factors that seemed to argue against
this possibility. When a giant meteor enters the atmosphere,
it often leaves behind a trail of electrified ("ionized")
particles, or "meteor trail," which remains visible for some
time. It resembles the contrail sometimes left in the wake of
high-flying jet aircraft. The United Air Lines crew had
reported spotting such a meteor trail while the airliner was
still near Iowa City, and the crew said the meteor trail was
still visible seventeen minutes later as the airliner flew under
it near Atlantic. Yet Rogers had volunteered in his first letter
that the sky had been perfectly cloudless. If the Rogers UFO
had really been the fireball, why hadn't he seen the meteor
trail which persisted for at least seventeen minutes and was
observed also by numerous witnesses on the ground in
western Iowa?

Also, the numerous witnesses in Iowa, including the airliner
crew, said the color of the fireball was red or reddish orange.
(I personally wrote to a number of the witnesses mentioned
in the Smithsonian and newspaper accounts for their descriptions.) Not a single observer in Iowa had reported the fireball
as being blue or violet, while Rogers had reported no red or
orange colors in the UFO, except that he once referred to
"gold." If the UFO and fireball were one and the same, the
position of the sun at 1:45 P.M. relative to the different
witnesses might have played a part in the different colors
reported. The observers in Iowa would be looking in a
westerly direction at the fireball, with the sun roughly behind
the meteor, while Rogers would be looking east with the sun
behind his back.

There was another seeming discrepancy: Rogers had insisted that the UFO hovered motionless in the sky, while all

of the Iowa observers reported seeing high-speed motion of the fireball which is characteristic of a meteor. But, here again, this might be explainable in terms of the viewing perspective of Rogers relative to the fireball's trajectory. In my next letter to Rogers, I asked if he would be willing to measure the magnetic bearing of his line of sight to the UFO when next he returned to the Crouter farm, and he agreed. He assured me that he knew precisely where he had been standing at one corner of the small lake and also the particular power-line pole near which the UFO had seemed to be hovering.

It was some weeks before Rogers had the opportunity to return to the Crouter farm. While awaiting his measurements, I plotted out the apparent location of the meteor trail, based principally on the detailed report from the United Air Lines crew, which had reported their position at the time the fireball was sighted and later when the airplane passed under the meteor trail. The magnetic bearing from the vicinity of the Crouter farm to Atlantic, Iowa, was *approximately 105 degrees*. Then I heard from Rogers, who reported that he had thought to bring along two magnetic compasses to assure an accurate measurement. The measured bearing from where he had been standing to where the UFO had been seen was *approximately 90 degrees*. This was a difference of only 15 degrees from the 105-degree bearing from Rogers' position to where the United Air Lines crew had reported passing under the persistent meteor trail—close enough to suggest that Rogers' UFO could have been the Omaha Fireball!

In an earlier letter, on October 11, 1968, I had decided it was time to inform Rogers that it seemed possible that his UFO had been a giant fireball and to get his reactions to this possibility. From extensive experience I knew that some persons who report UFO sightings are later very reluctant to accept a more prosaic explanation for what they first decided must be an alien spaceship. Would Rogers reject out of hand the possibility that he might have mistaken a fireball more than 110 miles away for a UFO hovering only a couple of hundred yards away?

Rogers promptly replied with the following observations: "The UFO could have been at ANY height and ANY distance . . . visual estimates away from fixed standards of comparison may well be compounded with illusion. I feel somewhat at fault for not acknowledging this previously, but my illusion was so clear. Yes, it is possible that the UFO *might* have been a meteor exploding at any distance and any altitude, but what put me off this possibility was the illusion, or impression, described again above [in his letter] that I saw it fixed in space, that the tear-drop outlines were clear and that there was NO movement as in a trajectory." It was clear that Rogers was willing to consider all plausible explanations and fully recognized the intrinsic limitations of human observation— including his own.

During the course of my investigation of this case, another possible explanation emerged. Some years earlier, a plasma physicist named Ferdinand de Wiess, then employed at Avco Corporation in developing reentry vehicles for intercontinental ballistic missiles (ICBMs), had proposed that some ball lightning reported during fair-weather conditions might be the result of meteors. He suggested that under certain conditions, the ionized trail created when a meteor enters the atmosphere, which constitutes a plasma, might form into a ball within a self-generated magnetic field which would sustain the plasma as it drifted earthward, perhaps following the Earth's magnetic field. In the fall of 1968, de Wiess was an associate professor at the University of Arizona, and soon after I learned of his theory, I sent him details on the Rogers case. He was delighted to learn of the incident which might confirm his earlier hypothesis.

If the de Wiess theory is correct, it then would be possible to offer an alternative explanation for the Rogers sighting— that what he saw was not the Omaha Fireball but a plasma formed out of the meteor trail as the meteor streaked over central Nebraska. This could explain why Rogers reported that the UFO hovered motionless until it disintegrated, while the numerous observers in Iowa reported seeing the fireball moving at high speed. It could explain why the fireball appeared red and orange to observers in Iowa, and why

Rogers' UFO was distinctly blue and violet. And it would indicate that Rogers' original estimate that the object was only a few hundred feet distant was not grossly in error. The object's proximity to the high-tension power line would also be explainable because of the magnetic field generated by such lines. And if Rogers did indeed see a plasma-UFO, and was not looking in the exact direction of Atlantic, it would explain why he failed to see the persistent meteor trail reported by so many witnesses in Iowa.

So this case is not fully explained, and the Rogers UFO is not completely "identified." No amount of additional investigation of this single case is likely to turn up additional evidence of value in resolving the issue. Hopefully, in time, there may be other sightings under similar circumstances which will shed new light on the question. For example, the St. Louis UFO/Fireball case, which occurred the following summer, provided useful perspective on the Rogers case by demonstrating that even experienced flight crews can mistake a large meteor more than one hundred miles away for a UFO which seems to be only a few hundred feet distant.

The Rogers case is useful because it demonstrates another important UFOlogical Principle:

> *UFOLOGICAL PRINCIPLE #8: The inability of even experienced investigators to fully and positively explain a UFO report for lack of sufficient information, even after a rigorous effort, does not really provide evidence to support the hypothesis that spaceships from other worlds are visiting the Earth.*

The Rogers UFO case may remain unexplained for some years, perhaps indefinitely, in terms of being able to establish beyond all doubt whether he saw a plasma-UFO, possibly produced out of the meteor trail of the Omaha Fireball, or whether it was the meteor itself. But one thing is certain: if the object was only a few hundred feet away, and disintegrated in a blinding flash without leaving behind any residue on the ground, it certainly was not an alien spaceship.

18 · UFOs on Radarscopes

One of the most remarkable inventions to emerge from World War II was radar, which can detect aircraft in darkness or bad weather at distances far beyond the range of human vision in broad daylight and good weather. Many laymen, and even a few of those who use radar equipment, believe that it is infallible. If a small spot of light—called a "blip" or "target"—appears on the radarscope, many persons believe that this necessarily indicates the presence of a solid, metallic object. If a blip moves erratically, or seems to indicate an object moving at extremely high speed, some persons conclude that this provides incontrovertible evidence that there must be extraordinary flying objects in our skies. *This misconception is not shared by engineers who are experienced in the design of radars, or by scientists and others who are experienced in the use of radar.*

Radar typically functions by transmitting brief pulses of high-power radio energy, some of which are reflected back to the radar antenna by objects within the radar beam at that instant. From the earliest days of radar, scientists quickly learned that radar echoes could be produced by moisture in the air. This has proved to be a great boon for certain applications, and weather forecasters now lean heavily on extensive networks of ground radars to detect and follow the movement of severe storms. All modern airliners carry a small radar to enable flight crews to detect severe storms ahead and to help the pilot select the smoothest possible flight path around or through such storms.

In the early days of radar experimentation and use during World War II, other mysterious targets would sometimes appear on the scopes during fair weather, which ruled out the possibility that they were reflections from moisture. Sometimes these targets would appear briefly, then disappear. Others would appear to hover in one area for extended periods of time—a characteristic which clearly ruled out the possibility that they were aircraft. These mysterious radar targets were dubbed "angels," and the name stuck, even though subsequent investigations have identified the causes of many of them.

During World War II, British radar specialists were puzzled by a radar blip that would appear just before dawn over one portion of London. The radar blip would quickly form into a circular ring that would expand in size until eventually it disappeared. In an effort to resolve the puzzle, observers were stationed on the ground in the vicinity of where the curious radar target appeared. As dawn approached, the observers saw hundreds of birds which had been nesting in the belfry of a large church suddenly emerge and take off in all directions in search of food—forming an expanding circle of birds. A similar type of expanding-ring-shaped radar target repeatedly spotted over Texarkana, Arkansas, in the 1950s, was found to be the result of thousands of red-wing blackbirds which would take off each morning just before sunrise to forage for their breakfast. A near-perfect ring would persist for distances of twelve to thirty-five miles from the roosting ground before it began to break up into small irregular-shaped blips, representing small clusters of blackbirds.

In the early 1950s the United States launched a major

program to strengthen its air defenses against possible enemy attack. To enable the air-defense system to cope with possible massive attacks, it was decided that electronic digital computers should be introduced to automatically track each radar target. But when a prototype facility was tested in the Boston area in the mid-1950s, scientists found that the computer was being saturated beyond capacity by spurious radar targets, or angels. At first, scientists suspected that most of the angels were the result of echoes off high ocean waves because the test radars were situated on Cape Cod, looking out over the Atlantic. But even after special circuits were devised to eliminate possible "sea clutter," many of the spurious targets persisted. It was then decided to maintain an airplane in readiness which could be dispatched to the scene of angels when they appeared. A few such on-the-spot investigations by the aircraft served to explain the source of these spurious targets; they were seagulls. Subsequent analysis showed that the high-power air-defense radar being used should be able to detect *a single bird* at ranges of up to one hundred miles! To avoid this source of angels, engineers later developed means to enable the computer to distinguish between echoes produced by slow-moving birds and stronger ones from fast-moving large aircraft.

Other investigations suggested the possibility that some angel targets might be caused by swarms of insects. In 1949, U.S. Navy and Bell Telephone Laboratories scientists jointly conducted extensive experiments in Arizona which conclusively demonstrated that insects were indeed another source of spurious radar blips. Subsequent experiments, conducted in the 1960s, in which a single bumblebee was released from an airplane in flight, showed that *even a lone insect* of this size could be detected at considerable distance by a very powerful radar. Still other experiments have shown that smoke and dust or mineral particles swept up into the air by a dust storm or thunderstorm can also produce spurious targets on radarscopes.

It is important to emphasize that the ability of a radar to detect smaller targets, especially those the size of insects, dust particles and moisture, is strongly influenced by the radio frequency at which a radar operates. The higher the radio frequency of the radar (and the correspondingly shorter its wavelength), the better it can detect small objects. *When two radars which operate at considerably different radio frequencies are searching the same area and a target shows up on the scope of one radar but not the other, then the target almost certainly is an "angel." A solid, metallic craft of even modest size would be detected by both.*

There is another general class of radar angels which is more difficult to identify so positively because even when an aircraft is dispatched to the scene to investigate, there is nothing to be seen. This class of angels is attributed to freak atmospheric conditions. Experiments have shown that at certain times a part of the radar energy may be reflected down to Earth, then reflected back to the radar antenna via the same bent path. Thus, even though the radar beam is aimed skyward, the antenna may—briefly—receive echoes from fixed or moving objects on the surface of the Earth. But there is no means by which the operator watching the radarscope can know that a target he sees is really on the surface of the Earth and not in the air. The situation is analogous to a mirage effect in which a human observer sees an object far beyond the horizon which may seem to be hanging suspended in the sky. Experiments have shown the sporadic existence of such reflecting layers in the atmosphere at various times. While they have been detected during all seasons, both day and night, *these reflecting-layer conditions occur most frequently during the warm, humid summer months—which, coincidentally, is when most UFO radar "sightings" occur.*

Still another source of radar angels is a localized area of turbulence in the atmosphere, although the basic mechanism involved is still the subject of scientific debate. Jet aircraft cruising at 30,000 to 40,000 feet altitude, in perfectly clear air, occasionally encounter very severe but brief turbulence which has come to be called "clear-air turbulence," or CAT. To learn more about clear-air turbulence, scientists have used powerful ground radars to search for echoes in the clear (nonrainstorm) sky. Then, jet aircraft have been dispatched to the area where an echo is detected to determine whether it encounters CAT, and usually the pilot does report severe turbulence. (The pilot never reports sighting a UFO.)

In the 1950s, when the principal military threat to the United States was that posed by an enemy bomber attack, there was growing USAF concern over spurious radar echoes. As the USAF increased the power of air-defense radars to extend the range at which they could detect enemy bombers, there was a more than proportional increase in the problem of spurious targets. Investigations were launched both by in-house laboratories and by outside companies experienced in radar propagation. In 1956 the Air Force Cambridge Research Laboratories published a report, written by one of its scientists, Vernon G. Plank, which attempted to summarize all that was known about the complex problem. The 117-page report referred to spurious-target experience and theories discussed in 113 technical papers that had previously been published on the subject—an indication of the complexity and long-standing recognition of the problem. Three years later, Plank published still another report on the subject.

Nor was the problem limited to long-range air-defense radars. Shorter-range airport surveillance radars, used to direct incoming and outgoing traffic at military and civil airfields, were also encountering difficulties with spurious targets, as evidenced by an extensive report issued by the USAF's 1800th Airways and Air Communications Service on April 9, 1957, to all its operating contingents. The report began: "The number of reported difficulties with 'Angels,' 'Anomalous Propagation,' and just plain false targets seems to be on the increase. . . . When and if this condition occurs at your location, a lot of worried people are going to want to know where the targets are coming from and what is causing them to appear . . . no one answer has been found that applies to all cases."

The report discussed the particularly acute case of spurious targets that had been experienced by the CPN-18 airport surveillance radar at Hamilton Air Force Base, California, in the vicinity of San Pablo Bay, near San Francisco. Spurious targets had appeared on the CPN-18 radarscopes during clear days, cloudy days, foggy days and even after a rain when the sky was clear and visibility was unlimited. Aircraft had been dispatched to the area where targets still appeared on the scopes, but they found *nothing*. Investigation at that base had shown that *spurious targets occurred most frequently at times when there was a temperature inversion present* over the San Pablo Bay area. The report quoted a Bendix radar field engineer as saying that he had personally encountered spurious radar targets over a wide range of geographic areas, from Montana to West Germany and Libya. Clearly the problem was universal.

The USAF report of April 9, 1957, cautioned that until means could be devised to ease the problem, "radar operators must learn to live with it." And it added that "considerable time has been expended by maintenance personnel in checking radar performance *when in reality the difficulty lay with the failure of all concerned to fully understand the limitations of their facility*." (Emphasis added.) In other words, even experienced radar operators and maintenance personnel often were not aware of the vagaries of radar propagation and freak effects that could result from unusual atmospheric conditions. The spurious-target problem had reached such proportions that the USAF prepared an hour-long motion picture, entitled "Radar Refraction and Weather," to better educate radar operators and maintenance personnel, and the report to all air bases described how to obtain a copy of the film.

Plank's two reports, much too erudite for the average radar operator, received limited circulation, which is unfortunate insofar as the radar UFO problem is concerned. In a conventional radar, the antenna does not look continuously in one direction, but rotates so as to scan essentially an entire hemisphere. Long-range surveillance radars usually scan at approximately 4 rpm, which means they get a fresh look in a particular direction only once every fifteen seconds. (Shorter-range airport radars rotate at 15 rpm, providing a fresh look every four seconds.) If a blip suddenly appears on the scope of a long-range radar in a position corresponding to a distance thirty miles east of the station, and on the next rotation of the antenna that original blip is gone but another shows up twenty miles west of the radar, an operator may easily leap to the conclusion that both blips are the result of echoes from a single object. If this assumption were correct, then the object would have covered fifty miles in fifteen seconds, corresponding to a speed of 12,000 mph—in which case the assumed object must be a UFO, for no conventional aircraft can travel at such speeds.

In reality, as Plank cautioned in his 1959 report, the two blips may be unrelated except that unusual atmospheric conditions are prevalent which are producing both spurious echoes. For example, at the moment that the radar antenna was pointed east on the earlier scan, atmospheric conditions may have been such as to refract (bend) some of the radar energy back toward the Earth, where it may have chanced to bounce off a large metal storage tank, then be returned via the same bent path to the antenna. On the subsequent scan, fifteen seconds later, atmospheric conditions may have changed slightly in the east so that the refracted echo was too weak to be detected by the radar. But during this scan, the same freak conditions may have occurred when the antenna was pointed to the west, producing a brief target in this location.

A tragic demonstration of the susceptibility of radar operators to being misled by spurious targets occurred during the war in Vietnam in mid-June of 1968. United States military radar operators spotted what appeared to be twenty to thirty targets on the scopes and concluded that they must be low-flying enemy helicopters that were preparing to attack friendly positions and ships. Observers outside were alerted, and they *reported seeing lights in the night sky that seemingly confirmed the radar targets.* United States anti-aircraft guns and artillery were promptly alerted to open fire, and fighter aircraft were directed to the radar targets and they too opened fire in the darkness. The heavy firepower *seemed* to take its toll because the radar operators noted that *twelve of the targets quickly disappeared from their scopes.* But the following day, airborne and ground reconnaissance failed to locate any wreckage of enemy helicopters that had seemingly been shot down the previous night. The only victims were a United States patrol boat that had been operating offshore, which was sunk, and an Australian destroyer that reportedly sustained two hundred holes from the attack. Subsequent investigation termed the tragic incident "Radar error."

This vulnerability of radar to being spoofed by angels has prompted corrective measures in newer designs, which make them somewhat less susceptible to spurious targets. (See Plates 15a, 15b.) But complete elimination of angels may never be possible, which explains why the U.S. Federal Aviation Administration and equivalent agencies in other countries are placing increased reliance on a basically different type of radar for air-traffic control. This "radar-beacon system" makes use of a small transmitter-receiver ("transponder") installed in an airplane which is triggered when it receives a specially coded interrogation from the ground. When this occurs, the aircraft transponder replies by transmitting back a specially coded message which not only positively identifies it as an aircraft but also indicates the airplane's altitude and its specific identity. This strong, coded signal cannot be mistaken for a spurious simple echo which can be produced by birds, insects and freak atmospheric conditions.

A typical UFO radar case, with visual sightings that seemed to confirm the radar, occurred near West Palm Beach, Florida, during the predawn and early postdawn hours of September 14, 1972. At approximately 4 A.M. (EDT), the West Palm Beach airport control tower began to receive telephone calls from persons asking about a very bright light they had seen hovering in the eastern sky out over the Atlantic Ocean. The tower controller, James Moon, Jr., as he recounted the incident, said he had looked and seen nothing. "Then, suddenly, there was this very bright light." He described it as being a "glowing circular object" that appeared to be approximately *two miles* east of the tower.

He then decided to examine the scope of the airport surveillance radar, which had recently been installed at West Palm Beach. It was a twenty-year-old ASR-3 that had originally been installed at a larger airport that had since been given a more modern radar, while the old ASR-3 had been reconditioned for use at West Palm Beach. After studying the scope, Moon said he spotted a curious radar blip that was approximately *ten miles east* of the airport, which, he assumed, was the glowing object he had seen. The blip was many times bigger than a conventional airplane blip, and it was moving very slowly—too slowly to be an airplane—at a speed of approximately five mph. The blip was moving toward the coast and subsequently took up a position northwest of the airport where reportedly it "remained more or less stationary."

The controller contacted the Miami International Airport and, reportedly, was told that the radar there also showed an unknown target. Further, that the Air Defense Command facility at nearby Homestead Air Force Base had already been alerted and that its height-finder-type radars showed an unknown target at an altitude of approximately 11,000 feet. The West Palm Beach tower operator contacted an Eastern Air Lines jetliner, then south of the airport, to ask if the crew could see the UFO. The crew soon radioed back that they too could see a bright light to the east. It would seem that here indeed was an impressive UFO case in which the presence of the UFO was confirmed by numerous visual sightings, including those of an experienced airline crew and an experienced tower operator, with confirmations from three different radars.

Because of Florida's proximity to Cuba, the Air Defense Command decided to scramble two F-106 jet interceptors at 6:13 A.M. (EDT), and the two jets were directed to the area where the radar UFO target was situated. Each of the F-106s had a powerful radar installed in its nose to help find the target. By this time the sky was becoming light, and this would simplify the task of spotting the unknown target. But the two F-106 pilots were unable to spot any target, either visually or on their intercept radars. However, the West Palm Beach tower operator reported that he could still see the bright UFO to the east, and it was agreed that one of the F-106 pilots would fly low over the tower so the controller could provide the bearing and elevation angle to the UFO

from his point of reference. Meanwhile, in response to the
UFO reports, West Palm Beach Sheriff William Heidtman
had taken off in a county helicopter shortly after 6 A.M., and
its pilot was directed to the vicinity of the curious target on
the West Palm Beach tower radar. The sheriff found nothing.
Then the tower directed his attention to the bright light to
the east and asked him to investigate, which he did.

Upon returning to Homestead Air Force Base, F-106 pilot
Major Jerry B. Smith reported he had managed to spot the
visual UFO after being assisted by the tower operator. He
identified the UFO as *Venus*, but added that the planet did
appear unusual because of two thin haze layers between it
and observers on the ground. When Sheriff Heidtman
returned, he too reported having seen the light to the east,
which he described as being "very bright, with occasional
flashes of red and green." What was it? Heidtman said, "In
my opinion, what I was looking at was the planet Venus." *
(It will be recalled from Chapter 9 that a brilliant Venus had
produced a rash of UFO reports in Kansas only several weeks
earlier.)

This case illustrates another important UFOlogical Principle, whose validity will be demonstrated in Chapter 21 in the
analysis of a famous radar-visual case that occurred in
England in the mid-1950s:

> *UFOLOGICAL PRINCIPLE #9: Whenever a light is sighted
> in the night skies that is believed to be a UFO and this is
> reported to a radar operator, who is asked to search his
> scope for an unknown target, almost invariably an
> "unknown" target will be found. Conversely, if an
> unusual target is spotted on a radarscope at night that is
> suspected of being a UFO, and an observer is dispatched
> or asked to search for a light in the night sky, almost
> invariably a visual sighting will be made.*

* When Donald E. Keyhoe described this incident in his latest book, he
criticized the USAF for trying to explain the UFO as a misidentification of
the planet Venus. *Keyhoe did not tell his readers of the careful search by the
two USAF pilots and by the helicopter-borne sheriff, nor that they all agreed
that the bright light in the east was Venus.*

In the excitement of the moment, it will seem unimportant that the radar target is to the west while the visual target may be east, north or south—the two "sightings" will seem to confirm one another. Even if the visual sighting is made many minutes, or even hours, after or before the radar sighting, it will be assumed by some that the presence of the UFO has been positively confirmed by what is usually called "two independent sensors."

19 · The Famous RB-47 Case (Part 1)

One of the strangest and most puzzling UFO cases on record involved the crew of an Air Force RB-47 jet bomber during a night training-test mission in the early morning hours of July 17, 1957. The University of Colorado UFO study group, after being personally briefed on the incident a decade later by the RB-47 pilot, could only say that the case was "unusual, intriguing and puzzling." Dr. Hynek, after more than two decades as a UFO investigator, calls it "a classic case . . . certainly one that must be considered seriously as illustrating an unquestionably strange phenomenon."

The most detailed investigation of the RB-47 incident, prior to my own, was conducted by Dr. James E. McDonald, an atmospheric physicist at the University of Arizona, before his tragic suicide in the summer of 1971. McDonald, who had personally investigated hundreds of UFO reports, and was one of the most outspoken proponents of the extraterrestrial spaceships explanation for UFOs, was especially impressed with this case. McDonald's RB-47 report was published in July, 1971, in *Astronautics & Aeronautics* magazine, the monthly journal of the American Institute of Aeronautics and Astronautics, upon the recommendation of the AIAA's UFO Subcommittee. In the article, McDonald summarized the incident as follows:

> An Air Force RB-47, equipped with electronic counter-measures (ECM) gear [equipment] and manned by six officers, *was followed by an unidentified object* for a distance of well over 700 mi. and for a time period of 1.5 hr., as it flew from Mississippi, through Louisiana and Texas and into Oklahoma. The object was, at various times, seen visually by the cockpit crew as an intensely luminous light, *followed by ground-radar* and detected on ECM monitoring gear aboard the RB-47. Of special interest in this case are several instances of simultaneous appearances and disappearances on all three of those physically distinct "channels" and rapidity of maneuvers beyond the prior experience of the aircrew. [Emphasis added.]

McDonald, Hynek, the AIAA UFO Subcommittee and others were especially impressed by the idea that the UFO had not merely been seen periodically in the form of a bright light in the night skies by the pilot and co-pilot, but seemingly had been spotted on an air-defense radar located at Duncanville, near Dallas, Texas, and that a very distinctive radio signal, presumably emitted by the UFO, had been monitored by one of three electronic intelligence ("Elint") receivers aboard the aircraft. If true, this seemed to rule out any possibility that the UFO could have been a meteor, weather or prankster's balloon, or misidentification of Venus or other celestial body.

The airplane involved in the incident was a type of B-47 bomber that had been modified to perform an electronic-intelligence-type reconnaissance mission, which explains the RB-47 designation. A primary purpose of such missions is to determine the location of air-defense radars in potential enemy countries so they can be quickly destroyed in event of war to prevent their use. A related function is to measure the limits of radar coverage and locate possible blind spots caused by local topography, to indicate the best approach path for attacking bombers to minimize their early detection. Elint missions are also performed so that bombers can be outfitted with equipment that can confuse or mislead such air-defense radars. Before such electronic countermeasures equipment can be designed, the signal characteristics, or "electronic fingerprint" of each type of radar must first be measured. Since radar signals do not stop at national borders, Elint missions can be conducted without crossing the borders of a potential enemy—at least insofar as the outer perimeter of air-defense radars is concerned.

Two of the three Elint systems carried on board the RB-47 were designed to monitor ground radar characteristics, and the third was intended to eavesdrop on enemy radio communications. The airplane involved in this incident was scheduled to be sent to West Europe to ply its trade. But before being sent overseas, the RB-47 had to be checked out on a practice mission to assure that its complex Elint equipment, its tail-mounted gun turret and its navigation system were all functioning properly. So, late in the evening of July 16, the RB-47 took off from Forbes Air Force Base, Kansas, situated near Topeka, and headed south. Its first destination was the Gulf of Mexico, where the tail turret could be fired over a gunnery range set aside for the purpose. Major Lewis D. Chase was the command pilot.

On reaching the Gulf, the RB-47 turned east and tested its tail turret over the gunnery range while the navigation equipment was also checked. When the airplane was south of Biloxi, Mississippi, the pilot turned north. His flight plan called for the airplane to proceed to Meridian, then turn west on a heading that would take the RB-47 across Louisiana into Texas. Near Waco, the airplane would head north to return to its home base. During the westbound flight from Meridian, the three Elint operators would exercise their systems, using USAF air-defense radars and communications stations which stretched along the Gulf Coast to protect the nation's southern flank against surprise attack.

Shortly after the RB-47 turned north from the Gulf, at least one of the three Elint operators, Frank B. McClure, decided to turn on his equipment and exercise it to assure that it was functioning properly before the aircraft reached Meridian and headed west. McClure's equipment, referred to here as Elint #2, consisted of an ALA-6 direction-finder, for taking bearings to a ground radar; an APR-9 receiver; and an ALA-5 pulse analyzer, for examining the radar-signal characteristics. The ALA-6 direction-finder consisted of a pair of antennas (to be discussed in more detail in the next chapter), mounted under the belly of the RB-47, and an operator's console which included a small cathode-ray tube like that used in a small portable TV set, to display the *approximate* bearing angle to the ground radar being monitored. The bearing to the radar was shown *relative to the airplane's heading*. For example, if the radar were directly ahead of the airplane, the display marker would point to the 12 o'clock position, and if the radar were abeam to the right, the marker would point to the 3 o'clock position.

As the RB-47 approached Biloxi, McClure tuned his APR-9 receiver to a portion of the frequency spectrum known as S-band (centered around approximately 3,000 megacycles) and observed a signal with the familiar characteristics of a CPS-6B-type air-defense radar. But, curiously, the bearing shown to this signal source was approximately 5 o'clock, i.e., southeast of the RB-47. This seemed to indicate that the radar was situated *in* the Gulf of Mexico, because radars along the Florida peninsula were too distant to be detectable, and besides they operated at a different frequency band. McClure knew there wasn't any air-defense radar sitting in the middle of the Gulf.

He was puzzled by another feature of the signal. As the airplane flew north, the bearing angle displayed should move "down-scope," toward the 6 o'clock position, unless the radar were directly ahead of the airplane. (For example, if you fix your gaze on a farm house as you drive along the highway, you must turn your head rearward—toward the 6 o'clock position—to keep it continuously in view.) Yet McClure observed that the bearing to the source of the radarlike signal was *moving "up-scope"—in the reverse direction to normal*. McClure concluded that his equipment was probably mal-

functioning—a not-infrequent occurrence for the complex
electronic equipment of that era. Later, as the RB-47
approached Meridian, McClure checked his equipment
against other radars, and it seemed to be functioning
properly, so he did not bother to report the earlier incident to
the airplane commander. *It is important to note that at the
time of this first incident in the general vicinity of Biloxi,
neither the pilot nor co-pilot saw anything unusual in the
night skies.*

The RB-47 turned west onto a course of 265 degrees (true)
as the aircraft neared Meridian. It was now flying at an
altitude of 34,500 feet, at a speed of nearly 500 mph; the
weather was clear, with almost no air traffic at that early hour.
The three Elint operators in the bowels of the airplane had
started to conduct their tests, monitoring air-defense radars
and military communications stations along the flight path.
The airplane was near Winnsboro, Louisiana, when, at
approximately 5:10 A.M. (CDT), the pilot suddenly spotted "a
very intense white light with a light-blue tint" coming toward
the aircraft out of the southwest. As the pilot and co-pilot
watched, the luminous object cut across the airplane's flight
path, zoomed off in a northerly direction and quickly
disappeared.

In the darkness the incident would be unnerving because
the luminous object at first seemed to threaten a head-on
collision. Normally, ground-based military and civil air-traffic
control operators warn an aircraft flight crew when there is
other nearby traffic, but there had been no such warning this
time. In 1957 the airlines were not yet flying jetliners that
could operate at the RB-47's altitude, and in the early
morning hours few military aircraft are normally aloft. So it is
not surprising that the pilot and co-pilot quickly began to
speculate as to what the luminous object might have been or
that UFOs came under consideration. During the first half of
1957 there had been a sharp increase in the number of UFO
reports, and the total for the year would be nearly double the
annual figure for the previous four years.

In the RB-47 the pilot and co-pilot sit in a tandem cockpit
inside a plastic bubble canopy and can talk with one another

only through the internal intercom system, which also provides communications between the cockpit and other crew members. As the pilot and co-pilot discussed the luminous object and began to speculate as to whether it might have been a UFO, their conversation was overheard by Elint #3 operator Walter A. Tuchscherer. When McClure observed Tuchscherer laughing and asked why, he was told, "They're chasing flying saucers up front," according to McClure's recent recollection. So McClure put on his earphones and began to listen too. Then McClure began to recall the curious signal he had detected some time earlier near Biloxi, and an alternative explanation to an equipment malfunction began to emerge in his mind. *If* the radarlike signal had been coming from an *airborne* vehicle—the UFO—which had been passing the RB-47 in flight, this could explain the up-scope movement of the bearing display. This prompted McClure to tune his APR-9 Elint receiver back to 3,000 megacycles, the approximate frequency of the curious signal he had detected near Biloxi. Within a few seconds he had retuned to this part of the spectrum and began to search for a signal—but without success.

For roughly twenty minutes McClure searched, but not until approximately 5:30 A.M. (CDT) did he detect one—a signal with the characteristics of a CPS-6B radar such as he had observed near Biloxi. The ALA-6 indicated that the approximate bearing to the signal source was around 70 degrees to the right of the airplane's heading (265 degrees), or roughly northwest of the airplane. McClure jotted down on a piece of paper the specific characteristics of the signal:

• Frequency: 2,995 to 3,000 megacycles.
• Pulse length: 2 microseconds (millionths of a second).
• Pulse repetition rate: 600 pulses per second.

The signal-source was even *scanning* at a rate of 4 revolutions per minute, indicating that its antenna was rotating at the same 4 rpm speed of a CPS-6B radar. That is, the signal would appear briefly on the ALA-6 display, as the rotating antenna of the source pointed toward the RB-47, and then it would disappear until approximately fifteen seconds later.

McClure recalled that the UFO sighted twenty minutes

earlier had seemed to cross the RB-47's path and head north. *If* the signal that McClure was monitoring was coming from the UFO, the northwest bearing to the signal-source seemed to suggest that the UFO had since turned west and was now pacing the RB-47 on a parallel flight path somewhat north of the RB-47. McClure informed the pilot and co-pilot of the newly discovered signal, its similarity to the earlier one received near Biloxi that had exhibited such unusual behavior, and asked if the flight crew could see the UFO to the northwest. The pilot and co-pilot strained their eyes, searching for the luminous object they had seen twenty minutes earlier, while McClure continued to monitor the radarlike signal on his ALA-6 and to jot down measurements which would later be turned over to wing intelligence officer Elwin T. Piwetz when the crew finally returned to their home base.

At 5:35 A.M. the signal-source showed a bearing of approximately 68 degrees, and at 5:38 A.M. the bearing was approximately 45 degrees, indicating that the UFO was accelerating. (All these bearings are relative to the airplane's flight path, unless otherwise indicated.) Then, at 5:39 A.M., *approximately nine minutes after McClure had first picked up the CPS-6B-type signal over Texas,* the pilot "sighted a huge light which he estimated to be 5,000 feet below the aircraft at about 2 o'clock," according to the Piwetz intelligence report. This would place the light at a bearing of roughly 60 degrees to the right of the RB-47 flight path, not too different from the 45-degree bearing to the radarlike signal-source noted several minutes earlier by McClure. Then, at 5:40 A.M., a curious thing happened. McClure now had *two* identical signals, one coming from a bearing of 40 degrees and the other at approximately 70 degrees. This seemed to indicate that there were now two separate signal-sources, i.e., that the UFO had split into two separate objects, *each* radiating a radarlike signal. The report by intelligence officer Piwetz, based on his interview with the crew after they returned to base, says: "Aircraft commander and co-pilot saw these two objects at the same time with the same red color." However, RB-47 pilot Lewis D. Chase, in discussing the case with me in 1971, did not recall ever seeing more than one light.

Shortly after 5:40 A.M., Chase decided to abandon his original flight plan so he could pursue the UFO, i.e., the light, and obtained permission from the civil air-traffic control center at Dallas to head northwest. The RB-47's heading of 320 degrees would take the airplane toward Dallas and Fort Worth. The flight crew then contacted the USAF air-defense radar station at Duncanville, a few miles southwest of Dallas, and "requested all assistance possible" in its UFO pursuit. Two minutes later, at 5:42 A.M., McClure was again receiving only a *single* signal, at a relative bearing of 20 degrees, suggesting that the two portions of the UFO had rejoined one another. But approximately thirty seconds later, there were two signals again at bearings of 40 degrees and 70 degrees. Meanwhile, aircraft commander Chase pushed his throttle forward in an effort to gain on the light (UFO). By 5:44 A.M., Elint #2 equipment once again was showing only a *single* signal, with a bearing of approximately 50 degrees. At 5:48 A.M., the crew later reported to intelligence officer Piwetz, the Duncanville radar called the RB-47 and asked that it turn on its radar transponder to a specific transmitting code so the controllers could positively identify the RB-47 on their scopes.

Then, despite the light traffic at that early hour, *the Duncanville radar operators asked Chase for assistance in locating the UFO.* He replied that the light (UFO) seemed to be approximately ten nautical miles northwest of Dallas. The radar station "immediately confirmed the presence of object on their scopes," according to the Piwetz intelligence report. At approximately 5:50 A.M. the light seemed to stop moving and disappeared from view of the RB-47 crew. At approximately the same time, McClure's radarlike signal disappeared from the ALA-6 display, and the Duncanville radar station radioed that its unknown target had also disappeared from its scopes! One can imagine the excitement in the RB-47 at that moment.

The RB-47 pilot concluded that he must have overshot the UFO as he was flying between Dallas and Fort Worth, and so he initiated a long, sweeping turn in a counterclockwise direction to try to reacquire the light. At approximately 5:51

A.M., McClure once again picked up the radarlike signal on his ALA-6, which showed that the signal-source was at a bearing of approximately 160 degrees—behind the RB-47 and *in the general direction of Dallas.* At 5:52 A.M., as the RB-47 continued its turn, the bearing to the signal-source was approximately 200 degrees, still in the direction of Dallas. At 5:57 A.M., as the airplane passed over the town of Mineral Wells, the bearing to the signal-source was 300 degrees, still in the vicinity of Dallas. *Yet the flight crew had not been able to reacquire visual contact with the light that had disappeared seven minutes earlier. Nor did the unidentified target show up on the Duncanville radarscopes.*

Finally, at 5:58 A.M., aircraft commander Chase spotted a curious light, *not* in the vicinity of Dallas, where the ALA-6 indicated the radarlike signal was coming from, but southeast of Dallas. Chase obtained approval to descend to 20,000 feet and maneuver to try to get closer to the newly sighted light. But, so far as the Piwetz report indicates, the crew found nothing, although the sky was beginning to get light with the approaching sunrise. The RB-47 was running low on fuel, and could have refueled at a nearby air base if the crew had spotted something to justify continued investigation, but around 6 A.M. the pilot decided to abandon the chase and head back to the base in Kansas.

During the maneuvers of the last few minutes, McClure apparently lost contact with the radarlike signal, but he continued to search for it as the RB-47 headed north. Then, at approximately 6:20 A.M., he once again spotted the signal on his ALA-6 display, which showed the signal-source to be at a bearing varying between 180 and 190 degrees, *in the general direction of Dallas.* But no unidentified target showed up on the scopes of the Duncanville radar, nor were there any reported sightings by ground observers despite the near-daylight conditions. McClure continued to monitor the signal until approximately 6:40 A.M., *with its bearing always in the general direction of Dallas to the south.* Then, as the airplane neared Oklahoma City, the radarlike signal "faded rather abruptly," according to the crew's later report to intelligence officer Piwetz.

From Oklahoma City the flight back to Kansas was uneventful. The weary crew landed and subsequently recounted the strange events of the previous night. The case would remain unexplained for nearly fifteen years, until the AIAA article in the summer of 1971 served to spark my own investigation, to be discussed in the following chapter.

20 · The Famous RB-47 Case (Part 2)

The RB-47 UFO case was unique in one respect. There are many UFO cases in which aircraft crews have reported seeing mysterious lights and luminous objects, as earlier chapters have demonstrated. And there are numerous reports of unidentified blips showing up briefly on radarscopes, as discussed in Chapter 18. There are even a few reports of UFOs that seemed to emit staticlike radio signals that reportedly caused interference in radio or television sets. But in the vast inventory of many thousands of UFO reports, the RB-47 incident was the only one in which the UFO seemed to emit "intelligently controlled" radarlike signals.

McDonald, and seemingly the AIAA's UFO Subcommittee, assumed that *all* of the incidents involved in the RB-47 case were *interrelated*—the anomalous behavior of Elint #2 near Biloxi, the luminous object sighted over Louisiana sometime later, and the radarlike signals and light encountered still later over Texas. If this was true, then there could be no plausible explanation other than an extraterrestrial spaceship, outfitted with a giant CPS-6B-like radar. If the signal monitored near Biloxi came from an airborne source, the vehicle's ability to rapidly pass the RB-47, cruising at nearly 500 mph, indicated the vehicle must have been able to fly at supersonic speed. And neither the United States nor the Soviet Union in 1957 had supersonic aircraft large enough to carry a CPS-6B-type radar, even if there were any good reason to so outfit such an aircraft.*

On the other hand, if the curious events of July 17, 1957, were *not* all related, there might well be a prosaic, terrestrial explanation for the case. Because the radarlike signal was the unique characteristic of this case, I focused my initial effort on this aspect. From the data jotted down by McClure during the events over Texas, it was clear that the signal he was monitoring was almost identical to that of a CPS-6B air-defense radar. The only discrepancy, I would subsequently learn when I obtained technical data from the CPS-6B instruction book, was that the radar emitted pulses whose duration was one microsecond, whereas the duration of the unidentified signal-source pulses, as measured by McClure, was two microseconds. But in later discussions with Rod Simons, an Elint specialist with the AIL division of Cutler-Hammer, which developed and produced the APR-9 receiver that McClure was using, I learned that this discrepancy was not consequential. Simons explained that ground reflections could cause "smearing," so that a one-microsecond pulse could appear to be two microseconds long. Thus for all practical purposes the signal that McClure was monitoring over Texas was *identical* to that of a CPS-6B air-defense radar.

This prompted me to wonder if there had been any CPS-6B air-defense radars in the vicinity of the RB-47's flight path at the time that McClure was obtaining the signal. If not, then one could quickly rule out any possibility that the radarlike signal might have been coming from a conventional

---

* During my investigation, I checked with Dr. George Rappaport, former technical director of the USAF's airborne electronic warfare laboratory, to determine if the USAF had ever built any airborne equipment which could generate a CPS-6B-type signal. He told me that he was not aware of any such equipment, or any good reason for building such a system.

CPS-6B radar. I called the Air Defense Command headquarters in Colorado Springs, Colorado, and asked them to dig back into their records and tell me if there had been any CPS-6B radars operating along the Gulf Coast and in Texas during July, 1957. In early August of 1971, ADC informed me that there had not been any CPS-6Bs in that region during mid-1957, but an improved version of the CPS-6B, with *identical signal characteristics*—called the FPS-10—*was* then being used in Texas. In fact, there were four such FPS-10 radars installed in Texas, *and one of these was located at Duncanville, near Dallas.* This indicated that there were a number of *possible* ground-based radar sources for the signal that McClure had monitored. It also meant that if a UFO outfitted with a powerful CPS-6B/FPS-10-type radar "mimic" had been flying over Texas during the early morning of July 17, 1957, it would almost certainly have caused intense interference with some or all of those air-defense radars. Yet no such interference had been reported, so far as I could learn!

Although one or more of the four FPS-10 radars in Texas could conceivably have been responsible for the radarlike signal that McClure observed on his Elint equipment, an extensive investigation would be required to determine if there was a direct cause-effect relationship, or lack of it. The first step would be to determine the flight path of the RB-47, to try to establish its approximate geographic location at key times. Then it would be necessary to obtain data on the coverage pattern of the CPS-6B/FPS-10 radar, and plot this for the four radars of this type which were operating in Texas in the summer of 1957. Only then could the signal-source bearings that McClure had jotted down be used to determine if they consistently "pointed" to one of the Texas radars. This seemed a relatively simple task when my investigation began, but it would prove far more difficult because of the complex nature of the CPS-6B/FPS-10 radar.

From the USAF Archives I obtained a copy of the RB-47 case file, including a copy of the report by intelligence officer Piwetz, who had interviewed the crew shortly after they had returned to base. Unfortunately, the crew never had an opportunity to check the Piwetz report for accuracy, and it contains two obvious errors, one of which may be typographical. But at least the information was obtained while the crew recollections were fresh. Additionally, aircraft commander Chase had filled out a detailed UFO report form on September 10, 1957, approximately two months after the incident, which proved extremely useful. In this UFO report form, Chase had drawn a rough sketch showing the RB-47's approximate flight path, and he had included important data on airplane speed, heading, winds aloft, etc., which would be needed to reconstruct the flight path more precisely. I corresponded extensively with Chase, now retired and living in Spokane, Washington, during the fall of 1971 as we jointly tried to reconstruct the airplane's flight path and resolve ambiguities in the Chase and Piwetz reports—especially during the more hectic part of the flight when the RB-47 headed northwest to pursue the UFO (light).

Chase was extremely helpful. He did not exhibit a deep commitment to the extraterrestrial hypothesis, but it was clear that he had been shaken by the incident at the time and remained mystified more than a decade later. I informed Chase of my basic views on UFOs and sensed some concern on his part that I was intent on "debunking" the incident at all costs. Yet he cooperated fully, if somewhat cautiously. From the Air Defense Command I learned that the CPS-6B and its improved FPS-10 version had been manufactured by General Electric's Heavy Military Electronics Department, whose general manager, Tom Paganelli, was an old friend. When I sought his assistance, he put me in touch with two engineers who had been involved in the design of the radars—Paul J. Teich and C. I. Robbins. They in turn provided photocopies of portions of the official instruction book for the CPS-6B and FPS-10 radars which described their key characteristics.

The CPS-6B/FPS-10 was really three separate radars combined into a single multifunction system, with three separate antennas rotating on a common pedestal. One radar antenna radiated a narrow beam designed to detect aircraft at very long range. The other two antennas worked as partners, with one being tilted so its beams converged with those from the other antenna to form a V shape. This made it possible to roughly determine the approximate altitude of a target by measuring the length of time required for the target to transit from one beam to the other. At low altitude, near the bottom of the V-beams, transit time would be short, while at higher altitudes passage time would be proportionately greater. The tilted antenna actually radiated *two* main beams which overlapped to provide coverage at high and low altitudes. Its companion antenna, which generated the vertical beam, actually consisted of *three* slightly overlapping main beams: a vertical-upper beam, a vertical-center beam and a vertical-lower beam.

Thus, as the CPS-6B/FPS-10 radar antennas rotated, they radiated a total of *six* main beams, each with its own distinctive coverage pattern. Each beam was generated by its own transmitter, and each had its own receiver to listen for echoes returned from targets. To prevent interference among the six transmitters, each operated in a different segment of the frequency spectrum. The frequency of the radarlike signal that McClure had monitored over Texas was 2,995 to 3,000 megacycles. If that signal came from one of the FPS-10 radars in Texas, it must have come from the *vertical-center beam* because the other five beams operated at much different frequencies. This emerged from my study of the instruction book, which showed that the vertical-center beam could be operated anywhere in the frequency band of 2,992 to 3,019 megacycles, depending on where its transmitter was tuned. (The transmitters of nearby radars would be set at slightly different frequencies to minimize the possibility of mutual interference.)

So my attention focused on the vertical-center beam. In reality, a radar antenna not only generates the main beam but it also produces some smaller, *unwanted* beams which are called "side-lobes" because they appear on each side of the main beam. Additionally, even the main beam may have imperfections due to energy spilling off the main beam, or what is called a "coma-lobe." To determine at what time during the RB-47's flight it should have been receiving a signal from one of the FPS-10 radars, and at what time it could not, it would be necessary to determine the radiation patterns of the side-lobes and coma-lobe as well as the main beam. GE's Robbins, who had originally been involved in the design and test of the FPS-10 antennas, dug into his dusty files and found the information needed. The data indicated that as the antenna rotated, it produced a vertical-center beam radiation pattern at the RB-47's 34,500-foot altitude that resembled three concentric doughnuts. (See Plate 15c.) The innermost and outermost doughnuts were very thin, because the side-lobes that produced them were thin, while the center doughnut, produced by the main beam and its coma-lobe, was very wide.

Whenever the RB-47 was in a geographic location illuminated by one of the three doughnut-shaped radar patterns, McClure's ALA-6 should have received a radarlike signal of the type he observed. When the airplane was not within one of the three doughnut-shaped regions, there should have been no radarlike signal. *If McClure received a CPS-6B/FPS-10 radarlike signal only when the RB-47 was within one of the three doughnut-shaped areas, then the signal was clearly coming from one of the ground-based air-defense radars and not from a UFO.*

It was during the fall of 1971 when I first plotted the RB-47's flight path on a standard aeronautical chart. Then I plotted the location of the four FPS-10 radars known to have been operating in Texas in mid-1957. At this point the finger of suspicion began to point to the Duncanville radar, just southwest of Dallas, for the other three Texas radars were beyond receiving range, especially during later portions of the RB-47 flight. Then, using small arrows, I began to plot the bearing angles to the signal-source that McClure had hurriedly jotted down, which were contained in the original Piwetz report. *It quickly became apparent that all of the arrows were pointing in the general direction of the Duncanville radar, near Dallas!* (See Plates 16–17.) Not every arrow pointed precisely toward Duncanville. But by this time I had borrowed a copy of the ALA-6 instruction book, through the assistance of Ken Klippel, an official of Hoffman Electronics, which produced the equipment, and it revealed that an ALA-6 operator could only obtain an *approximate bearing angle* to a signal-source because of the nature of the display itself. (See Plate 18a.) Additionally, because the bearing angle was measured and displayed relative to the airplane's fore-aft axis, brief maneuvers of the aircraft could introduce discrepancies.

If the Duncanville radar was indeed the source of the signal that McClure was monitoring over Texas, it would explain many curious aspects of the incident, including the following:

- Why the signal had not been detected shortly after 5:10 A.M., immediately after the encounter with the luminous object over Louisiana when McClure first began to search for a signal, and why it was not until 5:30 A.M. that he first detected the signal. It was not until approximately this time that the RB-47 would first have entered the outermost doughnut coverage of the FPS-10 radar at Duncanville.

- Why McClure's records showed no signal for the five-minute period between 5:30 A.M. and 5:35 A.M. During that time the RB-47 would have left the coverage of the outermost doughnut and would not yet have entered the center-doughnut coverage region.

- Why McClure lost the signal at approximately 5:50 A.M. as the airplane neared Dallas. At that time the RB-47 would have been too close to the Duncanville radar to be illuminated by even the innermost doughnut coverage.

- Why McClure reacquired the signal at approximately 5:51 A.M. The RB-47 had once again entered one of the doughnut-shaped coverage regions of the Duncanville vertical-center beam, and now the bearing to the signal-source was behind the RB-47 and thus pointing in the general direction of Dallas and Duncanville.

- Why the signal was later lost as the RB-47 approached Dallas, headed north to its home base, and then reacquired by McClure a few miles north of Dallas, and why the bearing to the signal-source was to the rear of the aircraft and in the general direction of Dallas and Duncanville.

· Why the signal "faded rather abruptly" as the RB-47 neared Oklahoma City. At that location the airplane would have flown beyond the most distant coverage of the Duncanville radar's vertical-center beam.

But what explanation is there for the brief periods when McClure reported that he was receiving the radarlike signal from *two* sources at slightly different bearings? The ALA-6 instruction book provides the explanation on pages 30 and 33, where it cautions the operator that he may briefly get *two* bearing indications from a *single* ground radar. The instruction book warns that the radar beam can be reflected from large metallic objects on the ground, such as a gasoline storage tank. (See Plate 18b.) When this happens, the ALA-6 will receive both a direct and a reflected signal, each at a different bearing, until the airplane position changes sufficiently.

However, all of this leaves unexplained the unknown target that had reportedly appeared briefly on the scopes of the Duncanville radar station, according to the crew account. As discussed in Chapter 18, there are numerous possible causes of spurious targets, but the formal report filed by the commander of the Duncanville radar station to Air Defense Command Headquarters suggests to me a case of mistaken identity. This official report, contained in the RB-47 case files, was sent by wire at 8:45 A.M. (CST), barely four hours after the incident. The commander's report states: "HAD NEGATIVE CONTACT WITH THE OBJECT." * In other words, the commander *denied that a UFO had been sighted on the radarscopes*—at least the one the RB-47 had been chasing. This seems to contradict the RB-47 crew report that station

---

* The McDonald/AIAA account of the RB-47 incident neglected to mention this official denial by the commander of the Duncanville radar station.

operators briefly had an unidentified target on their scopes. However, it is not necessary to question the veracity of the crew report to explain this apparent contradiction. If, in the excitement of the moment, the radar operators saw an unidentified target that was *later* identified, perhaps as a civil aircraft, the commander might be too embarrassed to admit the error and could try to dismiss his station's involvement with a brief "HAD NEGATIVE CONTACT WITH THE OBJECT."

Investigation showed that American Airlines flight #966 was scheduled to land at the Dallas airport (Love Field) at 6:00 A.M. The airport is located a few miles northwest of Dallas, in the general direction of the light the RB-47 was pursuing. And it was just northwest of Dallas where the RB-47 crew reported overflying the light. If American Airlines flight #966 was on time, it would have been approaching the Dallas airport at the time that the Duncanville radar operators noted an unidentified target in the same location. By 5:50 A.M., when the target disappeared from the Duncanville scopes, the airliner would have been on final approach and below the coverage of the Duncanville radar. On final approach, the airliner's landing lights would have been turned on, and this could explain the RB-47 crew's observation that it had overflown a bright light northwest of Dallas.

By 1971, when I launched my investigation, neither American Airlines nor the Federal Aviation Administration records were available to show whether flight #966 was on time that morning. But the weather was clear, except for some clouds to the south, and at that early hour the traffic would have been very light, so it seems safe to presume that the flight was preparing to land at the Dallas airport a few minutes before 6 A.M. Later, when the morning shift arrived at the Duncanville station, the commander, after being informed of the UFO incident, might have thought to check with the Dallas airport tower, only to learn that the unidentified target was American flight #966. By that time the RB-47 would already have been outside station communication range, and the commander would not be anxious to broadcast the fact that his operators had mistaken an ordinary airliner for a UFO.

At this point in my investigation, it was clear that the

radarlike signal that McClure had monitored while the RB-47 was over Texas, from 5:30 A.M. until it finally disappeared more than an hour later, had been coming from the FPS-10 radar at Duncanville. But it was equally clear that the Duncanville radar could not possibly have been the source of the signal that McClure first detected as the RB-47 had earlier approached Biloxi. The Duncanville and other FPS-10 radars located in Texas were too distant to be detected by the ALA-6 on board the RB-47. There were air-defense radars in Mississippi, Louisiana and Florida, but they were of a different type that operated at a different frequency. When I finally located McClure, who had since retired from the USAF and was living in Houston, Texas, he quickly resolved this problem. McClure told me that a CPS-6B radar was installed at Keesler Air Force Base, near Biloxi, and used for training electronic countermeasures equipment operators. It was operated by the USAF's Training Command, rather than by the Air Defense Command, which explained why it was not included in the list of radars which the ADC had earlier supplied to me. It was because McClure knew that there was a CPS-6B installed near Biloxi that he had tuned to its frequency as the RB-47 flew north from the Gulf.

When I plotted the flight path of the RB-47 and the approximate bearings to the source of the radarlike signal, as McClure had subsequently recalled them for intelligence officer Piwetz, it became apparent that the radarlike signal could have been coming from the CPS-6B at Biloxi *if* the ALA-6 had been malfunctioning in such a way as to display the reciprocal (direct opposite) of the true bearing to the radar. To determine whether a malfunction of this type was possible, I immersed myself in a detailed study of the ALA-6 instruction book to gain a better understanding of the operating principles of the equipment.

In addition to the characteristics of a radar signal discussed earlier, the signal is also "polarized," usually in a horizontal or a vertical direction to improve performance for the particular mission to be accomplished. For maximum possible sensitivity, the polarization of the receiving antenna in an Elint equipment such as the ALA-6 should be the same as that of the radar signal being monitored. For this reason, the ALA-6 employed two separate antennas, one of which was horizontally polarized while the other was vertically polarized. The Elint operator could select the one which provided optimum sensitivity. These two antennas are mounted "back to back" under the belly of the airplane on the same rotating pedestal which spins at 150 rpm or 300 rpm, as selected by the operator. When one of the two back-to-back antennas is pointing to the right broadside position, the other will be pointing to the left broadside position, so that they are always "looking" in *opposite directions.* But *only one* of the two antennas is in active use at any time. The choice of which antenna is to be connected to the APR-9 receiver is made by the ALA-6 operator by means of a small "toggle" switch on the panel of his equipment.

If the operator selects vertical polarization, then a twenty-eight-volt signal is sent to a device called a "relay" in the antenna assembly. This twenty-eight-volt signal is applied to an electromagnet in the relay which actuates a mechanism that connects the vertically polarized antenna to the APR-9 receiver. If the operator throws the toggle switch to the horizontal polarization position, this removes the twenty-eight-volt signal from the relay's electromagnet and allows a mechanical spring to exert a force to connect the horizontally polarized antenna to the APR-9 receiver. (For readers with a technical background, a schematic diagram of this portion of the ALA-6 is shown in Plate 19. The antenna switching relay is K-701.)

To enable the ALA-6 to display the correct bearing angle of the radar signal, two things are required. First, the control circuits for the cathode-ray-tube display must be "informed" of the angular position of the antenna at the instant the signal is detected, and second, the display-control circuits must know *which* of the two antennas is being used. A small electrical device called a "synchro," which is driven from the rotating antenna shaft, provides signals that indicate the angular position of the antenna shaft. But the signals supplied by the synchro must be switched to correctly indicate *which of the two antennas* is being used. Otherwise the display would not know whether, for example, to show the ground radar signal as coming from the right or the left side of the airplane.

This switching function, to reflect which antenna is in use, is performed by another relay, K-301 on the schematic diagram, which is operated by the same toggle switch used to actuate K-701, which selects the desired antenna. When the operator selects the vertically polarized antenna, the toggle switch sends a twenty-eight-volt signal to K-301 which actuates its electromagnet and causes a small metal arm to pivot and close metal contacts that connect the synchro signals to the display with the correct polarity for the vertically polarized antenna. When the operator throws the toggle switch to the horizontally polarized position, this removes the twenty-eight volts from relay K-301, enabling a mechanical spring to force the pivot-arm to change position and close another set of contacts which reverse the polarity of the signals from the antenna-shaft synchro.

If you have found the preceding technical details a bit heavy going, never mind. The significant thing is that *IF either one of these two relays should fail to operate properly, the ALA-6 display will be 180 degrees in error in showing the bearing angle to the radar being monitored.* That is, if *either* relay should malfunction, the ALA-6 could show the radar to be on the right-hand side of the airplane when in reality it was located on the left-hand side, or vice versa. Equally important, not only would the displayed bearing be 180 degrees in error, but as the airplane moves past the ground radar, *the displayed bearing would move up-scope, rather than the normal down-scope direction.* (To better understand this curious behavior, the reader is referred to Plate 20.)

If either one of these two relays had briefly malfunctioned during the RB-47's mission as it approached and flew past the CPS-6B radar installed near Biloxi, this would fully explain why McClure observed a bearing that pointed *away from* Biloxi, and why the bearing angle moved *up-scope* instead of down-scope. During World War II, I spent several years as a field engineer for General Electric working on aviation-electronics (avionics) equipment. From this first-hand experience, and more than thirty years spent in the avionics field, I knew that relays were one of the most unreliable devices used in avionics equipment in the early postwar years, when the ALA-6 was designed and manufactured. Today, relays are much more reliable, largely because they are now installed in hermetically sealed enclosures to prevent dirt, moisture and ice from interfering with their proper functioning. But at the time the ALA-6 was manufactured, relays were exposed to such contaminants and were a major source of equipment malfunctions. So it is not surprising that the ALA-6 instruction book, in the section devoted to possible equipment malfunctions, *specifically listed the type of symptoms that might be encountered if K-301 or K-701 malfunctioned.*

There was one obstacle to accepting this explanation for the anomalous behavior of the ALA-6 encountered by McClure near Biloxi. When the RB-47 was flying over Texas approximately an hour later, the ALA-6 bearing indications all pointed in the general direction of the Duncanville radar, which indicated that the Elint equipment was functioning properly at that time. Was it possible that relay K-301 or K-701 might have malfunctioned briefly in the vicinity of Biloxi, yet a short time later could have been operating properly? A relay is an electromechanical device which involves a small mechanical pivot movement to switch connections. The movement in one direction is produced by applying a voltage to an electromagnet, while movement in the opposite direction results from removing the voltage and depending on the force of a mechanical spring. The RB-47 took off from its Kansas air base on a hot, humid July day. As the airplane climbed to its 34,500-foot cruising altitude, the outside temperature to which the ALA-6 antenna assembly was exposed would quickly drop to sub-zero values, turning any accumulated moisture within the equipment into ice. If that ice formed in K-301 or K-701, it could freeze the moving element and prevent it from responding to the twenty-eight-volt signal—*initially.*

But as the equipment continued to operate, heat generated by voltage applied to the relay electromagnet when the operator selected vertical polarization would melt the ice, and in time would free the relay to function properly. So this is one possible explanation for an initial malfunction when the ALA-6 was first turned on near Biloxi, which could have cured itself a few minutes later. There are other possibilities, such as a poorly soldered connection which can give good electrical contact sometimes and be an open circuit at other times. (Perhaps the reader has, on occasion, "cured" a malfunctioning TV set by giving it a sharp blow.) Later, when I prepared a detailed report on my analysis of the RB-47 case and sent a copy of it to a Bendix official, he replied: "One of our engineers here, Jim Watson, read the RB-47 case write-up and asked that I convey to you his comments. He was an instructor for the Air Force, teaching maintenance on the ALA-6 unit, and he said, 'Had I been asked what could have caused the 180° ambiguity, I would have immediately responded that the most probable cause would have been a failure of the K-301 relay.' " Coming from a man who knew the ALA-6 intimately, and taught others how to troubleshoot it, this was a welcome endorsement.

If, as now seemed likely, the radarlike signal monitored by McClure near Biloxi had come from the CPS-6B radar near there and its anomalous behavior resulted from a temporary malfunction of a relay in the ALA-6, and if the radarlike signal monitored over Texas had come from the Duncanville radar, as now seemed certain, then the once-puzzling RB-47 case boiled down to the luminous object that had streaked across the airplane's path over Louisiana and the light to the northwest that the pilot had later spotted after McClure detected the radarlike signal over Texas. The luminous object sighted over Louisiana had the typical characteristics of a meteor/fireball—similar to those described in earlier chapters. The bright light that had been sighted to the northwest some twenty-nine minutes later (5:39 A.M.), and which subsequently prompted the flight crew to change plans and head in that direction, did not suggest a meteor. And at 5:39 A.M. the American Airlines flight #966 would not yet have been in the vicinity of Dallas. Could it possibly have been a celestial body, I wondered? Because Robert Sheaffer (Chap-

ter 15) is not only a UFO photo specialist but studied
astronomy, I enlisted his aid.

He wrote back to say that the star Vega would have been at
an azimuth of approximately 300 degrees for an observer in
central Texas at that hour—or roughly northwest of the
RB-47, at an elevation angle of approximately 27 degrees.
Vega would have been "a brilliant star, *brighter* than the first
magnitude," according to Sheaffer. Whether the bright light
to the northwest sighted at 5:39 A.M. was in fact the brilliant
star Vega, or something else, can never be established for
sure. Normally, an experienced flight crew would not mistake
a brilliant star for a UFO. But after the encounter with the
luminous object over Louisiana, and with McClure's ALA-6
indicating a source of a radarlike signal to the northwest and
the anxious flight crew searching for visual contact, under
those conditions Vega must be considered a possible candi-
date. Sometime later, after the RB-47 had flown past Dallas,
had circled around Mineral Wells and was heading southeast,
the flight crew had reported seeing another light. Sheaffer had
also checked his star charts and found that the star Rigel,
almost as brilliant as Vega, was just rising above the horizon
in the southeast at an azimuth of 105 degrees. The crew had
reported clouds to the south, and these could have given
Rigel an unusual appearance.

By mid-November I had completed my analysis of the
puzzling RB-47 case and had explained it, at least to my
satisfaction. But the acid test would be the reactions of
Chase, the aircraft commander, and McClure, the ALA-6
Elint operator. I mailed to both men an eighteen-page
analysis—slightly more detailed than the account here—and
invited their candid reactions. I had some doubts that Chase
would accept my conclusions, because he had "stuck his neck
out" in first reporting the incident on return to base, and
undoubtedly had been subject to some ridicule because some
people believe that only "kooks" report UFOs. Chase had
journeyed to the University of Colorado at his own expense
to present the case to its experts, and the case had been
hailed by Dr. McDonald as one of the most impressive of all

time. Finally, the American Institute of Aeronautics and Astronautics had recently singled out the RB-47 case for publication as one that seemed to defy explanation.

It was therefore a pleasant surprise to receive Chase's prompt response, in a letter dated December 8, 1971, which offered the following appraisal of my analysis:

> I think this study is an excellent work! I apologize for fearing you would not go in deep enough with your analysis. Congratulations, and my thanks, for giving me a plausible explanation for the events that happened to my crew that night in 1957.

McClure's reaction was equally heartening:

> I am certain that for some reason we had intercepted a ground signal that moved up-scope. I know that once we were near Dallas and [flying] North toward Forbes [Air Force Base], the signals were undoubtedly CPS-6B/FPS-10 air defense radars. I do not believe any UFO was emitting these signals.

Copies of my eighteen-page analysis-report, including the endorsements by Chase and McClure, were then mailed to the secretary of the AIAA's UFO Subcommittee for distribution to its members, and to Dr. Joachim P. Kuettner, the subcommittee chairman, on January 6, 1972. I fully recognized that Kuettner and his group might be a little embarrassed to discover there was a plausible terrestrial explanation for the RB-47 case. But I assumed that the UFO Subcommittee would, in the tradition of science, be anxious to publish an abbreviated version of my report so that thousands of AIAA members who had read the original account would at least have the opportunity to learn of a possible explanation that did not involve a spaceship from another world. It was more than a month later, on February 15, before Kuettner wrote to acknowledge receipt of the RB-47 analysis. (Kuettner was then director of advanced research projects for the environmental research laboratories of the National Oceanic and Atmospheric Administration, in Boulder, Colorado.) In

Kuettner's letter he said that while he would reserve final judgment, he was impressed by "your thorough analysis, especially of the radar observations," and he commented also on the "great amount of work and ingenuity" that had gone into the analysis.

On April 7, 1972, following my investigation of the St. Louis UFO/Iowa Fireball case (Chapter 5), I sent copies of my report on that case to the secretary of the UFO Subcommittee so they could be distributed to its members. Because I believed that the luminous object that had streaked across the RB-47's path over Louisiana was a meteor, I felt that the St. Louis case would demonstrate that experienced flight crews, even in broad daylight, could mistake a fireball for a squadron of UFOs. In sharp contrast to the prompt responses to my analysis that had come from Chase and McClure, there was no comment from the UFO Subcommittee. On May 19 I wrote Kuettner, pointing out that it had then been four months since the RB-47 report had been sent to him and the subcommittee members and that I was anxious to obtain their critical comments and to respond to any questions they had.

It was more than a month later, on June 22, before Kuettner replied. He said the reaction of subcommittee members "is generally quite positive, and actually complimentary concerning your radar analysis. Negative comments refer to the assumed self-recovery of the relay, the treatment of the various visual observations and the polemic style. . . ." Kuettner said he was moving to England for an assignment with the World Meteorological Organization and would send me more detailed comments once he got settled there. It was not until November 22, nearly five months later, that Kuettner found time to write and supply me with some of the specific comments and criticisms made by subcommittee members on my RB-47 analysis, which had been submitted to them nearly a year earlier.

Kuettner wrote that my explanation for the anomalous display and movement of the bearing indication on the ALA-6 when the RB-47 was in the vicinity of Biloxi was considered "rather convincing." And that my conclusion that

the CPS-6B/FPS-10-like radar signals monitored after 5:30
A.M. while the airplane was over Texas came from the
air-defense radar at Duncanville "makes a lot of sense."
Kuettner wrote that some members of the subcommittee
disagreed and considered it unlikely that relay K-301 or K-701
could malfunction briefly near Biloxi and then operate
properly later in the flight. "This is considered a little too
'far-out' by some of our committee members," he wrote. But
Kuettner added that "one should not object too heavily to
this as long as no further 'far-out' assumptions are needed.

"It is here where our committee members become quite
critical," Kuettner wrote. "That an experienced pilot would
[mis]take first a meteor for a UFO (an astronomer disagreed),
that the same pilot (who sees the landing lights of aircraft
every day) would then pursue a landing American Airliner as
an Unidentified Flying Object—after having sighted another
'huge light' 5,000 feet below the aircraft at 10:39 GMT [5:39
A.M. CDT] for which no interpretation exists—all at about
the same time at which the relay failure corrects itself—seems
just a little too much for my committee to accept. . . ."
Earlier chapters in this book have shown that experienced
flight crews can mistake a meteor for a UFO and, in at least
one case, can even imagine that the UFO has illuminated
windows (Chapter 1). The Navy/Gander case, discussed in
Chapter 6, illustrates that an experienced flight crew can even
mistake a partly illuminated moon for a giant UFO that
seemed to be zooming toward them. Chapters 9 and 18
presented cases that show that Venus and other celestial
bodies have often been mistaken for UFOs.

As for the relay malfunction, my own first-hand experience
with such devices as a field engineer and troubleshooter
during World War II has shown that such malfunctions can
be temporary. As noted in my detailed report to the
subcommittee, the relay malfunction appeared to have cor-
rected itself shortly after the RB-47 passed Biloxi, because
McClure used the ALA-6 after the airplane turned west near
Meridian, to take bearings to other air-defense radars (not of
the CPS-6B/FPS-10 type) in Mississippi and Louisiana, and
the equipment appeared to be functioning properly. I grant

that my explanation assumes a combination of several infrequent, but not rare, events. But the fact that a combination of infrequent events does occasionally occur is evidenced by the existence of the word "coincidence" to describe such a situation. For example, the chances of a person's being struck by lightning and surviving are slim, so it is not surprising that few living persons can boast of being struck *twice* by lightning. Roy C. Sullivan, a ranger in the Shenandoah National Park, Virginia, had the distinction of being the only person known to have survived being struck by lightning on *four* different occasions. On August 7, 1973, Sullivan saw a gathering thunderstorm, got into his car and began to drive in the *opposite* direction, for he is understandably fearful of being caught in a thunderstorm. Perhaps you have already guessed what happened next: a lightning bolt shot out of the clouds and hit Sullivan for the *fifth* time, and once again he survived!

The subcommittee members found my explanation "a little too 'far-out.' " Inasmuch as they have never offered any other, I am forced to conclude that they find it easier to accept the only alternative explanation—that a spaceship from another world had been outfitted with a large, powerful CPS-6B-type radar and sent on a long mission to Earth simply to play mischievous games with the RB-47. If *any* type of vehicle equipped with a CPS-6B/FPS-10-type radar was flying in the skies over Texas during the early morning of July 17, 1957, it should have produced intense interference with one or more of the similar air-defense radars then operating in the same area. Yet there were no reports of any such interference! Nor has there ever been a repetition of the RB-47 incident.

Finally, Kuettner's letter got around to the all-important issue of whether the many AIAA members who had read McDonald's original account of the RB-47 incident would be given comparable exposure to my proposed explanation: "Regarding publication of your article, half of the committee is against getting involved in it since it means breaking with our policy not to be drawn into controversial interpretations. The others are of the opinion that we may recommend to the AIAA the publication of a *very much shortened version* as a

'Letter to the Editor.' . . . My own conclusion—and the position I will take—is that your ECM [radar-Elint] interpretation is of such quality that it deserves publication, in a *very much shortened version*, as a 'Letter to the Editor.' Those interested in more details may write to you to obtain your fuller version." (Emphasis added.)

Kuettner and his UFO Subcommittee had recommended the publication of McDonald's long detailed account of the RB-47 incident, which claimed that the airplane "was followed by an unidentified object for a distance of well over 700 mi." McDonald's account had occupied *almost five full pages* in *Astronautics & Aeronautics* magazine. I had assumed that I would be given comparable space for the much more difficult task of offering an explanation and providing enough detail to support my analysis. Instead, all that Kuettner and his subcommittee were willing to recommend was a short Letter to the Editor! I replied to Kuettner's letter and politely turned down his offer. I had decided instead to write this book so that the results of many months of painstaking effort would not have to be boiled down to a short "Letter to the Editor." And AIAA members would at least have an opportunity to read an alternative explanation to the one suggested by the author of the RB-47 article.

Unless there is a change in AIAA policy, it will be Kuettner who decides whether this book will be reviewed in *Astronautics & Aeronautics*, and if it survives this hurdle, Kuettner will select the person who will appraise my book. But perhaps elected AIAA officials will take a fresh look at the AIAA's involvement and past approach to the UFO question.

21 · UFOs over England (Bentwaters and Lakenheath)

The Bentwaters-Lakenheath UFO incidents have been characterized as *"the most puzzling and unusual case in the radar-visual files"* by the University of Colorado UFO study group. Its final report added: *"The apparently rational, intelligent behavior of the UFO suggests a mechanical device of unknown origin as the most probable explanation of this sighting.* However, in view of the inevitable fallibility of witnesses, more conventional explanations of this report cannot be ruled out." (Emphasis added.) The case involved a reported series of radar and visual sightings at two air bases in England, one at Bentwaters, near the Channel coast, and the other some thirty-five miles to the northwest at Lakenheath. The incidents occurred in 1956 during the late evening of August 13 and the early morning of August 14. The late Dr. McDonald often cited this case to support his extraterrestrial views on UFOs, and Dr. Hynek has publicly hailed it as a "classic." The AIAA's UFO Subcommittee was equally impressed, and so the case was selected for publication and described in considerable detail in the September, 1971, issue of AIAA's *Astronautics & Aeronautics* magazine.

Gordon D. Thayer, who had investigated the Bentwaters-Lakenheath case for the University of Colorado, was selected to write the account for the AIAA. (Thayer, like UFO Subcommittee chairman Kuettner, is a scientist at the National Oceanic and Atmospheric Administration environmental research laboratories in Boulder, Colorado.) Thayer summed up his appraisal of the case as follows: "In conclusion, with two highly redundant contacts—the first with ground radar, combined with both ground and airborne visual observers, and the second with airborne radar, an airborne visual observer, and two different ground radars—*the Bentwaters-Lakenheath UFO incident represents one of the most significant radar-visual UFO cases.* Taking into consideration the high credibility of information and the cohesiveness and continuity of accounts, combined with a high degree of 'strangeness,' it is also certainly one of the most disturbing UFO incidents known today." (Emphasis added.)

The case was brought to the attention of the University of Colorado group in mid-1968 by a letter from the man who had been the watch-supervisor at the Lakenheath radar station at the time of the incidents. In his letter the former noncommissioned USAF officer recalled many of the events that had occurred twelve years earlier in great detail, but did not remember the date of the incident or even the month. When the original case file was located in the USAF's Project Blue Book office, it was found to contain telegraphic reports from the Bentwaters and Lakenheath USAF bases made shortly after the incidents, plus more detailed reports, based on interviews with some of the principals, that had been submitted several weeks later.

At one point in Thayer's AIAA article he described these original reports as being "confusing." They certainly are, especially some of the telegraphic reports submitted immediately after the incident. But they have the important advantage of being based on the recollections of events that had occurred only a few hours or a few days before. The confusion and ambiguities probably reflect uncertainties over exactly what had occurred. In any event it is difficult to understand Thayer's subsequent comment on "the high credibility of the information and the cohesiveness and continuity of accounts . . ." where he had earlier described them as "confusing."

Because these original reports are the only available source on what happened at Bentwaters, Thayer had no choice but to use them for this portion of his account. But for later events at Lakenheath, Thayer explained that he decided to rely primarily on the twelve-year-old recollections of the watch-supervisor because these were "the most coherent account of events at Lakenheath." This is true, but as Thayer himself admitted, there are a number of discrepancies between these twelve-year-old recollections and information obtained shortly after the incidents. For example, the watch-supervisor said the other radar station involved was at Sculthorpe when in fact it was at Bentwaters. Generally, I prefer the accuracy of the original reports to the coherency of twelve-year-old recollections, for reasons illustrated in the Gander case (Chapter 6). Therefore my reconstruction of events leans most heavily on the original reports. For incidents at Bentwaters there is scant difference from Thayer's account except for an unimportant variation of several minutes in the timing of one radar UFO sighting. There were three radar-UFO incidents at Bentwaters, involving an MPN-11 airport surveillance radar which has a maximum range of approximately sixty miles. These are referred to below, for convenience, as B-1, B-2 and B-3.

(B-1): At approximately 9:30 P.M. local time, Technical Sergeant Elmer L. Whenry, one of several radar operators on duty, spotted twelve to fifteen unidentified "blips" on his scope. These were located roughly eight miles southwest of the station and spread out over a distance of six to seven miles. (See Plate 21.) As he watched during subsequent scans of the radar, the cluster of blips moved at speeds of 80 to 125 mph in a northeasterly direction. When they reached a position approximately fourteen miles northeast of the station, the intensity of the blips "faded considerably." Then, at a distance of forty miles northeast of the station, the twelve to fifteen blips *merged* into a *single* large blip, which remained motionless for approximately ten to fifteen minutes. Then the single blip began to move northeast again for approximately five to six miles, then stopped again for three to five minutes before resuming movement in the same direction. Finally, at approximately 9:55 P.M., the blip moved off the display, corresponding to the maximum radar range of sixty miles. The incident had lasted for approximately *twenty-five minutes.*

(B-2): At approximately 9:30 P.M., as Whenry watched the slow-moving cluster of blips, another operator, Airman Second Class John Vaccare, Jr., spotted a single blip twenty-five to thirty miles southeast of the radar. During the next scan four seconds later, a blip appeared northwest of the previous position, and in subsequent scans the blip seemed to be advancing on a 295-degree heading at extremely high speed. After thirty seconds the blip was fifteen to twenty miles northwest of the radar, where it suddenly disappeared completely from the scope. If this series of blips which had appeared only briefly represented a legitimate target, the object would have been flying faster than 5,000 mph—far faster than any terrestrial airplane could fly.

(B-3): At approximately 10 P.M., roughly five minutes after Sergeant Whenry's first radar UFO had disappeared off-scope, he spotted another blip located roughly thirty miles east of the station. For each of the next three radar scans, the blip advanced westward until it was twenty-five miles west of the station, where the blip became weaker and disappeared. The total duration of this incident was only sixteen seconds. If this blip represented a solid object, it would have been flying at more than 12,000 mph!

The telegraphic reports on the incident submitted shortly afterward indicated that Bentwaters control-tower personnel, upon learning that UFOs were showing up on the local radar, had searched the night skies and had spotted a "bright light" that seemed to pass over the field "at terrific speed," moving from east to west at an altitude estimated to be 4,000 feet. Also, a pilot of a C-47 transport, flying at 4,000 feet altitude near Bentwaters, had reported seeing a bright light streak past "at terrific speed." The pilot said the light was "under" his aircraft, which could mean that it appeared to him to be at a lower altitude. During mid-August the Earth encounters a heavy meteor shower known as the Perseids, and the reports from Bentwaters mention that personnel had observed many "shooting stars" that night. As the St. Louis UFO case (Chapter 5) illustrates, even in broad daylight, experienced pilots can be grossly in error in trying to estimate the altitude and distance of a fireball/meteor. Two weeks later, when a more detailed report on the incident was filed from Bentwaters, there was no mention of the luminous objects that had streaked across the sky from east to west. This could indicate that these visual UFOs had subsequently been identified as meteors once the initial excitement had died down.

However, the more detailed account from Bentwaters reported that the control-tower shift-supervisor, Staff Sergeant Lawrence S. Wright, had sighted a more stationary visual UFO to the east-southeast. The bright light, which was described as being "pinpoint" in size, originally appeared at approximately 10 degrees above the horizon and *gradually rose during the hour it was in view* to an elevation angle of approximately 40 degrees. Wright said he viewed the light through 7 x 50 binoculars but could make out no details. Its color reportedly changed from amber to blue-white. From his description, the UFO's position and movement, the pinpoint light probably was the planet Mars, which was very bright at that time because of its proximity to the Earth. Because the UFO remained to the east-southeast, it could not possibly be related to the two rapidly moving radar-UFOs, which had disappeared after a few seconds to the west and northwest, or to the first (B-1) which had disappeared to the northeast.

A very significant event occurred at Bentwaters that same night, which is described in the case files but which Thayer chose to omit completely from his AIAA article. At approximately 9:30 P.M., as Sergeant Whenry was tracking the curious cluster of UFOs on his radarscope, a flight of two T-33 jet fighters from the 512th fighter-interceptor squadron, based at

Bentwaters, was returning to base. The Bentwaters radar station contacted the two pilots, First Lieutenants Charles V. Metz and Andrew C. Rowe, and asked them to make an on-the-spot investigation of the radar UFOs. Station personnel directed the two pilots to the area where the curious radar blips were located. According to the official report in the case files, the two pilots "searched the areas to the northeast, east, and southeast of Bentwaters *for approximately 45 minutes. . . . Results of this aerial search were negative.* Both officers reported that they observed *a bright star on the horizon to the East of Bentwaters* which might have been mistaken for an Unidentified Flying Object by the visual observer. Lt. Rowe also stated that a flashing beacon was flashing through *a low haze* along the East coast of England from the vicinity of the village of Orford." (Emphasis added.)

I was curious to know why Thayer had completely omitted any mention of this fruitless aerial search. Because I had first obtained a copy of the case file from Thayer, I knew he had access to these facts. During a telephone conversation with Thayer on May 20, 1973, I raised the question. His reply was: *"I didn't mention it in my article because I had to keep it down in length. I didn't want it to get too long."* His article, with illustrations, filled almost five full magazine pages and ran more than 6,500 words in length. It would have required no more than fifty words to have informed AIAA readers of the fruitless search by the two jet pilots, which cast doubts as to the presence of physical objects in the skies. But as Thayer explained, he "didn't want it to get too long."

In describing subsequent events, which all occurred in the vicinity of Lakenheath, Thayer turned to the "coherent" twelve-year-old recollections of the former watch-supervisor. He recalled that the Bentwaters radar station had called Lakenheath to ask if its CPS-5 long-range surveillance radar, or a shorter-range CPN-4 airport radar, had spotted any "4,000 mph targets." Curiously, they had not up to that moment, despite the fact that the CPS-5 coverage overlapped that of the MPN-11A at Bentwaters to a considerable extent. (See Plate 22.) Thayer quoted the watch-supervisor as recalling that he *"immediately* had all controllers start scanning the radar scopes . . . using full MTI (moving target indicator), which eliminated entirely all ground returns [echoes from fixed objects on the ground]. *Shortly after this search begun,* one of the controllers noticed a stationary echo on the scopes. . . ." (Emphasis added.)

Thayer's article emphasized that "the position of this initial contact . . . is almost directly in line with the path" of the last radar-UFO that had disappeared from the scopes at Bentwaters while heading in the general direction of Lakenheath. AIAA readers might logically conclude that the unidentified blip just spotted on the Lakenheath scopes was the same one that only moments earlier had disappeared from the radar to the east. But in reality, *the first radar-UFO was not spotted at Lakenheath until more than two hours after the last radar-UFO had disappeared from the Bentwaters radar.* There had been two fast-moving radar-UFOs headed in a westerly direction from Bentwaters: B-2, which disappeared around 9:30 P.M., and B-3, which disappeared at approximately 10 P.M. *The first radar-UFO detected at Lakenheath was at ten minutes past midnight on August 14,* according to telegraphic reports filed shortly after the incident. All of this information was contained in the case file in Thayer's possession.

As earlier noted, Thayer leaned heavily on the twelve-year-old recollections of the watch-supervisor, and this is reflected in the map he prepared to show the location of subsequent events. The map I have prepared to help the reader follow events (Plate 22) is based instead on the original telegraphic report, except as noted. But the differences are not of great consequence. For example, the original telegraphic report indicates that the Lakenheath radar operators first spotted a UFO-blip which was located approximately six miles west of the station and that it then moved to a position approximately twenty miles southwest of the radar. The watch-supervisor recalled that the radar-UFO was first spotted approximately twenty miles southwest of the radar.

The most curious characteristic of the UFO-blip when it was situated some twenty miles southwest of the Lakenheath CPS-5 is that the blip remained stationary. With the radar operating in the moving-target-indicator (MTI) mode, *only moving targets* should appear on the scope—IF the MTI is functioning properly. In radars of that early vintage, MTI was a relatively new feature and one that often caused problems. For example, the instruction book for the MPN-11A radar, which also had MTI, specifically warned radar operators and maintenance personnel of the possibility of *spurious signals* being caused by an MTI malfunction. In chapter 5, on page 12, the Technical Order (as the instruction book is called) warned that MTI "circuits are complex; the stability requirements are severe; the tolerances are close." And on page 18 of chapter 4, the same manual warns operators of still another potential source of spurious signals that can result from what is called "extra-time-around signals."

Without going into the complex technical details here, this condition can arise during anomalous-propagation weather conditions when echoes from distant fixed targets on the ground far beyond the selected maximum radar operating range defeat the MTI function. Under this condition, the Tech Order warned, "the signal from this distant fixed target may appear *as a false moving target. . . .*" (Emphasis added.) Clearly the engineers who designed the radar and helped write the instruction manual recognized the fallibility of radar under such conditions. The Lakenheath CPS-5 radar was not originally designed to include MTI. But this feature had later been added, which would increase the risk of operational problems.

The UFO-blip remained fixed for about five minutes on the Lakenheath scopes, then suddenly began to move north at high speed until it stopped two miles northwest of the radar, according to the original telegraphic reports, or twenty miles northwest, according to the watch-supervisor's recollections. The CPS-5 radar instruction book gives a minimum operating range of approximately seven miles. For this reason, the twenty-mile figure has been used in my map because the two-mile figure in the telegraphic report appears to be a typographical error.

The watch-supervisor recalled that at some point, exact time unknown, he called the local base commander and also

notified an air division command post near London to report
the incident. Authorities decided to scramble a Venom, a
two-man British interceptor, from a Royal Air Force base at
Waterbeach, roughly twenty miles southwest of Lakenheath.
The watch-supervisor recalled that it had taken thirty to
forty-five minutes for the Venom to become airborne and
approach Lakenheath. Subsequent events, as described in the
telegraphic report filed shortly after the incident, are as
follows: "Pilot advised he had a bright light in sight and
would investigate. At 13 miles west [of Lakenheath?], he
reported loss of target and white light."

The Lakenheath radar station then "vectored him to a
target 10 miles east of Lakenheath and pilot advised [that]
target was on [his] radar and he was *locking on.*' Pilot
reported he had lost target on his radar. Lakenheath RATCC
[radar] reports that as Venom passed the target on radar, the
target began a tail chase of the friendly fighter. *RATCC
requested pilot acknowledge this case.* Pilot acknowledged
and stated he would try to circle and get behind the target.
Pilot advised he was unable to 'shake' the target off his tail
and requested assistance. . . . Pilot [subsequently] stated:
'Clearest target I have ever seen on radar.' " By this time the
aircraft was running low on fuel, and the pilot decided to
return to base. Meanwhile, another Venom had been dispatched to the area, according to the original telegraphic
report: *"Second Venom was vectored to other radar targets
but was unable to make contact."* (Emphasis added.) Soon
the second interceptor returned to base, and no further
interception activities were undertaken, perhaps because all
of the mysterious targets had by then disappeared. All targets
evaporated from the scopes by 3:30 A.M.

Thayer's account, based on the watch-supervisor's recollections, is considerably more detailed and colorful. Shortly after
the Lakenheath radar informed the Venom pilot that the
UFO-blip was only one-half mile ahead of his aircraft's blip,
the pilot radioed back: "Roger, Lakenheath, I've got my guns
locked on him." But a few moments later, the pilot called in
to ask, "Where did he go? Do you still have him?" The
Lakenheath station informed the pilot that the UFO "had

made a swift circling movement and had gotten behind the Venom. The pilot then confirmed that the target was behind him and said that he would try to shake it." Thayer added: "Since no tail radar is mentioned, the pilot presumably saw [visually] the UFO behind him. The pilot of the Venom interceptor tried numerous evasive maneuvers, but he was unable to lose the [UFO] . . . which the Lakenheath RATCC radar continuously tracked as a distinct echo behind the aircraft echo." When the first Venom pilot decided to return to base, "he asked Lakenheath RATCC to tell him if the [UFO] . . . followed him on the radar scopes. According to the Lakenheath watch supervisor, the [UFO] appeared to follow the Venom only a 'short distance.' . . ."

The original telegraphic report also refers to a radar-UFO observed by the Lakenheath station "17 miles east of station, making sharp rectangular course of flight. This maneuver was not conducted by circular path but on right angles. . . . Object would stop and start with amazing rapidity." It is not clear whether this radar-UFO was the one that the first Venom tried to intercept east of the station or whether this radar-UFO showed up after both Venoms had returned to base. There is also a brief reference to UFO-blips appearing on the scopes of the CPN-4 airport surveillance radar at Lakenheath, but without any details. Unfortunately, the Lakenheath station, unlike Bentwaters, never responded to Project Blue Book requests for a more detailed follow-up report, so far as the contents of the case file show. The watch-supervisor recalled that he had written a detailed report on the incident for his superiors, but there is no reference to it in the Project Blue Book file. This could indicate that the Lakenheath base commander had second thoughts about the incident and preferred to forget the whole matter.

If it were not for the incident involving the first Venom pilot's reported radar-visual encounter with the UFO, this case would deserve scant attention because the erratic behavior of the radar-UFOs is so characteristic of spurious targets that have appeared on scopes since the earliest days of

radar. During my own investigation of the Bentwaters-Lakenheath case, I discussed it in considerable detail with E. P.
Hall, a radar specialist employed by Britain's Civil Aviation
Authority. Hall, who has been directly involved in the
installation and operation of numerous radars in Britain, told
me, "We have always had a terrible radar-angel problem
along our east coast" in the region where Bentwaters and
Lakenheath are situated. When there are temperature inversions over the North Sea and the Channel, he explained, so
much radar energy is bent Earthward that "our radars often
show us every ship in the English Channel." Still other
troublesome sources of radar angels, Hall explained, are flocks
of migrating geese, ducks and other birds, because "there is
an enormous bird sanctuary in the Anglican area." Hall was
quite unimpressed with the "unusual" behavior of the blips
on the Bentwaters and Lakenheath radarscopes because for
him it was a *familiar* experience.

Thayer himself acknowledged the possibility that the
multiple targets first spotted on the Bentwaters radar around
9:30 P.M. (B-1), which had moved northeast, could have
resulted from anomalous propagation conditions. He noted
that when angels are caused by radar energy being refracted
Earthward from a layer of air, the blips typically move at a
speed that is approximately *twice* the velocity of winds aloft,
and in the same general direction as these winds. The
Bentwaters weather report for the evening of August 13 shows
that the winds aloft were to the *northeast*—the direction that
the cluster of UFO-blips was moving. And the speed of blip
movement, 80 to 125 mph, is roughly twice the velocity of the
winds aloft that night. These ranged from 34 mph at 6,000
feet altitude to 80 mph at 20,000 feet.

Through the assistance of Bendix, which designed and
produced the CPS-5 radar, I established contact with Herbert
G. Forney, who had spent ten years as a Bendix field engineer
working on the CPS-5 and other such radars. I sent Forney a
copy of the AIAA article and asked if he had ever encountered unusual radar signals of that type on the CPS-5 or
similar radars. Forney wrote to say that during his ten years as
a radar field engineer "I've observed apparently fast-moving

echoes on the PPIs [displays] that turned out to be equipment malfunctions." Referring specifically to the CPS-5
radar, Forney said that the mercury delay line used in the
CPS-5 moving-target indicator (MTI) experienced "inherent
instability problems caused by temperature variations and
vibrations. In addition, the coherent oscillator (Coho) was
very susceptible to unstable oscillation caused by loss of
synchronism (lock-pulse). This condition would be very
apparent to an experienced operator; however, some of the
conditions produced by the mercury delay line [in the MTI]
may not be apparent."

If the UFO blips that first appeared on the Bentwaters
MPN-11A radar, and later on the Lakenheath CPS-5, were
produced by solid, craftlike objects, these objects should have
shown up on the other radars whose coverage extended to the
same area. For example, the targets first spotted on the
Bentwaters radar would have been within the range of
coverage of the Lakenheath CPS-5, the Sculthorpe airport
surveillance radar and even the long-range radar at the
London airport to the southwest. Yet there were no reports
of unidentified blips on the scopes of these other radars
during this time. Two hours after Bentwaters had alerted
both Lakenheath and Sculthorpe, the mysterious blips appeared on Lakenheath scopes, but they did not show up on
the Sculthorpe or Bentwaters radars, so far as the original
telegraphic dispatches indicate. There probably were still
other radars, at Royal Air Force bases, with overlapping
coverage. Yet my inquiry to the Royal Radar Establishment
(RRE) in late 1971 elicited the response that the incident had
never been brought to the RRE's attention. Nor could the
RRE locate any RAF officers who had been on active duty
during the summer of 1956 who could recollect the incident.

The same sort of atmospheric conditions that can cause
spurious targets on ground radars can play similar tricks on
airborne radars. For example, on January 21, 1951, two USAF
interceptors were running practice missions over Tennessee.
The time was approximately 4:20 P.M., still broad daylight,
when the radar operator aboard the interceptor that was
using the other as a tracking target suddenly noticed an

unidentified target on his scope which seemed to be ten miles ahead. He notified the pilot, who obtained permission to break off the training exercise to investigate. The interceptor radar, like the one in the Venom, had two displays, one of which showed target bearing and range while the other showed target elevation with respect to the interceptor's own altitude.

Initially the unknown radar target had appeared to be considerably higher than the interceptor, then flying at 7,000 feet. But as the interceptor closed to within four miles, the unknown blip seemed to change altitude rapidly and to drop beneath the interceptor's altitude. Still the pilot could see no physical airborne target ahead or below. Finally, to keep the unknown target within view of the radar, the pilot dropped the nose of his aircraft. To the pilot's surprise, he found his aircraft pointed directly at the X-10 plant area of the Atomic Energy Commission's nuclear processing facility! (The USAF report on its subsequent investigation does not identify the nature of this X-10 facility, but presumably it contained some large structures, used to extract fissionable uranium, which were reflecting radar echoes.)

The pilot obtained permission to retrace his original flight path to see if the mysterious radar blip would appear again, and if his radar would lead him to the X-10 plant area. Once again a blip appeared at a range of approximately ten miles, and once again the radar directed the interceptor toward the X-10 facility, with the pilot flying as close as security regulations permitted. The subsequent USAF investigation showed that there had been two temperature inversions in the region at the time; one was at 2,000 to 5,000 feet and the other was at 8,000 to 11,000 feet. Even a single temperature inversion can serve to reflect radar energy Earthward, and in this case there was a sharp double inversion. The effect had nothing to do with the radioactive materials being processed at the AEC facility, but was simply due to the fact that structures at the X-10 plant were reflecting the signals, via the double inversion, to the interceptor radar, creating the illusion of an airborne target.

Early in my investigation of the Bentwaters-Lakenheath

case, I sought to learn more about the technical characteristics of all of the radars involved in the incident. The Bentwaters MPN-11A radar had been built by Gilfillan (now ITT-Gilfillan), and the Lakenheath CPS-5 had been built by Bendix Corporation. Both companies dug into their files to locate copies of the instruction books that had originally been supplied to the USAF to provide operating and maintenance information. From Tom Holland, an electronics specialist at the British Embassy in Washington, I learned that the radar used in the Venom was an American design, the APS-57, produced by Westinghouse Electric in Baltimore, from whom I also obtained an instruction book on the airborne radar.

A telephone call to the embassy put me in touch with an RAF pilot in the air attaché's office who had flown Venoms himself. Wing Commander G. G. Farley told me that the pilot sat on the left side in the cockpit while the radar operator sat to the right of the pilot. Directly in front of the radar operator were the two scopes, one showing target bearing and azimuth and the other showing the target's relative elevation. Farley emphasized that it was extremely difficult for the pilot to try to operate the radar as well as fly the airplane because he would have trouble reaching the many controls and viewing the scopes. It was for this reason that the airplane was designed to carry the second crew member who was trained to operate the complex equipment and positioned to see its displays and reach its controls. Farley found it curious that none of the reports of the Venom's encounter with the UFO had made any mention of a *radar operator*. The original telegraphic report said, ". . . pilot advised target was on radar and *he* was 'locking on.' Pilot reported *he* had lost target on his radar. . . . Pilot stated: 'Clearest target *I* have ever seen on radar.' " (Emphasis added.) Never once did the words "we" or "radar operator" appear in the reports; only the words "I" and "pilot."

There is other circumstantial evidence that suggests that the pilot himself was trying to operate the equipment while flying the airplane and did not have an experienced radar operator along. Recall that the telegraphic report said the

pilot radioed in to say that he was "locking on" to the target
with his radar. And the watch-supervisor recalled the pilot
saying "I've got my guns locked on him." In 1956 there were a
few advanced radar fire-control systems that had the capability of locking onto a target and automatically tracking it, even
aiming the interceptor toward the target. *But the APS-57
used in the Venom did not have such lock-on capability.* The
APS-57 only had the ability to detect and display airborne
targets. This I learned from the Westinghouse instruction
book, and it was confirmed in my telephone conversations
with Harley B. Lindemann, a Westinghouse engineer who
had played a key role in designing the APS-57. If there had
been a trained radar operator on board, surely he would have
known the inherent limitations of the APS-57 and there
would have been no talk of "lock-on" by the radar. This
indicates that the first Venom pilot was alone, trying to fly his
jet fighter while simultaneously reaching across the cockpit
and attempting to manipulate a complex radar whose operation he did not fully understand, whose controls would be
difficult to see and operate in the darkened cockpit, to say
nothing of the difficulty of viewing the displays.

There is another important discrepancy in the account of
the first Venom's encounter with the UFO. Recall that the
pilot reported he had lost the target shortly after it had
appeared on his scope and he thought he had "lock-on." The
watch-supervisor recalled that the mystified pilot had radioed
in to ask, "Where did he go?" And that the Lakenheath
station had then informed the pilot that the UFO "had made
a swift circling movement and gotten behind the Venom." It
would have been physically impossible for the CPS-5 radar to
show a "swift circling movement" that would not have been
much more readily apparent on the Venom's own radar. The
reason is that the slow-scanning Lakenheath CPS-5 would be
"looking" in the direction of the UFO briefly only once *every
fifteen seconds,* whereas the Venom's own radar, which scans
at very high speed, would get *more than one hundred "looks"
in the direction of the UFO during the same fifteen-second
period.* (Depending on the scan-rate selected, the Venom
radar antenna would illuminate a target once each 0.09

seconds or each 0.13 seconds, compared to once each fifteen seconds for the Lakenheath CPS-5.) If the UFO-blip were a solid craftlike object, and if the pilot were watching the APS-57 scope, he would readily see any motion of the object, even at high speed. And if the pilot had been looking through his windshield, and if the UFO was visible in the form of a light as earlier and subsequently claimed, the pilot should have seen the UFO circle around his aircraft. Yet the pilot reported neither.

The watch-supervisor, in recalling the incident, conceded that "the first movement by the UFO was so swift (circling behind the interceptor) [that] I missed it entirely, but it was seen by the other controllers. However, the fact that this had occurred was confirmed by the pilot of the interceptor." This is a curious situation in which the pilot was prompted by reports from the Lakenheath radar operators to believe that the UFO had circled behind him, and so he reportedly looked and saw a light which he concluded must be the UFO. And the watch-supervisor, who himself had not seen the alleged encircling motion, concluded from the pilot's report that the blip on the scope previously thought to be the Venom must now be the UFO. In the excitement of the moment, this was understandable. But with the perspective of hindsight it would seem to be a case of the blind leading the blind.

What was the light that the Venom pilot reported seeing to the rear? The rearward visibility from the Venom cockpit is restricted by the seat-headrest except at higher elevation angles, which indicates that the light must have been at a moderate angle above the horizon. This raises the possibility that what the pilot saw was a bright celestial body. (Attempting to identify which one is impossible because the Venom's direction of flight at that moment is unknown.) Any military pilot who has, or thinks he has, a potentially hostile craft on his tail has reason for concern because he is in an extremely vulnerable situation. It would therefore be surprising if there was not at least a mild touch of panic in the cockpit of the Venom as its pilot executed evasive maneuvers intended to "shake" what seemed to be an extraterrestrial craft which apparently had maneuvered into a position that suggested that it might be preparing to attack the Venom from its vulnerable rear. In this state of mind, the Venom pilot, after executing a high-G turning maneuver, could quickly glance to the rear and find a light that seemed to be the UFO, for the night skies are filled with luminous objects—stars and planets. The weather report indicates that scattered clouds were beginning to move into the Lakenheath area about that time, which could facilitate the illusion.

If this explanation for the visual object seems strained, recall the six experienced Navy flight-crew members flying near Gander on an otherwise uneventful night who mistook a partly illuminated moon for a giant craft zooming toward them on a collision course (Chapter 6). And their imaginations had not been stimulated by reports from a ground radar that its scopes showed the presence of a UFO that seemed to be preparing for a tail attack. Recall also that the second Venom aircraft, which arrived as the first was departing for base, was directed by the Lakenheath station to the vicinity of the UFO-blip(s) on its scopes. But according to the official telegraphic reports shortly after the incident, *this second Venom failed to make either radar or visual contact with a UFO.*

Atmospheric conditions which result in spurious radar blips can occur at any time. But scientific studies have shown that the heaviest incidence of radar "angel" activity occurs during the warm, humid months of July and August—in the northern hemisphere. It is interesting to note that the Bentwaters-Lakenheath incident occurred during one of these two months. And the same warm, humid conditions were most conducive to causing malfunctions in the early-vintage ground radar MTI circuits.

Those who do not understand the basic limitations of radar—and this includes scientists from other disciplines who have never bothered to dig deeply into the subject—can be quite impressed by reports of mysterious blips that sometimes appear on radarscopes. But experienced radar designers and field engineers who have serviced radars, especially those of early vintage, are quite unimpressed. C. A. (Burt) Fowler, who directed the design of the MTI used in the CPS-5 radar installed at Lakenheath, and who has spent more than a quarter-century in radar engineering, is typical. After reading Thayer's AIAA account of the Bentwaters-Lakenheath case, Fowler told me that spurious blips are quite commonplace on radarscopes. He added that if an operator decides that a succession of such blips all derive from a single target, then he can easily conclude that the only possible explanation is a UFO which can fly at fantastic speeds, stop instantaneously, then accelerate to high speed in an instant and perform other seemingly impossible feats. Fowler added, "I'm surprised that the AIAA prints stuff like this."

This, then, is the case which Dr. Hynek has termed a "classic," and which Thayer, in his summary for the University of Colorado report, characterized as "the most puzzling and unusual case in the radar-visual files." This appraisal is not surprising because Thayer subsequently admitted during a telephone conversation that he had not obtained copies of the instruction books for any of the radars involved in the incident to make a detailed study of their performance characteristics and limitations. Nor had he attempted to learn about the radar characteristics from engineers who had designed or serviced the radars in the field.

This case, the RB-47 case and others analyzed in earlier chapters point up another important UFOlogical Principle, possibly the most important of all:

> UFOLOGICAL PRINCIPLE #10: Many UFO cases seem puzzling and unexplainable simply because case investigators have failed to devote a sufficiently rigorous effort to the investigation.

This is not really surprising because the vast majority of UFO investigators are persons who want to believe in extraterrestrial spaceships, either consciously or unconsciously. The larger the number of seemingly unexplainable cases, the stronger the apparent support for the extraterrestrial hypothesis.

22 · UFOs over New Guinea

Missionaries seldom achieve great fame, but Rev. William Gill is world-famous in UFO circles because of events he says occurred in mid-1959 at his station in New Guinea, near the village of Boianai in Papua. Thirteen years earlier Gill had come to his post with Rev. Norman E. G. Cruttwell, who directed the multistation Anglican mission from his own post at Menapi. In the mid-1950s, Cruttwell had become interested in UFOs and started reading books on the subject, and when he himself had a sighting, he wrote to report the experience to the editor of the British magazine *Flying Saucer Review*, in London. The editor replied by inviting Cruttwell to become the official UFO observer and investigator in New Guinea for the International U.F.O. Observer Corps. This must have been an exciting and flattering offer for a man in an obscure jungle mission. Cruttwell knew from his reading that UFOs might be spaceships from other worlds, and perhaps his own efforts could help solve the mystery. Cruttwell later described his assignment as "reporting any further sightings to them, and trying, if possible, to interview the witnesses. Little realizing what I was letting myself in for, I accepted, and started a U.F.O. file. I never imagined that within a year my file would be bursting with reports."

The reason for the bursting file was that Cruttwell enlisted the aid of his missionaries, including Gill, who were to report to him on all UFO sightings in their areas. The missionaries in turn alerted the natives to watch for UFOs. Within the next year, Cruttwell would receive more than sixty UFO reports, testifying to the fact that his missionaries and their natives responded well to his request. In March, 1960, Cruttwell could write an impressive forty-five-page (long-sheet) report in which he made a commendably scientific effort to categorize the many UFO reports by color, shape, time of day, *and by the mission that had reported the sightings.* In many of the reports, the UFO was said to resemble a "Tilley Lamp," which Cruttwell explained "is the most popular type of lamp in the Territory, where there is no electric light. Nearly all Europeans and quite a few of the better-off Papuans possess them. They burn kerosene under pressure . . . give out a brilliant white light equal to 300 candle-power. They are visible at a great distance and appear as an indefinite white blob of light, often with a halation of rays, due to the brightness. One often sees them far out to sea on a canoe, where the native people use them to attract fish."

Cruttwell's report shows that it was *almost six months* after he initiated the UFO "watch" *until Gill turned in his first report,* on April 9. On that date, at 6:50 P.M., Gill was returning home on a launch from a visit to an "out-station," and in the darkness he noticed a bright white light "like a Tilley Lamp" near the top of a nearby mountain. He was not unduly puzzled, assuming it was someone with a Tilley Lamp, and did not continue to watch the light. Five minutes later he looked up and the light had disappeared. Five minutes after that, he noticed a similar light shining from another position on the opposite side of the mountain, approximately a mile distant from the former location. Gill looked away and when he turned again to view the light, it had disappeared.

Cruttwell later observed: *"It was not until he [Gill] got a
letter from me about a later sighting from Giwa that it
occurred to him that it might have been a U.F.O."* (Emphasis added.)

Cruttwell concluded that the light(s) were not Tilley
Lamps, because there were no houses or trails on that part of
the mountain, and that the light that Gill had seen must have
been a UFO that was hovering near the mountain. "This
sighting was therefore of great importance to us at the time,"
Cruttwell wrote, "suggesting that some mysterious, apparently controlled, craft were flying about over Papua at night.
This was amply confirmed by subsequent sightings." What
had seemed rather commonplace to Gill at the time of the
incident obviously *loomed large in the mind of his superior.* If
Gill were anxious to please Cruttwell, he should in the future
be much more attentive to Tilley Lamp-like lights that might
really be UFOs.

On June 21, Gill could report a second UFO sighting, this
one by Papuan teacher-evangelist Stephen Gill Moi, whose
middle name suggests his close friendship with Gill. At
around 1 A.M. on June 21, Moi said, he had sighted a
luminous object descending from high in the sky which he
first thought was a "falling star" (meteor). But the object had
appeared to stop at one point and remained fixed for what he
estimated to be half a minute. Then, Moi said, the object
changed in brilliance and he said he could discern its
shape—that of an "inverted saucer"—the oft-reported shape
of UFOs. Then the UFO reportedly moved upward and
disappeared into the clouds. When Gill reported the incident
to Cruttwell, he wrote that "Moi claimed never to have heard
of 'Flying Saucers.' " (This seems surprising in view of the
UFO watch that Cruttwell had initiated many months earlier
and Gill's own reported Tilley Lamp sighting of April 9.) Gill
said he questioned Moi about the "inverted saucer" shape,
but Moi persisted in using this description.

Gill's own experience in combination with that of Moi
prompted Gill to write on June 26 to another Anglican
missionary who, like Cruttwell, was very interested in UFOs.
This was Rev. David Durie, head of a mission college at

Dogura. In the letter, Gill wrote: "I am almost convinced about the 'visitation' theory. . . . I do not doubt the existence of these 'things' (indeed I cannot now that I have seen one for myself), but my simple mind still requires scientific evidence before I can accept the from-outer-space theory. . . ." Before Gill dispatched this letter and before the night was over, he would seemingly get such evidence *firsthand*, judging from his later report.

The following are Gill's verbatim notes, which he told Cruttwell he had jotted down during the exciting events that reportedly occurred on the *evening* of June 26, 1959, beginning shortly after sunset:

6:45   Sighted bright white light from front door. Direction N.W. (Patches of low cloud. Clear over Dogura and Menapi.)
6:50   Call Stephen [Gill Moi] and Eric Langford.
6:52   Stephen arrives. Confirms not a star—like the other night. Coming closer, not so bright. Coming down. Orange? Deep yellow? (500 ft.?)
6:55   Send Eric to call people. One object on top, move—man? [*Sic*] Now 3 men—moving, glowing, doing something on deck. Gone.
7:00   Men 1 and 2 again.
7:04   Gone again.
7:10   Men 1, 3, 4, 2 (appeared in that order). Thin electric blue spotlight. Men gone. Spotlight still there. (Cloud ceiling covered sky c. 2,000 ft.)
7:12   Men 1 and 2 appeared—blue light.
7:20   Spotlight off. Men go.
7:20   U.F.O. goes through cloud.
8:28   U.F.O. seen by me overhead. Call station people. Appeared to descend, get bigger. Not so big, but seemed nearer than before. (Clear sky here; heavy cloud over Dogura.)
8:29   Second U.F.O. seen over sea, hovering at times.
8:35   Another one [UFO] over Wadobuna village. (Cloud forming again.)
?   Another to the east.
8:50   Big one stationary and larger—the original? Others coming and going through the clouds. As they

descend through clouds, light reflected like large
halo on to cloud—no more than 2,000 ft., probably
less. All U.F.O.s very clear—satellites? "Mother
Ship" still large, clear, stationary. (Clouds patchy.)

9:05   Nos. 2, 3, 4 gone. [Believed to be referring to UFOs.]
9:10   Mother ship gone—giving red light. No. 1 gone
       (overhead) into cloud.
9:20   "Mother" [ship] back.
9:30   "Mother" gone across sea to Giwa—white, red, blue,
       gone.
9:46   Overhead U.F.O. reappears, is hovering.
10:00 Still there, stationary.
10:10 Hovering, gone behind cloud.
10:30 Very high, hovering in clear patch of sky between
       clouds.
10:50 Very overcast, no sign of U.F.O.
11:04 Heavy rain. I Q A !!! (Wedau language! finished.)

Gill and his associates, according to this account, had stood
there watching for *more than four hours.* Even when the large
"Mother Ship" with manlike creatures on board had disappeared behind the clouds at 7:20 P.M., Gill and his associates
had *waited patiently for more than an hour* until the UFO
finally returned at 8:28 P.M. But who could blame them, for
seemingly they not only had been privileged to see UFOs, but
the manlike crew members of the craft! Nor is it surprising
that the following day, June 27, Gill wrote another letter to
fellow missionary David Durie. The letter, in its entirety,
follows:

Dear David:
    Life is strange, isn't it? Yesterday I wrote you a letter
(which I still intend sending you) expressing opinions of
U.F.O.s. Not less than 24 hours later I have changed my
views somewhat. Last night we at Boianai experienced
about four hours of U.F.O. activity, and there is no
doubt whatever that they are handled by beings of some
kind. At times it was absolutely breathtaking. Here is the
report. Please pass it round [*sic*], but great care must be
taken as I have no other and this, like the one I made out
re Stephen [Gill Moi], will be sent to Nor [Norman

Cruttwell]. I would appreciate it if you could send the lot back as soon as poss.

Cheers

Convinced

(signed) Bill

P.S. Do you think P. [Port] Moresby should know about this? (N. Cruttwell is at present in the Daga country, and will not be returning home until July 16th at the earliest.) If people think it worth while, I will stand cost of radio conversation if you care to make out a comprehensive report from the material on my behalf! *It's interesting Territory news if nothing else.* [Emphasis added.]

W.B.G.

The very next evening, shortly after sunset again, a Papuan medical assistant named Annie Laurie Borewa reportedly spotted the approach of a large UFO at approximately 6 p.m., according to Gill's account. She called Gill, and he hurried out to watch, along with several others. Although the sun had set, it was still light, Gill reported. "We watched figures appear on top [of the UFO]—four of them—there is no doubt that they were human. This is possibly the same object I took to be the 'Mother Ship' last night. Two smaller U.F.O.s were seen at the same time, stationary, one above the hills, west, and another overhead." The figures appeared humanlike except, Gill later observed, they seemed to be *enveloped in a luminous glow!* Gill's subsequent verbatim account continued: "On the large one [UFO], two of the figures seemed to be doing something near the centre of the deck—they were occasionally bending over and raising their arms as though adjusting or 'setting up' something (not visible). *One figure seemed to be standing, looking down at us* (a group of about a dozen). I stretched my arm above my head and waved. To our surprise, *the figure did the same.* [Emphasis added.] Ananias waved both arms over his head, then the two outside figures did the same. There *seemed* to be no doubt that our movements were answered. All the Mission boys made audible gasps (of either joy or surprise, perhaps both).

"As dark was beginning to close in, I sent Eric Kodawa for a torch [flashlight], and directed a series of long dashes toward the U.F.O. After a minute or two of this, the U.F.O. apparently acknowledged by making several wavering motions back and forth (in a sideways direction, like a pendulum). *Waving by us was repeated, and this was followed by more flashes of the torch, then the U.F.O. began slowly to become bigger, apparently coming in our direction.* [Emphasis added.] It ceased after perhaps half a minute and came no further. After a further two or three minutes the figures apparently lost interest in us, for they disappeared below deck.

"At 6:25 P.M., two figures reappeared to carry on with whatever they were doing before the interruption.(?) The blue spot light came on for a few seconds, twice in succession. The two other U.F.O.s remained stationary and high up— higher than last night (?), or smaller than last night (?)." If Gill's account is factual, he and his associates must certainly have felt a tingling sense of excitement and expectancy. Not only had they been privileged to be the first in New Guinea, if not on the entire Earth, to see the manlike creatures who operated the spaceships from alien worlds, but they had exchanged greetings with the UFO crew members, who indicated a friendly interest. Only a few moments earlier the UFO had started to move toward the beach where Gill and his friends were standing. Thus Gill and his friends seemed poised on the threshold of becoming the first humans to make contact with extraterrestrial visitors who flew the UFOs.

It was an incredible moment, but the most incredible part of Gill's account is the next entry in his log: *"At 6:30 P.M., I went to dinner."* (Emphasis added.) I simply could not believe my eyes when I read this in a photocopy of the original Cruttwell report. Furthermore, all of Gill's associates on the beach apparently were equally stricken with hunger, because not a single one was left behind to watch the UFO! Or to greet the crew if it came in and landed!

The very next entry in Gill's log is thirty minutes later, at 7:00 P.M.: "Number one U.F.O. still present, but appeared somewhat smaller. Observers go to church for Evensong." If Gill felt impelled to conduct the Evensong services, and believed they could not be delayed despite the exciting events of the moment, surely he could have relieved one or two of the natives of their obligation to attend so they could watch the UFOs. But this did not occur. The next entry in Gill's log reads: "7:45 P.M. Evensong over, and sky covered with cloud. Visibility very poor. No U.F.O.s in sight." If Gill felt any remorse at having abandoned his observation of the UFO for dinner and Evensong, there is no indication of this in his log of that night's events. Later that night, at 10:40 P.M., Gill's log noted: "A terrific explosion just outside the Mission House. Nothing seen. It could have been an atmospheric explosion, as the whole sky was overcast." At 11:05 P.M. he logged: "A few drops of rain."

The following night, June 28, Gill reported that a UFO was spotted about 6:45 P.M. very high in the sky, and that at 9:00 P.M. three were in view. At 11:00 P.M., Gill's log shows, there were *eight* UFOs, one "fairly low," but there was "no activity seen on board," i.e., no crew visible.

Because Cruttwell was not due to return to mission headquarters until July 16th, Gill had more than two weeks to weigh the deeper implications of what reportedly had transpired. The reported experience would seem to challenge at least some of Gill's long-held religious beliefs as a minister in the Anglican Church. I recall a letter I received a few years ago from the late Brother Cassian Brenner, a Franciscan at St. Joseph's Catholic Church in Los Angeles. Brenner himself had once had a UFO sighting and was therefore moderately interested in the subject. But he wrote me that he doubted that UFOs were from other worlds or that there was intelligent life elsewhere because, he explained, "If there were, Jesus would have told us and He only spoke of humans and angels." It is therefore interesting to study Gill's letter to Cruttwell for evidence of such soul-searching that would logically result from the incidents that Gill described. His letter follows in its entirety, as published in the Cruttwell report.

Dear Norman:

Here is a lot of material—*the kind you have been waiting for, no doubt;* but I am in some ways sorry that it has to be me who supplies it. Attitudes at Dogura in respect of my sanity vary greatly, and like all mad men, I myself think my grey cells are O.K. I am sorry you were not here with your telescope—the naked eye can be a hindrance when detail is essential. [Emphasis added.]

This is the original data. Please take whatever copies or photographs you like, but please send it back to me by return "Maclaren King" if possible, as I regard it with a sense of value which no copies could have.

There has been no [UFO] activity recently over here, but one report has come from Vidia (and others from Dogura, as you will see). Hope you had a successful walkabout,

Regards

(signed) Bill

P.S. Have a spare typed copy which I am sending you—you can keep it. (It contains most but not all the originals.)* W.G.

Gill's opening remark: "Here is a lot of material—the kind you have been waiting for, no doubt . . ." suggests that Cruttwell might have been pressing his missionaries for more reports, perhaps for more detailed reports than simply "Tilley Lamps" in the mountains and sky. If Gill and Boianai had previously been lagging behind other missions in turning in UFO reports, the enclosures with the July 15 letter more than made up for past deficiencies. As a result of the eight UFOs reported for the night of June 28, *Gill's mission at Boianai moved into first place* with a total of eighteen sightings for the fourteen-month period covered by Cruttwell's final report, compared to thirteen for Baniara. (The report gives a tabulation of the number of sightings from each mission.) Cruttwell's brief references to UFO reports from the Roman Catholic mission at Sideia also suggests the possibility that there might have been an unofficial competition in the field

* This is believed to refer to sketches of the UFOs and the occupants.

of UFOlogy as well as for the religious convictions of the New Guinea natives.

According to Gill's account, there had been a total of thirty-eight witnesses to events on June 26, the first night, and twenty-five of these signed his report to attest to their presence. *Cruttwell does not explain whether the other thirteen were unable or unwilling to sign the report.* At one point in the final report, Cruttwell wrote, "Many people are inclined to doubt the testimony of Papuan native witnesses, on the grounds that they are (a) uneducated (b) superstitious, (c) inclined to say anything to please the European. This is most unfair."

When Gill's account was brought to the attention of the Royal Australian Air Force and the RAAF analyzed the bearing and elevation angles of some of Gill's UFOs, the RAAF concluded that "at least three of the lights were planets, e.g. Jupiter, Saturn and Mars," Cruttwell wrote in his report. (Others have since pointed out that Venus was particularly bright at the time.) The RAAF also noted that "light refraction, the changing position of the planets relative to the observers and the unsettled tropical weather could give the impression of size and movement." In response to this, Cruttwell wrote, "Gill says that he is quite prepared to accept the possibility that some of the smaller objects [UFOs] could have been planets, though from their apparent size and behavior it is very hard to believe." (Obviously it would be very disappointing to Cruttwell if many of the UFOs in his report were no more than celestial bodies.)

It is interesting to analyze Cruttwell's appraisal of Gill's account of having seen UFOs with glowing humanlike creatures aboard that responded to hand-waving from Gill and his associates. "Many people are put off by the comparatively fantastic nature of the Boianai sightings and the appearance of men," Cruttwell wrote. "What they do not realise is that they were only three sightings out of a total of 79 so far reported. Many others were as fantastic as the Rev. W. B. Gill's." (My repeated reading of the Cruttwell report fails to show any others of a comparable nature.) "They stand or fall together," Cruttwell wrote. "No doubt some are explicable, but if only one is inexplicable, that one is significant. If these reports are to be rejected, they must all be proved erroneous, and many competent witnesses . . . must be judged either liars or fools. . . . I have faithfully recorded what they have told me without embellishment and the reader must judge the reliability of their statements."

Dr. J. Allen Hynek, who has characterized the Gill case as a "classic," says that he is "impressed by the quality and number of witnesses and by the character and demeanor of Reverend Gill as revealed by his report and tapes. . . ." My appraisal is quite the opposite, based on the old adage that "actions speak louder than words." I would only hope that if fate should ever offer you the potential opportunity to personally greet extraterrestrial visitors, you will be willing to suffer the inconvenience of a delayed dinner to avoid missing such a historic event.

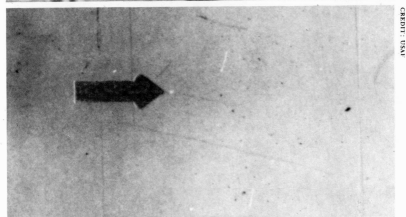

PLATES 13a, 13b:

A movie showing two "white blobs" seemingly flying in formation (Plate 13a), taken in Great Falls, Montana, on August 15, 1950, shortly before noon, is unquestionably authentic, but the question of what produced the images has persisted. A USAF investigation showed that two F-94 aircraft were in the area at the time and landed at a nearby airbase shortly after film was shot. The USAF concluded the images were caused by sunlight reflected off the fuselage of the two jet fighters which obscured fuselage details. The lower photo (Plate 13b) shows a similar image, taken with the same type of movie camera, caused by sunlight reflecting off a one-hundred-foot-long airliner at a distance of twelve miles, which is roughly equivalent to a forty-foot-long F-94 at a distance of five miles. (See Chapter 16.)

14a

PLATE 14a:
Another frame of the Great Falls movie film, showing two UFO images (arrows), as objects fly to the south of the cameraman. The lower part of the frame shows a portion of a nearby building which provided a convenient ground reference for film analysis.

14b

PLATE 14b:
Freak atmospheric conditions can produce a localized fog around an airplane which reflects sunlight to create a halo effect that might explain the brightness and long duration of the Great Falls images. This photo was taken of a Boeing B-52 during flight tests at 21,000 feet altitude. Air flowing around the wing has its relative humidity increased, causing water droplets to form and produce the localized fog which is illuminated by the sun.

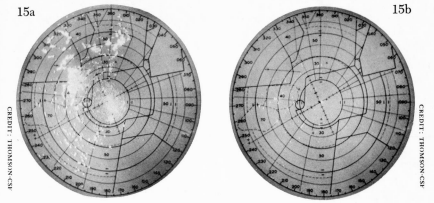

15a
15b

CREDIT: THOMSON-CSF
CREDIT: THOMSON-CSF

PLATES 15a, 15b:

Engineers who design radars know that spurious target-blips can result from many sources, including warm-humid conditions, freak atmospheric conditions, swarms of insects or birds, and even smoke and dust. These spurious targets have been observed since the earliest days of radar and are called "angels." Plate 15a shows the scope of an air-surveillance radar, operating in the mode of older-vintage models, with numerous angel-type target-blips. Plate 15b shows the same area when viewed by the same radar using special features to minimize spurious angel-type returns.

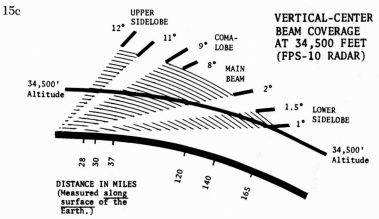

15c

UPPER SIDELOBE
12°
11°
9° COMA-LOBE
8° MAIN BEAM
2°
1.5° LOWER SIDELOBE
1°

VERTICAL-CENTER BEAM COVERAGE AT 34,500 FEET (FPS-10 RADAR)

34,500' Altitude

34,500' Altitude

28 30 37
120
140
165

DISTANCE IN MILES (Measured along surface of the Earth.)

PLATE 15c:

The UFO incident involving a USAF RB-47 electronic reconnaissance aircraft, which occurred during the predawn hours of July 17, 1957, is one of the most unusual on record. Electronic intelligence equipment on the RB-47 detected a signal, believed to have been radiated by a UFO, whose characteristics were identical with those of USAF ground radars of the CPS-6B and FPS-10 type used for air surveillance. The author's investigation showed that the "UFO signal" had same frequency as the *vertical-center* beam radiated by CPS-6B and FPS-10. This vertical-center beam actually consists of the main beam and associated "coma-lobe," plus an upper and lower side-lobe beam. As the radar antenna sweeps around in azimuth (out of the page), it produces three concentric doughnut-shaped radiation patterns in space. The radius of these patterns from the radar site, for the 34,500-foot altitude at which the RB-47 was flying at the time, is shown above and is illustrated in Plates 16-17.

16

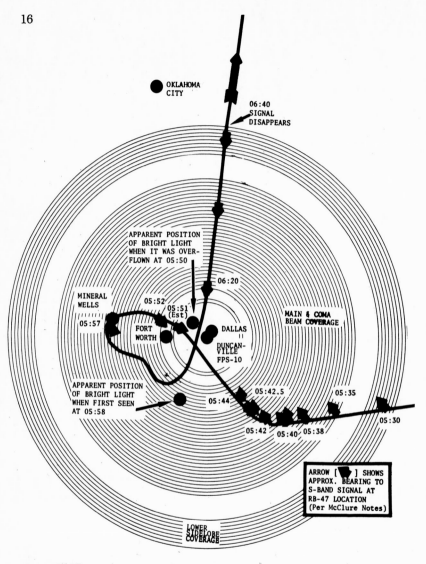

OKLAHOMA
CITY

06:40
SIGNAL
DISAPPEARS

APPARENT POSITION
OF BRIGHT LIGHT
WHEN IT WAS OVER-
FLOWN AT 05:50

06:20

MINERAL
WELLS

05:52
05:51
(Est)

05:57

FORT
WORTH

DALLAS

DUNCAN-
VILLE
FPS-10

MAIN & COMA
BEAM COVERAGE

APPARENT POSITION
OF BRIGHT LIGHT
WHEN FIRST SEEN
AT 05:58

05:44

05:42.5

05:35

05:42   05:40 05:38

05:30

ARROW [ ] SHOWS
APPROX. BEARING TO
S-BAND SIGNAL AT
RB-47 LOCATION
(Per McClure Notes)

LOWER
SIDELOBE
COVERAGE

PLATES 16-17:

When one RB-47 electronic intelligence (Elint) operator detected a CPS-6B/FPS-10-type signal as the aircraft approached Biloxi from the south (not shown on this sketch), he noted that the bearing to the signal-source indicated that the radar was in the Gulf of Mexico and that the bearing moved "up-scope," rather than normal "down-scope," prompting the operator to decide his equipment was malfunctioning. Later, at 5:10 A.M., as the RB-47 headed west, the flight crew observed a bright luminous object which zoomed across the airplane's flight path and disappeared to the north. When the pilot and co-pilot began to speculate on whether luminous object was a UFO, the Elint operator wondered if the signal near Biloxi might have come from the UFO, and

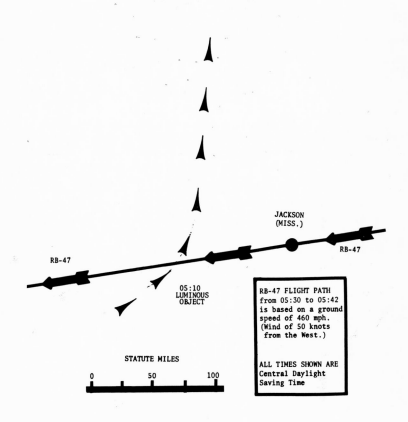

JACKSON
(MISS.)

RB-47

RB-47

05:10
LUMINOUS
OBJECT

RB-47 FLIGHT PATH
from 05:30 to 05:42
is based on a ground
speed of 460 mph.
(Wind of 50 knots
from the West.)

ALL TIMES SHOWN ARE
Central Daylight
Saving Time

STATUTE MILES

0   50   100

he immediately retuned his ALA-6 to the frequency of the original signal. After twenty minutes of fruitless search, he finally detected the same type of signal at 5:30 A.M. (For details, see Chapters 19, 20.) The bearings to the signal-source jotted down by the operator are shown on the map with small arrows. The author's analysis shows that the "UFO signal" was detected only when the RB-47 came within range of the FPS-10 radar at Duncanville, near Dallas, as shown by the shaded ring areas. The signal was not received when the RB-47 was in regions not illuminated by the vertical-center beams of the Duncanville radar. And in all cases, the bearing to the signal-source pointed in the general direction of the Duncanville radar. The luminous object sighted at 5:10 A.M. had the typical characteristics of a meteor-fireball. The lights sighted initially to the northwest and later to the southeast may have been celestial bodies. The light overflown northwest of Dallas is believed to have been American Airlines Flight #966, landing at the Dallas airport.

18a

CREDIT: USAF

PLATE 18a:

This is how a ground radar signal, and the "UFO signal," appear on the display of the ALA-6 Elint direction-finder on the RB-47. The display appears only briefly, then disappears as the ground radar antenna scans away from the RB-47, which increases the difficulty of obtaining a precise bearing measurement to the signal source. Additionally, the bearing angle is measured relative to the airplane's own flight path so that any aircraft maneuvers add to the difficulty of obtaining an accurate bearing measurement.

18b

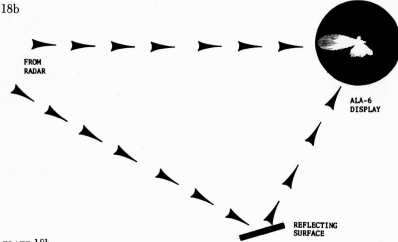

FROM
RADAR

ALA-6
DISPLAY

REFLECTING
SURFACE

PLATE 18b:

For two brief intervals during the RB-47 incident, the ALA-6 operator observed *two* identical signals, coming from slightly different bearings. If the signals were coming from a UFO, then the object must have divided into two segments—each of which was equipped with a powerful FPS-10-type radar. There is a more prosaic explanation if the signal was really coming from the Duncanville radar. The ALA-6 instruction book specifically cautions the Elint operator that the radar signal can be reflected off large metallic or other reflective surfaces and that the operator will then see displayed an identical signal that seems to be coming from two slightly different bearing angles, as shown in the sketch above.

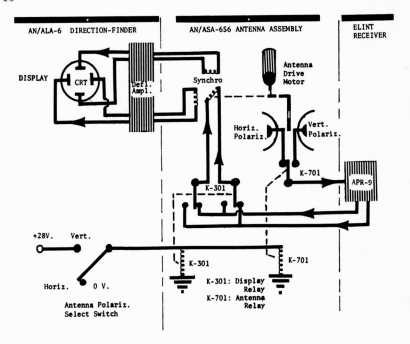

PLATE 19:

The ALA-6 and its associated Elint equipment, shown schematically here, provide two back-to-back antennas, one with horizontal polarization and one with vertical polarization. The operator can select the antenna which provides an optimum signal, using a panel switch on the ALA-6, shown schematically at lower left. When the operator selects the antenna, the switch applies or removes 28 volts from relay K-701, and simultaneously actuates or deactuates K-301. Relay K-301 applies the correct signal polarity to the synchro so that the ALA-6 will "know" which antenna is being used and can display the correct bearing. If K-301, or K-701, should fail to operate properly—and relays of the ALA-6 vintage were very unreliable—then the display will be 180 degrees in error in showing the bearing to the radar signal-source, and as the airplane flies past the radar, the bearing to the source will move "up-scope," rather than "down-scope." This was the anomalous behavior observed by the ALA-6 operator as the RB-47 approached and flew past Biloxi. (See Plate 20.)

20

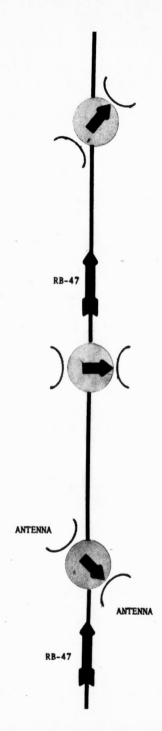

BILOXI

CPS-6B
RADAR

ANTENNA

ANTENNA

RB-47

RB-47

180° ERRONEOUS
BEARING INDICATION
RESULTING FROM A
MALFUNCTION OF K-301
OR K-701 RELAY IN
ALA-6 DIRECTION-
FINDER.

PLATE 20:

The anomalous behavior of the ALA-6 display as the RB-47 approached and flew past the CPS-6B radar located near Biloxi is readily explained if one of two electromagnetic relays (K-301 or K-701) in the ALA-6 malfunctioned briefly, perhaps because of ice formed at sub-zero temperatures at RB-47 cruising altitude. In such an event, the ALA-6 would erroneously "think" that the antenna in use was the one on the right-hand side of the RB-47, rather than the one on the left side. When the RB-47 was south of Biloxi, the ALA-6 would then show the bearing to the radar as being to the southeast (in the Gulf of Mexico), rather than to the northwest. And as the RB-47 flew past the Biloxi radar, the bearing the ALA-6 would display would move "up-scope" rather than "down-scope," exactly as the Elint operator reported observing.

PLATE 21:

One of the most famous radar-visual UFO cases involved USAF radars in England, installed at Bentwaters (center of darkened circular area) and at Lakenheath (north-east of Bentwaters.) At 9:30 P.M. the Bentwaters radar operator first noticed a cluster of slow-moving targets (1) that would occasionally stop and hover, then finally merged into single large blip before finally disappearing. Other operators briefly observed blips that shifted markedly (2) (3) before disappearing. Two jet fighters returning to base were directed to the location of the UFO-blips (1), searched the area extensively, but found nothing. During the same period, radar operators at nearby Lakenheath observed nothing unusual on their CPS-5 radar even though its coverage overlapped that of the MPN-11 radar at Bentwaters. (See Chapter 21.) The reported behavior of the radar blips indicates they were the result of anomalous propagation conditions which occur most often during the warm, humid summer months.

21

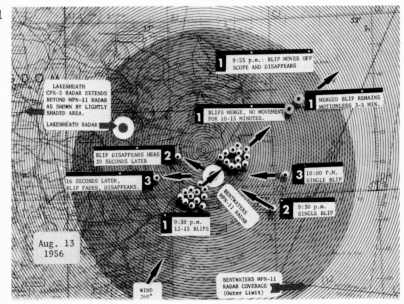

Although the Lakenheath radar station was alerted to the unusual targets on the Bentwaters radarscopes, it was not until more than *two hours later* that Lakenheath operators observed an unusual blip (4) on their scopes. The blip moved to the southwest of the Lakenheath radar and remained fixed in position for some minutes even though the radar "moving-target indicator" (MTI) being used should have eliminated all fixed targets from the scope. Later, a radar blip was observed (5) that seemed to be making right-angle shifts of position. During the time that the Lakenheath radar was observing unusual target activity, the blips were *not* being observed on the radars at Bentwaters or at Sculthorpe, northwest of Lakenheath, whose coverage included the region where Lakenheath was observing unusual activity. Discussions with engineers familiar with the radars and the MTI suggest that the Lakenheath radar-UFOs were the result of of a faulty MTI in combination with anomalous propagation conditions. (See Chapter 21.)

22

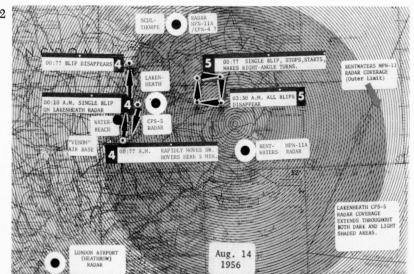

Scene of the Delphos (Kansas) UFO incident which was selected as the best case from more than one thousand entries by a "blue-ribbon panel" of experienced UFOlogists that included Dr. J. Allen Hynek and Dr. James A. Harder. According to the Durel Johnson family, a mushroom-shaped UFO was seen hovering in the middle of this grove of trees on the night of November 2, 1971, by teen-age Ronald (visible at right in Plate 23a, alongside Sheriff Ralph Enlow). According to Ronald, the UFO took off and flew over a low shed (to the right in Plate 23a), heading south. Because the site is surrounded by trees on three sides, the alleged UFO would have had to approach from the south as well as depart in that direction. The Johnsons claimed that the UFO knocked over the dead tree visible in Plate 23b, during either its arrival or its departure. Curiously, the tree fell in an east-west direction and shows no marks of impact. The metal fence surrounding the UFO site was erected after the incident was widely publicized to keep out curious tourists. (See Chapter 28.)

23a

REQUIRED PATH
FOR ARRIVAL
AND DEPARTURE

23b

UFO
SITE

DEAD
TREE

PLATE 24a:

This irregularly shaped ring of white crystalline material marks the spot where the UFO allegedly landed. This photo was taken less than 24 hours after the Johnsons reported the incident to the local newspaper. The twigs visible on the ring show no evidence of intense heat or burning, despite Ronald's report that the UFO emitted intense flame from underneath. Nor is there any visible depression to indicate that a large craft touched down on the site, despite the fact that heavy rains in the preceding days had made the area very muddy.

24b

PLATE 24b:

The Johnsons claimed that the irregular ring and the nearby trees "glowed" at night for some days or weeks after the UFO incident. This Polaroid print, taken by the Johnsons, purports to show the glowing ring. But the very bright illumination of the stick close to the camera, and portions of the ring in the foreground, compared with portions of the ring in the background, indicate that illumination was supplied by a flash lamp attached to camera and not by a glow from the ring. Samples of soil taken from the ring by Sheriff Enlow and others did not glow in the dark. Nor could the author find any witnesses who could substantiate the Johnsons' claim that the trees glowed brightly in the wake of the UFO visit.

23 • Famous "Contactees"

Some UFO reports go far beyond an account of a hand-waving exchange with occupants that allegedly fly the extra-terrestrial spaceships, and many come from what could be termed "basically honest, intelligent persons." One of the earliest and most colorful of these "contactee" cases was reported by George Adamski, the leader of a small religious cult in southern California. During the 1940s he shifted his operations to the vicinity of Mount Palomar, whose peak is the site of a famous observatory. Perhaps it was this proximity that sparked Adamski's interest in and speculation about the possibility of life on distant worlds.

In the fall of 1953, less than seven years after UFOs had first burst on public awareness, and only a year after a major "UFO flap" in 1952, Adamski coauthored a book entitled *Flying Saucers Have Landed* with a professional writer named Desmond Leslie. The success of this first book prompted an even more fantastic sequel, entitled *Inside the Space Ships*, which purported to describe Adamski's personal experience with extraterrestrial visitors aboard their flying saucers. Adamski said he had been transported, via a small "scout-ship," to a giant Venusian "mother-ship," cruising at 50,000 miles altitude, whose passengers included Martians and Saturnians as well as Venusians. Adamski's descriptions of these extraterrestrials contrast sharply with some later accounts by other "contactees" who would describe weird-looking creatures that allegedly operated the UFOs. Adamski's descriptions indicate that all of his extraterrestrial hosts, regardless of their native planets, were cast from the same mold that had fashioned Earthlings. In one account he described two "incredibly lovely young women," one with fair skin and long golden hair. The Venusian mother-ship, according to Adamski's account, was a spaceborne "Shangri-La" which included a "great teacher." He reportedly explained to Adamski the wisdom and philosophy of the very advanced extraterrestrial civilizations—a philosophy which was remarkably similar to that espoused by founders of Earth-based religions.

Adamski said that two months after his first exciting trip he felt an urge to visit Los Angeles, where he was contacted by a Martian who took him into the desert to board another scout-ship, which carried him to another mother-ship—this one from the planet Saturn. As Adamski described the Saturnian craft, it was a veritable Hilton Hotel in space—measuring nearly three-quarters of a mile long and as tall as a ten-story building. Naturally the giant craft was equipped with elevators. It also carried a "great teacher" as well as beautiful ladies and men with very handsome features, according to Adamski.

In the summer of 1954, Adamski said he learned from his extraterrestrial friends why there were so many UFO sightings. The extraterrestrials told Adamski that they had built UFO landing fields and even cities on the backside of the Moon, where they would be hidden from prying astronomers on Earth. Adamski wrote that he had been taken in a scout-ship for a firsthand look at the extraterrestrial bases for small UFO scout-ships on the backside of the Moon, where he said he saw "a fair-sized city" and people walking along the clean, narrow streets. Adamski said he saw lakes, rivers and even snow-covered mountains on the hidden face of the Moon, and he reported that the mountains contained heavy growths of timber. Had Adamski bothered to check with scientists at the Palomar Observatory, he would have learned that the Moon has no atmosphere and that the deep vacuum of space to which the lunar surface is exposed ruled out the possibility of open lakes, rivers and snow-covered mountains covered by timber. But for those who wanted to believe Adamski's remarkable story, astronomers could never hope to provide positive photographic evidence to disprove his account because in the mid-1950s it seemed that the backside of the Moon would forever remain hidden to Earthlings.

Even as Adamski was writing his fanciful story, powerful rockets were being developed in the United States and U.S.S.R. for long-range intercontinental ballistic missiles—rockets which would in the next decade serve to expose the backside of the Moon to detailed photographic scrutiny for the first time. By the early 1960s the United States had committed itself to land astronauts on the Moon. To help select suitable landing sites, small unmanned satellites were built and equipped with cameras that could photograph the lunar surface and transmit these pictures back to Earth. The first of these Lunar Orbiter satellites was launched on August 10, 1966, and by the time the fifth, and last, of these satellites had completed its mission in early 1968, the National Aeronautics and Space Administration had obtained photos of more than 99 percent of the Moon's surface, both front and backside. These pictures, all available to the public, demonstrated beyond any doubt that the astronomers were correct and Adamski was wrong—there are no rivers, lakes, or snow-covered mountains on the Moon, nor are there any flying-saucer bases or cities.

Less than two decades after Adamski's fanciful book was published, a total of twenty-one American astronauts in seven Apollo command modules would have made numerous orbits around the Moon in preparation for landings and return trips to Earth, and their personal observations and photos would confirm the pictures taken earlier by the unmanned Lunar Orbiter satellites. Adamski, however, never had the opportunity to see his story disputed by hard photographic evidence, for he had died, following a heart attack near Washington, D.C., in April, 1965—a year before the first Lunar Orbiter photos were obtained.

In a book first published in 1955, "Dr." Daniel Fry claimed that he had been given a ride in a flying saucer which predated Adamski's voyage. This red-letter date was July 4, 1950, according to Fry's book, *The White Sands Incident*, Fry said he had spotted the flying saucer one evening while strolling alone near the Army's White Sands Proving Grounds in New Mexico, where he was working at the time. According to Fry, the small craft was unmanned, remotely controlled from a distant "mother-ship," whose crew could communicate with him, apparently via radio link. Fry said he had been given a demonstration flight aboard the UFO, which speeded him to New York City and back at 8,000 miles per hour. Because the craft was unmanned, Fry was not obliged to try to describe the appearance of extraterrestrials, and because the flight was allegedly made over the United States, only an elementary knowledge of United States geography was required to describe the experience.

One might expect that an experience such as Fry describes would be an incident whose date of occurrence would be indelibly etched in the memory of the individual involved. Yet more than ten years after Fry's book was published, he acknowledged that he had made an error—the incident had occurred a year earlier than originally reported, in 1949 rather than 1950! Fry's book says he is "an internationally known scientist, researcher and electronics engineer who is recognized by many as the best informed scientist in the world on the subject of space and space travel." My own investigation showed that Fry was simply a skilled instrument-maker for Convair who had, during the late 1940s, designed and built several small devices used in missile-control systems.

The book notes that Fry has a Ph.D. from St. Andrews College of London, England, which was awarded for a "learned thesis." When I called the Library of Congress to obtain the address of Fry's "alma mater," they could not find it listed in any of their standard directories, although they did find the well-known St. Andrews University of Edinburgh, Scotland, with which Fry's "alma mater" may be confused. When I tried to place an overseas telephone call to Fry's alma mater, it could not be completed because the London information operator could not find a telephone listed for a St. Andrews College of London! Later, I learned that it was a sort of "correspondence school" that was operated by a small church, called St. Andrews Collegiate Church. From their standard application form I learned that anyone could apply for a Ph.D. by simply submitting a ten-thousand-word thesis and paying a modest fee which amounted to less than one hundred dollars.

Shortly after I met Dan Fry in late 1966, a new "contactee" appeared on the UFO scene named Woodrow Derenberger, a former preacher turned appliance salesman. He claimed that on the night of November 2, while he was driving home to Parkersburg, West Virginia, a UFO had landed on the highway, forcing him to stop his truck. He said a dark-skinned occupant emerged from the craft, approached the truck and motioned to Derenberger to lower the window so he could communicate with him. Then, using what Derenberger called "thought-waves" (which seemingly could not penetrate the car window), the UFOnaut said his name was "Indrid Cold," asked a few questions and then returned to his flying saucer and zoomed off into the night. Two nights later, Derenberger said, the UFOnaut made the first of numerous visits to his home. The extraterrestrial visitor reportedly explained that he came from a planet named "Lanulos," had a wife named "Kimi," two sons and a daughter. When I met Derenberger in early 1968 during his visit to Washington for lectures and we appeared together on a local television show, he told me that Lanulos was some three and one-half light-years away from Earth—corresponding to a distance of *20 trillion miles.* When Derenberger said he himself had made two visits to Lanulos in a UFO, and I asked how long the trip had taken, he replied, "About an hour and a half." I was too stunned to ask whether this was the one-way or round-trip travel time.

In another TV appearance in Washington, Derenberger

explained that the people of Lanulos, being far more advanced than Earthlings, had eliminated practically all of the problems that have for so long plagued Earth—disease, crime, poverty and war. The only problem that Lanulos had not solved was the domestic one between husband and wife, and so there were divorces in that distant near-utopia. During this TV appearance, Derenberger said his extraterrestrial friends often dropped in to visit him and sometimes brought along their wives and stayed for dinner. When the program moderator asked if persons who attended his lectures might be able to meet one of his extraterrestrial friends, Derenberger replied that he could not be sure but that "there is a very good possibility." However, he added, "The only way he [an extraterrestrial] would make himself known in a group of that kind, where there would be a large crowd, he would be standing close by the doorway, he would identify himself and leave immediately." If any of Derenberger's extraterrestrial friends showed up for his lectures in Washington, it was not reported in any of the local newspapers.

Possibly the most famous "contactee" case of all time is the one involving Betty Hill, and her late husband Barney, of Portsmouth, New Hampshire.* Their story of having seen a UFO and later of having been taken aboard a flying saucer and subjected to physical examinations was published as a two-part series in the October 4 and 11, 1966, issues of *Look* magazine. The series, entitled "Aboard a Flying Saucer," assisted by a widespread advertising and publicity campaign, reportedly resulted in the largest newsstand sales the magazine had ever achieved. The articles, and a book entitled *The Interrupted Journey* which appeared several weeks later, were written by John G. Fuller, who strongly leans toward the extraterrestrial spaceship hypothesis, judging from his three books on UFOs.

* The Hill case, covered in more detail in my earlier book *UFOs—Identified*, is highlighted here along with other colorful "contactee" cases for the benefit of readers who are unfamiliar with it, in order to provide perspective for the equally colorful accounts of contact with the occupants of "mysterious airships" in the 1890s, to be discussed in the next chapter, and the more recent Pascagoula "abduction" story in 1973, to be analyzed in Chapter 27.

The incident had allegedly occurred some five years before it achieved international fame—on September 19, 1961—as the Hills were driving home late at night through the White Mountains of New Hampshire. Betty, whose sister was quite interested in UFOs, spotted a light in the sky which seemed unusual and which, she concluded, was following their car. Finally, Barney stopped the car, got a gun from the car trunk, and went into a nearby field for a better view. He became extremely frightened and decided they ought to leave the main highway and take to some rambling back roads to "escape" the UFO. As a result, they did not arrive home in Portsmouth until the early hours of September 20, two hours later than they had originally expected when they had left Montreal some hours before.

Betty promptly called her sister later that day to tell of her own exciting UFO sighting and reported that the UFO had come quite close to the car, in dramatic contrast to her sister's sighting of only a distant UFO. The sister expressed concern that the proximity of the UFO might have exposed the Hills to some mysterious and deadly radiation. Later the sister called back to say she had checked with a physicist and that Betty could test for possible radiation effects using an ordinary magnetic compass. (This simply is not true; a compass reacts only to magnetic fields and to ferrous materials and cannot possibly indicate the presence of nuclear radiation.) When Betty brought a compass near the trunk of their car, she reported that the needle behaved strangely, although when Barney later repeated the test he did not observe any unusual behavior. Nevertheless, Betty was "haunted" by the fear that she and Barney had been exposed to radiation from the UFO and might be doomed to a horrible, lingering death, according to Fuller's account. Betty promptly went to the Portsmouth library and brought home a book entitled *The Flying Saucer Conspiracy*, filled with exotic flying-saucer stories. Betty next wrote to NICAP headquarters in Washington to describe the recent UFO sighting.

The letter to NICAP made no mention of being "abducted" because it was not until several days later, ten days after the incident, that Betty began to experience nightmares in which she *dreamed* that she and Barney had been taken aboard a flying saucer for an examination. *These frightening dreams continued for five successive nights.* When Betty described these nightmares to friends and her associates at work, one of the latter suggested that perhaps the dreams might have some basis in reality. When local NICAP investigators came to talk to the Hills, and were told of Betty's dreams, one of them suggested that perhaps an abduction actually had taken place and that this might explain why they had arrived home two hours later than originally expected. During the next two years the Hills described the incident and Betty's abduction dreams to local UFO and church groups.

During this period, Barney had sought psychiatric help from a doctor in Exeter, New Hampshire, for personal problems. Barney, a black, was divorced from his first (black) wife and now had an interracial marriage. In the fall of 1963 the Exeter psychiatrist recommended that he seek treatment from a prominent Boston psychiatrist, Dr. Ben Simon, a down-to-earth practitioner who had developed considerable skill in the use of hypnosis. And so, in the fall of 1963, Barney drove to Boston for his first visit with Dr. Simon, accompanied by Betty. It soon became apparent to the Boston psychiatrist, to use his own words, "that both needed help."

Simon noted that when Betty and Barney, individually under hypnosis, effectively "relived" their drive back from Montreal during the night of the UFO incident, both recalled the same details. This was quite natural, Dr. Simon later explained to me when I interviewed him in the fall of 1966, because both had undergone a common experience during the trip. But when Betty and Barney "relived" under hypnosis the alleged abduction and examination aboard the flying saucer, it was quite a different situation, Dr. Simon emphasized to me. Betty described many, many specific details while Barney seemed to recall almost nothing. This, Dr. Simon told me, indicated that the abduction incident was *not* a common, shared experience, and it suggested that Barney had acquired his knowledge of the abduction incident after repeatedly hearing Betty tell of her nightmare-dreams to friends and neighbors. Additionally, Simon said, many of the things that Betty reported as having occurred aboard the flying saucer had the typical characteristics of dreams with symbolisms, some of them sexual, that an experienced psychiatrist readily recognized.

Finally, I asked Dr. Simon for his candid appraisal of the abduction part of the Hills' story because he—an experienced psychiatrist—had spent more time in probing their account than anyone else. The doctor replied by telling me that he had been asked the same question only a couple of months earlier when a senior editor from *Look* magazine had visited him in Boston prior to deciding whether or not to publish the sensational Fuller articles. Simon said, "The first question he asked me was this: 'Doctor, do you really believe that the Hills were abducted and taken aboard a flying saucer?' " Simon told me he had replied, *"Absolutely not!"* The two men then discussed the case for an hour, and when the interview was finished, Simon said that the *Look* editor had said, "Doctor, if you had replied to my first question by saying that you really believed that the Hills had been abducted, I would have put on my hat and taken the next flight back to New York." (Yet from the way the articles were subsequently presented, *Look* readers might easily have concluded that the magazine endorsed the sensational story.)

Dr. Simon's dismissal of Betty's dreamlike account of the abduction did not surprise me. When he earlier had replied to my request for an interview, Simon had written that his interpretation was "somewhat at variance" with that emphasized by Fuller in the *Look* articles. During our later discussion, Simon told me that he and Fuller had had many sharp disagreements over Fuller's interpretations of the facts. Simon made an oblique reference to these disagreements in the introductory chapter which he wrote for Fuller's book. The doctor emphasized that Fuller's "reasoning and speculations are his own, based on his evaluation of my data . . . and his present convictions. . . . I have no doubt given him sleepless nights and many moments of despair."

Perhaps the most convincing indication of the viewpoint of

the Boston psychiatrist who treated the Hills is to be found in the introductory chapter that he wrote for the Fuller book. If Simon believed the abduction account to be fact and not fantasy, it would demonstrate beyond all doubt the existence of intelligent creatures on other worlds and that they were visiting Earth—surely the most exciting scientific discovery of all time. Yet Simon wrote: "Their existence (The UFO's) as concrete objects is of less concern to me than the experiences of these two people showing the cumulative impact of past experiences and *fantasies* on their present experiences and responses." (Emphasis added.)

24 • Mysterious Airships of the 1890s

Events that occurred eighty years ago in the United States provide invaluable insight into the UFO mystery. These events demonstrate that when the public has been conditioned by the news media to believe that there are strange flying objects in the skies, many persons will report having seen such objects—even when the objects do not really exist. During 1896 and 1897 many hundreds of persons reported seeing "mysterious airships," often said to have been flying at speeds of hundreds of miles per hour. Most of the reports came from the Midwest—from Texas to Michigan—and from the Pacific coast. Primitive powered airships of this type had been developed in Europe. For example, in 1884, a French airship measuring 165 feet long had managed to fly a five-mile closed course at an average speed of 13 mph. But at the time of the rash of "mysterious airship" sightings there were no large powered craft of this type in the United States. Numerous American inventors were trying to develop "flying machines," and on May 6, 1896, only a few months before the rash of "mysterious airship" reports, Samuel P. Langley had successfully flown a twenty-six-pound model airplane, a feat that made headlines.

Because of some similarities between the numerous reports of "mysterious airships" in the 1890s and the UFO flaps that began half a century later, there are those who suggest that the "mysterious airships" were really spaceships from other worlds that were erroneously described in terms of the emerging technology familiar to observers of that earlier era. But the fatal flaw in this hypothesis is that in the 1890s many persons reported having seen, and talked with, the very earthy members of the crews that allegedly operated the "mysterious airships." There were numerous reports of landings to enable the crew to replenish food and water. Not infrequently, it was said that the pilot sought directions to his destination. Some accounts said the pilot had confided to the "observer" that a revolutionary new airship design or "anti-gravity technique" was being tested that would be made public as soon as it had been patented. One of my favorite accounts involved an observer who claimed to have heard the crew of a "mysterious airship" singing "Nearer My God To Thee."

These accounts contrast sharply with some that would emerge half a century later in UFO "occupant" cases with their reports of strange-looking creatures that allegedly operated flying saucers. There were no more than a couple of "mysterious airship" reports that suggested that the alleged craft was of extraterrestrial origin, the most famous of which will be described subsequently. Many of the "mysterious airship" accounts can be characterized by Dr. Hynek's favorite description of many UFO reports: "Incredible stories told by credible people." For example, the April 28, 1897, edition of *The St. Louis Globe-Democrat* reported that a Kansas farmer named Alexander Hamilton who lived near Yates Center, had had an unnerving experience with a "mysterious airship" on the night of April 19. According to Hamilton, he was awakened by a commotion among his cattle around 10:30 P.M., got dressed and went outside to investigate, where he found one of the "mysterious airships" descending near the barn. He said he ran back, awakened his son and hired hand, and the three, armed with axes, returned to the farmyard. He said the craft was so close he could see two men and a woman inside the brightly illuminated "carriage" and claimed he could hear the three persons talking in an unknown tongue.

At that point, Hamilton said, the craft turned a huge, powerful spotlight on the three men on the ground, fired up its "great turbine wheel" (propeller) and began to ascend. Then the Kansas farmer reported that from an altitude of about three hundred feet, the crew of the "mysterious airship" lowered a heavy rope fitted with a slip-knot to form a lasso, looped it over the neck of a heifer and began to haul it aboard, despite the frantic efforts of Hamilton and his two companions to free the poor animal. The next morning, Hamilton said, he had found the hide, head and legs of the heifer in a nearby field; presumably the crew of the "mysterious airship" had devoured the remainder. Apparently there were some who doubted Hamilton's story, because on April 21 a dozen of the leading citizens from the area reportedly signed a sworn affidavit which testified to Hamilton's good reputation for "truth and veracity." The affidavit said that the undersigned "do verily believe his statement to be true and correct." The signers included the local sheriff, deputy sheriff, banker, postmaster and a justice of the peace. It would be difficult to find a more impressive list of character witnesses.

During the evening of April 11, 1897, a "mysterious airship" was reported by residents of Appleton, Wisconsin, and a few days later a farmer nearby came up with physical evidence to support the earlier reports. He said he had found a long iron rod sticking in the ground to which was attached the following unsigned letter, according to the local newspaper account:

> Aboard the Airship "Pegasus," April 9, 1897—The problem of aerial navigation has been solved. The writers have spent the past month cruising about in the airship "Pegasus" and have demonstrated to their entire satisfac-

tion that the ship is a thorough success. We have been
able to attain a speed of 150 miles an hour* and have
risen to a height of 2,500 feet above sea level.

The "Pegasus" was erected at a secluded point ten
miles from Lafayette, Tenn. . . . Within a month our
application for patents for a parallel plane airship will be
filed simultaneously at Washington and European capi-
tals. The ship is propelled by steam and is lighted by
electricity and has a carrying power of 1,000 lb.

An even more intriguing account appeared in the April 23,
1897, edition of *Modern News*, published in Harrisburg,
Arkansas: "The airship of which we have read so much of late
. . . anchored in Harrisburg Wednesday night (April 21).
Ex-Senator Harris was awakened about 1 o'clock by an
unfamiliar noise, and upon taking a peep out he spied a
peculiar looking object in the west. Instantly he thought of
the wonderful airship which had so mystified the people of
the west during the past few weeks, and hurriedly dressing he
took his field glasses and went out in the yard." Harris did not
need the field glasses because, according to his account, he
saw an airship gradually descending near his yard with an
elderly bewhiskered man, a woman and two young men
aboard. Harris said he approached the craft and struck up a
conversation with the pilot, who was busy taking on a supply
of fresh water from the well.

Harris said the pilot explained that some twenty-six years
earlier his uncle had devised means "by which the laws of
gravitation were entirely and completely suspended." Unfortunately the uncle had died before acquainting his nephew
with the full details, and it had taken the nephew—the
airship pilot—some nineteen years to rediscover the secret.
Harris said the pilot explained that he was "not quite through
experimenting and so I continue to travel at night to keep
from being detected. I will make an attempt to visit Mars
before I put the airship on public exhibition. . . . I have a
4-ton improved Hotchkiss gun aboard, besides about ten tons

---

* A speed of 150 mph is several times the maximum speed ever reported for
an honest-to-goodness gas-filled airship.

of ammunition. I was making preparations to go over to Cuba and kill out the Spanish army if hostilities had not ceased, but now my plans are changed and I may go to the aid of the Armenians. . . . I could take breakfast here, do my shopping in Paris, and be back here for dinner without inconvenience, as soon as I get my new propellers completed." Harris said he had been invited to take a ride aboard the craft but had declined.

During the month of April, 1897, "mysterious airships" were also reported over Michigan. According to the Lansing newspaper *State Republican*, William Megiveron reported that he had been awakened on the night of April 15 by a tap on the window. Opening his eyes, he said he was almost blinded by an intense light and that he heard a voice from above which explained that an airship was hovering overhead, concealed in the clouds. The voice explained that a round from a hunter's gun had damaged a wing and the crew was busy repairing it. The voice, Megiveron said, asked if he could prepare four dozen egg sandwiches and a kettle of coffee, which he agreed to do. Soon the airship reportedly lowered a scoop filled with Canadian coins to pay for the provisions, and hauled up the food. Megiveron said he had asked several times if he could be taken aboard, but that his requests were greeted with hoots of laughter. This prompted Megiveron to suspect that the airship crew had been drinking—especially since they had earlier asked for a corkscrew.

These are but a few of the many "incredible stories told by credible people" that were widely publicized during this period as newspapers sought to outdo one another in reporting "mysterious airships." During a five-day period between April 15 and April 19, 1897, *The Dallas Morning News* reported sightings from twenty-one different towns in Texas. During the next nine days the *Houston Post* carried nine others. One incident, which reportedly occurred on April 17 in the town of Aurora, Texas, would achieve fame more long-lived than the town itself. The incident, as reported in the April 19 edition of *The Dallas Morning News*, follows.

About 6 o'clock this morning the early risers of Aurora were astonished at the sudden appearance of the airship which has been sailing throughout the country. It was travelling due north, and much nearer the earth than before. Evidently some of the machinery was out of order, for it was making a speed of only ten or twelve miles an hour, and gradually settling toward the earth. It sailed over the public square and when it reached the north part of town [it] collided with the tower of Judge Proctor's windmill and went to pieces with a terrific explosion, scattering debris over several acres of ground, wrecking the windmill and water tank and destroying the judge's flower garden. The pilot of the ship is supposed to have been the only one aboard, and while his remains are badly disfigured, enough of the original has been picked up to show that *he was not an inhabitant of this world.* [Emphasis added.]

Mr. T. J. Weems, the U.S. [Army] Signal Service officer at this place and an authority on astronomy, gives it as his opinion that he [the pilot] was a *native of the planet Mars. Papers found on his person—evidently the records of his travels—are written in some unknown hieroglyphics, and cannot be deciphered.* This ship was too badly wrecked to form any conclusion as to its construction or motive power. It was built of an unknown metal, resembling somewhat a mixture of aluminum and silver, and it must have weighed several tons. The town today is full of people who are viewing the wreckage and gathering specimens of strange metal from the debris. The pilot's funeral will take place at noon tomorrow. Signed: E. E. Haydon. [Emphasis added.]

If the managing editor of *The Dallas Morning News* took the report at face value, as would appear to be the case, since the newspaper published the account, it seems strange that a reporter was not promptly dispatched to nearby Aurora for a firsthand investigation. In the year 1897 the crash of a "mysterious airship" with a strange-looking pilot who was thought to have come from Mars would seem to be an event of sufficient import to justify additional investigation and coverage. The reported pilot's log of his travels "written in some unknown hieroglyphics" would seem worthy of publication in subsequent editions. Yet the Dallas newspaper did not obtain a copy and publish it.

I first learned of the Aurora case from an article entitled "Airships Over Texas" written by Donald B. Hanlon and Jacques Vallee, which was published in the January–February 1967 issue of the British magazine *Flying Saucer Review*. At the end of the article was a letter from the two authors, evidently written after the original article had been submitted, which was published under a headline that read: "The truth about Aurora." Hanlon and Vallee wrote that an unnamed friend of Dr. Hynek, who lived in Texas, had volunteered to visit Aurora, or what remains of it, to make an investigation. The investigator first visited Brawley Oates, who operates a gas station and has a house on the site of the late Judge Proctor's farm. Oates explained that Aurora had once been the largest town in Wise County, and that Judge Proctor had been a justice of the peace. Oates declined to comment on the authenticity of the "mysterious airship" case, but suggested the investigator talk with Oscar Lowry, who had been a boy of eleven at the time, and who now lived a short distance away. Lowry also emphasized that Aurora had once been a very prosperous town until the railroad built new track which completely by-passed the town, and then its prosperity and population began to decline.

E. E. Haydon, who had written the original newspaper account, was a cotton buyer and a "stringer" (part-time reporter) for the Dallas newspaper. Haydon, understandably, was concerned over Aurora's decline and felt that something was needed to focus attention on Aurora and, hopefully, to make it a tourist attraction, Lowry suggested. This was speculation on Lowry's part, but he went on to point out several basic fallacies in Haydon's account. For example, Haydon had reported that the "mysterious airship" had collided with a windmill on Judge Proctor's farm, but Lowry said the farm did not have a windmill. T. J. Weems, whose expertise as an Army Signal officer and amateur astronomer had been invoked to establish the extraterrestrial nature of the pilot was neither an Army officer nor an astronomer. Weems was the local blacksmith, according to Lowry.

The town cemetery was operated by the Masonic Order, which maintained a chart to show the location and identity of each person buried there. If an unknown pilot had been buried in the Aurora cemetery, there ought to be one grave whose occupant was listed in the records as "unidentified." But each grave's occupant was named. Despite Haydon's report that there had been many visitors to Aurora to pick up scraps from the "mysterious airship," none of these ever showed up as family heirlooms or in museums. The alleged pilot's log, with its mysterious "hieroglyphics," had also disappeared, despite the obviously great value of such a document—if it existed. But old myths do not die easily. On May 24, 1973, newspapers around the country published the following United Press International story:

> Aurora, Tex.—(UPI)—A grave in a small north Texas cemetery contains the body of an 1897 astronaut who "was not an inhabitant of this world," according to the International UFO Bureau.
>
> The group, which investigates unidentified flying objects, has already initiated legal proceedings to exhume the body, and will go to court if necessary to open the grave, director Hayden Hewes said Wednesday.
>
> "After checking the grave with metal detectors and gathering facts for three months, we are certain as we can be at this point [that] he was the pilot of a UFO which reportedly exploded atop a well on Judge J. S. Proctor's place, Apr. 19, 1897," Hewes said. "He was not an inhabitant of this world."

How had the investigators in 1973 been able to find the plot in which the "mysterious airship" pilot had been buried, when the cemetery records did not show any "unidentified" grave? Very handily. A large rock had been discovered in the tiny cemetery on which had been scratched the vague outline of an arrow with three small circles—a rock that for some strange reason had never been noticed by previous investigators. If this was indeed the tombstone that the citizens of

Aurora had provided for the poor victim from a distant world, it could hardly be said that they had given him a "decent Christian burial," as Haydon had reported in a follow-up story. On the night of June 14, 1973, after there was talk of analyzing the rock to determine the age of its scratched arrow, the rock mysteriously disappeared.

The Reuters news service, which had been scooped by the UPI on the Aurora case, supplied its clients with a story of the case that also included a report from a housewife in suburban Dallas who had discovered a mysterious "blob" in her backyard that was growing at a wild pace despite her efforts to kill it. (Later the mysterious blob was identified as a type of fungus.) In late May the UPI had still another story datelined Aurora which quoted a ninety-one-year-old woman, who had been a girl of fifteen in Aurora at the time of the reported incident. She said she "had all but forgotten the incident until it appeared in the newspapers recently." She said her parents had gone to the site of the crash, but had refused to take her along. She recalled that the remains of the pilot, "a small man," had been buried in the Aurora cemetery.

The Associated Press, not to be outdone, in a story datelined Denton, Texas, reported that a North Texas State University professor had found some metal fragments near the Oates gas station (former Proctor farm). One fragment was said to be "most intriguing" because it consisted primarily of iron which did not seem to exhibit magnetic properties. The professor also said he was puzzled because the fragment was "shiny and malleable instead of dull and brittle like iron." (Subsequent analysis of the fragments by scientists at the National Aeronautical Establishment of Canada reportedly showed the metal fragments to be commonplace, without unusual composition or structural characteristics.)

The national publicity, and even more in the local press, brought hordes of curious visitors, some of whom hauled off old gravestones as mementos. Fortunately, the Aurora Cemetery Association succeeded in blocking attempts to dig up the grounds in search of the "Martian pilot." Hopefully, the occupants of the Aurora cemetery can rest in peace until, perhaps on the one hundredth anniversary of the alleged incident, national attention once again will focus on Aurora as some young newsman or aging managing editor searches for something to liven up an otherwise dull news day!

Not all of the "mysterious airship" reports should be dismissed as simply tall tales intended to achieve local fame for an individual or publicity for a town in need of a tourist attraction. Once the public had become conditioned to believe that there were strange flying objects in the skies, nature provided enough "trigger-mechanisms." For example, some reports suggest that the stimulus was a bright meteor/fireball, or perhaps a ball-lightning-type plasma. The April 15, 1897, edition of *The Dallas Morning News* reported: "That Denton is not behind the other towns and cities in North Texas is shown by the fact that the mysterious airship of which so much has been said and written in the last few days, has been seen here by at least two credible persons. . . . The airship is described as cigar-shaped with a light, moving slowly. Then it accelerated 'at a terrific rate.' There was a row of windows along one side. . . ." This description brings to mind the UFO reported in 1948 by Eastern Air Lines pilots Chiles and Whitted, and the reports sparked by the flaming debris from the Zond-4 rocket, described in Chapter 1. If the object was a meteor and it was initially headed toward the observers, this would account for what appeared to be its slow motion at the start.

The April 16, 1897, edition of *The Dallas Morning News* carried a report from Corsicana which said that a "mysterious airship" appeared as "a bright light a long distance from the earth and was moving at rather a fast speed across the firmament." On March 31, 1897, a report from Galesburg, Michigan, told of a brilliant white object seen about 10 P.M. that was accompanied by a sharp crackling sound as the brilliant object soared over the city and disappeared after approximately thirty seconds. From Manistique, Michigan, in April, came a report of a cigar-shaped object "with a bright light in the center of it," which zoomed overhead at a speed

estimated at 1,000 mph. These and similar accounts suggest
the object was a meteor/fireball.

Still other "mysterious airship" reports, where the object
appeared as a bright light that remained in view for many
minutes or several hours, suggest that Venus, Mars or another
bright celestial body was responsible. For example, the April
10, 1897, edition of *The Evanston [Illinois] Index* reported
that "five hundred reputable citizens gazed with astonish-
ment at the spectacle of a bright light in the heavens to the
west. It was first seen at about 8:15 o'clock, very low down on
the horizon and had the brightness of fifty ordinary electric
street lights . . . it was in plain view for fully forty-five
minutes. A great many people viewed it with opera glasses
. . . and were certain it was the famous airship about which
so much fun has been made in the papers." This "mysterious
airship" was promptly identified as the star Alpha Orionis by
Professor George W. Hough, then director of the Northwestern University Dearborn Observatory—a post that Hynek
would later assume.

Finally, the 1890s had their pranksters too. For example,
on April 10, 1897, many persons in southern Iowa, from
Ottumwa to Burlington, reported they had seen not one but
several "mysterious airships." Later, pranksters admitted they
had constructed hot-air balloons out of tissue paper, with
candles used to supply both the hot air and the illumination.
On November 24, 1896, shortly after midnight, persons in
downtown San Francisco saw what was first assumed to be a
"mysterious airship." It later proved to be a prankster's
hot-air balloon. The famed newspaper publisher William
Randolph Hearst, in a penetrating commentary on the role
the news media had played in "brain-washing" the public into
believing and reporting mysterious airships, wrote the following in an editorial carried in the December 5, 1896,
edition of the *San Francisco Examiner*:

> "Fake journalism" has a good deal to answer for, but
> we do not recall a more discernible exploit in that line
> than the persistent attempt to make the public believe
> that the air in this vicinity is populated with airships. It

has been manifest for weeks that the whole airship story is pure myth.

More than half a century later, the news media—including radio and television—would play a similar role, albeit unwittingly, in perpetrating another myth—that there are, or might be, extraterrestrial vehicles in our skies. This will be discussed in the two following chapters.

I acknowledge my indebtedness for many of the "mysterious airship" accounts and references to research conducted by others, including Jerome Clark, Harold H. Deneault, Jr., Lucius Farish, Donald B. Hanlon, Gordon I. R. Lore, Jr., and Jacques Vallee.

25 • The Interactive Effect

The news media play a very significant and interactive role in the UFO mystery, periodically breathing new life into it, which generally is not recognized, even by many of the journalists involved. This is the result of two special characteristics of the UFO issue.

The first is that the prospect of there being intelligent life elsewhere in the vast universe has great intrinsic appeal—understandably—for a large segment of the public. The discovery of such intelligent life would be one of the most exciting events of all time, not only for the public but for the scientific community as well. Even if there is only a *small* possibility that UFO reports involve extraterrestrial visitors, the fact that anyone who is willing to scan the skies may be lucky enough to see a UFO and thereby become a firsthand participant in this exciting possibility* presents an opportunity that is hard

---

* One woman, describing her UFO sighting during an interview on a national TV show, was asked, "What was it like when you saw this thing?" She replied, "It's spectacular. It's magnificent. It's beautiful . . . something

to resist. When the news media indicate that UFOs are being seen by others in the area, they supply the motivation for the general public to keep an alert eye on the skies.

The second special characteristic of UFOs is that there are so many natural and man-made stimuli that can become UFOs when observers are led to believe that "they" are in the vicinity and when the observers—perhaps unconsciously—are anxious to participate in the great UFO adventure. This was demonstrated by the rash of "mysterious airship" reports in the 1890s—an era when there were far fewer stimuli in the skies than are available today. Even so, the bright celestial bodies, meteors, ball lightning, prankster's hot-air balloons and outright hoaxes, in combination with news media publicity, were quite sufficient. Today we have many more stimuli, principally man-made. Some of these have already been discussed in earlier chapters—such things as space debris entering the atmosphere, giant scientific balloons and the smaller weather types, aircraft conducting experimental tests, military aircraft engaged in mid-air night refueling operations or exercises, and little-known USAF reconnaissance aircraft which fly at speeds faster than 2,000 mph at extremely high altitudes. Brightly illuminated blimps used for aerial advertising provide still another type of stimulus.

Even experienced UFO investigators can be fooled, if only temporarily. When NICAP headquarters in Washington sent three top investigators to South Hill, Virginia, to investigate that "landing" case in the spring of 1967 (Chapter 13), they spotted what seemed to be a fast-moving UFO the first night. It proved to be a man-made Earth satellite in orbit. During the University of Colorado UFO study, its scientists were testing a device whose inventor claimed it could detect the proximity of a UFO, when the detector sounded its alarm. Two staff members rushed outside and sure enough they quickly spotted a UFO. After watching the UFO for some time, they finally realized that they were looking at Venus! In another instance an experienced NICAP UFO investigator

_____

really marvelous. . . ." From her account and the reported position of the UFO in the sky at the time, she may well have been looking at Venus.

from Boston, while driving near the lower Chesapeake Bay, saw an airplane that was being followed by what he described to me as a triangular-shaped UFO. I pointed out to him that the Naval Air Test Center is located in that region and suggested that this UFO might be an aerial gunnery target being towed on a cable behind the airplane. He followed up on this suggestion and later informed me that the UFO was indeed a towed target.

Several years ago, shortly before sunset, a neighbor called excitedly to tell me to hurry outside to see a giant, colored UFO as large as the Moon. This UFO turned out to be a man-made cloud produced at an altitude of approximately 120 miles by a rocket which had released barium and other chemicals. The rocket had been launched by the National Aeronautics and Space Administration from its facility at Wallops Island, Virginia, located more than one hundred miles southeast of Washington. In the summer of 1971, police in Washington, D.C., began to receive a number of UFO reports from persons who told of sighting blinking lights in the night skies. The police explained that these were three new helicopters which had recently been acquired to help them track down criminal suspects. At the present time there are several hundred police helicopters in use in the United States, and they are usually equipped with intense spotlights, which often help to generate UFO reports.

Following one of my UFO lectures, a member of the audience came to the podium to describe his own encounter with a most unusual UFO while in the Army. He had been stationed in the Philippines, on guard duty one night, when he and a companion saw a large glowing object moving slowly and silently through a dense jungle toward them. When the UFO had moved sufficiently close, the two men were able to identify it as a colony of fireflies moving as a cluster. When I mentioned the incident in a subsequent lecture, a member of the audience came forward to tell me that he had had a similar encounter with a colony of fireflies while hunting in Canada. During the summer of 1973, a UFO sighted near Butte, Montana, proved to be a giant man-carrying kite that was being towed by an automobile preparatory to being released for flight. In at least several instances a UFO which reportedly seemed to zig-zag back and forth in the sky has turned out to be a gasoline-powered model airplane being flown on a tether-line.

Several years ago, shortly after sunset, a friend pointed out to me a glowing orange-colored, cigar-shaped UFO which was moving silently at high altitude a few miles to the west. As we watched, the glowing UFO executed a gradual turn in the still-light sky. I asked the friend to keep the UFO under surveillance while I obtained my binoculars. When I returned, we quickly identified this UFO as an unusual short-persistence vapor trail from a jet airplane which itself was visible only with the binoculars. Because of unusual atmospheric conditions, the vapor trail was dissipating completely only a few seconds after it formed, leaving in the wake of the airplane a short trail that was being illuminated by the rays of the setting sun. Although I have seen hundreds of jet aircraft vapor trails through the years, this was the first and only one of such short persistence I have ever observed. Recently, Frank D. Marrow, of Ulster, Pennsylvania, wrote to describe a similar experience, except that in his case the vapor trail had expanded into more of an egg or saucer shape.

A UFO survey of American Institute of Aeronautics and Astronautics members* in the San Francisco area, conducted by Dr. Peter A. Sturrock, revealed still another class of stimuli for UFO reports which may be more common than generally recognized. One AIAA member, an amateur astronomer, reported that he was star-gazing in his backyard one night with a friend when they observed three luminous objects that appeared to be flying silently in precise formation at very high altitude, estimated to be 100,000 feet. A week later, he reported, the incident occurred again. But this time, he reported, one of the UFOs "broke formation" and made a noise which gave away its identity. These UFOs were white owls, gliding in complete silence. The luminous effect was

* One AIAA member who responded to the UFO survey described two occasions when he said he had received "telepathic communication" to alert him to the upcoming appearance of UFOs.

caused by diffuse lights from the city illuminating the underside of their wings.

In 1961, R. G. Button, then employed by General Dynamics Corporation, was driving alone on a dark night, returning from a business trip to an Atlas ICBM missile site in Wyoming. Suddenly, to use his own words, "a bright, disc-like object zoomed at the car from the right front, then did an abrupt right-turn." The object seemed to pace his car, always slightly ahead, and appeared to pulsate and periodically change altitude. When he accelerated the car to more than 90 mph, the UFO did the same; and when he slowed down, the UFO followed suit. "Now I was frightened, and pretty well convinced there was something out there," he told me. The highway was deserted and there were no houses in sight. Finally, Button stopped the car only to find that the UFO seemed to be hovering just ahead of him. He turned off the engine, rolled down the window and thought he heard a "sizzling sound," which presumably came from the UFO.

Button said he finally mustered his nerve and decided to get out of the car for a close-up inspection. "By now I couldn't tell if it was huge and a few hundred yards away, or small and close." As he walked toward the UFO, it began to fade and almost disappeared. Then he identified the UFO that had been pacing his car: a copper-coated wire strung on poles to the right side of the highway, which had been reflecting the light from the headlamps of his car. If Button had not stopped to investigate, at some point the UFO would suddenly have veered off and disappeared, where the path of the power line and the highway were no longer parallel, and this UFO case would forever have been listed among the unexplained.

The foregoing examples of the wide variety of stimuli that can generate UFO reports are probably only a small percentage of the total. But they suffice to illustrate that when the news media condition the public to believe that there are UFOs to be seen, there are many stimuli that can readily generate numerous UFO reports. When this media-induced rash of UFO reports is published, it will impact on a still wider segment of the public and prompt still more persons to scan the skies hopefully for UFOs, producing still more reports and publicity.

But the news media traditionally lose interest in any subject that fails "to build," to provide new and more exciting details that lead to a conclusion or climax. In time, a local or even a national UFO flap runs out of steam when news media editors tire of simply running additional stories about mysterious lights in the night skies or publishing more UFO photos which are suspected hoaxes. As media interest declines, there is less incentive for pranksters to launch helium-filled or hot-air balloons. As media coverage declines, the public concludes that the UFOs have stopped coming, so fewer persons scan the skies. Now UFOs enter a period of dormancy until circumstances combine a few years later to arouse media interest again.

This interactive effect is clearly evident from an analysis of UFO flaps of the past, including the one during the fall of 1973, to be discussed in the next chapter. For example, following the nationwide burst of publicity given the first UFO report on June 24, 1947, by private flyer Kenneth Arnold, there was a flurry of other reports. But during the five-year period from 1947 to 1951, the number of UFO reports submitted to the USAF averaged fewer than *fifteen* per month. This included a modest surge during 1950 when Donald E. Keyhoe, the principal early publicizer of the extraterrestrial hypothesis, published his first UFO book, filled with extravagant claims and charges of a high-level government conspiracy to withhold the "truth" from the public.

The year 1952 started quietly enough in terms of UFO reports submitted to the USAF. Then the April 4 issue of *Life* magazine carried a major feature story entitled "Have We Visitors From Space?" and excerpts from the article were featured in more than three hundred newspapers throughout the country. During the same month the number of UFO reports to the USAF skyrocketed to more than five times the previous monthly average. May was also a bumper-crop month. Then in June, *Look* magazine ran two feature stories on UFOs and *Life* published still another. During that month a total of 148 UFO reports, *or nearly ten times the previous monthly average*, were submitted to the USAF.

Then, in July, UFOs made headlines around the nation when mysterious blips were spotted on the Washington National Airport radarscopes. The hot, humid weather conditions were precisely those that often cause spurious "angel" blips. But radar was then a relatively new device, especially for civil air traffic controllers, and its technical shortcomings were not well understood. There was considerable speculation in the news media stories that extraterrestrial spaceships might be conducting reconnaissance of the nation's capital. Not surprisingly, a total of 536 UFO reports were submitted to the USAF during July, an all-time peak corresponding to a *3700 percent increase* over the earlier monthly average.

In September even the urbane *New Yorker* magazine published a feature story on UFOs. And in January, 1953, the then very popular television program "Robert Montgomery Presents" featured a drama about a pilot who had been captured by a flying saucer. But the UFO story did not continue to build. There were additional reports of mysterious lights in the skies and of curiously behaving blips on radarscopes, but nothing significantly different from previous reports and nothing that provided substantiation for speculation about extraterrestrial visitors. More important issues dominated the news, such as whether the new Eisenhower Administration could end the increasingly unpopular war in Korea, and so there was a sharp decline in the UFO reports published in the national news media. And the number of UFO reports submitted to the USAF also declined sharply to about one-third the 1952 figure.

By the mid-1950s the United States was engaged in a desperate race with the Soviet Union to develop giant rocket boosters for intercontinental ballistic missiles. Once such rockets were perfected, they would be powerful enough to launch a man-made satellite into orbit around the Earth. And still larger versions could be built to carry scientific payloads out into space—to the Moon and even the planets of our solar system. Space travel—the dream of visionaries and science-fiction writers—was close to becoming reality. Growing numbers of articles on these prospects began to appear in the general news media as well as the technical press.

This served to lift the idea of space travel out of the realm of science fiction and to condition the general public to its approaching reality. And it provided a rationale that UFO believers could use to argue that much more advanced civilizations on other worlds might already be engaged in space travel and be visiting Earth. During 1955 and 1956 a total of ten books on UFOs, espousing the extraterrestrial hypothesis, were published in the United States—*five times as many as had been published here in the preceding eight years since UFOs had been "discovered."* One of the most influential of the 1955–1956 crop of books was written by the late Edward J. Ruppelt, who, as a captain in the USAF, had earlier briefly headed the Project Blue Book office. Judging from the book, *Report on Unidentified Flying Objects*, Ruppelt seemed inclined to suspect that UFOs might be extraterrestrial visitors.

These are some of the factors that appear to have motivated the national news media to once again take an interest in the UFO issue. And with this renewed coverage of the subject, the number of UFO reports submitted to the USAF once again rose dramatically, reaching 1,006 or an average of nearly eighty-four per month. But after a brief period, when the story again failed to build, the national news media again lost interest and turned their attention to more pressing matters, such as the then-projected Missile Gap which might enable the U.S.S.R. to wreak sudden thermonuclear devastation on the United States.

The subsequent hiatus in national news media interest lasted until 1966, when reported UFO sightings by University of Michigan students achieved widespread publicity. (Dr. Hynek, who investigated the case, suggested swamp gas as a possible explanation. Although I was not active in the UFO field at that time and did not investigate the case myself, I have long suspected a student hoax-prank.) This incident, and other UFO reports that followed in its wake, sparked a short inquiry in April, 1966, by the House Armed Services Committee, whose membership included a Michigan congressman.

National interest was whetted by the publication of six new UFO books during 1966—three times as many as the average published during each of the previous ten years.

In addition to the top USAF officials who testified during the House Armed Services Committee hearings on UFOs, Dr. Hynek appeared as the USAF's consultant on the subject. During his testimony, Hynek acknowledged that "puzzling cases exist, *but I know of no competent scientist who would say that these objects come from outer space.*" (Emphasis added.) A few months after these hearings, *Look* magazine carried its sensationalist account of the Barney and Betty Hill UFO "abduction." In December of 1966, Hynek wrote a feature story in *The Saturday Evening Post* in which he seemed to dismiss all possible explanations for UFOs except extraterrestrial spaceships, suggesting a radical change in his attitude in recent months. However, the article revealed that Hynek had, by his account, undergone several such flip-flop changes in his views on UFOs during his years as a UFO consultant. Hynek wrote more feature stories during 1967 in such diverse publications as *The Christian Science Monitor* and *Playboy* magazine. In the latter, Hynek wrote of his "fear" that the Russians might beat the United States in solving the UFO mystery and might be the first to make "contact with an alien civilization conducting reconnaissance missions to our planet."

In January, 1967, the American Broadcasting Company initiated a new network television show, entitled "The Invaders," whose theme was that extraterrestrial visitors from UFOs had already landed and infiltrated Earth and were outwardly indistinguishable from Earthlings except for their inability to bend their little fingers. The hero, a young architect, and his girl friend were among the handful of Earthlings who had discovered the "truth," but their efforts to alert the world were frustrated each week by the extraterrestrial "invaders." ABC said it had sold the new UFO television series to fifteen foreign countries. The year 1967 also saw publication of ten UFO books in the United States, all promoting the extraterrestrial viewpoint, a new high-water mark for this subject during a single year. Not surprisingly, the number of UFO reports submitted to the USAF also remained very high, reaching a total of 937 for the year.

In 1966 the USAF—after years of criticism that it had failed to do an adequate job of investigating UFOs or that it was holding back information from the public—decided to fund an independent investigation. In the fall of 1966 the University of Colorado was selected to make the study, which was to be directed by Dr. Edward U. Condon, a highly respected member of the faculty who had once headed the National Bureau of Standards.* As the new effort got under way during 1967, national news media coverage began to slacken a bit, perhaps in the expectation that the Colorado investigation would produce a definitive answer to resolve the issue of whether Earth was playing unwitting host to extraterrestrial spaceships.

The report of the Colorado investigation was made public on January 8, 1969, along with an endorsement of its conclusions by a review panel that had been established by the National Academy of Sciences. Condon reported that investigation of numerous UFO cases had turned up no evidence of extraterrestrial visitors, although he conceded that it had not been possible to explain every case. Condon also recommended against any further expenditure of government funds for UFO studies. The USAF later announced that it would close down its Project Blue Book office and later shipped off its many UFO reports to the Air Force archives at Maxwell Air Force Base, Alabama. *The USAF also terminated its long-standing contract with Dr. Hynek for consulting services.*

Condon's conclusions were sharply criticized by UFO groups, such as NICAP and APRO, and others with a commitment to the extraterrestrial hypothesis. This included two scientists who participated in the Colorado study and were fired for secretly taking documents from the files and "leaking" them to NICAP and other proponents of the extraterrestrial viewpoint. Hynek also lashed out at the Condon conclusions, especially the recommendation against

---

* Dr. Condon died on March 25, 1974.

any further government-funded UFO investigations. (Even while the Colorado study was in progress, Hynek apparently questioned its ability to resolve the issue and believed that a follow-up study would be required, according to scientists with the Midwest Research Institute at Kansas City, Missouri. They told me that Hynek had suggested to them that he and MRI join forces and submit a proposal for such a study. When they sought my advice, I recommended against the idea. MRI subsequently decided against such a joint effort.)

Condon's general conclusion that there was not a shred of evidence to indicate alien spaceship visitations and its endorsement by the National Academy of Sciences panel were widely accepted at the time by the national news media. And so UFO reports were soon relegated to the same category as stories about haunted houses by the national news media, except for sensationalist publications such as the *National Enquirer*. Even the minor UFO flap in Kansas in mid-1972 (Chapter 9) failed to generate national interest—perhaps because the conclusions of the Condon report were still fresh and there were more important matters, such as the 1972 Presidential campaign.

By early 1973, with the continuing depressing disclosures about the Watergate scandal, editors welcomed anything that would lighten the news—even stories about the search in the tiny Aurora cemetery for the body of the poor pilot of the "mysterious airship" that had allegedly crashed into the nonexistent windmill on Judge Proctor's farm in 1897. This series of wire service articles in the spring of 1973, which appeared in numerous newspapers around the country, would help set the stage for the UFO flap of 1973, to be discussed in the next chapter. It provides still another example of UFOlogical Principle #6 at work.

26 · The 1973 UFO Flap

The 1973 UFO flap, which originated in Georgia during late August, proved an illustrative microcosm of the previous quarter-century of the UFO issue. A year before, a similar rash of UFO reports from Kansas stirred scant interest among the national news media, but the 1972 Presidential campaign was then in progress. The late summer of 1973 provided quite a different context. The Senate Watergate investigation, which had so completely dominated the news for months, had recessed, leaving the media in the late-summer doldrums and its editors, along with the general public, weary of the sordid disclosures coming out of Washington. The reaction of the news media to the UFO reports from Georgia is aptly described by NICAP's account in the October issue of its publication *UFO Investigator*.

NICAP reported, "The wave of sightings brought widespread reaction from national and local news media, and flooded many Southern newspapers with front-page stories. . . . At the same time, both major wire services, AP and UPI, were transmitting reports to papers and broadcast stations around the country . . . newspapers as far as California and Connecticut began to cover the story, sometimes running several articles over a three or four day period. By happenstance, NBC-TV broadcast a rerun of its popular [hour-long] special on 'Ancient Astronauts' * . . . Sept. 6, which added further impact. . . . During the first week of September, NICAP was contacted by media in many parts of the East Coast. . . . Interviews were done with . . . multiple radio and TV stations. . . . By the end of the month [September], news stories from all across the country had been received . . . and more were arriving daily." NICAP, which had almost gone bankrupt in the wake of the Colorado/Condon report, was clearly delighted at the resurgence of news media interest, and the prospect of expanded membership.

As I read the initial reports from Georgia in 1973, I recalled the very similar rash of UFO reports from the same region just six years earlier. Then too, many of the reports had come from police officers who had told of chasing, or being chased by, a UFO. When the University of Colorado had sent a team of scientists to Georgia to investigate, they found to their surprise that the planet Venus and other celestial bodies, together with stimulated imaginations, were responsible for the reports (Chapter 9). My thoughts went back to the mid-1960s when I had first become interested in the UFO question, when I would have found it difficult to believe that police officers and others could mistake Venus for a UFO. But during the intervening years, like other UFO investigators, I had discovered that bright celestial bodies, especially when viewed through a thin transparent haze layer, are responsible for producing more UFO reports than any other single source.

Even experienced pilots can mistake a bright celestial body for a moving craft that seems to be headed toward them on what appears to be a collision course. Max Karant, a senior

---

* This TV show was based on the full-of-nonsense best-selling book *Chariots of the Gods*, by Erich Von Daniken, a former Swiss hotel manager, which suggests that Egypt's pyramids and other such achievements of the ancients were really the products of extraterrestrial visitors.

official of the Aircraft Owners & Pilots Association and long-time general aviation pilot, tells of two such encounters, one of which occurred while he was flying the North Atlantic at night. During the latter incident both Karant and his co-pilot decided that the bright light was headed toward their own aircraft at approximately the same altitude, and they thought they could even make out the characteristic red-green wing-tip lights carried by aircraft. When Karant climbed above some nearby cloud-tops, it seemed that the other craft had done the same. But after a few minutes it became apparent that the object was simply Venus.

In the late summer of 1973 I learned after checking with the U.S. Naval Observatory that Mars and Jupiter were especially brilliant in the night skies in addition to a bright Venus. NICAP's own regional investigator in Savannah, Georgia, himself an astronomer, conceded that as many as 50 percent of the UFO reports he had investigated could be explained as misidentifications of stars and bright planets. I was inclined to suspect that the figure was probably considerably higher.

By early September the Georgia flap had spread to nearby states. For example, a United Press International story told of a sighting by a woman in Nashville, Tennessee, who had gone to a police station to report a curious object in the night skies which not only changed color but also seemed to change from a cigar shape to a triangular shape. The police officer who went outside with her to look at the UFO subsequently told the UPI, "I saw what she was looking at. But it looked like a star that wasn't doing anything but flickering." Another bright, pulsating UFO was photographed by the son of the publisher of a small-town Georgia newspaper. Subsequent analysis showed this UFO to be a bright star.

The following week a UPI story which some newspapers headlined as a "UFO landing" told of a farmer living near Griffin, Georgia, who reported seeing a golden, egg-shaped object float to Earth near his house and then take off. His account seemed to be supported by a small burned hole in the ground, measuring several inches deep and about twelve inches long. A soil chemist from the local University of

Georgia agricultural experiment station visited the site to make an analysis. His conclusion was that the hole could conceivably have been made by a small meteorite or piece of space debris, but he also acknowledged the possibility that the report was a hoax. Near Manchester, Georgia, a glowing object reported as a UFO was recovered by the police and analyzed. It turned out to be an ordinary emergency road flare, apparently planted by a prankster.

Several weeks later, thousands of persons in South Carolina reported seeing a truly strange UFO slowly drifting through the sky. When the UFO subsequently landed in the yard of a woman near Camden, South Carolina, it was identified as a large helium-filled balloon, measuring approximately sixty feet in length, to which were attached thin sheets of metalized plastic—along with cards asking the finder to return the object to Professor Howard Woody of the atmospheric sky sculpture research project, in the art department at the University of South Carolina. Woody told the Associated Press he had been launching such "atmospheric sculptures" for some years.

A few days later, the sheriff at Longview, Texas, began to receive reports of "strange objects" that were landing at the local airport. When he dispatched deputies to the site to investigate, they found the UFOs were only migrating snow geese which, apparently, had mistaken the concrete runways for a lake. A series of UFO reports from the San Jose, California, area were subsequently identified by an astronomer as an extremely bright bolide—a meteor which explodes with a brilliant flash as it enters the atmosphere. When the deputy sheriff of Renfroe, Alabama, received a rash of telephone calls telling of a UFO that had landed in a tree, and went to investigate, he found an ordinary weather balloon.

Dozens of motorists driving near Greenwood, Delaware, were startled one night to see a bright-orange disk glowing in the nearby woods. It proved to be a hoax staged by five local volunteer firemen who had built a seven-foot-diameter hoop which was outfitted with orange light bulbs and powered by a small engine-driven generator normally used for more impor-

tant fire department purposes. A few days later, many of the
68,000 football fans watching a night game in Baton Rouge,
Louisiana, saw a brightly glowing UFO float over the stadium
with a police helicopter in sharp pursuit. The helicopter crew
subsequently identified the UFO as a hot-air balloon, fabricated from a plastic garment bag by student pranksters. How
many other UFOs reported during the 1973 flap were of the
same genre will never be known. A few days before the Baton
Rouge incident, a giant, 150-foot-diameter scientific balloon
was launched from Palestine, Texas, and prevailing winds
carried it over the southeastern states to provide still another
stimulus for UFO reports.

If there were a few extraterrestrial spaceships intermixed
with the many misidentified UFOs, it is strange that they
were not detected and tracked by the very extensive government radar networks. For example, the Navy operates a
"radar fence" that extends across the United States from the
Atlantic to the Pacific Ocean to detect objects in space out to
distances of several thousand miles that pass over the United
States. This Navy Space Surveillance System is so sensitive
that it has detected objects as small as a six-inch-long metal
strap released from an early American satellite. In addition,
the USAF has a giant radar, with an antenna the size of a
football field, situated near Eglin Air Force Base, Florida,
whose primary mission is to detect and track objects in space
that pass over the eastern part of the United States. This
FPS-85 radar, the most powerful in the western world, is used
to maintain a continuous and precise catalog of every object
in space, including hundreds of small fragments from spacecraft that have exploded in orbit.

For surveillance of the airspace closer to Earth, the Federal
Aviation Administration operates an extensive radar network
whose coverage is continuous over the southeastern states
down to 10,000 feet, and in portions of this area it extends
much lower. Additionally, the USAF now operates its own
extensive air-defense radar network in this same region to
guard against any possible attack from Cuba. Finally, all large
and medium-size airports have radars that scan the skies out
to a distance of approximately fifty miles. Yet somehow the

numerous UFOs being reported during the fall of 1973
seemed to avoid being detected and tracked by these
extensive radar networks—a point that was occasionally
mentioned in a few news stories but invariably "buried" far
down in the article.

The UFO flap of 1973 had begun to ebb by early October
as more important news emerged: the scandal that was
engulfing Vice President Spiro Agnew and the outbreak of
another war in the Mid-East. Then, on October 11, a UFO
blockbuster hit when two shipyard workers from Pascagoula,
Mississippi, reported to the local sheriff's office that they had
been abducted that night and taken aboard a flying saucer for
an examination by three strange-looking creatures with clawlike hands. It was the first major "abduction" story since the
incident involving Barney and Betty Hill made headlines in
1966. And it was a fresh lead for news media editors who had
begun to lose interest in continuing reports of flickering lights
in the night skies. Within twenty-four hours the two obscure
men—who said they had been fishing at the time of the
incident—were nationally famous and new life had been
injected into the 1973 UFO flap. (This case will be analyzed
in the next chapter.)

Several days later, a taxicab driver from Gulfport, Mississippi, reported that he too had had an encounter with a flying
saucer and a strange creature with crablike claws. The man
said the UFO had landed directly in front of his taxi, causing
its engine to stall and his radio to become inoperative—phenomena that are occasionally reported to be caused by the
proximity of a UFO. Then he said he heard a tapping against
the car's window and observed the creature with claws similar
to those reported by the two Pascagoula men a week earlier.
The account, which seemed to provide support for the
Pascagoula case, was widely publicized. Much less widely
publicized was the cab driver's subsequent admission that his
story was a hoax which he contrived when another taxi driver
found him sleeping on the job in his cab.

By the second week in October, UFOs had begun to
attract the interest of news media in Ohio, as the focal point
of reports shifted from the southeast states to nearby

Kentucky, Tennessee and Indiana. Until a UFO flap achieves national attention, its center of activity tends to move outward to adjacent areas, like ripples caused by dropping a rock into a pool of water. By the time that the local news media and public in the originating region have lost interest, it is peaking in other areas to the east, south, west and north. By the second week in October, Ohio began to emerge as the "storm center" for the 1973 flap, with the bulk of the reports of sightings coming from the southern and central portions of that state, in the general vicinity of Dayton.

For this reason it is instructive to examine the coverage given to UFOs by the Dayton press. It is ironic that Dayton is the site of the USAF's largest technical facility, which in turn had housed the Project Blue Book UFO investigations office that was closed down in early 1970. One of the first major feature stories appeared in the *Dayton Daily News* on October 10, under the headline "UFOs Reported in Louisiana, Indiana." If UFOs were as close as Indiana, perhaps they might be visible to Dayton residents who were willing to scan the skies that night. This proved to be true, as the October 11 edition of the Dayton newspaper reported: "Wednesday was a good night for Unidentified Flying Object spotters in this vicinity." The article included a photo of a UFO that reportedly had been taken the previous night by a police officer from a nearby town. It showed a glowing "blob" of light. The newspaper reported that the Montgomery county sheriff's office had received about a dozen telephone reports of UFO sightings the previous night.

Not to be outdone, the October 11 edition of Dayton's *Journal Herald* also carried a major story headlined "UFO sightings reported in area." These Ohio reports were picked up and distributed nationally by the UPI and received wide play in other Ohio newspapers. The very next day *The Journal Herald* carried another feature on UFOs, citing more recent UFO sightings in the state, including one by a college student. He described this UFO as being a high-flying object with three blue lights which had swept across the sky at very high speed in a few seconds. A few months earlier the object would have been dismissed as simply a bright meteor, but in October of 1973, the object was clearly a UFO.

The same day, the *Dayton Daily News* published another UFO feature under the headline "Planet Clue Offered as UFOs Move North." The article told of hundreds of additional UFO reports that had been received. It quoted Roger Hoefer, curator of astronomy at the Dayton Museum of Natural History, as suggesting that some UFO reports might be due to Venus, Mars and Jupiter, which were particularly bright. Hoefer noted that at approximately the same time that area residents were reporting seeing a UFO in the southwest sky, he had personally been watching Venus in the same location from the museum's observatory. He also commented, "Any time anyone keeps staring at a bright object, it is sure to appear to move."

On October 13, *The Journal Herald* carried the UPI story on the Pascagoula incident under the headline "Two 'captured' by UFO's crew." Two days later, the newspaper reported additional UFO sightings in Ohio, while the *Dayton Daily News* of the same date carried a major feature headlined "UFOs Flying Over Union [Ohio] Photographed, Police Say." The same day, the nearby *Fairborne [Ohio] Daily Herald* published a UPI story, datelined Dayton, headlined "Hysterical Woman Says UFO Lands, Kills 2 Cows." The article told of eighty additional UFO reports made the previous night, including the account of the death of the two cows. The story noted that police, in response to this report, had searched the area but were unable to find the bovine victims. Both Dayton newspapers also carried major UFO features on October 16. One included a picture of a fuzzy light that reportedly had been seen over Union on an earlier night. The other, in *The Journal Herald*, was a major story headlined "Astronomers, AF discount UFO reports." A UPI story, datelined Columbus, Ohio, told of additional UFO sightings within the state.

Several dozen Dayton area motorists who chanced to be driving near the suburb of Xenia during the night of October 16 received the shock of their lives when they were stopped on a main highway by a flashing red light being operated by three "creatures" with wrinkled aluminum "skin" and antennas atop their heads. When the police came to investigate, the creatures turned out to be three ingenious teen-age pranksters who had wrapped their bodies with aluminum foil and fashioned antennas out of old coat hangers. The youths were released by the police with a reprimand. The story and a picture of the aluminum-clad UFOnauts appeared the following day in the Dayton newspapers and were distributed nationally by the wire services. A few days later, stimulated by the Dayton-Xenia incident, two young men repeated the hoax in Jonesboro, Arkansas, and were fined for "malicious mischief."

Several days later, the police department in the small town of Falkville, Alabama, received a telephone report that a UFO had landed in a pasture and that its aluminum-clad occupant was loose. When the local police chief went to investigate, he found a six-foot-tall aluminum-covered "creature" with an antenna atop his head, who "moved stiffly," as if it were a robot, the officer later reported. The officer photographed the creature with his Polaroid camera, and when he turned his patrol-car spotlight on the UFOnaut, "it" began to run down the highway with the officer in pursuit in the patrol car. The officer explained he was unable to catch the UFOnaut because "he was running faster than any human I ever saw." When the *National Enquirer* asked the police chief for his evaluation of the incident, the officer reportedly replied, "I didn't believe in men from outer space, but I do now."

The October 17 edition of *The Journal Herald* carried still another UFO feature headlined "Even Reds see little green men." The accompanying story, released by the Soviet news agency Tass, said that Russian scientists had detected an unusual radio signal from space which, according to Tass, might be coming from a distant civilization. Coming in the midst of the UFO flap, the Russian story got wide coverage in the national news media. For example, the widely viewed National Broadcasting Company's evening news program on October 16, with the respected John Chancellor as anchorman, followed its brief report on recent UFO sightings with the Tass story.

My own investigation indicates that the Tass story had as little validity as the UFO accounts with which it was so widely linked. Leading American radio astronomers, who maintain close liaison with their foreign counterparts, including the Russians, told me that no respected Soviet astronomers had announced the discovery of any new radio signals whose characteristics suggested they might be coming from a distant civilization. Nor have they done so in the months since the Tass release. My own investigation suggests that the signals reported by Tass probably came from a new type of military communications satellite with which the USAF has only recently begun to experiment. This class of satellite, designed to provide communications with Strategic Air Command forces in the Arctic, employs an unusual orbit— for United States spacecraft—which results in the satellite's remaining over the U.S.S.R. for eight hours every day before departing.

The same October 17 article in *The Journal Herald* told of new UFO sightings and of a report from Clarksville, Arkansas, that students and faculty from College of the Ozarks had reported seeing a "ghost-like bearded creature with long gray hair who foams at the mouth." Meanwhile, when Ohio Governor John J. Gilligan was asked, during a press conference, what he thought about the UFO flap then raging in his state, the governor responded that he and his wife had seen a UFO two nights earlier, October 15, while driving back from a weekend in Michigan. His statement clearly dispelled any possibility that UFOs are reported only by kooks and "little old ladies in gym shoes." Gilligan's "endorsement" of UFOs was featured on NBC's network newscast by John Chancellor that night, as well as by Walter Cronkite on the Columbia Broadcasting System's evening news report. And it was featured the following morning on the NBC "Today Show," as well as on the CBS Morning News program. *The Cleveland Plain Dealer* featured the story on its front page in a box with a red border, and a brief news item even appeared in *The New York Times*. The Ohio governor was invited to appear on the American Broadcasting Company's "Dick Cavett Show," but he declined.

In describing the UFO sighting, Gilligan said he and his wife had spotted the object while driving south toward Ann Arbor. "It was a vertical beam of light, amber colored," according to Gilligan, and it seemed to remain relatively fixed in the sky in a south-southeast direction for about thirty-five minutes. The governor said he had no idea what the light was but that it would "fade out and [then] get brighter" as seen through the broken clouds. On the night that Gilligan saw the bright UFO, the planet Mars was at its closest and brightest—closer to Earth than it will be until 1986. And it was to the east-southeast in the sky, near the reported position of Gilligan's UFO.

Both Dayton newspapers carried feature stories on the Gilligan sighting on October 18, and on the following day *The Journal Herald* published a follow-up article which disclosed that the governor had gotten a good deal of national coverage and exposure in the news media—a not unwelcome thing for anyone in public office. That night, a helicopter being flown by Army Reservists from Columbus to Cleveland had an encounter with a UFO which, understandably, unnerved its crew and made front-page news in Cleveland and elsewhere in Ohio. The incident, which seemed to involve the threat of a mid-air collision between the helicopter and the UFO, will be considered in detail in Chapter 29.

The October 19 edition of the *Dayton Daily News* carried another feature which told of a "giant sparkler in the sky" that had been reported by numerous Ohio residents, providing the ninth consecutive night of UFO reports. The October 21 edition of the same newspaper carried a UPI story datelined Cincinnati. It reported that the Cincinnati police department had received an anonymous communiqué from its regional crime information center that read: "The most recent scare of UFO's is now over. They have been destroyed by the combined force comprised of Buck Rogers, Flash Gordon, Superman and the Flying Nun. We hope you can return to chasing criminals rather than UFO's." The unknown author of that communiqué proved to have the gift of prophecy, or perhaps a keen appreciation of how quickly the news media's interest fades. The Ohio UFO flap was about to enter a period of sharp decline.

The two major newspapers in Washington, D.C., understandably preoccupied with the Watergate scandal, Vice President Agnew's resignation and the Mid-East war, had all but ignored the UFO flap of 1973. But by mid-October, with events in Ohio and Pascagoula being publicized by the radio-TV networks, the UFO flap no longer could be ignored. The October 17 edition of *The Washington Post* carried a major UPI feature headlined "UFOs Return With a Vengeance," with a subhead that read: "Sightings Reported in Four States, Signals on Moscow Radio." The same day the *Washington Star-News* published a five-column feature story, from the AP, under the headline "UFOs: Is Anybody O-o-out There?" Included was a large artist's sketch of one of the alleged Pascagoula UFO-creatures, complete with clawlike hands.

Once the newspapers in the nation's capital had prominently publicized the fact that a major UFO flap was under way in the United States, the local citizens promptly responded with reports of Washington-area sightings. The next day, the *Washington Star-News* carried a follow-up feature headlined "UFOs—Local 'Sightings.'" One man, the article said, reported watching flashing blue lights pass across the southern horizon for nearly an hour the previous night. (The Orionids meteor shower begins at this time of the year, and its meteors usually give off a blue-green light.) A local woman recalled that *several weeks earlier* she had seen three flashing lights moving toward a very large white light in the sky. (Some airliners now carry bright flashing white Xenon "anticollision" lights as well as the more familiar rotating red beacon and red/green wing-tip lights.) *The Washington Post* apparently decided not to become involved in reporting mundane local UFO sightings. Its October 19 edition carried only a short article under the headline "Weather, Publicity Spur UFO Reports."

The New York Times also had all but ignored the UFO flap. But finally, on October 21, several days after it had carried a brief item on the Gilligan sighting in Ohio, the newspaper finally succumbed. Science editor Walter Sullivan wrote a thoughtful capsule summary of the long-standing mystery which offered several terrestrial explanations for UFO reports. The article was headlined: "Despite Lack of Data From Pilots and Officials, Reports of UFO Sightings Are Many and Widespread." A month later, police in New York and in many Long Island communities were deluged one night with reports of a long, glowing UFO. It turned out to be a commercial advertising aircraft outfitted with strings of multicolored lights that was being flown to promote a local bank.

The Los Angeles Times, which had also resisted pressures to publicize the current UFO flap, succumbed on October 21, in the wake of widespread publicity on the Pascagoula case, by running two major feature stories. One no-nonsense article, by science writer George Alexander, was headlined: "Scientists, Engineers Doubtful About UFOs." The subhead was "Don't Question Sightings but Disbelieve Control by Extraterrestrial Intelligence." But Alexander's debunking story appeared on *page 25.* The other feature story, headlined: "UFOs: Odd Things Going On in Mississippi, Most Agree," appeared on *page 1.* Those who took time to carefully read the full story, written by Nicholas C. Chriss, would recognize that the author was somewhat skeptical of the Pascagoula case. But many readers would only read the headline.

One factor that had helped to sustain earlier UFO flaps was missing in 1973. Before the USAF had closed down its Project Blue Book office in 1970, it had been obliged to try to explain every UFO report. Some, involving hoaxes by otherwise honest, respectable citizens, were embarrassing for a taxpayer-supported agency to candidly expose. Whatever explanation the USAF advanced, some of which admittedly were ill-conceived, it was usually attacked by the "believers," and this generated heated controversy which in turn produced more news media coverage, which in turn helped generate more UFO reports. But in 1973, in response to news media and other inquiries, the USAF replied that it was no longer in the UFO business, forcing the media to look elsewhere for UFO expertise. And so the media often turned to Dr. Hynek, the USAF's former UFO consultant, whose views were widely quoted in the press. By late October, in the wake of the Pascagoula case, Hynek was quoted as warning against "undue national panic." Hynek was also urging still another government-sponsored UFO investigation and the formation of a national clearing house to receive UFO reports, which he volunteered to head. The "undue national panic" of which Hynek warned did not develop, perhaps because other matters seemed to the national news media to be of much greater import—matters such as the impact of the Arab oil embargo, the prospect of gas rationing, widespread unemployment and cold homes during the coming winter months.

A final feature story on UFOs that appeared in *The Washington Post* on October 20, quoted Ms. Irmgard Lincoln, director of a Washington "institution" called the Cosmic Academy, who claims that she communicates regularly with the occupants of flying saucers via telepathy. Ms. Lincoln was quoted as predicting that "they are going to land very soon here in Washington . . . and all over the earth." I recalled that Ms. Lincoln had made exactly the same prediction some six years earlier when she and I appeared together on a local radio program on UFOs.

Several days earlier there had been a rash of UFO sightings reported in western Maryland and northern Virginia. Two days later, an AP story from Front Royal, Virginia, quoted a local farmer as saying that his farm had been used late one night as a launching site for helium-inflated balloons that carried battery-operated lights or burning flares. The young men who had used his farm, he said, told him the operation was part of a weather experiment being conducted by the University of Pennsylvania. But a subsequent check by the AP failed to provide confirmation by University of Pennsylvania spokesmen. In mid-November, a rash of UFO reports in the general vicinity of Elmira, New York, were explained several days later when three helium-filled luminous-painted balloons bearing aluminum foil descended and became entrapped in the trees of a local citizen.

By late in November, just three months after the 1973 UFO flap had started in Georgia, it was all but over. Venus, Mars and Jupiter were still there, almost as bright as before. But with the approach of winter weather and more frequent overcast skies, far fewer people were inclined to stand watch outside in the hope of seeing an honest-to-goodness UFO. Besides, judging from the coverage given to the subject in the national and most local news media, it was obvious by early December that the UFOs were no longer coming in droves. There are those who have suggested that the Earth is being visited by extraterrestrial spaceships from civilizations that have long ago depleted their own natural resources, which they hope to replace here. If so, perhaps the headline news telling of our Earth's fast-diminishing energy and mineral resources prompted the UFOs to seek other sources of supply.

If there were citizens in Northport, Washington, who were disappointed that the great UFO flap had come and seemingly gone without their being able to share in the excitement, this disappointment vanished in early January, 1974, when local residents reported seeing a large, glowing UFO in the night sky. Some observers reported that the UFO was twenty-five feet in diameter, or larger, and zoomed across the sky at speeds of sixty miles per hour. The UFO was not seen again for a week, but then it reappeared, and startled one local woman when it landed nearby and then mysteriously took off again. The Northport UFO was such a dramatic success that its creators could not resist taking a public bow. Like so many other UFOs, this one had been fabricated out of a plastic bag, converted into a hot-air balloon by means of candles, but this time by seventeen-year-old twin *girls*. Although the plastic bag was only several feet in diameter, it had generated reports of a UFO many times that size. According to the UPI account of the incident, the girls explained: "We just wanted to get people's imaginations going—and we did."

27 • "Abduction" in Pascagoula

The most famous UFO case to emerge during the 1973 flap involved two shipyard workers from Pascagoula, Mississippi, who claimed that while fishing in the Pascagoula river on the night of October 11, they had been abducted by three strange-looking creatures, carried aboard a flying saucer for examination and then released unharmed. Coming in the midst of a nationwide UFO flap, at a time when the national news media had begun to tire of publishing simply more reports of strange lights in the night skies, the Pascagoula case had great appeal. Within forty-eight hours, thanks to wire-service and TV network coverage, the two men were internationally famous—and they had acquired an attorney who would serve as their agent. The attorney, Joseph Colingo, told me that during a single day he had received "some three hundred phone calls right in this office—television stations, radio stations. I even got calls from London, South America, Canada, Mexico and all over the country inquiring about this."

The incident involved Charles Hickson, age forty-two,

employed in the small Walker Shipyards, and nineteen-year-old Calvin Parker, who had recently come to work in the same shipyard from his home in Laurel, Mississippi. Parker was living with the Hicksons at the time. The men's story, told principally by Hickson, was extremely sketchy and lacked the detail that had characterized the Barney and Betty Hill UFO abduction story that had achieved similar fame just seven years earlier. Nor was the Pascagoula account as colorful as another abduction story, well known to UFO-logists, told nearly a decade earlier by a Brazilian farmer named Antonio Villas-Boas. He said he had gone outside his house one night to investigate a UFO that had landed there and that he had been set upon by several men who carried him aboard a flying saucer. Inside, Villas-Boas reported, he had been *forced* to make love to a spacewoman whose body was "much more beautiful than that of any woman I have ever known before."

Hickson said the two men had been fishing after dark, within several blocks of downtown Pascagoula, when they heard an unusual buzzing or zipping sound. When they turned toward the sound, Hickson said, they saw a flashing blue light coming from a craft that was hovering several feet above the ground. In a "first-person account" published in the December 2 edition of *The National Tattler*, Hickson said the craft was "sort of rounded or oval, was about eight to 10 feet wide and about eight feet high." When Hickson appeared on the "Dick Cavett Show" on the American Broadcasting Company's television network, he said the craft was "around twenty foot long, the overall of it." But several weeks later, on the National Broadcasting Company's "Mike Douglas Show," Hickson said the UFO was "twenty or thirty feet long." In an earlier interview with an Aerial Phenomena Research Organization investigator on October 13, Hickson said the UFO was sixteen to eighteen feet long. The first newspaper accounts said the incident had occurred around 7 P.M., but during the Cavett show Hickson said it was between 8 P.M. and 9 P.M. Later, on the Douglas show, Hickson said the incident had occurred "around nine o'clock."

In any event, as soon as the UFO appeared nearby,

Hickson said, three strange-looking creatures suddenly emerged from the craft and "floated" toward the two men. Two of them, he said, grabbed him, and the third was left to handle young Parker. According to Hickson, he and his friend were "floated" into the UFO through a door which "didn't open like a door opens—it just appeared, the opening just appeared." Hickson said he was floated into a very intensely illuminated room and that Parker, apparently, was taken to another. Hickson said he was "levitated" in a horizontal position while a large round object floated back and forth over his body as if giving him a physical examination. At one point, according to Hickson, the two creatures left the room, but he made no attempt to escape because he seemed to be completely paralyzed except for the ability to move his eyes.

The most detailed part of Hickson's account was his description of the space creatures, although it is difficult to understand how he could have observed so much detail. Outside, the night was dark and the abduction had occurred so quickly. Inside, Hickson said, it was so intensely illuminated he could not make out any details of the room. In fact, more than a month after the alleged incident, when Hickson and Parker appeared on the Douglas TV show, Hickson disclosed for the first time that the interior illumination was so bright that he had suffered severe eye injury, which he compared to "a welding flash." Hickson said it persisted "for about three days." *

Despite the intense illumination and reported eye injury, Hickson somehow managed to note that the creatures were about five feet tall, with no necks, had gray wrinkled skin "like an elephant," long arms and lobsterlike claws for hands. Their legs never separated for walking; instead they "floated," Hickson said. On their heads, where human ears and a nose would be located, were small cone-shaped appendages. Below the "nose" was a "mouth" which Hickson first described as being a "hole," but in a later interview as a "slit." When

---

* Hickson never mentioned an eye injury when he was being examined for possible radioactivity by USAF doctors at Keesler Air Force Base the day after the incident had allegedly occurred.

Hickson was interviewed by an APRO investigator shortly
after the incident, he reported that the creatures had "slits"
where human eyes would be located. but later on the Cavett
show, he said they had "no eyes. I didn't see any eyes." When
Cavett asked whether Hickson had heard anything resembling speech, he replied "no." But later, when Cavett asked if
the creatures had tried to communicate with the two men,
Hickson replied, "I did hear some mumbling, some type of
mumbling from one of the things. . . ."

After the two men were carried aboard the UFO, Hickson
reported, he did not see his friend until sometime later when
the two men were floated out and deposited on the riverbank.
Parker proved unable to supply even sketchy details of his
experience because, as Hickson explained, the youth had
fainted at the start of the incident and had not regained
consciousness until it was over. Hickson said the creatures
had quickly boarded their UFO and it had zipped off into the
night. All this, allegedly, had occurred within several hundred
feet of U.S. Highway #90, yet none of the passing motorists
had reported seeing the glowing flying saucer hovering a few
feet above the ground where it should have been readily
visible.

During the next several hours, according to Hickson, the
two men had debated whether they should even report the
incident because "people wouldn't believe us." After bol-
stering their nerve with a few nips of liquor from a bottle that
Hickson had in his car, he said they first visited the offices of
the local newspaper, only to find them closed for the night.
Finally, around 11 P.M., Hickson called the Jackson County
sheriff's office, which dispatched a deputy to bring the two
men in to make a firsthand report.

Hickson says that he "asked the sheriff not to let it out to
the news [media]," despite his earlier statement that he had
first tried to report the incident to the local newspaper. In
any event, by the following day the abduction story was being
publicized widely, not only in Pascagoula but across the
nation. A UPI dispatch quoted Sheriff Fred Diamond as
saying "something" had happened to the men because they
were "scared to death and on the verge of a heart attack."

Another newspaper account quoted Deputy Sheriff Conrad Clark as saying that Hickson's employer described him as a "good steady worker." Had reporters checked with Hickson's former employer, the large Ingalls Shipyards, they could have learned that he was fired on November 20, 1972, for "conduct unbecoming a supervisor," involving financial hanky-panky whose details Ingalls officials decline to discuss.* Then on July 6, 1973, Hickson had filed for bankruptcy because of his hopelessly high personal debts, in the U.S. District Court at Biloxi. This I learned from Richard Glacier, a reporter for *The Daily Herald* in Gulfport.

Pascagoula attorney Colingo told me that he became involved when the head of the Walker Shipyards, which was his client, called for his help because newsmen were hounding the company in seeking interviews with Hickson and Parker† I learned that Colingo now had a contract with the two men to handle their TV appearances and other commercial ventures.

APRO headquarters learned of the Pascagoula incident the morning of October 12, when the news first broke, and asked one of its most experienced and distinguished investigators to hurry to the scene. This was Dr. James A. Harder, professor of civil engineering at the University of California at Berkeley, who arrived in Pascagoula later that same day. Dr. J. Allen Hynek, hearing of the incident, also hurried to Pascagoula, and the two famous investigators jointly interviewed the principals in the presence of Colingo and members of the sheriff's office. Harder later reported his opening remarks to the two shipyard workers: "I said that they were one of a very

---

* According to a penetrating account of the Pascagoula case, written by Joe Eszterhas, that appeared in the January 17, 1974, edition of *Rolling Stone*, Hickson had been fired "because his superiors alleged that Charlie Hickson, expert shipfitter, was borrowing money from the boys working under him, then paying them back by trying to finagle them promotions."

† A different version of how Colingo got involved is described by Eszterhas in *Rolling Stone*. He said that when Colingo chanced to call his brother-in-law, an executive at the Walker Shipyards, the latter suggested that Hickson and Parker might need an "adviser." He went on to explain, "Hell, if they seen what they says they seen, it's probably worth only about a million dollars." Colingo promptly arranged to meet with the two men.

small number of persons who had had such an experience."
(*The A.P.R.O. Bulletin*, September–October, 1973.) This
would indicate that Harder already accepted their story as
fact even before the interview. Later, Harder said, he told the
two men about other famous UFO abduction cases, including the one involving Villas-Boas.

Harder, who has acquired some skills in hypnosis for use in
his UFO investigations, to probe for details which the
principals might not otherwise recall, employed this technique during part of the Pascagoula interviews. He admitted
in his APRO report that "both Hickson and Parker were
fearful of hypnosis." After Harder had demonstrated hypnosis
on an attending doctor and a fellow shipyard worker, he said,
Hickson was finally persuaded to try it "but only as a dry run.
He was very nervous but finally did calm down." On October
14 the two men were again interviewed by Harder and Hynek.
After two days of interviews the two experienced UFO
investigators reported their conclusions. Harder said: "*There
was definitely something here that was not terrestrial. . . .
Where they come from and why they were here is a matter of
conjecture, but the fact that they are here is true, beyond a
reasonable doubt.*" Hynek was slightly more qualified in his
endorsement. "*There is no question in my mind that these
two men have had a very terrifying experience.*" (A UPI
dispatch erroneously attributed Harder's statement to Hynek
and vice versa. The attributions and appraisals here are
correct, as verified by my discussions with both men.)

These ringing endorsements by the two experienced UFO
investigators were carried by the wire services and published
around the nation. One typical newspaper story carried the
headline "Two Men Claim to Have Been on UFO; Scientist
Believes Them." Newspaper readers could not help being
impressed with the academic credentials of the two scientists,
especially since Hynek had been a long-time UFO consultant
to the USAF (which invariably was mentioned in the
newspaper articles) and since he was the head of the
astronomy department at Northwestern University.*

* In the spring of 1974 Hynek acquired still another impressive-sounding
title: Director of the "Center of UFO Studies." According to one newspaper

It is hardly surprising that the citizens of Pascagoula developed a case of the jitters. If the story was true, as Harder and Hynek believed, and if the same UFO was still in the area, it might return for more victims at any moment. But the next victims might be carried off to a distant world, perhaps to be exhibited there before crowds of strange-looking creatures of the type that Hickson had described, or worse, the victims might be stuffed and placed in a museum. An unknown prankster filled a large plastic balloon with helium, painted it with psychedelic colors and released it to float across downtown Pascagoula. The minister of one local church posted a sign announcing that his next sermon would be entitled "Visitors from Outer Space: What Sayeth the Lord?" Later, the minister offered a tape-cassette recording of his sermon for sale for the modest price of two dollars.

Some of the early press accounts on this case reported that Hickson and Parker were willing, even eager, to take a polygraph examination ("lie-detector test") to verify the truthfulness of their story. Yet during the subsequent days there was no follow-up report that the two men had done so. Then, on October 31, the national news media reported that *one* of the men, Hickson, had finally taken the test. And he had passed it with flying colors, according to the New Orleans polygraph operator, Scott G., who had administered the examination. One typical newspaper headline for the UPI story reporting this remarkable new development read: "UFO Story Stands Up in Lie Test." The article quoted a statement issued by the polygraph operator: "It is my opinion that he [Hickson] told the truth when he stated that he believes he saw a spaceship, that he was taken into the spaceship and that he saw three creatures." The test had been run just in time so that Dick Cavett could read the impressive-sounding statement before introducing Hickson on November 2, on the latter's first feature TV network appearance. The UPI story said the tests had been "administered in cooperation with the Jackson County sheriff's office at the request of an attorney for Hickson and Parker."

account of March 17, 1974, the new organization was set up by Hynek himself and is "currently [a] one-man operation [run] out of his home. . . ."

The fact that Hickson had been willing to take a polygraph examination suggested that he had nothing to hide. There was no explanation for the fact that Parker had *not* taken a test at the same time, but when Hickson appeared on the Cavett show, he explained that the young man was in the hospital. Later, Colingo informed me that the young man had suffered a "nervous breakdown" and this explained why he had not taken a lie-detector test.

When I returned from a month-long trip in mid-December, I launched my own investigation of this now-famous case. The announced results of the polygraph tests on Hickson gave this case an element of respectability and credibility that other such fantastic UFO "contactee" cases lacked. From my very limited knowledge of polygraph tests, I knew that it is not an infallible technique for determining if the subject is telling a falsehood. (If it were even close to being infallible, polygraph tests could eliminate the need for many long court trials and could be substituted for a jury.) But before I could probe the Pascagoula case and the validity of Hickson's examination, I needed to strengthen my knowledge of polygraphy. To do this, I sought the assistance of a long-experienced specialist in the Washington area—Glenn Maggard, who operates the Atlantic Security Agency. Maggard is a licensed examiner and a member of the American Polygraph Association.

Maggard emphasized to me that the "charts" which are generated by a polygraph, to show the subject's physiological reactions to questions, are not in themselves the sole mechanism that indicates whether the subject is telling the truth. The *effectiveness of the polygraph depends principally on the skill and experience of the human examiner, and on the questioning techniques he employs,* Maggard emphasized. He told me that some persons, for physiological or psychological reasons, are not "good subjects" because they can tell a falsehood without having physiological responses that can be detected on the charts. For this reason, Maggard said, each subject must first be tested by the examiner to be sure that he responds when telling what is known to be a falsehood. Maggard then gave me approximately a dozen questions to

pose to the New Orleans polygraphist who had tested
Hickson, so that Maggard could evaluate his expertise.

When I telephoned the New Orleans polygraphist on
December 28 and posed Maggard's first question, asking
whether he was a member of the American Polygraph
Association, the operator replied that he was "not yet."
Where had he been trained? At the National Training
Center of Lie Detection in New York. Later Maggard told
me that this was a respected polygraph school. When I asked
the New Orleans polygraphist how long he had been practicing, he replied, "Approximately a year." Later I would
discover that the New Orleans polygraph operator had *not*
been "certified" by the school in which he had trained and
would not be "certified." The reason was explained to me by
Richard Arthur, director of the National Training Center of
Lie Detection in New York City. Arthur told me that each of
his graduates, like those of other recognized schools, operate
as an "intern" during his first year, and every new graduate is
expected "to return his cases" to Arthur for his analysis and
review. This is to assure that the new operator is following
prescribed procedures and demonstrating good judgment.
Arthur explained that the New Orleans operator who had
examined Hickson "did *not* complete this phase of his
training." When I asked if he would have another opportunity to submit his work for review and certification, Arthur
replied, "No, his year is up. He has to comply within one year
and he has not." *

Returning again to my telephone interview with the young
New Orleans operator, when I posed to him the more
complex questions on technique and procedure that Maggard
had supplied, I was glad that I had decided to tape-record the
entire conversation so I could provide Maggard a precise,

---

* In an article published in the September–October, 1973, issue of *The
Journal of Polygraph Studies,* Arthur discusses some of the problems that
arise in this profession, especially because many states do not require
examination and licensing of polygraph operators. Arthur said he knows "one
rather famous [polygraph] 'expert' who—as far as I know—has never
rendered a 'lying' opinion for a lawyer . . . the unscrupulous attorney can go
from one expert to another until—at last—his client comes up truthful."

verbatim transcript of the New Orleans operator's answers. Later, after Maggard had had an opportunity to study my typed transcript, he called me to say that it was clear that the New Orleans polygraphist was "an inexperienced operator." Then Maggard told me, "Judging from what he told you, I doubt whether he can tell whether the subject is telling a lie or telling the truth."

I was becoming increasingly curious about why the polygraph test which had served to give so much credibility to the story of the Pascagoula "abduction" had been given by an examiner of limited experience who was uncertified by his own school—especially one who had been imported from New Orleans, which is one hundred miles from Pascagoula. My check of the Yellow Pages in the telephone directory for Mobile, Alabama—which is only thirty miles from Pascagoula—showed that there were two licensed commercial polygraph operators there, one of whom I later learned had had more than seventeen years' experience in the field. On January 4, when I talked by telephone with attorney Colingo about these and other aspects of the case, he assured me that he too originally had doubts about the Hickson-Parker story. He added that he had not been impressed by the endorsement given by Harder and Hynek after their two days of interviews with the two shipyard workers. Colingo said his reaction was "The hell with that, I want a lie-detector test taken."

I asked if the attorney had had any previous experience with polygraph examinations. Colingo replied, "I was public defender down here for a while, some years ago, and I've seen them operate. I have had people take them on numerous occasions." Based on this experience, Colingo would fully understand the important role that the expertise of the polygraph operator necessarily plays in the reliability of the test results. Without revealing at that point what I had already learned about the New Orleans polygraph operator, I asked whether he was an experienced examiner. The attorney replied, "Oh, Lordy, he's a graduate of Purdue University and has given *thousands* of them [polygraph tests]." When I asked how long he had been practicing, Colingo replied,

"Hell, several years." Then he quickly transitioned into a discussion of the thoroughness of the test that had been given to Hickson. Colingo said that the "normal, average polygraph test will take between thirty and forty-five minutes after you go through the formality of kind of briefing them [subject] to some extent. This one *took about three hours.*" I asked whether this "three hours" included the preparatory briefing of Hickson before the actual test questioning. Colingo replied, "The questioning." I did not tell him that during my conversation with the New Orleans polygraphist he had told me that he had run a series of *four* tests, each of which lasted for only three to five minutes. Based on this, the total duration of the time that Hickson was connected to the polygraph could not have exceeded *twenty minutes!* The remainder of the time, the polygraphist explained to me, was devoted to talking to Hickson "so he understands the questions and I understand what he means [by his answers] and we are just talking about things and explaining things."

When I began to explore with Colingo how he had happened to select the New Orleans polygraphist, he explained, "We have *only one* [polygraph operator] in the state and that is the state agency in Jackson, the capital. And they were reluctant to want to give a polygraph test to anyone who is not accused of crime, *so I had to go out of the state.*" Colingo said that he "not only tried in the state of Mississippi, I had the local sheriff's office try in the state of Alabama. We have an operator in Mobile, which is only twenty miles [away]. *They wouldn't agree to give it.*" Later he reemphasized this point: "I tried first through the sheriff's department to see if we could get either Mobile or Jackson to do it. The sheriff's department's answer to me was No."

Colingo acknowledged that he had been "referred to a man in Montgomery, Alabama, who wanted to charge two or three hundred dollars to come down here and take [i.e., give] a lie-detector test. I told him No. I said I don't want to pay anything." Colingo explained that he thought the test should be given without charge: "I said it's a matter of national . . . it's for the good of the country . . . I think the country should know." Meanwhile, Colingo said, as he fruitlessly

searched for a patriotically motivated polygraph operator
who would be willing to come to Pascagoula and run the test
free, "all the newsmen kept hounding us, wanting to know
why they couldn't take a lie-detector test." It was at this
point, Colingo explained, that he called a friend and former
law-school classmate in Jackson whose two brothers operate
detective agencies—one in Jackson and the other in New
Orleans. The Jackson agency, which Colingo told me he had
previously employed in other matters, did not have a
polygraph operator on its staff, but the one in New Orleans
did.

Colingo explained to me that he had "made the arrangements for them to come over here [to his own office], but
prior to doing it, it was well understood with the president of
the detective agency that there would be no compensation
for it." Colingo then explained another reason why he had
not wanted to pay for the lie-detector test. If the attorney
paid for the test, he told me, some persons might infer that
this could influence the results. So, on October 30, Hickson
had taken the test in Colingo's office while the attorney,
another member of the New Orleans detective agency, the
local sheriff and a deputy monitored the proceedings in
another room by means of an intercom. After the *first* in the
series of tests, the attorney told me, the New Orleans
polygraph operator had left Hickson and come into the room
where Colingo and the others were sitting to announce,
"Hell, they're telling the truth!"

As I listened to Colingo describe his difficulties in finding a
polygraph operator to conduct the examination on his terms,
and the pressures from newsmen to have Hickson and Parker
take the lie-detector tests to which they had agreed, it might
have seemed that the attorney had been lucky at last to find
even a young, inexperienced, "uncertified" operator in New
Orleans who worked for his friend's brother.

When I called Jack N. Wood, one of the two commercial
polygraph operators listed in the Yellow Pages of the Mobile,
Alabama, telephone directory, I asked him if he had been
contacted during Colingo's search for someone to test
Hickson. *Wood told me he had not!* I learned that Wood

had practiced his trade for seventeen years, after being
trained by the Army. He suggested I call Frank Schottgen,
another experienced Mobile polygraph operator, the son of
the owner of the Allied Secret Service detective agency where
Wood himself had previously worked until he had recently
gone into business for himself. I called Schottgen and asked if
he or his agency had been approached by Colingo or the
Pascagoula sheriff's office. *He told me they had not,* but he
said he had heard that the chief polygraphist of the Mobile
police department—Captain Charles Wimberly—had been
contacted. Wimberly, I learned, has thirteen years' experience in this field and is a member of the State Board of
Examiners of Alabama, which, like Mississippi, requires that
all polygraph operators pass rigorous tests for licensing.
(Louisiana, I discovered, does not require that its polygraph
operators be licensed. One Mississippi state law enforcement
official told me that operators who fail to pass licensing tests
in his state or in Alabama sometimes set up practice in
Louisiana, where no examination is required.)

When I called Captain Wimberly, he told me that he had
been approached by the Pascagoula sheriff's office to see if he
would test Hickson and Parker. When I asked him, "Did you
turn them down?" he replied, "I didn't turn them down in
that sense. I turned them down in the sense that if I was
involved in running a polygraph test on those individuals it
would have to be [done] in my environment and on my
terms." Wimberly wanted the tests run in his office, not in
Colingo's, which other polygraphists confirm is the standard
practice to accentuate the psychological impact of the tests.
In other words, Wimberly simply wanted to conduct the
examination in the conventional manner in which he normally ran lie-detector tests.

This hardly seemed an unreasonable requirement. Nor did
Wimberly's other conditions under which he would be
willing to run the test. Wimberly wanted to bring in another
experienced commercial operator to participate in the tests,
and the results released in the name of the commercial
operator because "I didn't want my police department
switchboard lighting up with all those phone calls" (from

UFO buffs), the officer told me. He said he explained to the
Pascagoula sheriff's office that "I would physically run it, but
it would have to be on my terms." In response, Wimberly was
told that the test was being arranged for attorney Colingo,
who would have to decide whether to accept the tests under
Wimberly's conditions. *The Mobile police polygraphist told
me that he never heard further from the Pascagoula sheriff's
office or from Colingo.* When I asked Wimberly if he was still
willing to test Hickson and Parker, he replied he was,
providing he could "run the examination the way I felt it
should be run."

The Pascagoula sheriff's office had earlier released an
official statement saying it "has no public or private opinion
about whether the [UFO] report was true or false. The
responsibility of the sheriff's department is not to prove
people right or wrong in their complaint."

Police chief Craig M. Monroe, Jr., of Gulfport, Mississippi,
took quite a different position on October 16, five days after
the Hickson-Parker incident, when a Gulfport taxi driver
reported that he had also had an encounter with a strange-
looking creature from a UFO at 3 A.M. Chief Monroe
decided he *did* have a responsibility to try to prove or
disprove the driver's story, in view of growing UFO hysteria in
the area—if only to calm local citizens, or to prepare for more
UFO abductions! While Colingo and the Pascagoula sheriff's
office were, according to Colingo, vainly searching for an
experienced polygraph operator, the Gulfport police chief
had no trouble finding one. He called Truth Incorporated, in
Jackson, Mississippi, a company that specializes in polygraph
examinations. Within forty-eight hours after the cab driver
had reported his UFO encounter, he had taken a test in
Jackson, administered by Truth Incorporated, and had
flunked it badly. The taxi driver then admitted it was all a
hoax that had been concocted to explain why he had been
found asleep in his cab by a fellow driver. Thanks to police
chief Monroe's good judgment and prompt action, the
citizens of Gulfport could relax—while the citizens of Pascagoula were still jittery.

If the Pascagoula sheriff's office was not familiar with

Truth Incorporated, despite its national reputation, the sheriff could have learned of the company as I did when I called the Mississippi State Identification Bureau and talked with Dewey Weames, an experienced polygraph operator and past secretary of the state polygraph examiners' board. When I asked Weames if he or his associates had been called by the Pascagoula sheriff's office, Weames said he was not aware of any such inquiry. He acknowledged that state operators would not have been able to give Hickson and Parker an examination because it was not a criminal matter.

Robert Alexander, who runs Truth Incorporated, has ten years' experience as a polygraph operator, and his part-time associate is Max Burleson, with twelve years' background and more than twenty thousand examinations under his belt. Burleson told me that he operates a similar business in Memphis and that he and Alexander often collaborate on important cases—such as the one involving the Gulfport taxi driver. Burleson told me that he and Alexander had followed the Pascagoula case casually in the newspapers and that when they read that the two men were eager to take a polygraph examination, they had thought that Truth Incorporated might be asked to give the test—especially in view of their experience with the Gulfport case. But Burleson told me that the call never came either from Colingo or from the Pascagoula sheriff's office. Instead, more than a week later, the young, inexperienced polygraphist from New Orleans and his boss journeyed to Colingo's office to test Hickson and then make the widely publicized pronouncement that the lie-detector tests seemed to substantiate the UFO abduction.

Perhaps none of these many experienced commercial polygraph operators would have been willing to conduct the examination without charge—but Colingo could not have known this without at least asking them. Burleson explained to me that for a case of this type, the subject ought to be tested for a *full day*, and that both he and Alexander would have participated (providing a total of twenty-two years' experience). Under these circumstances, he said, the fee would probably have been around five hundred dollars. To me, this does not seem like an excessive price to pay to determine whether extraterrestrial visitors are abducting innocent victims, or whether instead the citizens of Pascagoula and the nation were the real victims—of a hoax.

During my January 4 telephone conversation with Colingo, the attorney repeatedly stressed the great difficulty he had encountered in his search for a polygraph operator to test Hickson and Parker: "Everyone kept saying, 'When are they going to take a polygraph? When—if they're telling the damn truth—? Why don't they take a lie-detector test?' " Then, Colingo's voice became tense as he said, *"Well, I could not and would not make it publicly known that I couldn't get anyone to give them the damned test!"*

When I asked Colingo if Hickson would be willing to take another test from a different polygraph operator, the attorney retorted sharply, "Why should he? Why should he?" When I posed this question again later, the attorney said he had already raised the issue with Hickson: "I've talked to him. I've said, 'Now, we've had one test . . . if there are any more tests that they can think of throwing at us I want 'em to do it.' " Colingo told me Hickson had replied, "Joe, as far as I'm concerned, I went through the hypnosis. I've gone through this. I've taken every test imaginable, and to hell with it. If people don't want to believe me, to hell with them. I don't give a damn." To this Colingo added, "And that's just the way he feels, and it's a very, very sensitive area."

Then I inquired about a polygraph test for young Parker, who by this time had recovered sufficiently from his "nervous breakdown" to appear with Hickson on NBC's Mike Douglas TV show, telecast on December 31. Parker had by this time quit his job in Pascagoula and returned to his home in Laurel. Colingo replied, "Parker is ready, willing and able. I would say that as far as—if there were any more lie-detector tests to be taken, I would be more prone to say that, since Mr. Parker didn't take one the first time, I've told him sometime down the road I'm going to give him one. So if there was one taken, I'd be more—we'd be more—it would be much more favorable if Parker took it." Because of Colingo's aversion to paying for a polygraph test, I told him I would be willing to underwrite the cost for both Hickson and Parker and that he would have full access to the results. Colingo replied, "Why should I—for *your* benefit—subject my client to a lie-detector test when *I* am satisfied, and that's the only one that counts right now."

But later in our conversation, Colingo admitted that I was not the only one to suggest that Parker take a lie-detector test and that Hickson take another. He said he was currently negotiating with companies that "want to buy a story on this." One of the prospects, he said, had insisted on a new polygraph test for both men as a condition to the contract. But the attorney said he had told the prospect that the two men would take such a test only after there had been an agreement on financial arrangements.

When Colingo once again asked why he should have the two men take a new polygraph test, I acknowledged that there was the risk that "if they fail, then you have lost a client." Colingo replied indignantly, "I'm not making any money out of it anyway. . . ." When I asked whether he wouldn't share in the proceeds of the deal he said he was currently negotiating, the attorney replied, "But the time and money that I have had to, that I've lost in this office, there would be no way on that penny-ante thing that I would be halfway compensated—if I got *all* of the money." Then he added, "There's been no money, absolutely none." * As our long telephone interview came to a close, Colingo said, "Well, I'm certainly not saying that I won't give them another test. That's not my position at all. But I'm not sure I would do it at *your* request. I'm sure I would do it *when I get ready to do it*. And I will be happy, if and when I do it, to notify you and you can come down here and sit and watch it."

---

* In the *Rolling Stone* article of January 17, 1974, reporter Eszterhas says that Colingo asked him: "How much do you think we can make on their Exclusive Story?" Eszterhas said he replied that it would depend on how well the Hickson-Parker story could be verified. To this, Eszterhas said, Colingo replied: "A million, you think? I figure if we sell magazine and book and movie rights to one of the big studios, that can be a lot of money. I wish to hell *Life* magazine was still in business."

When five months had elapsed without hearing from Colingo, I took the initiative to contact him to determine if there had been any new developments in the case. When we talked by telephone on June 7, 1974, Colingo said he had not seen or talked with Parker for four or five months because he had moved to Laurel, Mississippi. The only significant new development, Colingo said, was that a team from the National Broadcasting Company had recently visited Pascagoula to talk with Hickson in preparation for a special UFO television program that NBC planned to produce. Colingo volunteered: "I don't want you to get the impression that either one of these fellows has made any money off this because they have not."

If Hickson and Parker do submit to a rigorous polygraph examination, given by a team of experienced operators, there is no way of knowing what the result will be even if the case is a hoax, as I firmly believe it is. Burleson told me that once a subject has gained confidence that he can "beat the machine," it makes a falsehood more difficult to detect. Burleson also described another technique that can be used to enable a subject to tell falsehoods without being detected even by an experienced examiner. (I will not divulge it here lest it be used to handicap polygraph examiners in their important work.) Even if the two men take a test and fail it, news of this event will never receive the widespread publicity given to their original account. (I doubt that the polygraph examiners will be invited to tell their story on the Cavett or Douglas shows.) As a result, many people who were exposed to the original UFO abduction account will never learn the full story.

If the Pascagoula case is positively exposed as a hoax by such tests, it will leave a void in the "Land of UFOria"—but only temporarily. Within a few years, two campers in Colorado, or perhaps two hunters in Minnesota, will report an equally fantastic encounter with space creatures that allegedly were only two feet tall, or stood ten feet high. Like all previous accounts, there will not be a single shred of physical evidence to support the story. But UFO investigators with impressive-sounding credentials will quickly arrive to interview the principals. And then they will issue their pronouncements to the news media, certifying the authenticity of the latest wild UFO case. These "experts" will make headlines because journalists, under pressure of deadlines, will not take time to investigate their past record of similar pronouncements on cases that turned out to be hoaxes. Overnight, the campers or the hunters will be catapulted from obscurity to international fame. You will see and hear them on all the network talk-shows.

It will happen again and again unless law-enforcement officials and national news media—including network radio and television—show the same good sense demonstrated by police chief Monroe of Gulfport, and promptly ask the principals to submit to a rigorous polygraph examination conducted by a team of experienced, licensed operators. They are not hard to find. One need only look in the Yellow Pages of the telephone directory for any sizable city, either under "Lie Detection Services" or under "Detective Agencies."

28 · Delphos:
Blue-Ribbon Panel's Choice

A prize of $50,000 was offered on March 12, 1972, to anyone who could submit a UFO report or other evidence that offered positive proof that at least one extraterrestrial spaceship had visited the Earth. The offer came from the *National Enquirer*, a sensationalist tabloid newspaper, which later announced that it would pay $5,000 for the best UFO case submitted if it failed to qualify for the $50,000 prize. Some UFOlogists claim that the best cases are never reported for fear of personal ridicule, despite the many thousands of reports on record which would indicate that this is not a strong deterrent. But certainly the prospect of winning $50,000, or $5,000, could be expected to bring forth the best reports, even from the reluctant. So it is not surprising that by the contest closing date, January 1, 1973, the *National Enquirer* had received *more than one thousand entries*, it later reported.

To judge the entries, five university professors—all with Ph.D.'s—were selected on the strength of their long experience as UFOlogists and investigators. James Lorenzen, the international director of the Aerial Phenomena Research Organization (APRO), the nation's second-largest UFO group, was named as a consultant-advisor to the panel, four of whose members were long-time technical advisors to APRO. One of these, Dr. James A. Harder of the University of California at Berkeley, would later play a key role in the Pascagoula case (Chapter 27). The fifth panel member was Dr. J. Allen Hynek, considered by some to be the nation's leading UFO expert because of his twenty-five years in the field, most of them as a paid consultant on UFOs to the USAF.* It is not, therefore, surprising that the *National Enquirer* characterized this illustrious group of UFOlogists as a "blue-ribbon panel."

I was delighted to learn of the contest and the famous UFO experts who would judge the entries. For some years I had attempted—without success—to get leading proponents of the extraterrestrial viewpoint to designate a single "best case" which they had rigorously investigated and were *certain* could not be explained other than as an extraterrestrial visitation. It had been frustrating for me through the years to investigate and explain a case such as Socorro, which Hynek had once categorized as the most crucial one in eighteen years of UFO reports, only to be told by some that I had spent my time on an "unimpressive case." Or to spend months investigating the RB-47 case, which had so impressed the AIAA and the late Dr. McDonald, only to be informed that I had "picked an easy one." After more than a quarter-century of UFO incidents, during which time the UFO investigators who lean toward the extraterrestrial view have had time to sharpen their investigative skills and presumably their ability to sort fact from fiction, it seemed to me that it was time for them to designate a "make-or-break" UFO case.

Now, thanks to the *National Enquirer*'s $50,000 prize and

---

* Dr. Joachim P. Kuettner, chairman of the AIAA's UFO Subcommittee (Chapter 20), writing on Hynek's UFO expertise, observed: ". . . there is little doubt that he knows as much about UFOs as any scientist in the world."

its choice of so distinguished a panel of experienced UFO-logists to select the winning entry, we could expect the strongest possible case for the extraterrestrial hypothesis to emerge. Hynek, who prides himself on his expertise in spotting hoaxes, would, presumably, assure that such a case could never be selected as the panel's choice. The May 27, 1973, edition of the *National Enquirer* announced that the panel of experts had decided that none of the entries deserved the $50,000 prize because no case submitted had been able to provide positive proof of extraterrestrial visitations. But from the more than one thousand entries, the panel had voted *unanimously* (with one member abstaining*) to award the $5,000 prize to a farmer named Durel Johnson, who lived just outside the small Kansas town of Delphos. The Johnson incident, also known as the Delphos case, was characterized by the panel as "a major scientific mystery—the most baffling case the panel encountered in a full year of investigation."

Dr. Hynek, acting as spokesman, said the panel had selected "the Johnson case because of the great number of individual items of 'strangeness' involved which remain unexplained even after a long series of chemical, optical, electronic and other physical tests carried out by eleven university and private laboratories. Among the *facts* that make the case *of great scientific interest* are: the sighting of the luminous object itself [UFO], observed clearly by the Johnsons' 16-year-old son and at a distance by his parents; and the presence at the landing site of a ring of soil of altered chemical composition, extending more than a foot below the surface.†

"*This ring of soil and the bark of surrounding trees glowed brightly for several days.* Also the ring of soil differed markedly from its immediate surroundings, not only in chemical composition but in appearance. The soil was dried out and powdery. For more than a year after the sighting, this

---

* The abstaining member was Dr. Robert Creegan, professor of philosophy at the State University of New York in Albany.

† Copyright: NATIONAL ENQUIRER; Lantana, Florida.

soil would not accept water, nor could anything be grown in it." (Emphasis added.) According to the *National Enquirer*, "*Dr. Hynek emphasized that the panel had carefully investigated the possibility of a hoax, but are* [sic] *completely satisfied that the sighting was real.*" (Emphasis added.) If this panel of experienced UFOlogists had rigorously explored the possibility of a hoax and found nothing suspicious, then this was THE case for which "believers" (and I) had waited so long.

The most detailed report on the Delphos case was written by Ted Phillips, of Sedalia, Missouri, who specializes in cases where a UFO allegedly has left behind traces or physical evidence of its presence. Phillips, who had worked with Hynek previously on "trace cases," received a telephone call from him on the evening of December 2, 1971, telling of the Delphos incident, which reportedly had occurred a month earlier on November 2, 1971. Phillips responded to Hynek's request that he make an on-the-spot investigation, and two days later he arrived in Delphos. Hynek did not go.

Phillips, who leans toward the extraterrestrial view on UFOs, is a rather thorough investigator but seems inclined to accept testimony at face value, judging from his account of the Delphos case. Because he was one of the first experienced investigators to visit the site, his account of the incident, based primarily on his interviews with members of the Johnson family, will be used here unless otherwise noted. Phillips was told that on the night of November 2, the sixteen-year-old Ronald was tending his sheep alone in the backyard several hundred feet north of the Johnson house. The time was 7 P.M., more than an hour after darkness. When Mrs. Johnson came to the back step of the house to call Ronald for dinner, the youth hollered back to say he would be in soon. His parents began to eat dinner without him, and when they had finished without Ronald's appearance, Mrs. Johnson said, she again went out to call him. This time, she said, the boy did not reply, but this did not seem cause for concern, so she returned to the house.

While the parents had been eating dinner inside, exciting events were occurring in the backyard, according to Ronald's account. He said that it was shortly after his mother had first called him to dinner that he heard a "rumbling sound" to the northeast. Looking in this direction, Ronald said he saw a "mushroom-shaped" object that was "illuminated from top to bottom by multicolored light." The object was sitting in the middle of a belt of Chinese elm trees a few dozen yards away. Ronald said the strange-looking object was hovering about two feet off the ground and that he could see a bright glow underneath it—presumably coming from some sort of propulsion unit that enabled the object to hover above the ground.

Ronald was in such a position that he could have run away from the UFO and sought refuge in a nearby barn or the house. But instead he said he watched the UFO for several minutes. Then it suddenly became intensely illuminated underneath and began to ascend and head south at what the youth said was considerable speed. As the UFO took off, it passed directly over a low shed, and as it did so, Ronald said, the sound changed from a "rumble" to a "high-pitched whine" similar to a jet aircraft. As the UFO flew south, it passed near the west side of the Johnson house, where the parents were eating dinner. But despite the silence that prevails on a Kansas farm after dark in the late fall months, the parents said they heard nothing.

Phillips, again quoting the youth, reported that "as the sound changed, the boy was suddenly unable to see—*he claimed to have lost his vision completely.*" (Emphasis added.) This would have been a terrifying experience for the youth, who, he later acknowledged, *had read some books on flying saucers* and thus knew that if spaceships from other worlds were visiting Earth, they might be armed with mysterious radiation weapons. Phillips speculates that it was probably at this point—while Ronald was standing there temporarily blinded—that his mother came out to call him a second time for dinner, and this could explain why Ronald failed to reply.

"After what seemed to be several minutes," Phillips reported, "the boy began to regain his sight. *He saw the object in the sky* and ran to the house. He told his parents that a flying saucer or something had landed and was still visible in the sky. Mr. and Mrs. Johnson both stated that the boy was frightened and excited when he entered the house. They said they didn't believe the boy at first and he became very aggravated." When the Johnson family finally went outside to check on the youth's story, and looked to the south, they told Phillips that they "saw a bright light *in the southern sky.*" (Emphasis added.) (During my interview with Mr. Johnson, however, he said that when the family emerged they saw the UFO "was right up between those trees, by the road . . ." only a couple of hundred feet away.) The Johnsons told Phillips that the UFO was "at least half the apparent diameter of the full moon . . . the color of an arc-welder . . . decreasing in size, moving into the distance." They said they had decided to walk back to the grove of trees to examine the spot where Ronald said the UFO had been hovering. They told Phillips that as they walked around a low shed, "they saw in the darkness a glowing circle. The soil surface was glowing a bright grey-white. Portions of the nearby trees reportedly glowed also," according to the Phillips report.

If the Johnsons' account is factual, the glowing circle on the ground and the glowing bark on the trees would seem to confirm Ronald's story and erase all doubt about the UFO's visit. Presumably the glowing ground and tree bark were caused by some mysterious radiation given off by the UFO, perhaps the same thing that had temporarily blinded Ronald. This might have prompted most persons to remain a healthy distance away from the glowing circle on the ground—but not the Johnsons, according to their account. Both Mr. and Mrs. Johnson said they even reached down and touched the glowing soil and found that it was not warm, but that the soil did have a crusty, crystalline texture. Shortly after touching the glowing soil, Mrs. Johnson said, she felt a "numbing in her fingertips," which she compared to the effect of a local anesthesia. In an effort to get the finger-numbing soil off her hands, she said, she rubbed them against her leg, and now "her leg also became numb." Mr. Johnson reported that his fingers became numb too after touching the glowing soil. (Mrs. Johnson said that the numbness in her fingers persisted

for about two weeks, while Mr. Johnson said his was much
shorter lived.) Ronald told Phillips that his eyes remained
sore and bloodshot for several days after the incident and
that he had experienced headaches.

If the account is factual, it must have seemed to the
Johnsons that night that the whole family had been exposed
to some mysterious radiation from the spaceship from distant
worlds that had landed in a grove of trees behind their house.
It would be understandable if the Johnsons had developed at
least a mild case of panic and had gotten into the family car
and rushed to see their doctor. But instead the entire family
remained cool as a cucumber. Mrs. Johnson said she calmly
returned to the house, got a Polaroid camera and went back
to the glowing circle that had reportedly numbed her fingers
and took a photograph of it. Mr. Johnson and Ronald got
into their car and drove into nearby Delphos—not to see a
doctor, but to visit the local weekly newspaper, which Mr.
Johnson thought would be interested in seeing the Polaroid
print of the "glowing ring," and hearing about the exciting
incident.* But the editor of the Delphos *Republican*, Willard
Critchfield, was "on deadline" that night, and he decided it
was more important to stay on the job and get out the town's
weekly newspaper than to take off twenty minutes and go out
to see where the UFO had reportedly landed and left behind
a glowing ring.

So Mr. Johnson and Ronald returned home and the next
issue of the Delphos *Republican* came out on schedule, but it
carried not a single word about the exciting UFO incident on
the outskirts of town—an incident that would later be
selected as the most impressive UFO case from more than
one thousand entries by the *National Enquirer's* "blue-
ribbon panel" of experts. Undiscouraged by this lack of local
newspaper interest, Mr. Johnson drove into town the next
day and had lunch at the town's principal restaurant, near the

---

* According to the Phillips account, Mr. Johnson "called" editor Critchfield
shortly after the incident. But Critchfield, his reporter Mrs. Smith and later
Mr. Johnson confirmed that Johnson and his son had driven into town to see
the local editor.

newspaper office, where Critchfield normally ate. Mrs. Lester (Thaddia) Smith, a local newspaper reporter who had known the Johnsons for many years and had heard of the UFO incident from her boss, walked over to ask Johnson about it. He invited Mrs. Smith to come and see for herself the curious white ring on the ground. After lunch, Mrs. Smith, her husband and her son-in-law all drove to the Johnson farm. Mrs. Smith's account of what she observed is as follows: "Upon arriving at the scene I knew instantly that something had left evidence that it had been there. The circle was still very distinct and plain to see. The soil was dried and crusted. The circle or ring was approximately 8 ft. across, the center of the ring and *outside area were still muddy from recent rains.* The area of the ring that was dried was about a foot across and *was very light in color.*" (Emphasis added.)

Mrs. Smith, with a reporter's eye for detail, observed that a dead tree, which would have been directly in the path of the reported UFO during its arrival and departure, had fallen or had been knocked over. IF the dead tree had been standing before the incident, then almost certainly it would have been knocked over by any object that had landed and taken off from the "site." (See Plates 23a, 23b.) When the Johnsons assured her that the tree had been standing before the incident, Mrs. Smith wrote: "The object had crushed a dead tree to the ground either when it landed or took off." She also noted a broken branch on a live tree adjoining the site and naturally concluded that it too had been a victim of the UFO. When she noted that this limb had a "whitish cast," she decided that it "looked as though it had been blistered," presumably from intense heat emitted by the UFO.

Mrs. Smith took a photo of the area and, using her words, "went back to the newspaper office to write my story. Thinking about the almost unbelievable things I had seen, I decided to call the Concordia Weather Bureau to find out if they had seen an unidentifiable object on radar." She learned that the radar had not been operating that night, but the Weather Bureau office suggested that she notify the Ottawa County sheriff in nearby Minneapolis (Kansas), which she did. (Mrs. Smith later told me that *she had suggested to Mr.*

Johnson that he report it to the sheriff, but that Johnson had declined.)

Sheriff Ralph Enlow, undersheriff Harlen Enlow and Kansas Highway Patrolman Kenneth Yager arrived at the Johnson farm on November 3 at approximately 2 P.M., shortly after Mrs. Smith's visit. After talking with members of the Johnson family, the officers went back to inspect the site. What they found is described in a report by undersheriff Harlen Enlow: "We observed a ring shaped somewhat like a doughnut. . . . The ring was completely dry with a hole in the middle and outside of the ring [there was] mud. There were limbs broken from a tree and a dead tree broken off, there. There was a slight discoloration on the trees. We were given a picture taken the previous evening by Mrs. Johnson which showed that the ring glowed in the dark. Undersheriff Enlow took a soil sample from the dried ring and photographed it.

"The soil sample taken was almost white in color and very dry. We used a Civil Defense Radiological Monitor to determine that the soil was not radioactive." The report noted that the soil samples and photos were stored in the sheriff's office. Finally, the report said that a man named Lester Ernsbarger, of Minneapolis, had reported to the sheriff's office on November 3 that he had "observed a bright light descending in the sky in the Delphos area at approximately 7:30 P.M. on the night of November 2." Some UFO investigators quickly concluded that this was an independent substantiation of the Johnson account. But at 7:30 P.M., the alleged Johnson UFO would either have been hovering in the grove of trees or would just have taken off and have been *ascending,* not descending.

From a photo taken by the law-enforcement officers on November 3, within twenty-four hours of the alleged incident, and from measurements made by Phillips a month later, it is evident that the so-called ring should more accurately be described as an *irregular horseshoe shape, with an open space to the northwest.* The outer diameter was approximately 90 inches in a north-south direction and 99 inches in an east-west direction. The thickness of the horseshoe/ring varied from *12 inches* to *30 inches*. (See Plate 24a.) When I later interviewed Sheriff Enlow, he told me that when he had visited the Johnson farm most of the backyard was mushy mud because of recent heavy rains—except within the horseshoe-shaped ring, which was relatively hard and dry. And when Phillips visited Delphos a month later, he noted that recently fallen snow which had melted elsewhere in the yard was unmelted over the horseshoe-shaped ring. He reported that when he poured water on this soil, it tended to run off rather than be absorbed as with soil inside and outside the ring.

Phillips took some soil samples from the site during his first visit, and when he returned on January 11, 1972, he and Mr. Johnson probed more deeply. At that time, Phillips reported, he found that traces of the white material extended down from the top to a depth of as much as fourteen inches, where the soil still seemed dry. During the next few months, many UFO investigators and others would scoop up samples, eventually prompting Johnson to fence off the site area. Fortunately, the photo taken by Sheriff Enlow during the early afternoon of November 3 shows how the site appeared shortly after the incident and makes it possible to draw several significant conclusions, which will be discussed shortly.

It was not until some months later that I learned of the Delphos case and began to brief myself on the details prior to its selection by the *National Enquirer* panel, using Phillips' report as well as that of another UFO investigator, a Kansas City lawyer named Clancy D. Tull, now deceased. When I studied the photo of the site that had been taken by Sheriff Enlow, two things were evident. (See Plate 24a.) First, the dried-out condition of the soil could not have resulted from the proximity of an extremely hot object, because the photo revealed numerous small twigs on the ground, some of them within the horseshoe-shaped ring, *none of which showed the slightest evidence of heat or burning.* Later, when I inter- viewed Sheriff Enlow, he told me that he saw "no evidence of burning of any kind."

The second thing that was clearly apparent from the Enlow photo was that *if* any sort of craft had been hovering over the

site, *it had not at any time landed or touched down.* Because
of the heavy rains in late October, most of the backyard had
been very wet and muddy, including the soil on either side of
the horseshoe-shaped ring. *Unless* the horseshoe-shaped ring
had been there for some time *before* November 2, this soil
too would have been mushy. If any craft had landed there, its
weight would have made a depression in the mud and would
have pushed the small twigs into the soil. *Yet the Enlow
photo does not show even the slightest indentation, and the
twigs are lying flat atop the whitish soil with no sign that a
large object landed on them.*

If the Johnson boy's account was factual, then clearly the
alleged UFO must have been *hovering over the site for the
full duration of its visit.* Ronald said that while the UFO was
hovering about two feet above the ground, it had made a
rumbling noise and given off intense illumination. Yet if the
object made its presence so obvious when it hovered, and if it
must have been hovering for the full duration of its visit, why
hadn't Ronald seen and heard the UFO long before, and why
had it not been spotted earlier by Mr. Johnson when he too
was working in the backyard? If the UFO had flown in only a
short time before Ronald said he first spotted it, why hadn't it
attracted his attention at the time of arrival? Especially since
the UFO reportedly made so much noise while flying!

The fallen dead tree posed another curious riddle. Mr.
Johnson insisted that the tree had been standing just south of
the site before the incident, although he acknowledged that it
already was dead. The grove of trees that surrounds the site
from three directions meant that a UFO would have to
approach from the south and depart in the same direction, as
Ronald had reported. If a UFO had knocked over the tree
during arrival, the tree should have fallen in *a northerly
direction,* or in *a southerly direction* if it had been knocked
down when a UFO departed to the south. But instead the
*dead tree had fallen to the west and was lying in an east-west
direction.* Furthermore, there were *no signs of impact on the
tree,* according to Sheriff Enlow, who had inspected it the day
after the alleged incident. Investigators Tull and Phillips

confirmed that there was no visible sign of impact on the fallen tree.

Another aspect of the case which repeatedly aroused my curiosity was that despite the mysterious aftereffects that all three members of the Johnson family claimed to have experienced, none of them had ever bothered to seek treatment or examination by a doctor—so far as I can determine. (A family of modest means certainly would not want to waste their money seeking medical attention for nonexistent injuries if the UFO incident were simply a tall tale.) Sheriff Enlow told me that he and the other officers, during their November 3 visit to the farm, had handled the white substance in the horseshoe-shaped ring. But he said that none of the law-enforcement officers had experienced any numbness—even within twenty-four hours of the reported UFO incident.

The only person other than the Johnsons known to have reported experiencing numbness from handling the soil is Dr. James A. Harder, one of the members of the "blue-ribbon panel." Harder had visited the Johnson farm in August, 1972, some *nine months after the UFO incident*, in the company of Ted Phillips. As Durel Johnson later described the incident to me, Harder had bent over to feel the soil in the ring when suddenly he complained that his fingers felt numb, and he had run to the house to wash the dirt off his hands. (Johnson chuckled as he recounted the incident.) Later, Phillips confirmed that Harder had experienced a slight numbing of one finger but had walked, not run, to the house. Johnson claimed that Phillips had "tested [ring soil] with eight men for thirty minutes and *every one of their hands got numb*." Phillips said this was not true. He said he had heard that someone had conducted such a test, but he had not been able to confirm it or get any details.

After Durel Johnson and I had inspected the UFO site area at length, he invited me in to see his collection of Polaroid color prints which he claimed showed how "the whole place glowed up." He assured me *all* these pictures had been taken in "pitch dark." One print did indeed show a golden-orange glow along nearby tree trunks—but the *glow was on the west side, facing away from the UFO ring and toward what obviously was the setting sun.* When I suggested that the picture had been taken in the late afternoon, not in "pitch dark," Johnson at first held to his original story but later acknowledged that I might be correct. Then he reached into his collection for a picture that showed only the UFO ring in close-up. The ring did appear white, but certainly not "glowing." Johnson agreed to let me take this picture outside and photograph it with my own camera. (See Plate 24b.)

Later, I enlisted the expertise of my photo-consultant, Robert Sheaffer (Chapter 15), for his appraisal of the picture. Sheaffer told me that he was convinced that the white illumination came from an ordinary flash lamp on or near the camera and not from an internal glow or illumination provided by the ring. This was apparent because portions of the ring closest to the camera (and flash lamp) were most intensely illuminated while those a couple feet more distant were less bright. The most brightly illuminated object visible was the surface of a small stick, facing *away* from the ring but toward the camera (and flash lamp).

According to Johnson, the ring and nearby trees glowed for several days after the alleged UFO visit—so brightly that the whole area was illuminated. But I was able to locate only two witnesses outside the Johnson family who had bothered to come out at night to see the curious phenomenon, and they did *not* substantiate this part of Johnson's story. Mrs. Smith and her husband told me that they had returned to the Johnson farm on the night of November 3, roughly twenty-four hours after the alleged UFO visit. When I asked Mrs. Smith if "the whole area was lit up," as Mr. Johnson had told me, she replied, "Not the night we were there." When I sought a fuller description of the "glow" from the ring, and asked if it resembled a fluorescent light, Mrs. Smith replied, "No, it didn't look like a fluorescent light. The rest of the ground was dark, but here was this gray ring with a center of dark." When I inquired whether she had tried to photograph the ring that night with her own Polaroid camera, she responded that it never occurred to her.

Another curious aspect of the story that the soil in the ring glowed at night is that *none* of the soil samples taken by any of the investigators, including that obtained by Sheriff Enlow less than twenty-four hours after the incident, ever showed the alleged fluorescent properties in darkness—so far as I can determine. There is no doubt that the horseshoe-shaped ring was covered with some sort of white substance. This is clearly evident from the Johnson photos and the one taken by the sheriff. As a skier, I know how brilliantly snow-covered mountains can glow on the darkest night if there is a nearly full moon, and I wondered if this might possibly explain the visibility of the ring that Mrs. Smith and her husband had observed that night. When I asked her whether the moon had been bright the night of her visit, she said she thought it had not because it had been so dark in the grove of trees where the ring is located. But later I learned that there had indeed been a full moon on the evening of November 3, 1971.

The most startling part of my interview with Durel Johnson came when he informed me that all of his mail "that comes from any distance at all" was being "censored right in here at the [Delphos] post office." The Johnsons had become internationally famous in UFO circles even before the *National Enquirer* award (which at the time of my interview had not yet been made). And so they had received many letters, some from far-off places. It was conceivable that a curious postal employee who handled a letter for the Johnsons that might have arrived with its flap poorly sealed could be tempted to ease it open to read the contents. But when I probed Johnson for more details, he told me that the local post office "censorship" was much more deliberate *and obvious.* He told me that they would slit open his mail and then *seal the envelope again with a piece of tape.* Johnson offered to show me examples, but explained that he could not find any because his wife "puts all those letters away" and she was not home at the time. Curiously, Johnson had never complained to the local postmaster about the illegal procedure which he claimed was so commonplace with his incoming mail.

Durel Johnson's story about his problems with the Delphos
post office struck me as improbable, but certainly not as
improbable as the story about the UFO incident. Johnson's
allegation offered the opportunity to determine if he was
occasionally inclined to spin "tall tales." If his charges were in
fact true, then certainly the matter ought to be brought to
the attention of the postal authorities. So I decided to write
to the Delphos postmaster, and sent him a verbatim transcript of Johnson's allegations together with a duplicate of
that portion of my tape-recorded interview. The postmaster
promptly informed me that the matter had been turned over
to the regional postal inspector in Kansas City. On August 14,
1973, the postal inspector wrote me to say that a full
investigation showed "there were no grounds for the allegation."

During my interview with Durel Johnson, he would occasionally switch to financial aspects of his UFO incident. I
learned there was some basis for his preoccupation with this
consideration. Two months *after* the UFO incident, he
learned that the farm, which he had long rented and thought
he had an option to buy, was about to be sold out from under
him. He had only a few days to raise a very large sum of
money which the local bank declined to supply. He finally got
the necessary mortgage in a nearby town, but its size was such
that I wondered if Johnson could pay it off during his
lifetime. Two months *after* Johnson had assumed this large
debt, the *National Enquirer* announced its $50,000 UFO
contest. If Johnson could win that prize, he could pay off the
mortgage and have a little left over. At the time of my visit,
the winner of the contest was expected to be announced soon
and Johnson—having been told by some UFO investigators
that his case was a leading contender—was a bit edgy.

But Johnson also believed that others were profiting from
his UFO case while he had so far received nothing. For
example, Johnson showed me a newspaper clipping telling of
a recent UFO lecture at nearby Concordia College by
Stanton Friedman, who earns his living in this fashion.
Friedman, understandably, had devoted part of his lecture to
the nearby Delphos incident. Johnson, as he showed me the

newspaper clipping, said, "He got one thousand dollars or better from Concordia College that night." The tone of Johnson's voice indicated that he thought that was a lot of money for a brief lecture. Johnson was also irritated because the president of the Delphos bank had collected a seventeen-dollar fee from a Salina, Kansas, newspaper for alerting it to Johnson's UFO incident, but he had not offered to share the fee. Johnson further charged UFO-investigator Phillips with "making himself a little money" on the case, and cited an article Phillips had written for Britain's *Flying Saucer Review* magazine, without realizing that the publication does not pay for such articles. My own investigation suggests that the allegations against Phillips were as ill-founded as those against the Delphos post office.

It was during one of Johnson's occasional, brief diatribes on this subject that he made a slip of the tongue which was especially revealing: "If I don't get anything out of *this circle*—I mean if I don't get something out of the *Enquirer* . . . Ted Phillips is going to be sued." Johnson had unwittingly singled out the one thing that seemed to give substance to the otherwise flimsy verbal account of the UFO incident— the irregular horseshoe-shaped ring of some unknown white substance. During the time that Johnson and I had talked, I had "caught him off-base" enough times to shake my confidence in the veracity of his account of the UFO incident. Some months earlier, the late Clancy D. Tull had informed me, in his letter of July 22, 1972, that during his visit to investigate the case he had asked the Johnsons if they would be willing to take a thorough polygraph (lie-detector) test, and he said *they had declined!* They also had refused, he said, to allow young Ronald to undergo hypnotic evaluation and regression intended to draw on his subconscious recollections of the alleged incident.

I vividly recall my first impression when I arrived at the UFO site in the Johnson backyard—that the spot was the most unlikely location for any craft to try to land. It is surrounded on three sides by trees and on the fourth (south) side by a shed which stands about five feet high. (See Plates 23a, 23b.) Additionally, if Mr. Johnson's story was correct, the dead tree was standing south of the site, which would have posed still another obstacle. If an extraterrestrial spaceship had needed or wanted to come down for a "hovering," there were inviting open fields in every direction—no more than a few hundred feet away, where there would be no risk of collision with an obstacle. If the craft was anxious to hover in a grove of trees so it would not be seen by Earthlings, why had it picked this grove, so close to an illuminated farmhouse, when there was a much more secluded belt of trees only several hundred yards further north?

Then there was the white material that formed the irregular ring, which must have been ejected or emitted from the underside of the UFO, presumably from its glowing propulsion unit, if the Johnson story was true. Since the UFO had passed over the metal roof of the low shed immediately south of the site both when it had allegedly arrived and again when it had departed, one should expect to find a similar white substance atop the roof. *Yet nobody ever reported finding such white material atop the shed roof!* Tull had written me, in response to my question, that he had made it a point to examine the shed roof but had "found no evidence of anything" except for oxidation and accumulated grime from many years' exposure to the elements.

All of this prompted me to believe that the irregular horseshoe-shaped ring had been there *prior* to November 2, 1971, when the UFO was alleged to have come. Phillips' report that he had found traces of the white material many inches below the surface suggested that the ring might have been there for months or years before the November 2 date. I wondered if there might have been some sort of circular structure on the site. The U.S. Department of Agriculture periodically takes aerial photos of all the farmland in the country to determine what portion is under cultivation. The photos for the western half of the United States are stored in the USDA's Western Photo Laboratory, at Salt Lake City, Utah, and copies can be purchased for a modest fee. With the assistance of Miss M. L. Caulfield of that facility, I obtained an extreme enlargement of an aerial photo showing the Johnson farm that had been taken on June 27, 1971—

roughly four months before the alleged UFO incident—and another that had been taken in 1965. When I explained the intended use of the photos, Miss Caulfield and her associates provided the maximum possible enlargement of the tiny area on the original negatives. It was possible to pinpoint the location of the UFO site relative to the low shed and other landmarks. A comparison of the aerial photos taken in 1971 and in 1965 showed there had been a significant reduction in the number of trees growing near the UFO site during the six-year period. This suggested that something had been taking a toll of the Chinese elm trees—perhaps the same disease that has destroyed so many elm trees throughout the Middle West during the same period. During my visit to the Johnson farm, I had observed the whitish substance on the trunks of some of the trees near the UFO site that some investigators had concluded was evidence of heat from the UFO. But when I examined other trees in the grove—far from the UFO site—I found a similar whitish growth.

Both aerial photos had been taken in the summer, and the full foliage of the trees made it difficult to examine the UFO site in detail. The problem was made more difficult because of extreme graininess of the prints due to the high degree of enlargement that I needed and had requested. The photos were adequate to show that no large structure, such as a silo, had been located at the UFO site, at least not in 1965 or 1971. Another possibility suggested itself. Perhaps the unusual ring might have resulted from a circular livestock feeder that had been sitting on the site for some years, where it would be close to the shed that housed a large flock of sheep. If a circular livestock feeder or watering trough was responsible, this could explain the "break" in the ring where the feed or water would have been loaded into the device. The sheep, or other livestock, would have gathered around the remaining periphery of the feeder, and the whitish ring might have resulted from feed or drinking water—perhaps containing a food supplement—which would have "slopped" out. Because eating livestock often urinate in the excitement of being fed, there might be considerable organic content in the ring soil.

Such a feeder would not be visible in the aerial photos because of graininess and overhanging foliage.

Tull had taken samples of the whitish ring soil and had had them analyzed using carbon spectrographic techniques. This analysis, he told me, showed *"a great deal of organic material."* (Emphasis added.) This would indicate that the ring had been caused *by animal or plant life*, rather than by the exhaust of an extraterrestrial spacecraft. Tull's analysis also showed the presence of considerable silicate, *ferrous oxide* and aluminum.

Stanton Friedman had also obtained samples from the ring and a sample from the surrounding area for comparison, and he had them analyzed by the Agri-Science Laboratories of Hawthorne, California. When Friedman later published the results, he noted that the *salinity* of the soil taken from the ring area was nearly *four times* that of soil taken from outside the ring. This helped explain why plants did not grow in soil samples. (The high salinity could have been caused by animal urine.) The Friedman-sponsored analysis also showed that the trace-element concentration of *zinc in the ring soil was 111 times that found in soil from outside the ring.* One possible explanation for this very high zinc content is that the ring had been produced by an animal feeder constructed from galvanized iron which contains zinc to protect it from rusting. It would also explain the high content of iron oxide reported by Tull.

Seeking outside expertise, I contacted Dr. Roger J. Gerrits, a senior scientist in the Department of Agriculture's Agricultural Research Service, located just outside Washington, D.C. I discussed the Delphos case with him, told him of my speculation that the ring might have been caused by an animal-feeding device, and sent Dr. Gerrits a copy of the published Friedman-sponsored analysis. Dr. Gerrits subsequently told me that galvanized-metal feeders are not widely used for dispensing food because the zinc might contaminate the food. But he added that a galvanized-metal container can be used to dispense water to livestock without such risk.

Commenting on the Friedman-sponsored analysis, Dr. Gerrits said that *many* samples of soil from outside the ring should have been taken to obtain a meaningful representative average of the prevailing soil conditions for comparison with a sample taken from the ring. He said it was "unfortunate that a well-designed scientific approach and scientific methods were not used in the attempt to obtain meaningful information." By the time of my visit to Delphos, more than a year after the alleged incident, the whitish material was no longer present—having apparently been dissolved or carried off by curious investigators—making it impossible to conduct the sort of precise scientific analysis that was needed.

And so my efforts to positively "nail down" the source of the whitish ring and the curious composition of the soil underneath have been frustrated. In this respect, the Delphos case is not 100 percent explained. But I would hope that the other evidence turned up by my investigation is sufficient to cause you to question the conclusions of the *National Enquirer*'s panel of experts. Recall that the newspaper said: "Dr. Hynek emphasized that the panel had carefully investigated the possibility of a hoax, but are completely satisfied that the sighting was real."

In the early summer of 1972, long before the Delphos case had been selected as the winner and before I had visited the area, I had written to the editor of the *National Enquirer*, pointing out that I had exposed some previously unexplained UFO cases as hoaxes and had found prosaic explanations for others. I suggested that after the panel had selected a winner that the newspaper withhold payment until I had investigated the case. I offered to conduct this independent investigation without charge other than my out-of-pocket travel expenses to make an on-the-scene investigation. I promptly received a brief acknowledgment informing me that the editor involved was out of town but that I would hear from him upon his return. When several months went by without hearing further, I wrote again, this time to the managing editor, and repeated my offer. I never heard further in reply to my offer.

In the spring of 1973, when I learned that the Johnsons had won the $5,000 "best-case" prize, I was delighted because I was certain they could put the funds to good use. If the *National Enquirer* had paid $5,000 for a tall tale and a

whitish ring in a grove of trees, that profitable newspaper
could well afford it. The newspaper had, unwittingly, made a
useful contribution to the UFO controversy by demonstrating the quality of the best case submitted out of more than
one thousand entries, as appraised by a group of distinguished, experienced UFOlogists who lean toward the extraterrestrial hypothesis.

In reporting the choice of the Johnson/Delphos case, the
National Enquirer disclosed that it had extended the $50,000
offer in a new sweepstakes. The closing date for entries would
be January 1, 1974. In the spring of 1974, the blue-ribbon
panel met again, this time in New Orleans, to select the best
from the hundreds of UFO cases that had been reported
during the previous year. The Pascagoula "abduction" case
might have seemed like an odds-on favorite, perhaps a serious
contender for the $50,000 grand prize or at least the $5,000
award, because of the earlier strong public endorsements
given by two of the five panel members. Recall that Hynek
had said: *There is no question in my mind that these two
men have had a very terrifying experience."* And Harder had
stated: *"There was definitely something here that was not
terrestrial . . ."*

Yet when the panel met, the Pascagoula case was not even
a serious contender, I was told. This suggests that the other
panel members did not share the confidence earlier expressed
by Hynek and Harder in the veracity of the Hickson-Parker
story, and perhaps that the two scientists themselves had
begun to have some doubts. In any event, there was no
$50,000 prize voted, but the panel did recommend the $5,000
award for best case of 1973 to the four-man crew of an Army
Reserve helicopter, based on the crew's account of a curious
incident that had occurred in central Ohio during that state's
UFO flap. This case will be analyzed in detail in the next
chapter.

29 • Army Helicopter Incident: Best Case of 1973

The four-man crew of an Army helicopter, flying near Mansfield, Ohio, on the night of October 18, 1973, had a frightening encounter with a brightly glowing object moving at very high speed that seemed to threaten a mid-air collision. The incident, which occurred during the height of the UFO flap in Ohio, involved a Bell Helicopter Corporation UH-1H, operated by an Army Reserve crew that was returning to Cleveland from Columbus. The weather was clear, the helicopter was cruising at a speed of ninety knots (103 mph) on a heading of 30 degrees (northeast) at a barometric altitude of 2,500 feet. (This figure and other altitude figures are relative to mean sea level unless otherwise indicated, rather than indicating actual helicopter height above the terrain.) The pilot was Captain Lawrence Coyne, commanding officer of the Army Reserve's 316th medical detachment, based in Cleveland. Coyne described the incident when he appeared on the ABC Network's "Dick Cavett Show" on November 2, 1973. He supplied additional details when I talked with him later by telephone on several occasions.

It was several minutes past 11 P.M. local time when the crew
chief spotted a bright red light to the east and called it to
Coyne's attention, suggesting that it might be an obstruction-
warning light atop a TV antenna tower. The pilot told him to
keep an eye on the light. The light seemed to maintain a
constant bearing angle, which prompted the crew chief to
conclude that it was flying a course parallel to the helicopter
and "was pacing us," Coyne said. But soon the red light
seemed to get larger and brighter, causing the crew chief to
warn the pilot that the object seemed to be "converging on us
on a collision course." Coyne said, "I looked to my right,
through the right window, and I observed the light coming at
a very fast speed, in excess of six hundred knots" (684 mph).
The helicopter was not far from the Mansfield airport, where
Coyne knew an Air National Guard detachment of F-100 jet
fighters was based. Although aircraft are not supposed to fly
at such high speed at low altitude, Coyne said he called the
Mansfield control tower to ask if one of the F-100 jet fighters
was approaching for a landing, but he received no reply.

The glowing red object was continuing to close toward the
helicopter, and so Coyne decided to descend rapidly to avoid
a possible mid-air collision. First he reduced the helicopter
rotor's "collective pitch," which decreases lift, causing the
helicopter to descend at a rate which Coyne told me was
1,000 feet per minute. When the object still seemed headed
for the helicopter, the pilot also changed the rotor blades'
"cyclic pitch," which put the aircraft into "about a twenty-
degree angle of dive." This, he explained to me, increased the
rate of descent to approximately 2,000 feet per minute.
When Coyne last observed his barometric altimeter, he said,
it read 1,700 feet, yet the glowing red object seemed still to
be headed directly toward the helicopter, and so the pilot
told the crew to "brace for impact."

It must certainly have been a moment of terror for the
crew. Nothing is more frightening to an aircraft crew than the
prospect of a mid-air collision, especially at night with an
unknown craft whose crew shows no sign of taking evasive
action to try to avoid the catastrophe. But there was no
impact. Instead, as Coyne described events to Cavett, "We

looked up and there was this object, right over us. Stopped!
The best way I can describe the object is it was approximately
fifty to sixty feet long, was about as big as our aircraft. The
leading [front] edge of the craft was a bright-red light. The
trailing edge had a green light, and you could delineate where
the light stopped and the gray metallic structure [began]. You
could see because there were reflections of the red and green
off the structure itself. It—the trailing light on the aft end of
the craft—swung about ninety degrees and came [shown
down] on the helicopter . . . and flooded the cockpit with a
green light."

"And this only existed two or three seconds," Coyne
continued, "because we all saw the craft hovering over us, but
it moved out of my field of vision and the co-pilot and flight
medic [John Healey] still had visual contact with the craft."
Coyne later estimated that the object had been only five
hundred feet above the helicopter. As the co-pilot and flight
medic on the left side of the helicopter watched, the glowing
object headed west over the Mansfield airport, then appeared
to turn northwest, with the green light turning to white. Then
the object appeared to make a climbing turn and disappeared.

When Coyne next looked at his cockpit instruments, he
said he was shocked to find that the barometric altimeter
showed the helicopter to be at 3,500 feet and *climbing* at a
rate of 1,000 feet per minute. As he explained on the Cavett
show, "We were supposed to be going down, but we were
going up!" When Cavett asked, "You were being sucked, or
drawn, or magnetized, or what?" Coyne replied, "I really
don't know. It was just a matter of seconds we were at 1,700
feet and then we were [at] 3,500 feet, climbing a thousand
feet per minute, with no power—I mean the collective [pitch]
was down and I was in a shallow dive." Another curious
aspect of the UFO encounter, Coyne explained, was that the
crew had "felt the G-forces [gravity forces] as we began
descending, but we had *no feeling* of our climbing a thousand
feet a minute until I observed the altimeter." (The forces to
which Coyne referred are those familiar to airline passengers
during a rapid climb or descent, or during turbulent air

conditions.) Coyne was equally mystified by the fact that although the object had seemed to pass within five hundred feet of the small aircraft, "there was no turbulence, no vortex. There was no engine sound!"

Still another mysterious effect occurred when the co-pilot tried to make radio contact with the control towers at the Cleveland, Columbus, Akron-Canton and Mansfield airports to report the incident. Coyne said the co-pilot was *rapidly changing frequencies* in an effort to reach one of the control towers, but for several minutes after the UFO had passed over, no radio contact was established. Coyne said, "We were going through the radio panel [tuning] quite fast, and when you change frequencies you do hear the channeling tone, and the radio was functioning [in this respect] except that when you keyed the mike [pushed button to switch radio from receive-mode to transmit-mode], there was no keying sound, even though we transmitted." Cavett asked, "And that equipment was out of commission then?" Coyne replied, "No, the equipment was functioning, but *we just couldn't transmit or receive!* We finally got ahold of Akron-Canton approach [control] about six to seven minutes later, but the keying sound was back again." (There are a number of UFO cases in which it is reported that the proximity of the UFO has caused a malfunction or blackout of radio equipment.)

Coyne described his experience on the same TV show in which Cavett interviewed Charles Hickson, one of the two Pascagoula shipyard workers, but Hickson appeared on a segment separate from Coyne. In some respects, Coyne's story seemed almost as incredible as Hickson's account of his abduction. But there was a very sharp contrast in the manner in which each man described his alleged experience. Hickson was as calm and casual in describing his abduction by two strange-looking space creatures as if he had been telling of a trip to a local drugstore, while Coyne's manner revealed that he was very distressed and puzzled by what he described. If I had grave doubts about Hickson's story, I was very much inclined to believe that Coyne and his crew had actually experienced the chilling encounter he described.

Captain Coyne and his crew, unlike the two Pascagoula

shipyard workers, had not debated for several hours as to whether to report the incident for fear their story might not be believed. Shortly after Coyne landed at the Cleveland airport, he had reported the incident to Federal Aviation Administration officials there—as I subsequently confirmed in an interview with one of them. The report which the FAA tower supervisor wrote for his superior, after talking with Coyne, said that the pilot "sounded emotionally shaken. . . ." And the following day, Coyne had called an officer in the Air National Guard at the Mansfield airport to determine if one of the F-100 jet fighters based there might have been the source for the incident. Coyne said the officer told him that all the jet aircraft had landed by 10:47 P.M. the previous night—more than fifteen minutes before the helicopter's UFO encounter.

I first learned of the Mansfield case on November 1 when I visited New York City to tape a TV show on UFOs for David Susskind. One of the other panelists was John Healey, the flight medic on the Army helicopter involved in the UFO incident. Healey's regular job is that of a detective with the Cleveland police department. When I learned from him that the pilot would appear on the Cavett show the next night, I made it a point to watch and to tape-record his account. As I studied the transcript of my tape recording, my attention began to focus on the *possibility* that the UFO might have been a bright meteor-fireball. If the glowing red object had indeed been a fireball, this would *not* explain why the helicopter apparently had ascended from 1,700 feet to 3,500 feet without any conscious action by the pilot, nor the apparent brief outage of the helicopter radio equipment. But my experience with several previous UFO cases, and especially the RB-47 incident (Chapters 19–20) had taught me that seemingly mysterious things that are reported to have occurred during a UFO sighting, with its attendant excitement, are not always directly related.

Captain Coyne and his crew had estimated that the UFO had passed only five hundred feet above the helicopter. But recall the "UFO squadron" sighted by three experienced flight crews flying near St. Louis on June 5, 1969 (Chapter 5).

The American Airlines cockpit observers had also thought
that the UFOs posed a collision threat, and that it had come
within a few hundred feet of their jetliner—in broad daylight.
But in fact the fireball was 125 *miles* to the north. If an
experienced airliner flight crew could make an error of 125
miles in broad daylight in estimating the distance to a fireball,
then the Army helicopter crew, at night, might also be
seriously in error in their estimate that the object had come
within five hundred feet. If the object was a meteor, and if in
reality it was at a considerably higher altitude, this could
explain why there had been "no turbulence, no vortex . . . no
engine sound."

Without an accurate fix on the distance to the object, the
crew's estimate that the object was fifty to sixty feet long
could be grossly in error, for it is basically impossible for the
human brain to accurately estimate the size of an *unfamiliar*
object in the sky, especially at night, unless its distance is
known at least approximately (UFOlogical Principle #5). As
the photograph of the "Iowa Fireball" taken by the Peoria
newspaper photographer (Plate 3b) shows, a fireball has a
long luminous tail of glowing ionized air and gases. It is
impossible to estimate its length, even from the picture,
because the distance to the fireball is unknown.

The Army helicopter crew might honestly think that they
could make out a "gray metallic structure." But recall the
multiple observers in Tennessee on the night of March 3,
1968, watching the flaming debris from a Zond-4 rocket enter
the atmosphere, who thought they could make out a fuselage
that "was constructed of many pieces of flat sheets of
metal-like material with a 'riveted-together look.'" One could
not exclude the possibility that the helicopter crew, like the
Zond-4 observers and so many other UFO observers, were
unwitting victims of spurious details supplied by their brains
—details which had not actually been observed by their eyes.

My initial investigation included an attempt to determine
if there had been any other pilot reports of a UFO or fireball
sighting on October 18, around 11 P.M., that might have been
submitted to FAA control towers in the vicinity of Mansfield.
With the assistance of Dennis Feldman, assistant director of

the FAA public affairs office in Washington, arrangements were made for me to interview tower officials at several airports. From Donald Jones, an FAA supervisor in the Columbus airport tower, I heard a firsthand account that demonstrates the extreme difficulty of accurately estimating the distance to a fireball, even for an observer on the ground. Several years earlier, Jones told me, when he had been a tower controller at the Peoria airport, at around 3 A.M. the interior of the glass-enclosed tower cab had suddenly been illuminated with an intense green glow. When Jones turned toward the source of the illumination, he said he saw a bright fireball that was moving from west to east. The fireball seemed to be so close, Jones told me, that he thought it was in the airport traffic pattern. The fireball seemed to be turning and descending, and he was sure it was going to impact in the outskirts of Peoria, near a brewery.

A few moments later, Jones said, he learned he had erred by something more than *fifty miles* in his estimate. A pilot flying fifty miles east of Peoria radioed in to say that the fireball had just flashed past his aircraft, and was still headed east. The pilot reported that he had expected a mid-air collision and had taken evasive action, Jones told me. Returning to the Mansfield incident, Jones had talked to the watch-supervisor who had been on duty in Columbus the night of October 18, and he told me that there were no pilot reports nor had any of the tower operators spotted anything resembling the Mansfield UFO. When the Cleveland tower checked its records, it found nothing other than the Coyne report. The tower supervisor at the Mansfield airport, Robert Bohnlein, who had been on duty that night, had seen nothing unusual and said he did not even recall the Army helicopter incident, which had occurred nearly a month prior to our conversation.

Recalling that the Volunteer Flight Officer Network (VFON), discussed in Chapter 6, sometimes gets meteor-sighting reports as well as those involving reentering satellites and space debris, I called Herb Roth, VFON director, in Denver. After checking his records, he said there were none whose date and time corresponded to the Mansfield incident.

But Roth suggested that I call Dr. David D. Meisel, director of the American Meteor Society, in Geneseo, New York, whose members collect and submit meteor-sighting reports. Although Meisel had no reports that corresponded to the time and date of the Mansfield incident, he expressed interest in obtaining some details on the Ohio encounter.

Meisel explained that a major meteor shower, the Orionids, occurs every October. The peak activity usually occurs on the nights of October 21 and 22, but he emphasized that "there is considerable activity for a week before and after those dates." This would encompass the date of the Mansfield incident. He told me that the Orionid meteors always come from the east, and asked the origin of the UFO. I told him it had come from the same direction—east. Then he asked the specific time of the Mansfield UFO encounter, and I told him it was a few minutes past 11 P.M. That was interesting, Meisel said, because the Orionid meteor shower usually begins between 11 P.M. and midnight. Then he asked if there had been any predominant color. I told him that the leading edge was an intense red—which is characteristic of the extremely hot ionized air produced by any object entering the atmosphere at very high speed—but that the crew had said the helicopter cockpit was flooded with green light.* Dr. Meisel replied that the characteristic color of the Orionid meteors is blue-green.

During our discussion, Dr. Meisel volunteered that even experienced meteorists are sometimes so startled by the sight of a large fireball that they later have trouble in agreeing on the direction from which the meteor came and its trajectory. He said he had seen this happen during an expedition to Florida to watch a major meteor shower, despite the fact that all of the observers had come expecting to see meteors. If the crew of an Army helicopter, never expecting to see a giant fireball, suddenly had spotted one that seemed headed

---

* Subsequently I discovered that the overhead portion of the helicopter's transparent canopy is tinted green for protection against intense sunlight. This means that even a white luminous tail of a fireball could have caused the green illumination inside the cockpit.

toward their craft on a collision course, surely they could be
expected later to have as much difficulty as experienced
meteorists in accurately recalling what had happened. If the
Mansfield UFO was in reality a large fireball, this could
explain the crew's recollection that the object seemed to stop
briefly and hover over the helicopter for a couple of seconds.
The long luminous tail of the fireball would be overhead for
several seconds, illuminating the helicopter canopy and
cockpit for this period. In trying to reconstruct what had
happened, the crew would recall that the canopy and cockpit
had been brightly illuminated for several seconds and might
logically *deduce* that the object must have stopped and
hovered for that time period.*

But what explanation is there for the pilot's recollection
that just before that it seemed that the UFO would collide
with the helicopter, its barometric altitude was 1,700 feet and
it was *descending* at 2,000 feet per minute; yet shortly after
the UFO had departed, the pilot reported that the altimeter
showed the aircraft to be at 3,500 feet and a separate vertical
velocity indicator showed it was *climbing* at 1,000 feet per
minute? This was a real puzzler. I discussed the case with
Dave Brown, Washington bureau chief for *Aviation Week &
Space Technology* magazine, who is an experienced pilot
with some hours in helicopters. Brown suggested that perhaps
the pilot or co-pilot might *unconsciously* have pulled back on
the collective- and/or cyclic-pitch control(s) as he leaned back
in his seat to view the luminous object overhead. Later, when
I discussed this case with Dan Tisdale of Bell Helicopter
Corporation, he agreed that Brown's idea was a distinct
possibility. Tisdale is a former Marine Corps helicopter pilot
with more than three thousand hours of flying time.

During another telephone conversation with Captain
Coyne, I asked him for his best estimate of how long it had
been after the glowing object passed overhead before he had

* Dr. Meisel subsequently informed me that he had received reports of five
major fireball incidents that had occurred during the October Orionids
meteor shower between the fifteenth and twenty-fifth of the month. But
none of these coincided with the October 18 incident near Mansfield.

looked at the instrument panel and discovered that the helicopter was climbing at 1,000 feet per minute and was at 3,500 feet altitude. He replied, "It is pretty hard to guess . . . I would say maybe thirty seconds, maybe thirty to forty seconds." Then I asked him what his reactions had been at that point—what had he done to stop this unwanted ascent? Coyne replied, "I pulled the collective [pitch] up . . . and put cyclic [pitch] back to neutral." Coyne seemed a bit hesitant in this response because I'm sure that he realized, as I did, that *under those conditions the actions he described would have increased the helicopter's lift and rate-of-climb when in fact he was trying to reduce both.* When I asked him what happened next, Coyne said that after about twenty seconds the helicopter stopped climbing, and later he had descended to his previous 2,500-foot cruise altitude. If Coyne's reactions had been as he recalled them, the helicopter should have continued to climb, for increasing collective-pitch would increase, not decrease, the helicopter's lift. (Since the UFO had long since disappeared over the horizon, one need not consider any possible mystical effects that would cause a helicopter to level out when its basic aerodynamics call for it to climb.)

Suddenly the pieces of the puzzle began to fall into place. It will be recalled that just before the glowing object passed overhead, Coyne said that his instruments showed a barometric altitude of 1,700 feet and that the craft was descending at a rate of 2,000 feet per minute. This 1,700 feet is with respect to sea level, but central Ohio is not at sea level. An aeronautical chart for that region shows that the nearby Mansfield airport is at an elevation of nearly 1,300 feet above sea level. This means that at the moment that Coyne last looked at his instruments, his helicopter was *only 400 feet above the ground and at its descent rate, the craft would have crashed against the ground within twelve seconds!* For the moment, the flight crew's attention was focused on the UFO, which was zooming toward the helicopter and would continue on toward the west. But certainly the flight crew's subconscious must have been warning them not to forget to pull back on the collective-pitch and/or cyclic-pitch immediately, once the UFO collision threat had passed, or the helicopter would soon crash to the ground.

Under these perilous conditions, it would have been instinctive for Coyne, or co-pilot Ariggo Jezzi, to have quickly pulled the craft out of its rapid descent to climb back to a safer altitude—even if this was done unconsciously while the four-man crew was still in a state of near-shock from the frightening encounter. Only if the pilot and co-pilot knew this had been accomplished would they dare to spend the next thirty to forty seconds, by Coyne's own estimate, watching the UFO disappear to the west. My conclusion is that the flight crew reacted precisely as it should have done at the time, and hauled back on the collective-pitch and cyclic-pitch. Some time later, when Coyne looked at his instruments and the panic of earlier moments had passed, he was confused over the sequence of events that were responsible for the helicopter's climb and higher altitude and, understandably, concluded that the UFO had caused the effect.

There is solid physical evidence, or to be more precise, a lack of it, to support this explanation that the helicopter was operating normally and that it had not been "sucked" upward by some mysterious force at extremely high speed. The day after the incident, Coyne had the helicopter and its rotor blades carefully examined by five mechanics and a certified Federal Aviation Administration inspector to determine if there had been any structural damage. A special instrument was used to detect any strains that might not be visible to the eye. The inspection showed that there was *no* evidence of structural damage which would have occurred if the helicopter had been "sucked" upward at extremely high velocity.

If this change from a 2,000-foot-per-minute descent to a 1,000-foot-per-minute climb was due to the unconscious reaction of the flight crew to avoid ground impact, then the whole incident must have consumed a somewhat longer time than the crew later estimated. For example, if the helicopter's descent had been converted into a 1,000-foot-per-minute climb in only ten seconds, then it would have required nearly *two minutes* for the craft to have reached a 3,500-foot altitude—where Coyne first studied his cockpit instruments after the UFO had passed. This would be four times the thirty seconds that Coyne had estimated. Similarly, where Coyne estimated that his original descent from 2,500 feet to 1,700 feet occupied about ten seconds, Tisdale's calculations show that the helicopter would require about thirty seconds for this maneuver. Thus there appears to have been a three-fold or four-fold "distortion of time" in the recollection by the crew of events that transpired during those hectic moments—a distortion of time caused simply by the difficulty of recalling the time-duration of unexpected and frightening events.

But what explanation is there for the radio communications difficulties reported by the helicopter crew in the wake of the incident? The most basic one is that the helicopter was approximately fifty to sixty miles away from the airports at Cleveland, Columbus and Akron at the time of the incident. At the helicopter's relatively low altitude it was simply below and beyond the effective range of those airport radio facilities. To check this, I asked Coyne to run a test the next time he flew near Mansfield, by trying to contact the Cleveland, Columbus and Akron-Canton airport towers from the same altitude at which the helicopter was flying at the time of the UFO incident. Coyne later made such a test, and he reported back to me that *he was not able to make contact with any one of these three airports*—simply because he was beyond the range of their radio coverage at this relatively low altitude. He was, however, able to make contact during the test with the nearby Mansfield tower.

Thus the mysterious behavior of the radio on the night of the UFO incident really boils down to why the Mansfield tower had not responded. Every experienced pilot will confirm that there have been instances when his radio call to an airport tower has failed to elicit a reply. Perhaps the controllers are busy talking to other aircraft at the moment and they know that if another pilot fails to get a reply he will call in again. During the late shift the Mansfield tower usually has two controllers on duty, but occasionally it has only one. Another possible explanation, if an aircraft is maneuvering at the time it calls the tower, is that its fuselage may be shielding its own antenna in the direction of the tower. Perhaps the microphone button itself occasionally fails to function properly.* The point is that there are numerous instances every day throughout the country when a pilot's call to a tower fails to bring back a reply.

Coyne's description of how the co-pilot was rapidly tuning the helicopter radio in a desperate effort to make radio contact suggests still another possible explanation. The helicopter was equipped with a Model 807A very-high-frequency (VHF) radio, built by Wilcox Electric Company, whom I called to learn more about the equipment. Engineer Robert Piper explained to me that in changing frequencies, the radio set may require up to five seconds—under certain conditions—to settle down on the newly selected channel. Thus it is conceivable that the co-pilot, in his anxiety to make radio contact, did not allow sufficient time for the radio tuning mechanism to settle down to the Mansfield tower frequency.

It is interesting to speculate on what might have happened if the flight crew had failed to act promptly and instinctively to pull the helicopter out of its rapid descent after the collision threat had passed, and if the craft had crashed as a result, killing all on board. A team of experienced Army investigators would have been dispatched to the scene to sift through the debris to try to explain why the helicopter— under full power, during perfectly clear weather conditions— had flown into the ground. Unable to find an apparent cause, the Army might have issued a public request for possible witnesses to the accident. Coyne told me that following his appearance on the Cavett program, he had received a telephone call from a man living near Galion, Ohio, who had reported seeing the incident. (My subsequent attempts to locate this witness have proved fruitless.) If this witness had

---

* Malfunctions of the microphone on-off button are sufficiently common-place that the Federal Aviation Administration has proposed that a warning light be installed in the cockpit to alert the flight crew to a malfunction that results in the radio transmitter being turned on without the pilot's knowledge, thereby causing interference to other aircraft.

responded to the Army request, and had described the
seeming near-collision of a bright glowing object and the
helicopter, at a time when Ohio was experiencing a rash of
UFO reports, it would undoubtedly have resulted in another
"Mantell-type" incident, with black newspaper headlines
reading: "UFO Knocks Down Army Helicopter."

This would have caused understandable concern among
the nation's civil and military pilots, who would henceforth
keep their eyes peeled for UFOs. And for weeks or months
there would be numerous reports from pilots of misidentified
meteor-fireballs and weather balloons—all reported as UFOs.
This would have generated pressures for still another Congressional hearing, and for another government-funded UFO
investigation, etc. Contemplating this likely aftermath, we
should all be grateful for the instinctive, if unconscious,
reactions of pilot Coyne or co-pilot Jezzi in pulling their
helicopter out of its steep descent barely four hundred feet
above the ground.*

Now that the Mansfield incident has been selected as the
best UFO case of 1973 by the *National Enquirer's* panel of
experts, and the four-man crew is $5,000 richer as well as
being internationally famous UFO celebrities, it will not be
easy for them to accept the explanation that the UFO was
merely a bright fireball, that the seemingly mysterious behavior of the helicopter was due to the unconscious, instinctive
reactions of well-trained pilots, and that the seemingly
curious behavior of the radio was due to quite normal causes.

---

* Although Coyne told me that he understood that the Army planned to
make a formal investigation of the Mansfield UFO incident, my query to
Army Aviation headquarters disclosed that no such action was expected.
Rather, I was told, the Army was somewhat embarrassed over the considerable publicity that had resulted from the incident.

30 · Congress, UFOs and N-Rays

Anyone who read newspaper accounts of a one-day Congressional "Symposium on Unidentified Flying Objects," held in Washington on July 29, 1968, would logically conclude that most American scientists believe that extraterrestrial spaceships are making regular visits to Earth, judging from the views expressed by all six of the scientists who testified. In name, the symposium had been held under the auspices of the House Committee on Science and Astronautics, but it had really been arranged and organized principally by one committee member, Congressman J. Edward Roush of Indiana.

Roush's carefully selected roster of experts who were invited to appear included the late Dr. James E. McDonald, then the nation's most outspoken proponent of the extraterrestrial viewpoint; Dr. J. Allen Hynek; and Dr. James A. Harder, a committed "believer" whose efforts on the Pascagoula and Delphos cases have been discussed in recent chapters. The other three Ph.D.'s who testified offered slightly less pronounced leanings toward the extraterrestrial viewpoint. The roster of experts that Roush had selected was so one-sided that one of them, Dr. Carl Sagan, a Cornell University astronomer, was finally prompted to observe: "I might mention that, on this symposium, there are no individuals who strongly disbelieve in the extraterrestrial origin of UFOs and therefore there is a certain view—not necessarily one I strongly agree with—but there is a certain view this committee is not hearing today, along those lines." (Sagan is coauthor of a book entitled *Intelligent Life in the Universe*, dealing with the scientific prospects of finding such life rather than with UFOs.)

The symposium need not have been so one-sided.* A member of the committee's staff with whom I had worked in connection with my position at *Aviation Week & Space Technology* magazine and who knew of my considerable experience in UFOlogy, had suggested to Roush that I be invited to testify. But this staff member told me later that Roush had rejected this suggestion. After a day of listening to only one side of the UFO issue, Roush concluded the symposium with the following observation: ". . . I think the time will come when certain people will look back and read what has been done here today and realize that we have pioneered in a field insofar as the Congress of the United States is concerned. They will be very mindful that something worthwhile was done here today . . . I would like to say this has been one of the most unusual and most interesting days I have spent since I have been in the Congress. . . ." (Subsequently, Congressman Roush was named to NICAP's Board of Governors. Still later, former top NICAP official Donald E. Keyhoe, in a new book, wrote that "NICAP had played the leading role in securing the so-called hearings. . . .")

When the testimony presented at the symposium was published by the Government Printing Office, the document also contained long written statements from six additional

---

* Many network TV programs and talk-shows on UFOs are nearly as one-sided as Congressman Roush's symposium, and usually allot much more time to those offering the extraterrestrial spaceship viewpoint than to the skeptics.

scientists and UFOlogists who had been invited to make submissions. Five of these six were also proponents of the extraterrestrial viewpoint. The only dissent was voiced by Dr. Donald H. Menzel, a world-famous astronomer and an experienced UFOlogist. John G. Fuller promptly wrote a new UFO book, based largely on the Roush-sponsored symposium testimony. The public, judging from the Congressional hearings and the Fuller book, might logically conclude that the prevailing opinion of the scientific community was 11 to 1 in favor of the extraterrestrial viewpoint.

If this apparent ratio had been just the reverse, it would have been much more representative of prevailing opinion among United States scientists and engineers. And in terms of "hard-core believers," the ratio would be even more lopsided. There are those who are open-minded to the possibility of extraterrestrial spaceships, but this view derives in large part from the fact that a handful of scientists with impressive-sounding academic credentials, like Hynek, Harder and the late McDonald, have been unable to explain some UFO cases, such as the Socorro, South Hill, RB-47 and Bentwaters-Lakenheath incidents. It is assumed that these UFO investigators have made rigorous, scientific probes for hoaxes and terrestrial explanations before pronouncing these cases to be "unexplainable." The cases discussed in earlier chapters reveal this to be a faulty assumption.

The colorful history of science offers numerous examples showing that even practitioners with impressive credentials occasionally become unwitting victims of self-delusion and wishful thinking. For example, at the turn of the last century the world of science was bubbling with excitement over recent discoveries of mysterious radiation that was invisible to the human senses. First it was Germany's Wilhelm Roentgen who had discovered X-rays, and then in 1896, France's Henri Becquerel discovered the radiation emitted by pitchblend, known today as radioactivity.

In the fall of 1903, Professor R. Blondlot, a respected member of the French Academy of Sciences and head of the physics department at the University of Nancy, announced the discovery of still another type of radiation, which he

named "N-rays" in honor of his university. In a paper
published by the French Academy of Sciences, Blondlot
disclosed that N-rays were emitted spontaneously by many
different metals, but never by wooden objects. He said that
the presence of N-rays could be detected by the human eye in
a nearly darkened room. When they were present, the N-rays
enabled the eye to see objects not otherwise discernible.
Within several months, the Academy had published a dozen
more papers that confirmed Blondlot's remarkable discovery.
One reported that N-rays also improved an observer's sense of
hearing and smell. Another disclosed that N-rays were
emitted by the human brain, nerves and muscles as well as by
metals.

Jean Becquerel, son of the famed discoverer of radioactivity, reported an experiment he had conducted that showed
that N-rays could be transmitted over a wire, like electricity.
When one end of the wire was placed near a human brain,
N-rays were seemingly emitted from the other end of the wire
and caused a change of intensity in a faintly luminous
detector. Young Becquerel reported that if the human
subject was anesthetized with ether, there was a change in the
intensity of N-rays emitted by the subject's brain. *An even
more curious effect reported was that metals themselves
could be anesthetized with ether or alcohol, which caused
them to stop emitting N-rays!*

Soon a variety of French scientists were experimenting with
N-rays, including biologists, physiologists, psychologists,
chemists, botanists and even geologists. Still more exciting
discoveries were being reported. For example, that N-rays
were emitted also by growing plants, by a vibrating tuning
fork and even by a human corpse. All investigators confirmed
Blondlot's original findings that *N-rays were never emitted by
wooden objects.* Blondlot constructed a spectrometer—an
instrument which could diffract N-rays into a line spectrum—
to enable him to measure their wavelength. When he
reported that he had made such measurements, this seemed
to confirm beyond any doubt the existence of the mysterious
rays. Within a year of Blondlot's original paper, *the French
Academy had published nearly one hundred papers on the*

subject. It came as no surprise when the Academy announced that Blondlot would receive its Lalande prize of 20,000 francs and a gold medal for his discovery of the remarkable N-rays.

Blondlot's reported discovery of N-rays sparked feverish activity in other European countries as scientists there sought to repeat his experiments. But neither German nor British scientists seemed able to detect the effects of N-rays that Blondlot had reported. One was an American-born scientist, Dr. R. W. Wood, then working in Britain. Finally, Wood decided to arrange for a visit to Blondlot's own laboratory so he could observe a demonstration by the discoverer himself. Because N-ray effects always had to be observed in a very dimly lighted room, this provided Wood with an opportunity to conduct tests of his own without Blondlot's knowledge.

For example, during one experiment-demonstration with Blondlot's spectrometer, Wood secretly removed its aluminum prism, without which diffraction was impossible if N-rays did in fact exist. Despite this missing prism, Blondlot reported that he was observing the normal diffraction effect! When Dr. Wood held up a metal file in the darkened room, Blondlot demonstrated that the N-rays it emitted enabled him to read the hands of a dimly illuminated clock which he said he could not read otherwise. But when Dr. Wood secretly substituted a wooden ruler of approximately the same size as the metal file, leading Blondlot to believe it was the metal file, Blondlot was still able to read the dimly illuminated clock. Yet Blondlot and other French scientists agreed that wooden objects never emitted N-rays.

These and other tests convinced Dr. Wood that Blondlot was sincere but that he had unwittingly become the victim of his imagination, and perhaps an unconscious desire to become famous as a discoverer of still another mysterious radiation. The other French scientists, eager to participate in the excitement of scientific discovery, had also been victims of self-delusion and unscientific methodology. Dr. Wood exposed N-rays as fantasy in the September 29, 1904, issue of *Nature* magazine. Three months later, when the French Academy presented the Lalande prize to Blondlot, there was no mention of N-rays. Instead, the presentation was given "for his life work, taken as a whole." A short time later, Blondlot committed suicide. In the early 1920s another type of mysterious radiation was reportedly discovered. These "Mitogenetic rays," as they were called, were said to be emitted by growing plants and living things. But Mitogenetic rays proved to be a member of the same family as N-rays.

At the time that UFOs were "discovered" in 1947, and when there was some basis for speculation that there might be alien spaceships in our skies, it seemed sensible to turn to physical scientists, such as astronomers, physicists and engineers, to serve as UFO investigators. Today, with the wisdom of hindsight, the UFO mystery emerges as a more complex issue that involves both physical science and human psychology. For this reason, the average physical scientist is seriously handicapped as a UFO investigator both by training and by experience. In the world of physical science, two scientists may disagree sharply over the interpretation of data, or the manner in which it was measured. But one scientist need not suspect that his associate has intentionally falsified the data and that he is dealing with a hoax.*

An experienced trial lawyer, who is familiar with the often widely divergent testimony of eyewitnesses, a criminal investigator or investigative journalist who is intrinsically wary of accepting statements as fact without deep probing and perhaps some "discounting," is much better qualified in many respects for the role of a UFO investigator than is a physical scientist. An experimental psychologist, experienced in the inherent limitations of human perception and recall, would place far less credence in UFO reports from pilots, police officers and airport-tower operators than would a physicist or an astronomer, and with good reason. Yet relatively few persons with these types of expertise have become UFO investigators, compared with those whose backgrounds are in

* A notable exception, which achieved national prominence in the spring of 1974, involved a respected scientist at the Memorial Sloan-Kettering Center in New York who was accused of having falsified the results of his experiments in making skin transplants on mice.

physical science. The few who have entered the field of UFOlogy often find themselves seriously handicapped for lack of a background in physical science in dealing with cases such as the RB-47 and Bentwaters-Lakenheath incidents.

But perhaps the most basic problem is that the majority of the scientists who have been sufficiently attracted to the field of UFOlogy to become investigators are those with a very strong desire to believe in extraterrestrial visitations. This is not surprising. A scientist who dismisses "ghosts" as pure fantasy is not usually interested in spending his time investigating reports of "haunted houses." And so the great majority of UFO cases are investigated and reported on by scientists and by NICAP or APRO investigators with a deep-seated hope of finding positive evidence of alien spaceships. Or, short of that, of finding another "unexplainable" case which can be added to the list of other such cases and thereby seem to provide circumstantial evidence to support the extraterrestrial hypothesis. The results of their investigations should not be surprising.

If this appraisal is correct, does it mean that I, Dr. Menzel and other skeptics have a deep-seated, perhaps unconscious, aversion to the idea of there being intelligent life in other worlds? Surely no man who has devoted his life, as Menzel has, to the study of distant stars, galaxies and planets in our solar system could fail to be excited over such a possibility. And in my own case, as a senior editor for a magazine that serves the aerospace industry and has reported in great detail every step of our space program, I can think of no more exciting story that could be written than one telling of intelligent life from distant worlds that had reached Earth. I should be terribly embarrassed if I ignored or "debunked" a UFO case that later turned out to provide evidence of such extraterrestrial visitations. That kind of a "goof" could easily cost me my job.

31 · The $10,000 Offer

During my years in the field of UFOlogy, I have often been asked whether I have ever encountered a UFO case that was sufficiently puzzling to prompt me to wonder if it might involve an extraterrestrial spaceship. In other words, just how confident am I that *not one* of many thousands of UFO cases involves an extraterrestrial visitation? My reply is that when I was a boy in Iowa we used to employ a very effective means to test the strength of a youthful friend's convictions. It was summarized in the expression "Talk is cheap. Put your money where your mouth is." This is precisely what I have repeatedly done to demonstrate my own confidence that there are no spaceships from other worlds in our skies, in what has come to be known as my "ten-thousand-dollar offer." It has been extended on nationwide radio and TV programs, in *Parade* magazine (Sunday supplement), and in numerous lectures. The offer, in brief contract form, is shown below:

> 1. Parties to this agreement are Philip J. Klass, 560 "N" St. S.W., Washington, D.C., hereinafter referred to as Klass, and the undersigned Party of the Second Part.

2. Klass hereby agrees to pay the Party of the Second Part the sum of TEN THOUSAND DOLLARS ($10,000) within thirty (30) days after *any one* of the following events occurs:

(A) Any crashed spacecraft, or major piece of a spacecraft, is found whose design and construction clearly identify it as being of extraterrestrial origin in the opinion of the U.S. National Academy of Sciences; or

(B) The U.S. National Academy of Sciences announces that it has examined other evidence which conclusively proves that the Earth has been visited during the 20th Century by extraterrestrial spacecraft, in the opinion of the National Academy of Sciences; or

(C) The first bona fide extraterrestrial visitor, who was born on a celestial body other than the Earth, appears live before the General Assembly of the United Nations or on a national television program.

Provided that Party of the Second Part shall have made all of the payments provided for in Par. 3 of this Agreement.

3. Party of the Second Part agrees to pay Klass the sum of ONE HUNDRED DOLLARS ($100) each and every year from the date of this agreement until the occurrence of any one of the events described in Par. 2 above or until his total payments amount to ONE THOUSAND DOLLARS ($1,000), whichever occurs first, at which time such payments shall cease. In the latter event, Klass's obligations to pay the $10,000 under this agreement shall remain in force until the death of either one of the two parties to this agreement. (The first annual payment shall be made upon execution of this agreement by both parties.)

It is important to stress that *the other party to this agreement need not himself find or supply the evidence.* Also, that the maximum amount that the other party risks is one thousand dollars, whereas I stand to lose ten thousand dollars *with each and every contract signed.* Thus, when the offer is extended repeatedly to large audiences, if only ten people were to accept the offer and if subsequent events proved me to be wrong, I would lose every cent I have managed to save in more than thirty years of labor. In other words, every time I make this offer I risk complete bankruptcy! While this does not prove my views on UFOs are correct, it certainly is a meaningful measure of my own willingness to "put my money where my mouth, or typewriter, is."

The first time I extended such an offer was in the fall of 1966 when the late Frank Edwards and I appeared on a local television interview program in Washington. Edwards had come to town to publicize his latest UFO book, *Flying Saucers—Serious Business.* It would become a best seller, with more than a million copies in soft cover. Edwards and the TV program moderator were old friends from the days of radio, and so it was not until late in the program that I managed to interrupt their reminiscing long enough to test the strength of Edwards' convictions on UFOs.

Turning to Edwards, I said, "In the closing pages of your book, you write that there seems to be a build-up of these UFOs, and that we're approaching a climax. And you predict that maybe tomorrow, or certainly within two or three years, we may see landings—or we *will* see landings." At that point the moderator interrupted to read directly from the final page of the Edwards book in which he predicted that "overt landing" or formal contact "cannot be far away" and seemed "due in the next two or three years." I proceeded by offering "to pay you ten thousand dollars at such time as bona-fide extraterrestrial visitors either present themselves to any Earth government representatives—I mean federal government—or appear live on television . . . providing that for every year that goes by that they don't present themselves you send me a check for one thousand dollars. Now, if it happens within two years, as you feel confident it will, you will be eight thousand dollars ahead. If it happens tomorrow, you're ten thousand dollars ahead. But if it should take fifty years or longer, then you're in trouble." Edwards promptly declined.

At the time of the incident, Edwards had started to write still another UFO book, which would be published the following year after his death. In this book, *Flying Saucers— Here and Now!*, Edwards described our meeting and my offer. Edwards wrote that I had offered to pay him ten thousand dollars if he "could bring a living space creature" to my office. My version of what transpired is based on a verbatim transcript of a tape recording which I made of the TV program involved.*

Edwards would prove to be the first of many who have profited handsomely by promoting the myth of extraterrestrial visitors to decline to risk even a tiny fraction of their financial gains by accepting the offer, despite my reduction of the annual payment to one hundred dollars. Another is John G. Fuller, author of three popular UFO books, including one on the Hill case. When I handed him the simple ten-thousand-dollar contract, quoted earlier in this chapter, during the David Susskind TV show on UFOs, Fuller crumpled the sheet and called it "the biggest, confusing double-talk I have ever experienced . . . This is the great hoax of all time." Stanton Friedman, who earns his living as a UFO lecturer promoting the extraterrestrial view, had earlier rejected the offer, as had Dr. Hynek and Dr. Harder. Friedman and Hynek, who are usually paid one thousand dollars or more for a one-hour talk on UFOs, were unwilling to risk the fee for a single lecture. NICAP and APRO officials have also declined the offer.

In the spring of 1969, when the offer was included in my *Parade* magazine article, a Seattle man became the first person to take me up on it, and for two years he fulfilled his end of the agreement. Then, in the spring of 1971, he tried to collect the ten thousand dollars simply on the strength of his own statement that the Norwegian government had, nearly

---

* Considering this gross error in Edwards' account of an incident in which he was directly involved, it is not surprising that there are similar inaccuracies in his accounts of UFO incidents.

twenty years earlier, recovered an extraterrestrial spaceship
that had crashed in Spitsbergen. My attorney, Irvin M. Davis,
of Boston, replied by calling his attention to the terms of the
contract. Davis said that if and when the contract terms were
met, the Seattle man would receive the ten thousand dollars.
We never heard further from him and he let the agreement
lapse. There have been no subsequent takers.

Let me extend a similar offer to you. If, at any time during
my lifetime, any evidence of extraterrestrial visitors is found
that meets the simple conditions specified in Paragraph 2 of
my ten-thousand-dollar offer, then I am willing to refund to
you the *full purchase price of this book if you will mail the
book back to me.** Because an author receives a royalty of 10
to 15 percent of the selling price (of a hard-cover book),
depending on the quantity sold, I am risking up to ten times
the total royalties I will receive on this book in extending this
offer. If this book is well received, and if subsequent events
show that my views on UFOs are in error, this offer could
bankrupt me. Even if I am correct as of this moment—that
not one of the thousands of UFO reports involves an
extraterrestrial spaceship—it is entirely possible that an
honest-to-goodness extraterrestrial craft could land, or crash,
tomorrow, or next year. It certainly is possible that there is
intelligent life elsewhere in the vast universe.

But a visitation to Earth is not likely to happen, even once,
simply because of the gigantic distance that separates our
planet from all possible sources of intelligent life. American
and Russian space probes have shown that the environments
of Venus and Mars—the only two planets in our solar system
whose distance from the Sun might possibly permit the
existence of intelligent life—are really much too hostile to
support intelligent life-forms. The next closest source, the star
Alpha Centauri, is more than 26 *trillion miles away*. There is

* Ralph and Judy Blum, whose UFO book dealing principally with the
Pascagoula case was published in the spring of 1974, predict "that by 1975
the government will release definite proof that extraterrestrials are watching
us." If their prediction comes true *in any year*, I will refund the purchase
price to those who return my book.

no evidence that this star has even one planet, or if it does, that there is intelligent life there. But if it were so blessed and if its residents had spaceships that could travel at a speed of *67 million miles per hour,* a single trip to Earth and back home would require almost a *century* to accomplish. (At a speed of 67 million miles per hour, a craft could circumnavigate our Earth in less than two seconds!)

It is because of these vast distances that astronomers and exobiologists who are interested in possible intelligent life elsewhere in the universe are generally agreed that the most we can hope for would be to communicate with distant civilizations via radio waves or laser beams which travel at the speed of light—186,000 miles per second (670 million miles per hour). Even at this velocity, simple communications between Earth and a distant civilization will be difficult. A radio message sent to a planet of the closest star outside our solar system would require four and a half *years* to arrive there, and a reply would consume the same transit time. It now seems more likely that if intelligent life is someday found, it will prove to be at a vastly greater distance, so that a two-way exchange of messages could require a century to accomplish, or many centuries. In this event, the scientist or government official who prepares our original transmission will not be alive to receive the reply.

If this, together with my debunking of the myth of UFOs as extraterrestrial visitors, leaves you a bit sad and feeling lonely in a cosmic sense, you are in good company. One scientist, for whom I have great respect, wrote me to express his own disappointment: "I guess I wanted the UFOs to be machines under intelligent control. It seems more exciting. However, your logic is unassailable." I hope this book will not discourage you from sky-watching on a pleasant evening. If you watch long enough and carefully enough, in time you will see something whose appearance or behavior seems unusual and inexplicable. If you are willing to devote enough effort, you can probably find a prosaic explanation, although luck sometimes plays a key role in finding such an answer. Perhaps you will decide instead that you have seen a UFO, setting free your hopes and fantasies to imagine that you have been privileged to see a spaceship from a distant world, operated by intelligent creatures.

I would hope not. But I acknowledge that the idea of visitors from distant worlds is a fascinating myth for adults. It is especially so because it fills the void left many years ago when we outgrew the fanciful and wonderful fairy tales of our childhood, when an ugly frog could suddenly become a handsome prince. If UFOs are spaceships from a distant world whose civilization is vastly more advanced than our own, it is automatically assumed that they long ago learned how to overcome all of the seemingly immutable laws of physics that now constrain our own technology, and the social problems that blight our Earth. Dr. Carl Sagan phrased it aptly during his appearance on the "Dick Cavett Show"—in the role of a debunker—when he observed, "UFOs can do anything we want them to."

The idea of wondrous spaceships from a distant civilization really is a fairy story that is tailored to the adult mentality—a fairy story in which anyone can become a firsthand participant simply by keeping an alert eye peeled toward the skies. The myth of extraterrestrial visitors will persist—this book notwithstanding—if only because there are so many natural and man-made "UFOs" to be seen, and because so many people *want* to believe.

My thanks and appreciation to the following, in addition to those mentioned in the body of this book, for their thoughtfulness in sending me newspaper and magazine clippings on UFO matters, which have proved so useful in my research and in the writing of this book:

David Ashkin, the late Brother Cassian Brenner, Margot Busak, Kenneth L. Calkins, Gerald L. Dawson, Fred C. Durant III, Dennis S. Feldman, Joe Frizzell, Hal Gettings, Jack Grover, Jerry Hannifin, Woods Hansen, Wally Knief, John E. Kumpf, Lily and Bernard Levine, Frank D. Marrow, Bernard Pfefer, Fred G. Pratt, David J. Shea, Earl E. Spencer, Mina and Bruno Spiegler, Robert E. Steele, Tirey K. Vickers, Frank Wright, and my mother, Mrs. Raymond N. Klass.

My special thanks to Robert Sheaffer for his review of my manuscript and useful suggestions, and my apologies to any other contributors through the years whose names have been omitted unintentionally.

Index